This is the last page!

In keeping with the original Japanese comic format, this book reads from right to left—so action, sound effects, and word balloons are completely reversed. This preserves the orientation of the original artwork—plus, it's fun! Check out the diagram shown here to get the hang of things, and then turn to the other side of the book to get started!

DENGEKI DAISY
VOL. 10
Shojo Beat Edition

STORY AND ART BY
KYOUSUKE MOTOMI

© 2007 Kyousuke MOTOMI/Shogakukan
All rights reserved.
Original Japanese edition "DENGEKI DAISY"
published by SHOGAKUKAN Inc.

Translation & Adaptation/JN Productions
Touch-up Art & Lettering/Rina Mapa
Design/Nozomi Akashi
Editor/Amy Yu

The stories, characters and incidents mentioned in this publication are entirely fictional.

Printed in the U.S.A.

Published by VIZ Media, LLC
P.O. Box 77010
San Francisco, CA 94107

10 9 8 7 6 5 4 3 2 1
First printing, July 2012

www.viz.com   www.shojobeat.com

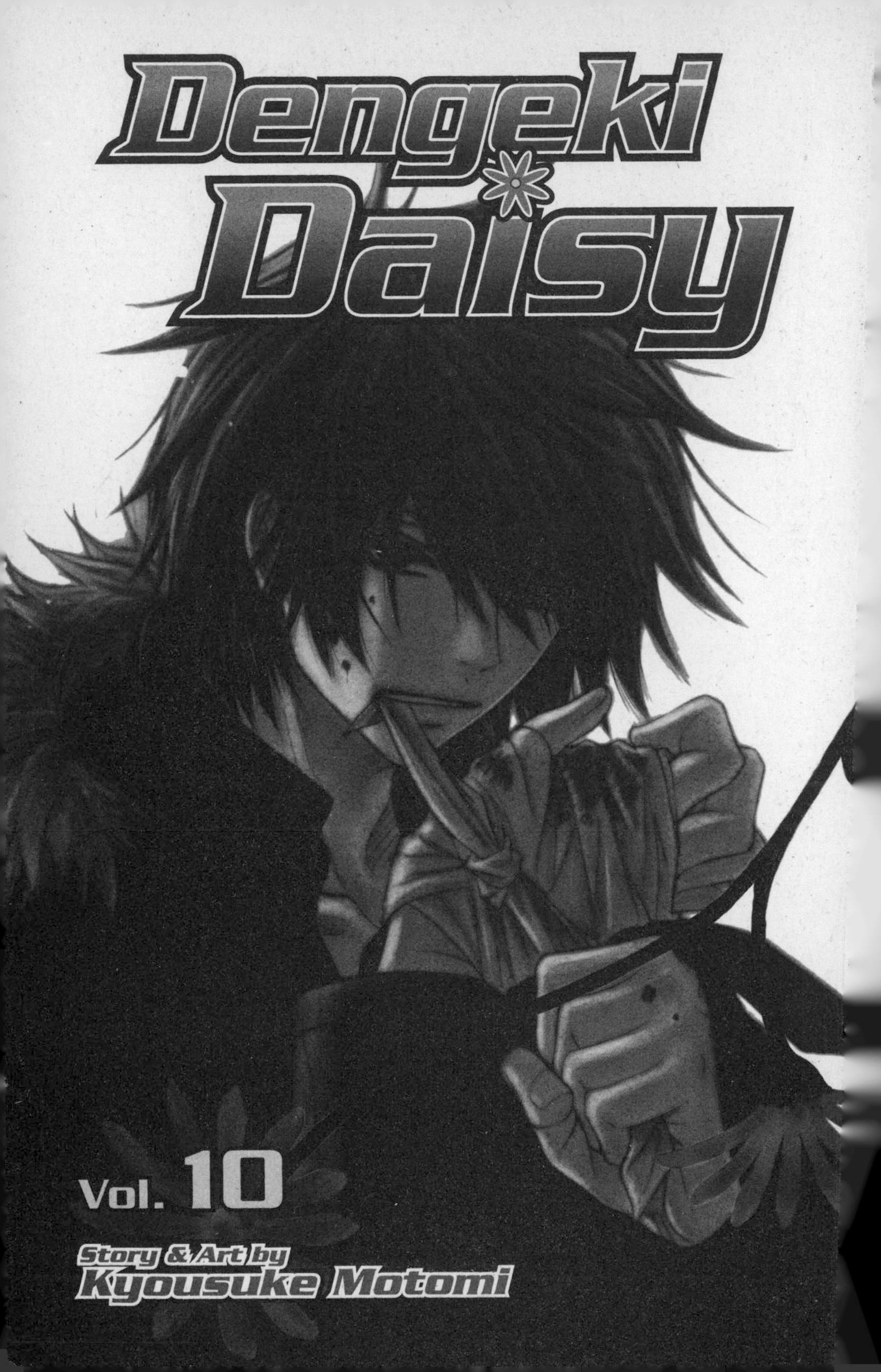
Dengeki Daisy
Vol. 10
Story & Art by
Kyousuke Motomi

Dengeki Daisy

Volume 10 CONTENTS

DAISY

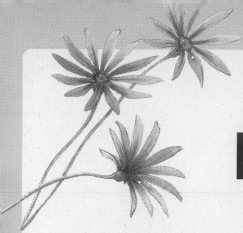

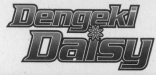

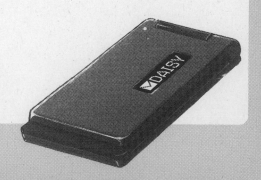

Dengeki Daisy Vol. 10

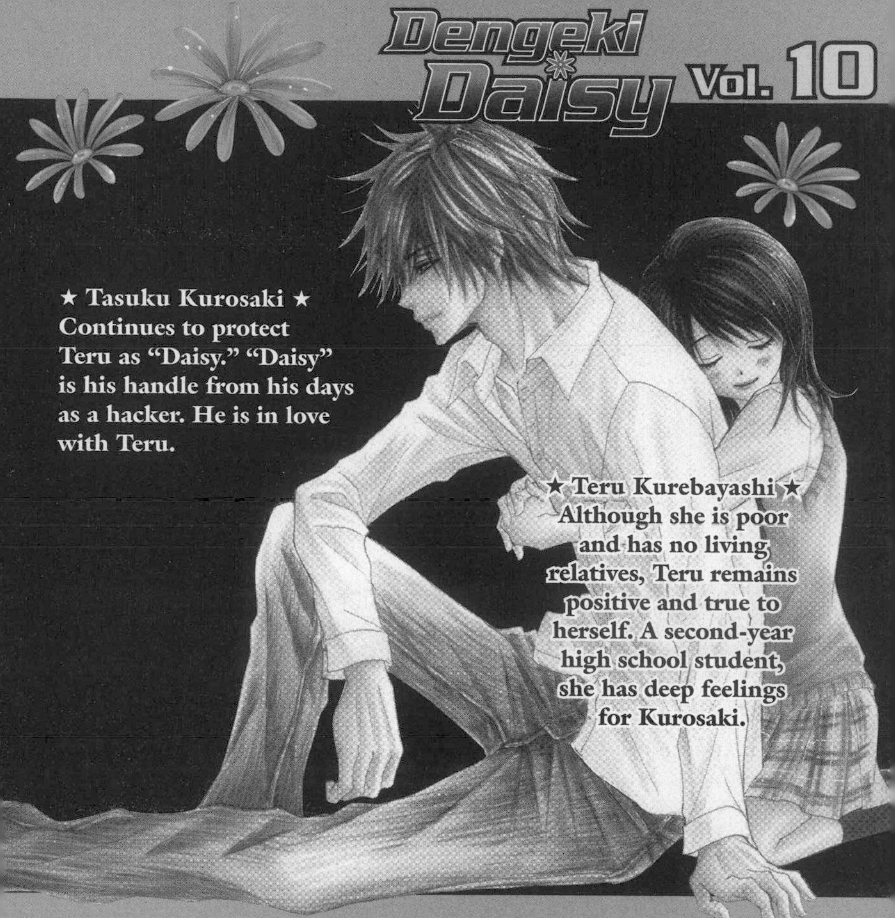

★ Tasuku Kurosaki ★
Continues to protect Teru as "Daisy." "Daisy" is his handle from his days as a hacker. He is in love with Teru.

★ Teru Kurebayashi ★
Although she is poor and has no living relatives, Teru remains positive and true to herself. A second-year high school student, she has deep feelings for Kurosaki.

★ Teru discovers that Kurosaki is Daisy, the mysterious person who supported and encouraged her after her brother's death. Thinking that there must be a reason why Kurosaki has chosen to hide his identity, Teru decides to keep this knowledge to herself.

★ During this time, Teru's life is threatened, and strange incidents involving Teru and Kurosaki occur. Kurosaki decides to disclose the truth to Teru, but Akira beats him to it and tells her about Kurosaki's past "sin." Learning what Akira has done, Kurosaki disappears from sight. Seeing Teru so despondent, the Director and Riko tell her about Kurosaki's past.

★ Teru learns that Kurosaki's father was involved with the development of a top-secret government code, and his death was shrouded in mystery. Kurosaki became a hacker to clear his father's

CHARACTERS...

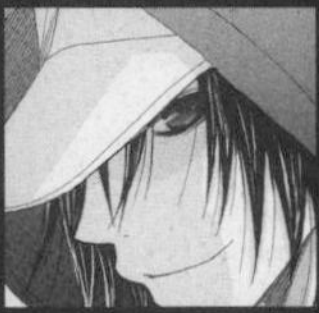

★ Akira ★
Chiharu Mori's partner-in-crime. He continues to stalk Teru and Kurosaki.

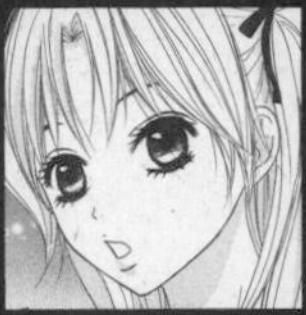

★ Rena ★
Teru's friend. Certainly not the docile type, but she tends to value her friends.

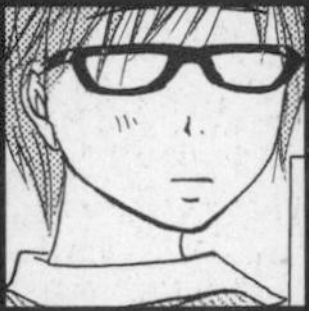

★ Kiyoshi Hasegawa ★
Teru's friend since grade school and Kurosaki's number two servant.

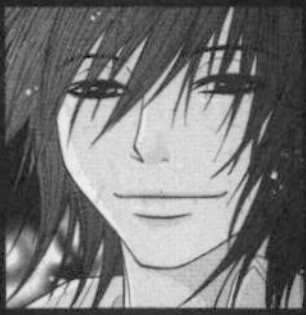

★ Soichiro Kurebayashi ★
Teru's older brother and a genius systems engineer. He died after leaving Teru in Kurosaki's care.

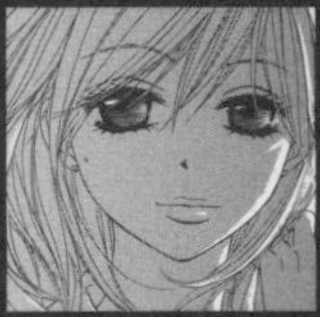

★ Chiharu Mori ★
She used to work at Teru's school. Teaming up with Akira, she continues to target Teru and Kurosaki.

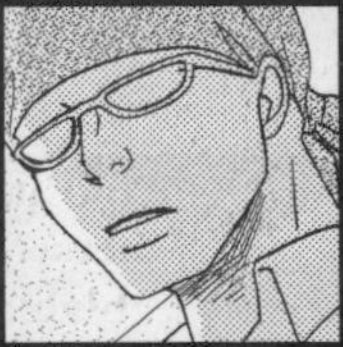

★ Boss (Masuda) ★
Currently runs the snack shop "Flower Garden" but used to work with Soichiro.

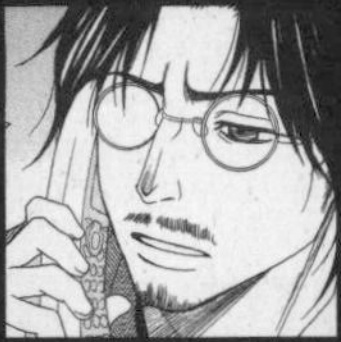

★ Director (Kazumasa Ando) ★
He used to work with Soichiro and is currently the director of Teru's school.

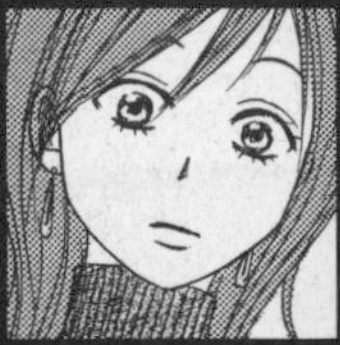

★ Riko Onizuka ★
She was Soichiro's girlfriend and is now a counselor at Teru's school.

STORY...

name and created the code virus known as "Jack Frost." In order to save Kurosaki from being charged with a "Jack Frost"-related murder, Soichiro worked nonstop to decipher the code and died in the process. Teru accepts this newfound knowledge about Kurosaki and decides to search for him.

★ Teru manages to lure Kurosaki out of hiding by lying to him about going to see Akira. Then she thanks Kurosaki for all that he has done for her and asks him to stay by her side.

★ Idyllic days pass, then one day, the duo find out that the organization that had been trying to revive the "Jack Frost" virus has been shut down. But Akira, who was involved in this incident, warns Kurosaki that things are not over...

CHAPTER 45: TRIAL AND TRIBULATION

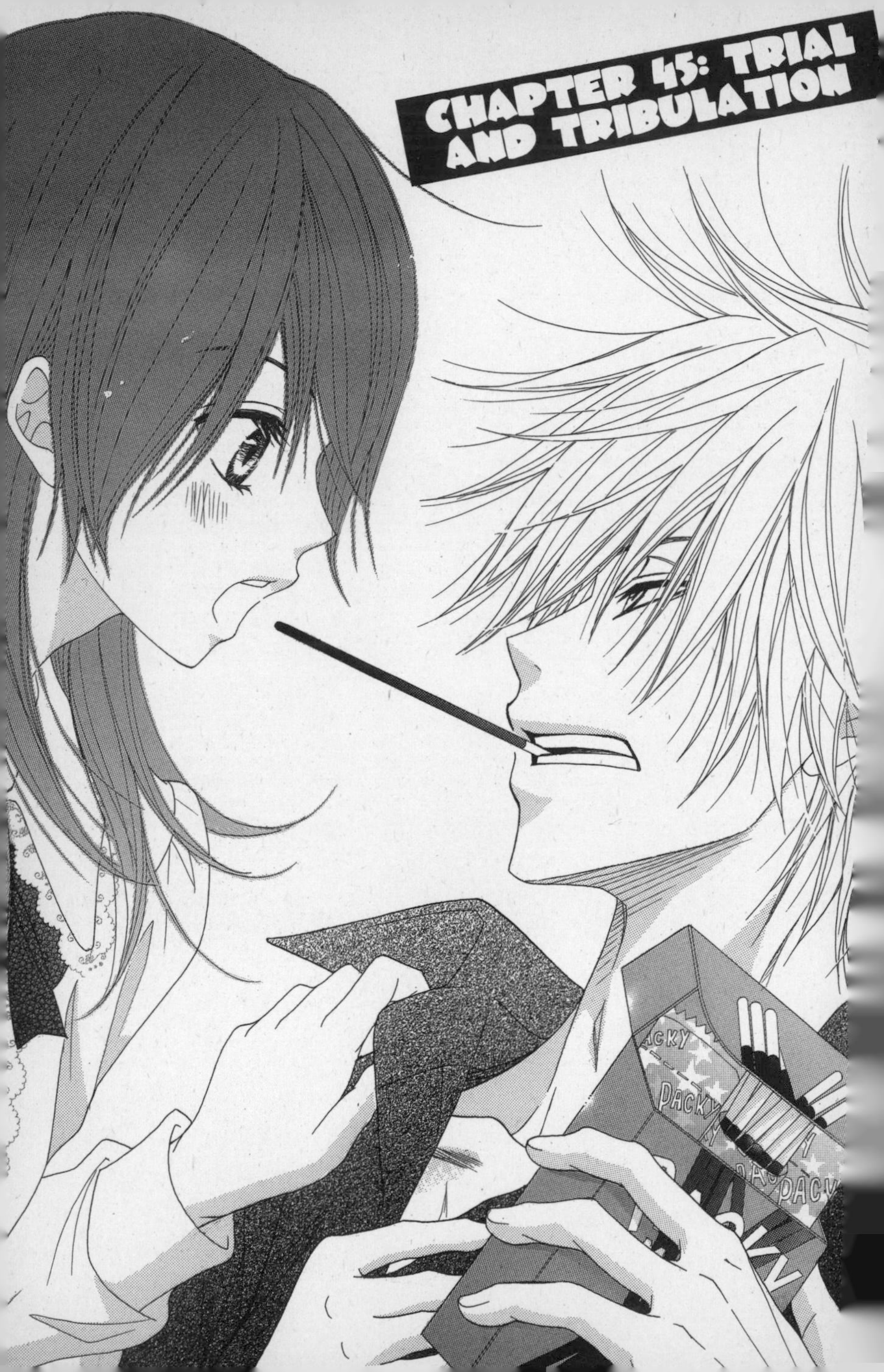
PACKY
PACKY
PACKY

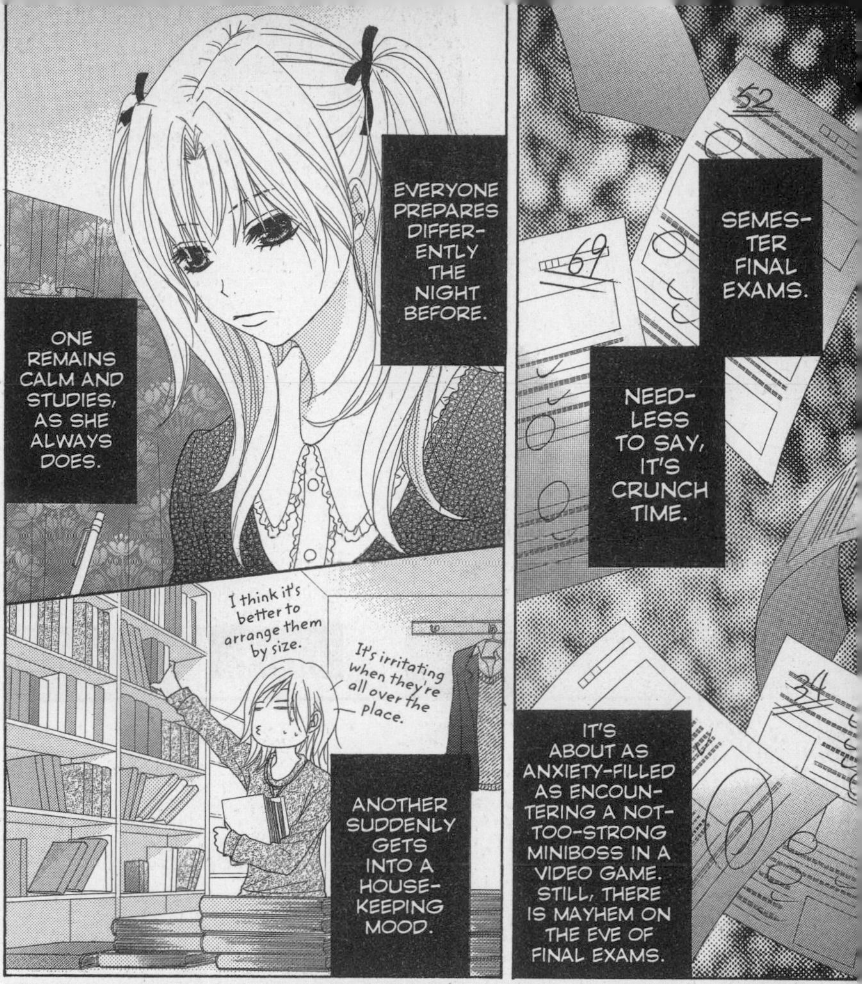
SEMESTER FINAL EXAMS.
NEEDLESS TO SAY, IT'S CRUNCH TIME.
IT'S ABOUT AS ANXIETY-FILLED AS ENCOUNTERING A NOT-TOO-STRONG MINIBOSS IN A VIDEO GAME. STILL, THERE IS MAYHEM ON THE EVE OF FINAL EXAMS.
EVERYONE PREPARES DIFFERENTLY THE NIGHT BEFORE.
ONE REMAINS CALM AND STUDIES, AS SHE ALWAYS DOES.
It's irritating when they're all over the place.
I think it's better to arrange them by size.
ANOTHER SUDDENLY GETS INTO A HOUSEKEEPING MOOD.

HELLO, EVERYONE! IT'S KYOUSUKE MOTOMI.

WELL... *DENGEKI DAISY* IS...IN ITS...
...TENTH VOLUME! THANK YOU SO MUCH! I'M ABSOLUTELY DELIGHTED!!!

THIS IS POSSIBLE THANKS TO ALL OF YOU WHO PURCHASED THIS VOLUME.

IF YOU ENJOY IT EVEN A LITTLE, I WOULD BE EVEN MORE PLEASED.

THANK YOU VERY MUCH!!

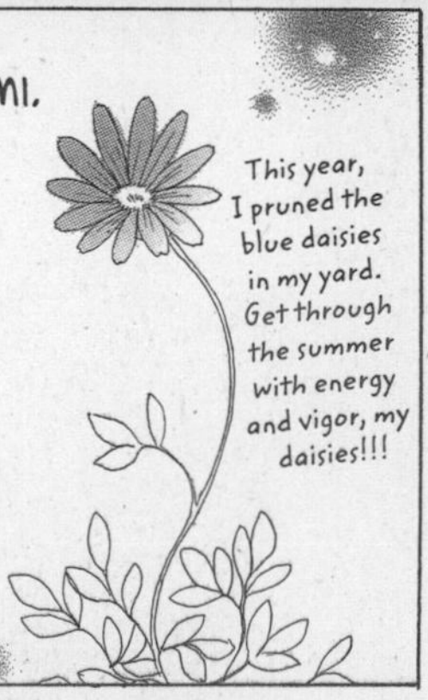
This year, I pruned the blue daisies in my yard. Get through the summer with energy and vigor, my daisies!!!

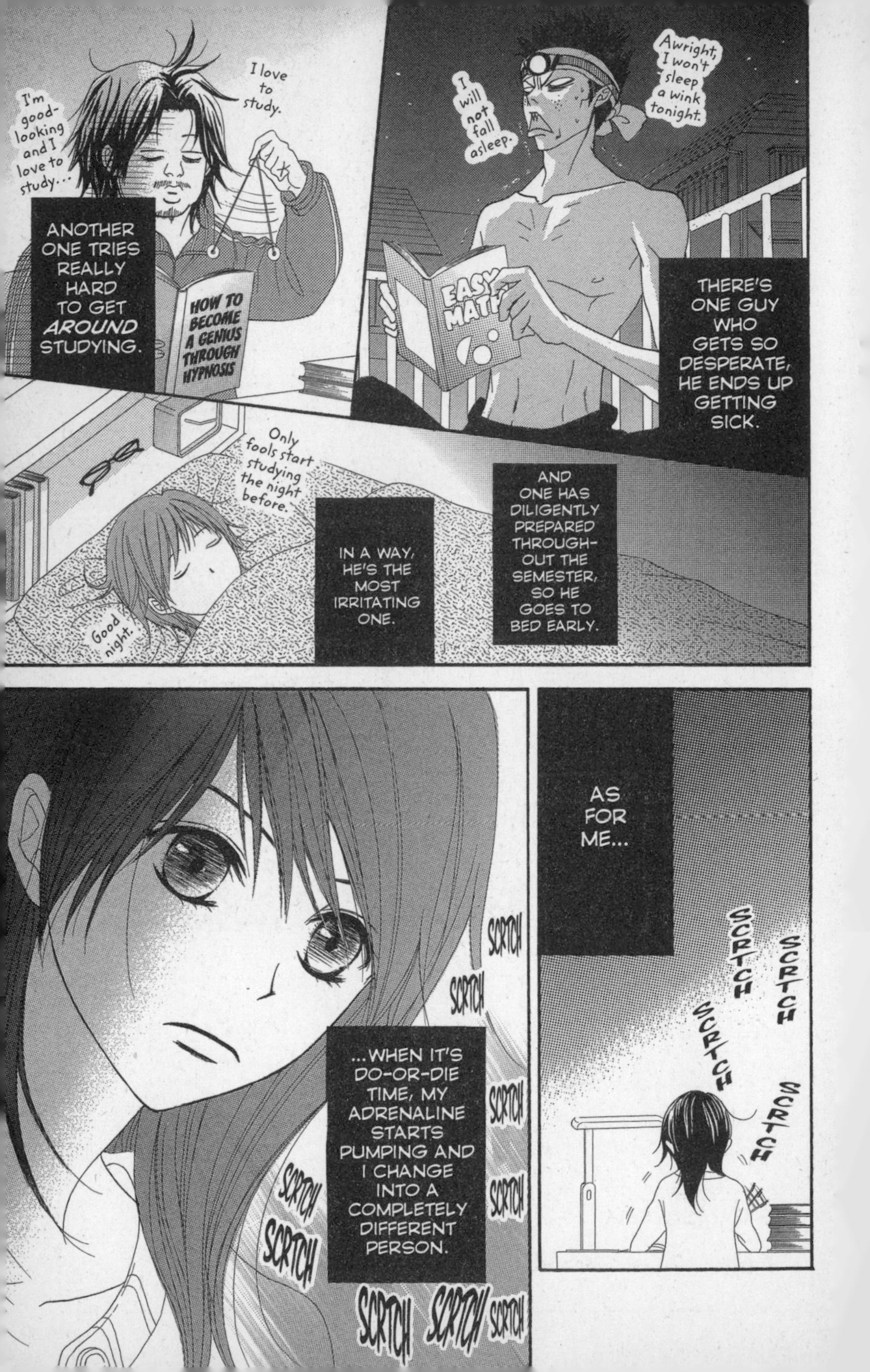
Awright, I won't sleep a wink tonight.
I will not fall asleep.
EASY MAT
THERE'S ONE GUY WHO GETS SO DESPERATE, HE ENDS UP GETTING SICK.
I love to study.
I'm good-looking and I love to study...
ANOTHER ONE TRIES REALLY HARD TO GET *AROUND* STUDYING.
HOW TO BECOME A GENIUS THROUGH HYPNOSIS
AND ONE HAS DILIGENTLY PREPARED THROUGH-OUT THE SEMESTER, SO HE GOES TO BED EARLY.
IN A WAY, HE'S THE MOST IRRITATING ONE.
Only fools start studying the night before.
Good night.
AS FOR ME...
SCRTCH
SCRTCH
SCRTCH
SCRTCH
SCRTCH
SCRTCH
...WHEN IT'S DO-OR-DIE TIME, MY ADRENALINE STARTS PUMPING AND I CHANGE INTO A COMPLETELY DIFFERENT PERSON.
SCRTCH
SCRTCH
SCRTCH
SCRTCH
SCRTCH
SCRTCH
SCRTCH

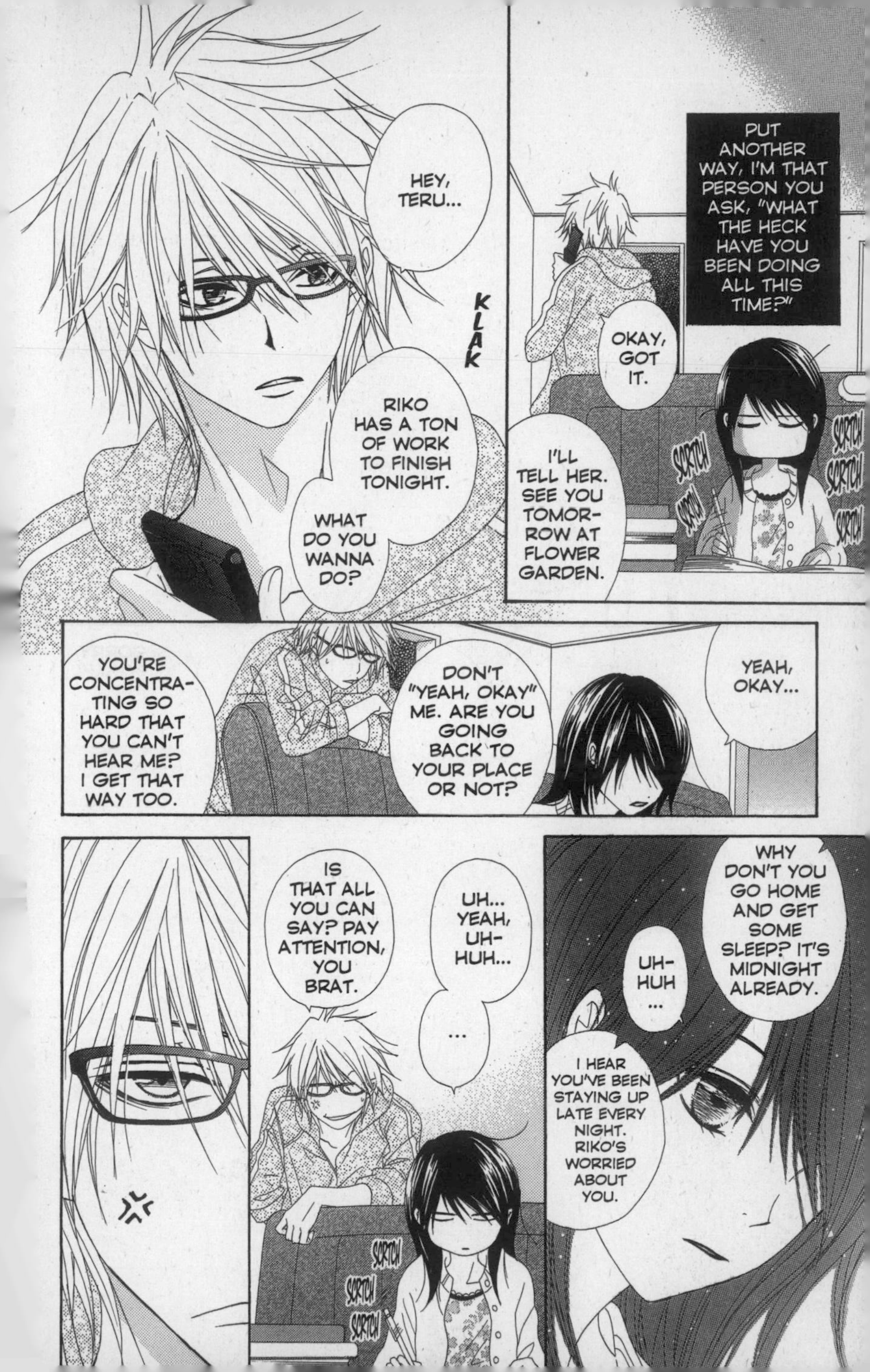
PUT ANOTHER WAY, I'M THAT PERSON YOU ASK, "WHAT THE HECK HAVE YOU BEEN DOING ALL THIS TIME?"
OKAY, GOT IT.
SCRTCH SCRTCH SCRTCH
SCRTCH SCRTCH SCRTCH
I'LL TELL HER. SEE YOU TOMOR-ROW AT FLOWER GARDEN.
HEY, TERU...
KLAK
RIKO HAS A TON OF WORK TO FINISH TONIGHT.
WHAT DO YOU WANNA DO?
YEAH, OKAY...
DON'T "YEAH, OKAY" ME. ARE YOU GOING BACK TO YOUR PLACE OR NOT?
YOU'RE CONCENTRA-TING SO HARD THAT YOU CAN'T HEAR ME? I GET THAT WAY TOO.
WHY DON'T YOU GO HOME AND GET SOME SLEEP? IT'S MIDNIGHT ALREADY.
UH-HUH ...
I HEAR YOU'VE BEEN STAYING UP LATE EVERY NIGHT. RIKO'S WORRIED ABOUT YOU.
UH... YEAH, UH-HUH...
IS THAT ALL YOU CAN SAY? PAY ATTENTION, YOU BRAT.
...
SCRTCH SCRTCH SCRTCH

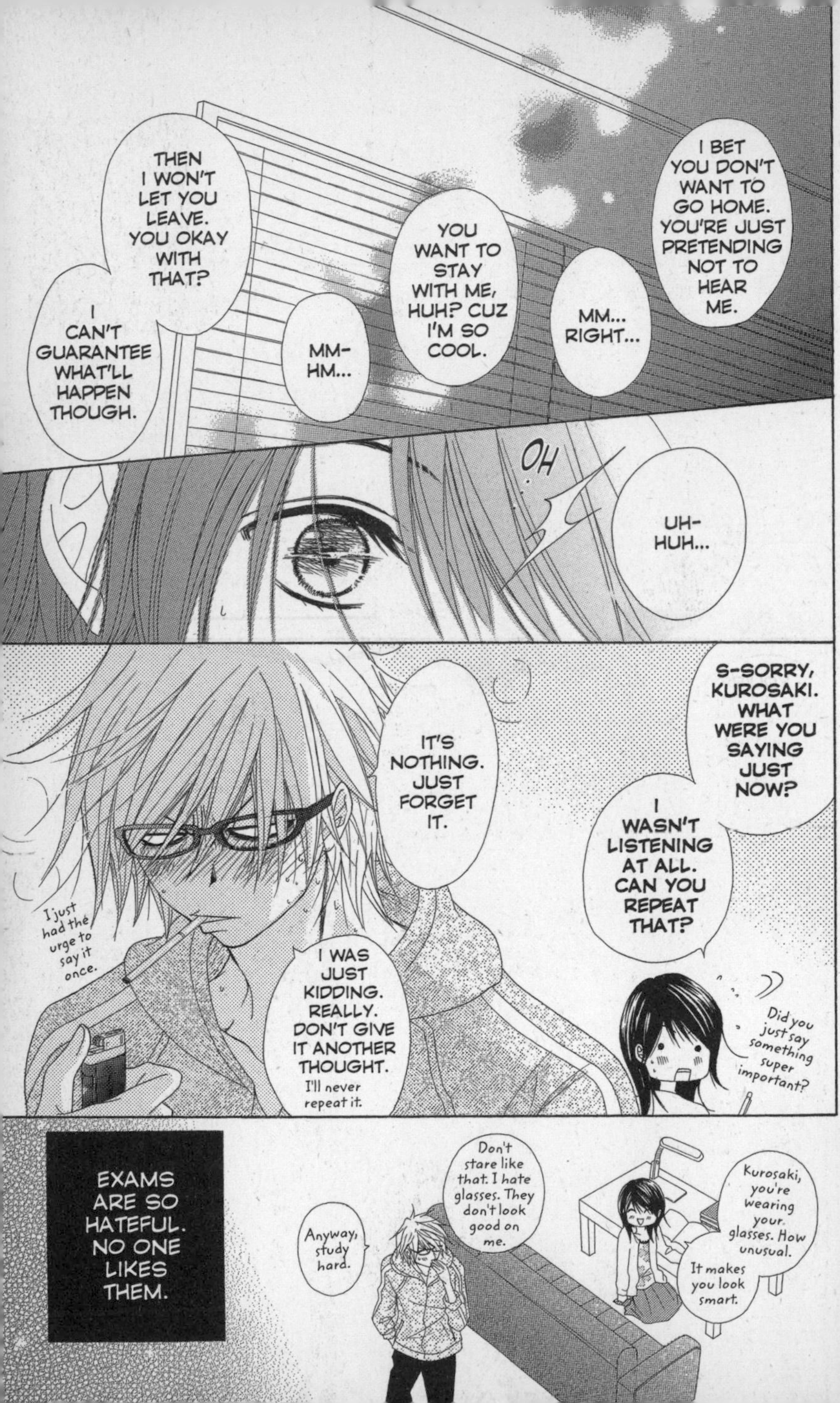
I BET YOU DON'T WANT TO GO HOME. YOU'RE JUST PRETENDING NOT TO HEAR ME.
MM... RIGHT...
YOU WANT TO STAY WITH ME, HUH? CUZ I'M SO COOL.
MM-HM...
THEN I WON'T LET YOU LEAVE. YOU OKAY WITH THAT?
I CAN'T GUARANTEE WHAT'LL HAPPEN THOUGH.
OH
UH-HUH...
S-SORRY, KUROSAKI. WHAT WERE YOU SAYING JUST NOW?
I WASN'T LISTENING AT ALL. CAN YOU REPEAT THAT?
Did you just say something super important?
IT'S NOTHING. JUST FORGET IT.
I WAS JUST KIDDING. REALLY. DON'T GIVE IT ANOTHER THOUGHT.
I'll never repeat it.
I just had the urge to say it once.
Kurosaki, you're wearing your glasses. How unusual.
It makes you look smart.
Don't stare like that. I hate glasses. They don't look good on me.
Anyway, study hard.
EXAMS ARE SO HATEFUL. NO ONE LIKES THEM.

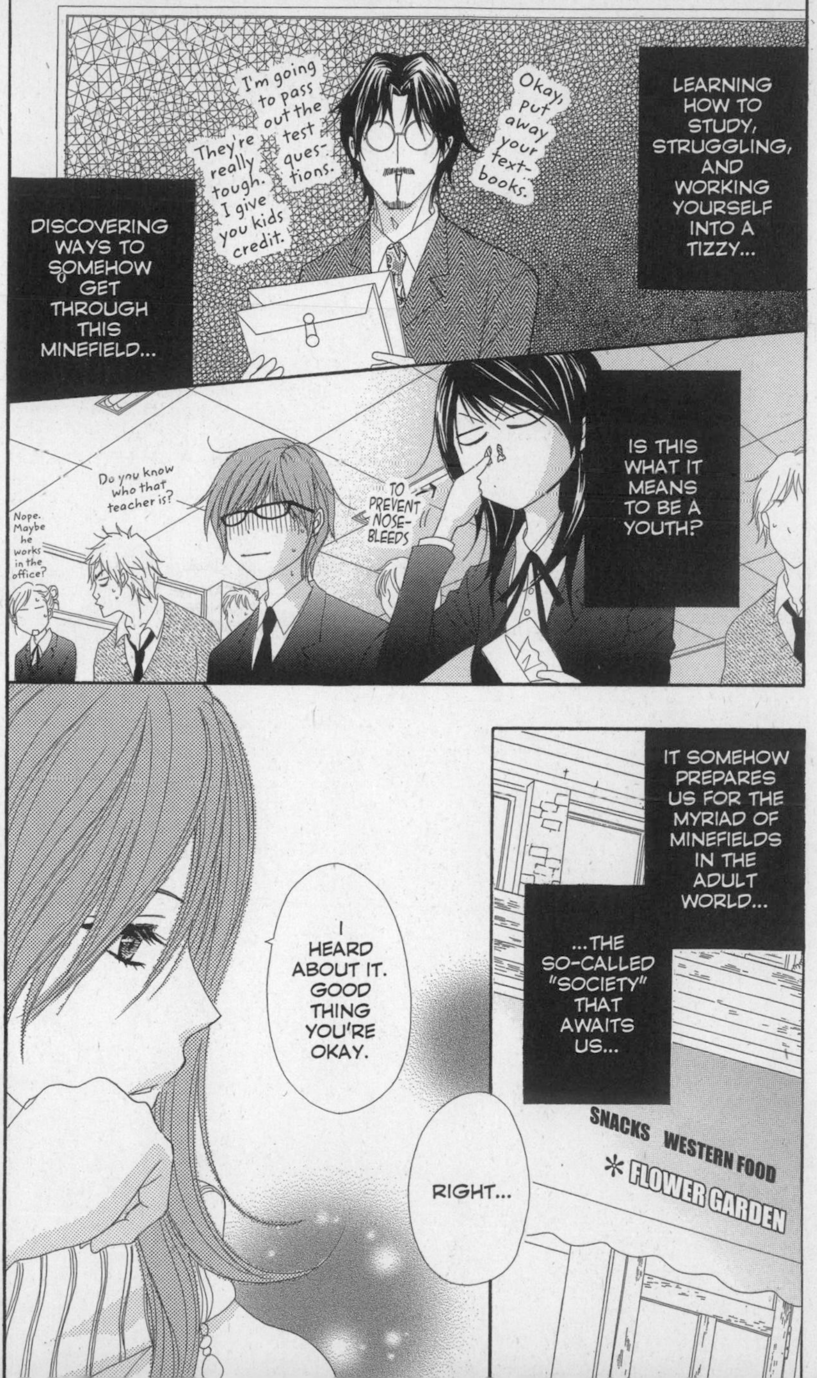
LEARNING HOW TO STUDY, STRUGGLING, AND WORKING YOURSELF INTO A TIZZY...
Okay, put away your text-books.
I'm going to pass out the test ques-tions.
They're really tough. I give you kids credit.
DISCOVERING WAYS TO SOMEHOW GET THROUGH THIS MINEFIELD...
IS THIS WHAT IT MEANS TO BE A YOUTH?
TO PREVENT NOSE-BLEEDS
Do you know who that teacher is?
Nope. Maybe he works in the office?
IT SOMEHOW PREPARES US FOR THE MYRIAD OF MINEFIELDS IN THE ADULT WORLD...
...THE SO-CALLED "SOCIETY" THAT AWAITS US...
SNACKS WESTERN FOOD
FLOWER GARDEN
I HEARD ABOUT IT. GOOD THING YOU'RE OKAY.
RIGHT...

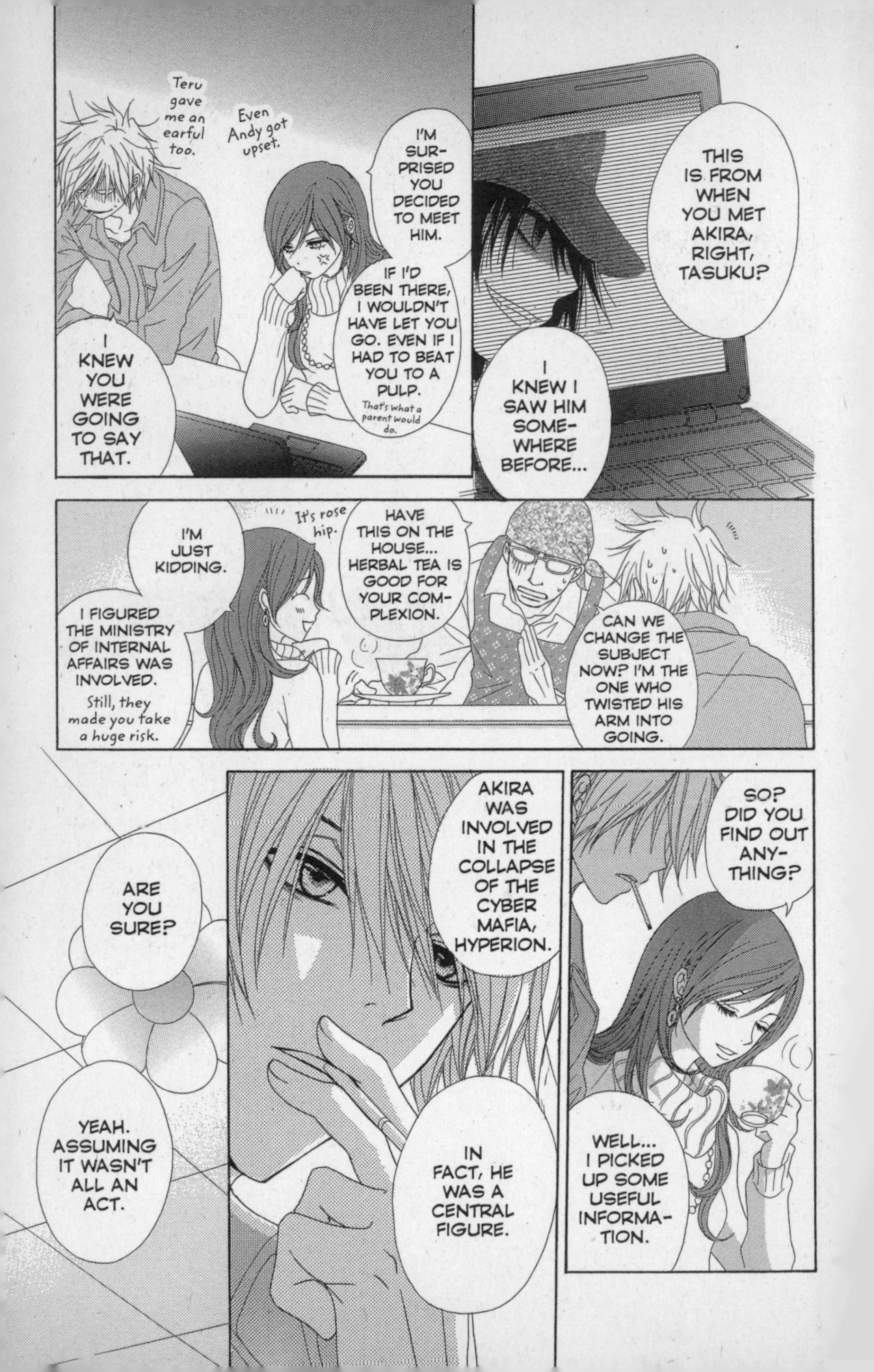
THIS IS FROM WHEN YOU MET AKIRA, RIGHT, TASUKU?
I KNEW I SAW HIM SOME-WHERE BEFORE...
I'M SUR-PRISED YOU DECIDED TO MEET HIM.
Even Andy got upset.
Teru gave me an earful too.
IF I'D BEEN THERE, I WOULDN'T HAVE LET YOU GO. EVEN IF I HAD TO BEAT YOU TO A PULP.
That's what a parent would do.
I KNEW YOU WERE GOING TO SAY THAT.
HAVE THIS ON THE HOUSE... HERBAL TEA IS GOOD FOR YOUR COM-PLEXION.
It's rose hip.
CAN WE CHANGE THE SUBJECT NOW? I'M THE ONE WHO TWISTED HIS ARM INTO GOING.
I'M JUST KIDDING.
I FIGURED THE MINISTRY OF INTERNAL AFFAIRS WAS INVOLVED.
Still, they made you take a huge risk.
SO? DID YOU FIND OUT ANY-THING?
WELL... I PICKED UP SOME USEFUL INFORMA-TION.
AKIRA WAS INVOLVED IN THE COLLAPSE OF THE CYBER MAFIA, HYPERION.
IN FACT, HE WAS A CENTRAL FIGURE.
ARE YOU SURE?
YEAH. ASSUMING IT WASN'T ALL AN ACT.

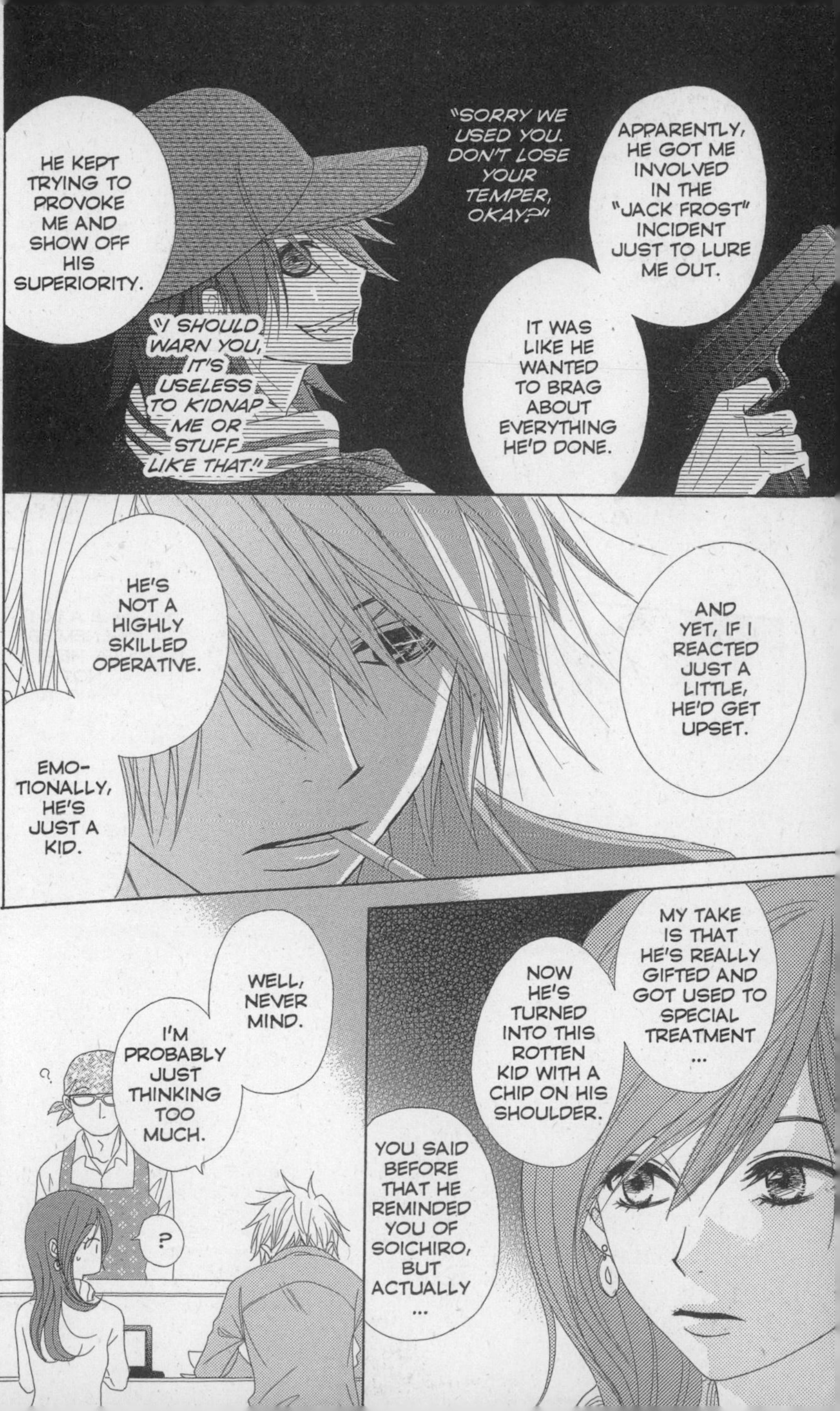
APPARENTLY, HE GOT ME INVOLVED IN THE "JACK FROST" INCIDENT JUST TO LURE ME OUT.
"SORRY WE USED YOU. DON'T LOSE YOUR TEMPER, OKAY?"
HE KEPT TRYING TO PROVOKE ME AND SHOW OFF HIS SUPERIORITY.
IT WAS LIKE HE WANTED TO BRAG ABOUT EVERYTHING HE'D DONE.
"I SHOULD WARN YOU, IT'S USELESS TO KIDNAP ME OR STUFF LIKE THAT."
AND YET, IF I REACTED JUST A LITTLE, HE'D GET UPSET.
HE'S NOT A HIGHLY SKILLED OPERATIVE.
EMO-TIONALLY, HE'S JUST A KID.
MY TAKE IS THAT HE'S REALLY GIFTED AND GOT USED TO SPECIAL TREATMENT ...
NOW HE'S TURNED INTO THIS ROTTEN KID WITH A CHIP ON HIS SHOULDER.
YOU SAID BEFORE THAT HE REMINDED YOU OF SOICHIRO, BUT ACTUALLY ...
WELL, NEVER MIND.
I'M PROBABLY JUST THINKING TOO MUCH.
?
?

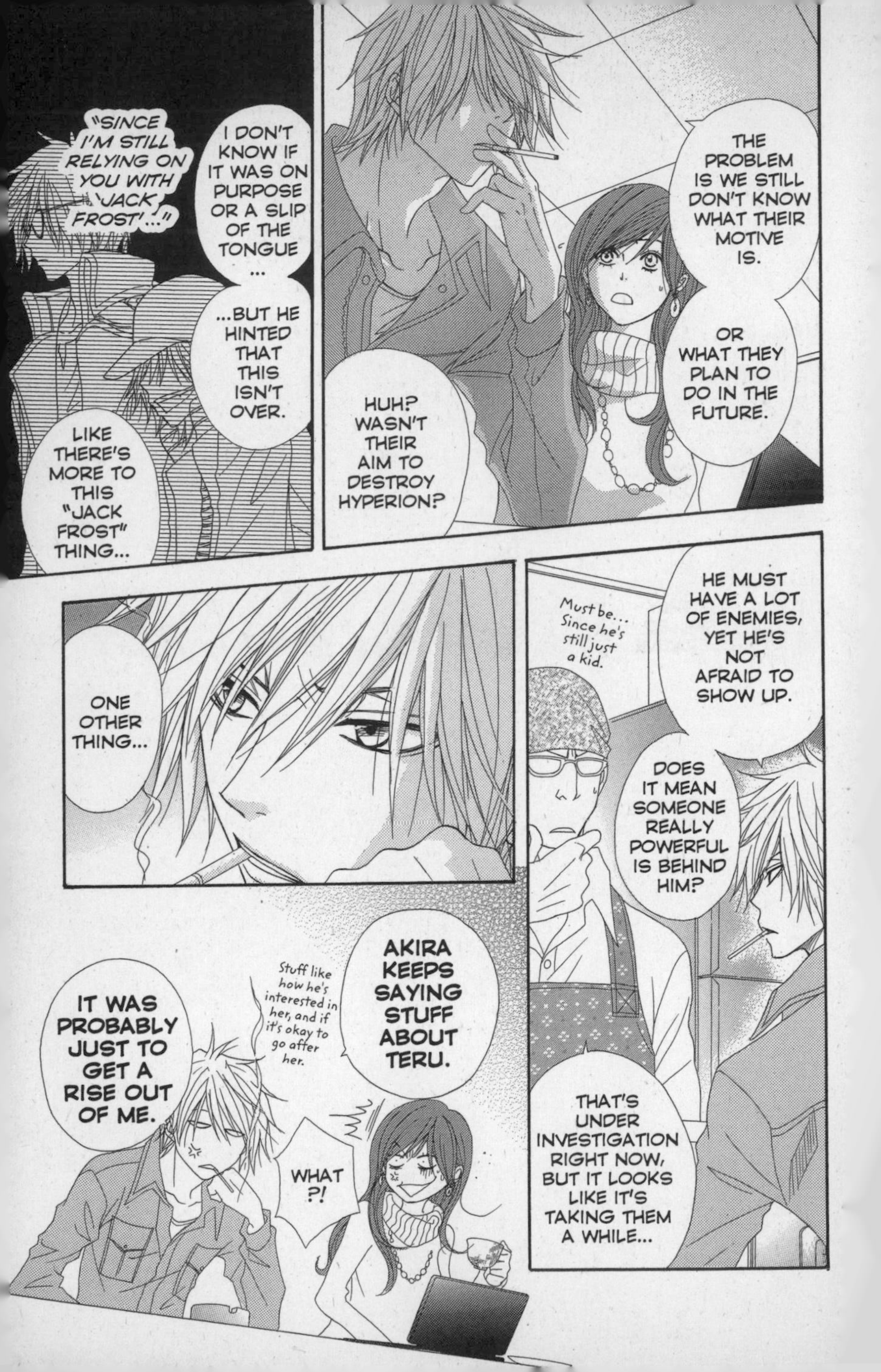
THE PROBLEM IS WE STILL DON'T KNOW WHAT THEIR MOTIVE IS.
OR WHAT THEY PLAN TO DO IN THE FUTURE.
HUH? WASN'T THEIR AIM TO DESTROY HYPERION?
I DON'T KNOW IF IT WAS ON PURPOSE OR A SLIP OF THE TONGUE...
"SINCE I'M STILL RELYING ON YOU WITH 'JACK FROST'..."
...BUT HE HINTED THAT THIS ISN'T OVER.
LIKE THERE'S MORE TO THIS "JACK FROST" THING...
HE MUST HAVE A LOT OF ENEMIES, YET HE'S NOT AFRAID TO SHOW UP.
Must be... Since he's still just a kid.
DOES IT MEAN SOMEONE REALLY POWERFUL IS BEHIND HIM?
THAT'S UNDER INVESTIGATION RIGHT NOW, BUT IT LOOKS LIKE IT'S TAKING THEM A WHILE...
ONE OTHER THING...
AKIRA KEEPS SAYING STUFF ABOUT TERU.
Stuff like how he's interested in her, and if it's okay to go after her.
IT WAS PROBABLY JUST TO GET A RISE OUT OF ME.
WHAT?!

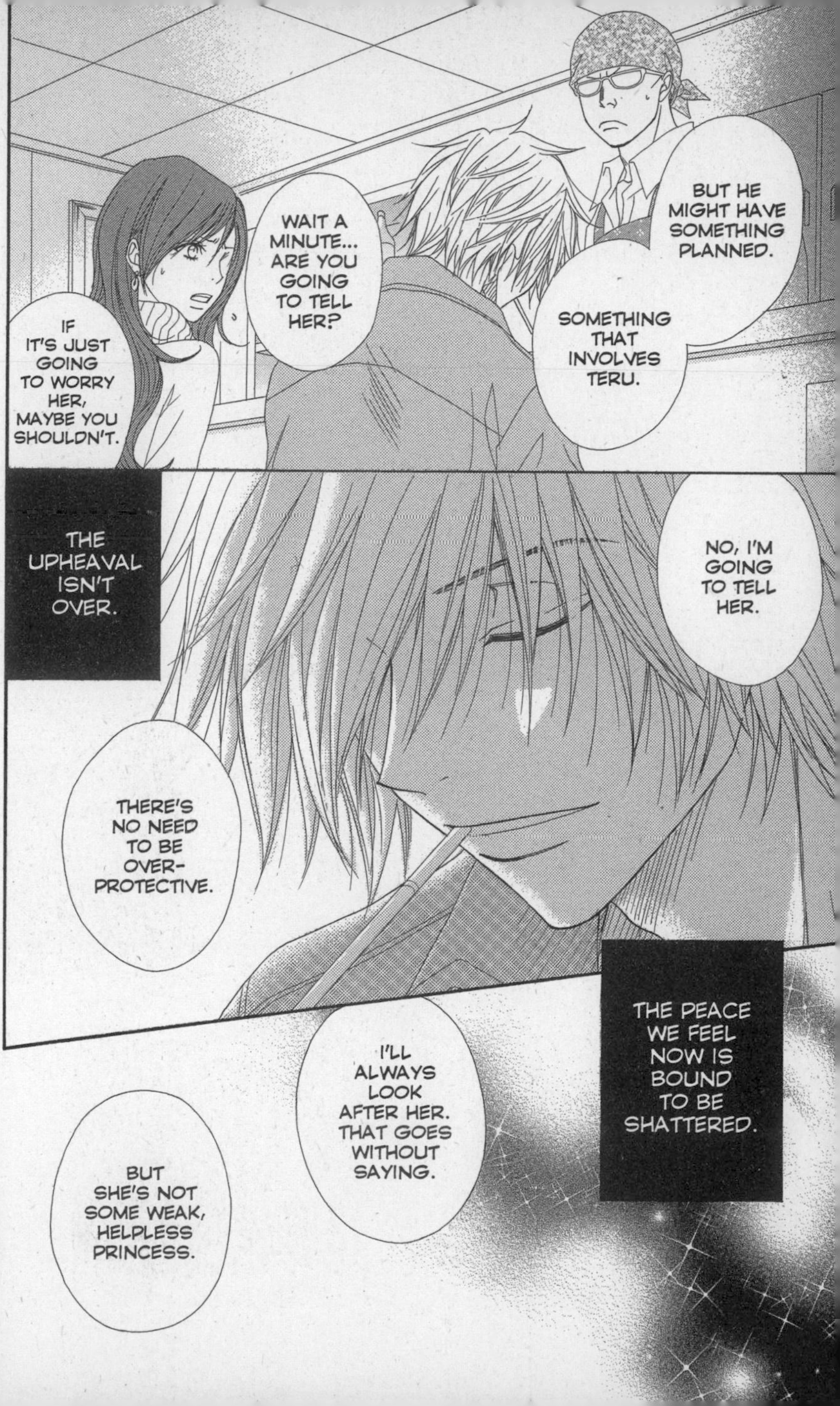
BUT HE MIGHT HAVE SOMETHING PLANNED.
SOMETHING THAT INVOLVES TERU.
WAIT A MINUTE... ARE YOU GOING TO TELL HER?
IF IT'S JUST GOING TO WORRY HER, MAYBE YOU SHOULDN'T.
NO, I'M GOING TO TELL HER.
THE UPHEAVAL ISN'T OVER.
THERE'S NO NEED TO BE OVER-PROTECTIVE.
THE PEACE WE FEEL NOW IS BOUND TO BE SHATTERED.
I'LL ALWAYS LOOK AFTER HER. THAT GOES WITHOUT SAYING.
BUT SHE'S NOT SOME WEAK, HELPLESS PRINCESS.

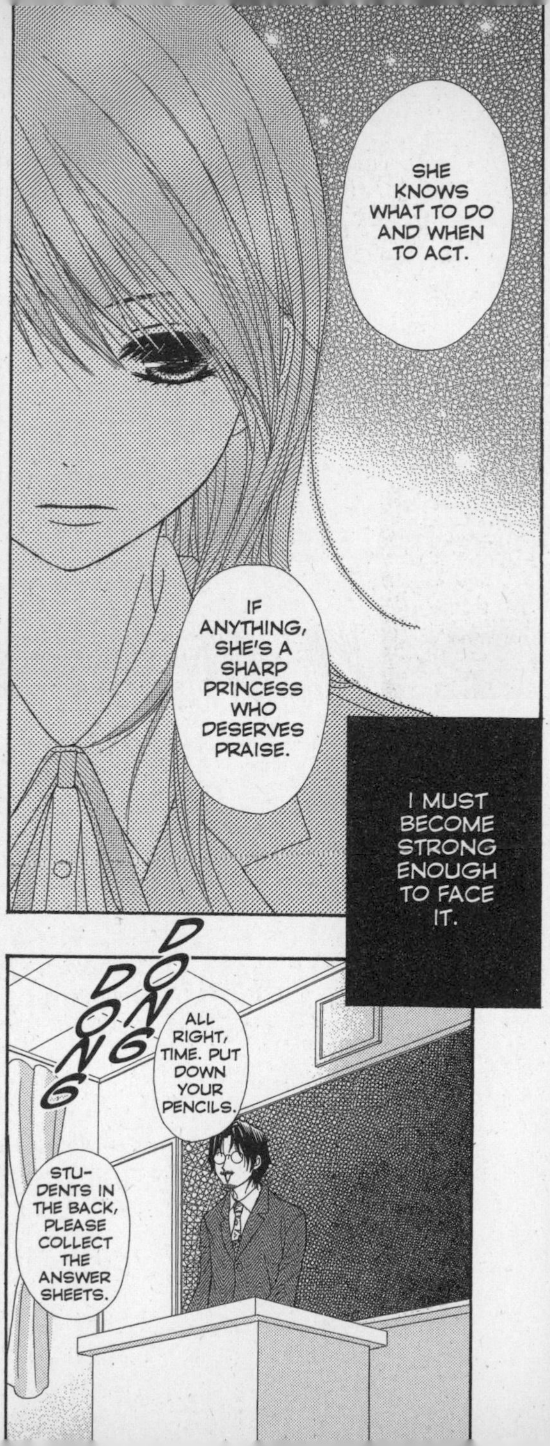
SHE KNOWS WHAT TO DO AND WHEN TO ACT.
IF ANYTHING, SHE'S A SHARP PRINCESS WHO DESERVES PRAISE.
I MUST BECOME STRONG ENOUGH TO FACE IT.
DONG DONG
DONG DONG
ALL RIGHT, TIME. PUT DOWN YOUR PENCILS.
STU-DENTS IN THE BACK, PLEASE COLLECT THE ANSWER SHEETS.

DENGEKI DAISY QUESTION CORNER

BALDLY ASK!!

①

...HELLO! I BRING YOU THIS CORNER, WHICH IS SUSTAINED BY THE KIND AND SENSIBLE QUESTIONS OF OUR READERS. WE RECEIVED SO MANY WONDERFUL QUESTIONS THAT IT WAS HARD TO CHOOSE. THANK YOU VERY MUCH!!

NOW, AWAY WE GO!!!

Q.
I HAVE A QUESTION, KYOUSUKE SENSEI. CAN YOU TELL US WHICH SCENES ARE FUN TO DRAW AND WHICH ARE TEDIOUS FOR YOU?

(SARABUREDDO, AICHI PREFECTURE)

A.
WELL, I HAVE IT IN MY HEAD THAT I'M NOT GOOD AT DRAWING, SO EVERY CRUCIAL SCENE IS NERVE-WRACKING FOR ME TO DRAW. IN PARTICULAR, FACIAL EXPRESSIONS—THOSE SCENES WHERE I WANT LOOKS TO CONVEY A RANGE OF EMOTIONS—TAKE A LOT OF EFFORT. TAKE A CRYING FACE, FOR EXAMPLE. IF I LOSE FOCUS FOR JUST A MOMENT, THE LOOK CONVEYS NOTHING MORE THAN IRRITATION, SO I EXPEND A LOT OF ENERGY ON THESE. I REALLY WISH MY CHARACTERS WOULDN'T CRY... TERU'S WAILING IN VOLUME 7, KUROSAKI CRYING IN THE REUNION SCENE IN VOLUME 9... I FEEL SUCH SCENES WERE EXTREMELY DIFFICULT TO DRAW. I HAD FUN DRAWING KAORUKO P●PING IN VOLUME 6. I DID A GOOD JOB ON THAT ONE.

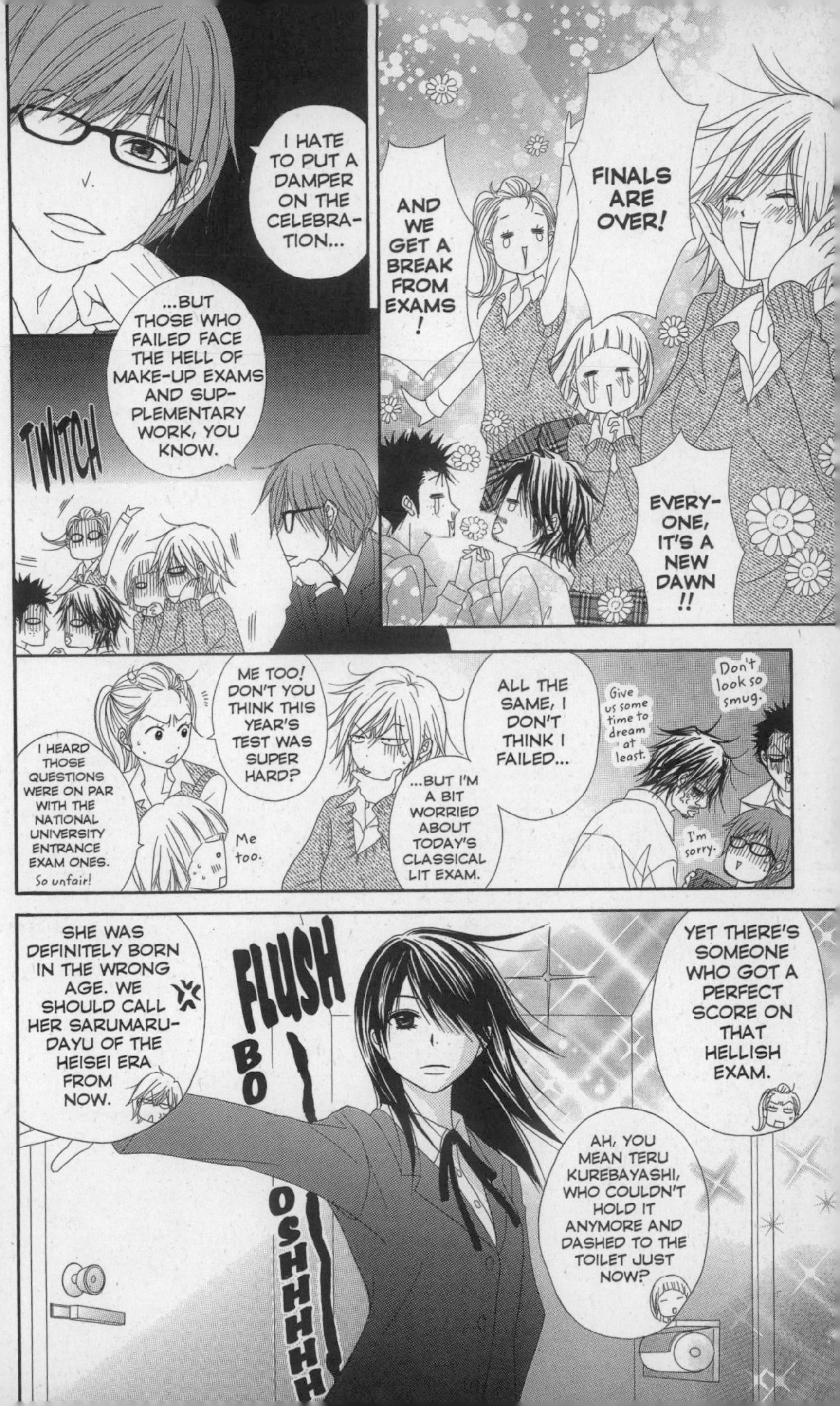
FINALS ARE OVER!
AND WE GET A BREAK FROM EXAMS!
EVERYONE, IT'S A NEW DAWN!!
I HATE TO PUT A DAMPER ON THE CELEBRATION...
...BUT THOSE WHO FAILED FACE THE HELL OF MAKE-UP EXAMS AND SUPPLEMENTARY WORK, YOU KNOW.
TWITCH
Don't look so smug.
Give us some time to dream at least.
I'm sorry.
ALL THE SAME, I DON'T THINK I FAILED...
...BUT I'M A BIT WORRIED ABOUT TODAY'S CLASSICAL LIT EXAM.
ME TOO! DON'T YOU THINK THIS YEAR'S TEST WAS SUPER HARD?
I HEARD THOSE QUESTIONS WERE ON PAR WITH THE NATIONAL UNIVERSITY ENTRANCE EXAM ONES.
So unfair!
Me too.
YET THERE'S SOMEONE WHO GOT A PERFECT SCORE ON THAT HELLISH EXAM.
AH, YOU MEAN TERU KUREBAYASHI, WHO COULDN'T HOLD IT ANYMORE AND DASHED TO THE TOILET JUST NOW?
SHE WAS DEFINITELY BORN IN THE WRONG AGE. WE SHOULD CALL HER SARUMARU-DAYU OF THE HEISEI ERA FROM NOW.
FLUSH
BO
OSHHHHH

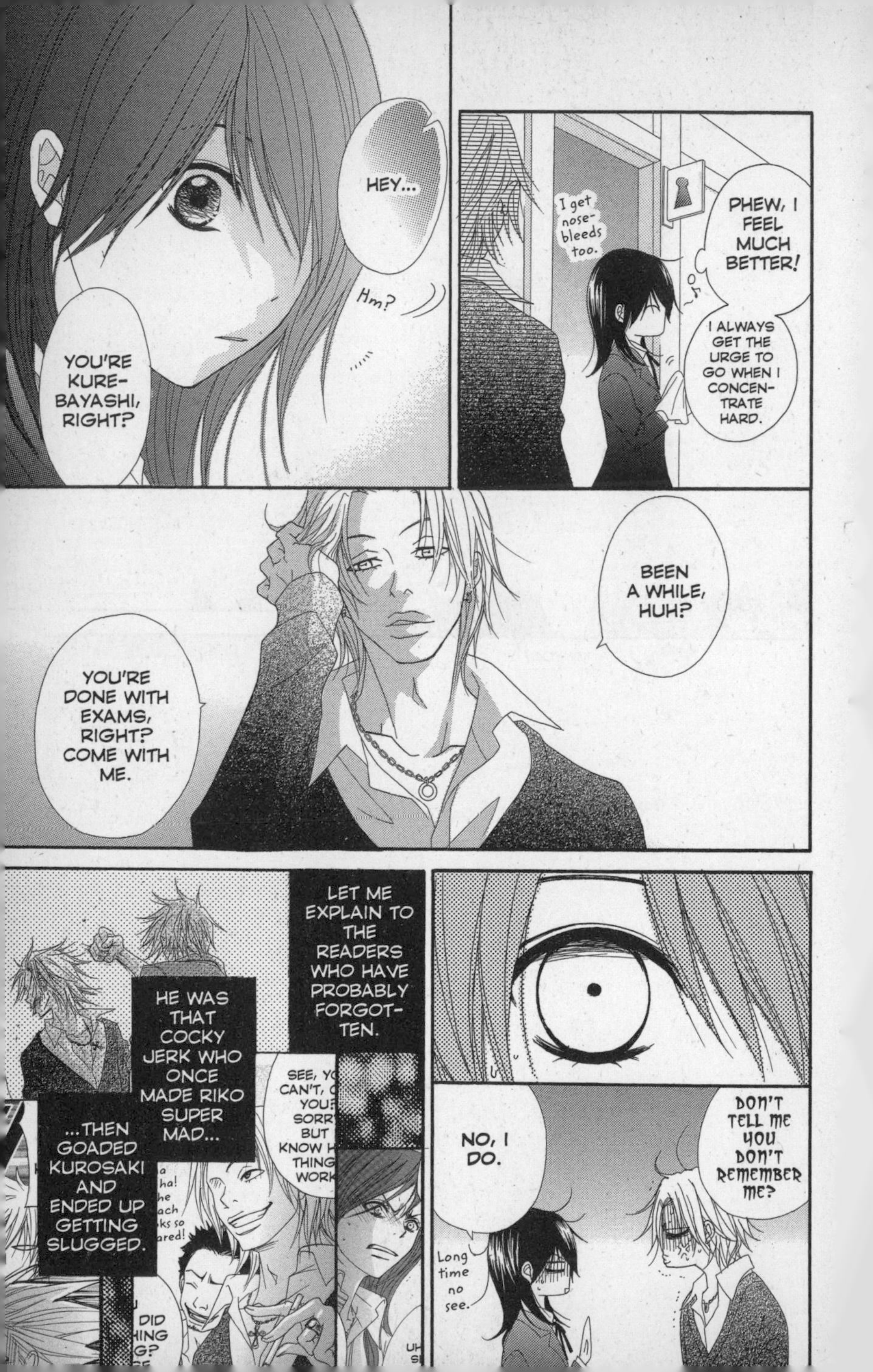
PHEW, I FEEL MUCH BETTER!
I ALWAYS GET THE URGE TO GO WHEN I CONCENTRATE HARD.
I get nose-bleeds too.
HEY...
Hm?
YOU'RE KURE-BAYASHI, RIGHT?
BEEN A WHILE, HUH?
YOU'RE DONE WITH EXAMS, RIGHT? COME WITH ME.
DON'T TELL ME YOU DON'T REMEMBER ME?
NO, I DO.
Long time no see.
LET ME EXPLAIN TO THE READERS WHO HAVE PROBABLY FORGOT-TEN.
HE WAS THAT COCKY JERK WHO ONCE MADE RIKO SUPER MAD...
...THEN GOADED KUROSAKI AND ENDED UP GETTING SLUGGED.

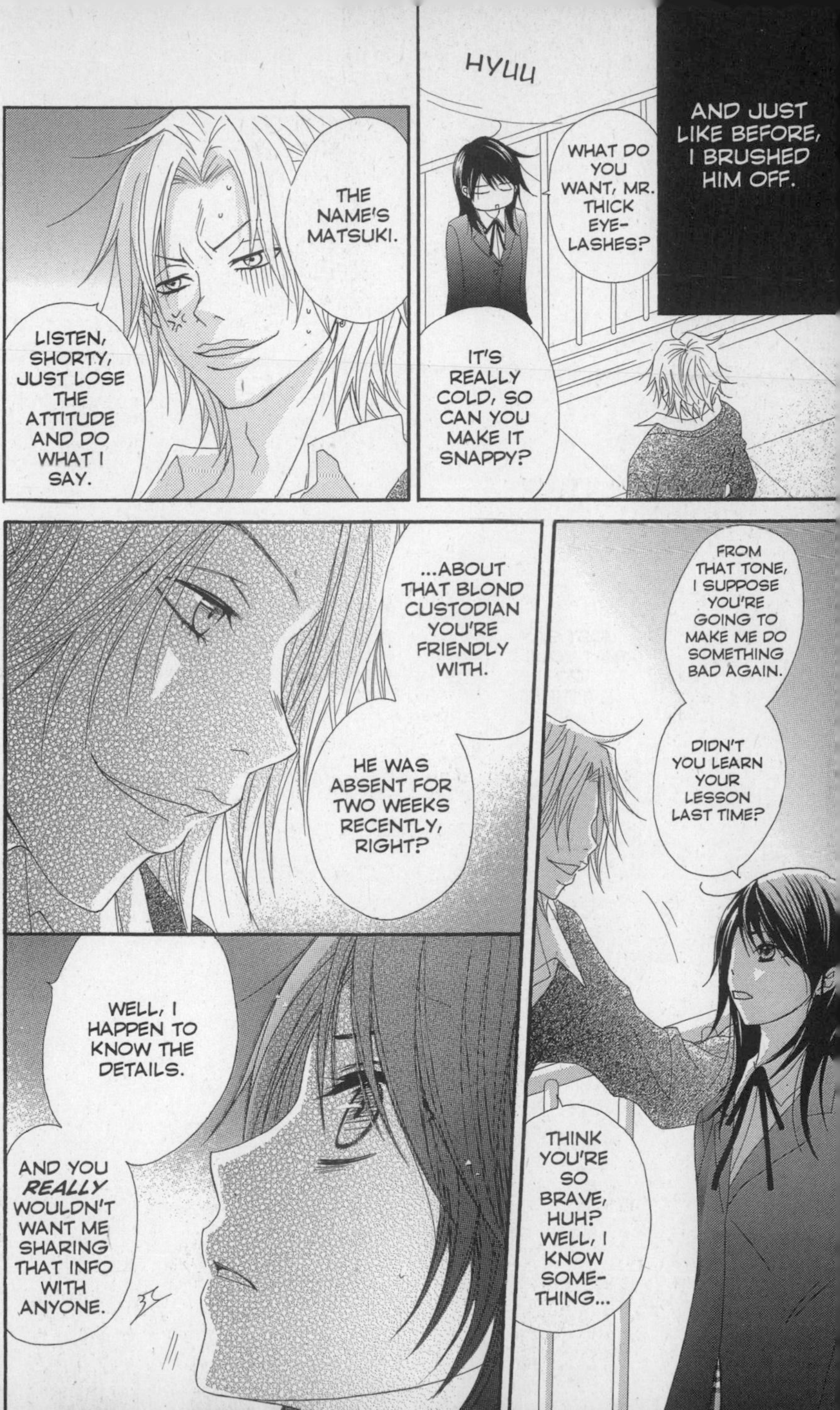
AND JUST LIKE BEFORE, I BRUSHED HIM OFF.
HYUU
WHAT DO YOU WANT, MR. THICK EYE-LASHES?
IT'S REALLY COLD, SO CAN YOU MAKE IT SNAPPY?
THE NAME'S MATSUKI.
LISTEN, SHORTY, JUST LOSE THE ATTITUDE AND DO WHAT I SAY.
FROM THAT TONE, I SUPPOSE YOU'RE GOING TO MAKE ME DO SOMETHING BAD AGAIN.
DIDN'T YOU LEARN YOUR LESSON LAST TIME?
THINK YOU'RE SO BRAVE, HUH? WELL, I KNOW SOME-THING...
...ABOUT THAT BLOND CUSTODIAN YOU'RE FRIENDLY WITH.
HE WAS ABSENT FOR TWO WEEKS RECENTLY, RIGHT?
WELL, I HAPPEN TO KNOW THE DETAILS.
AND YOU *REALLY* WOULDN'T WANT ME SHARING THAT INFO WITH ANYONE.

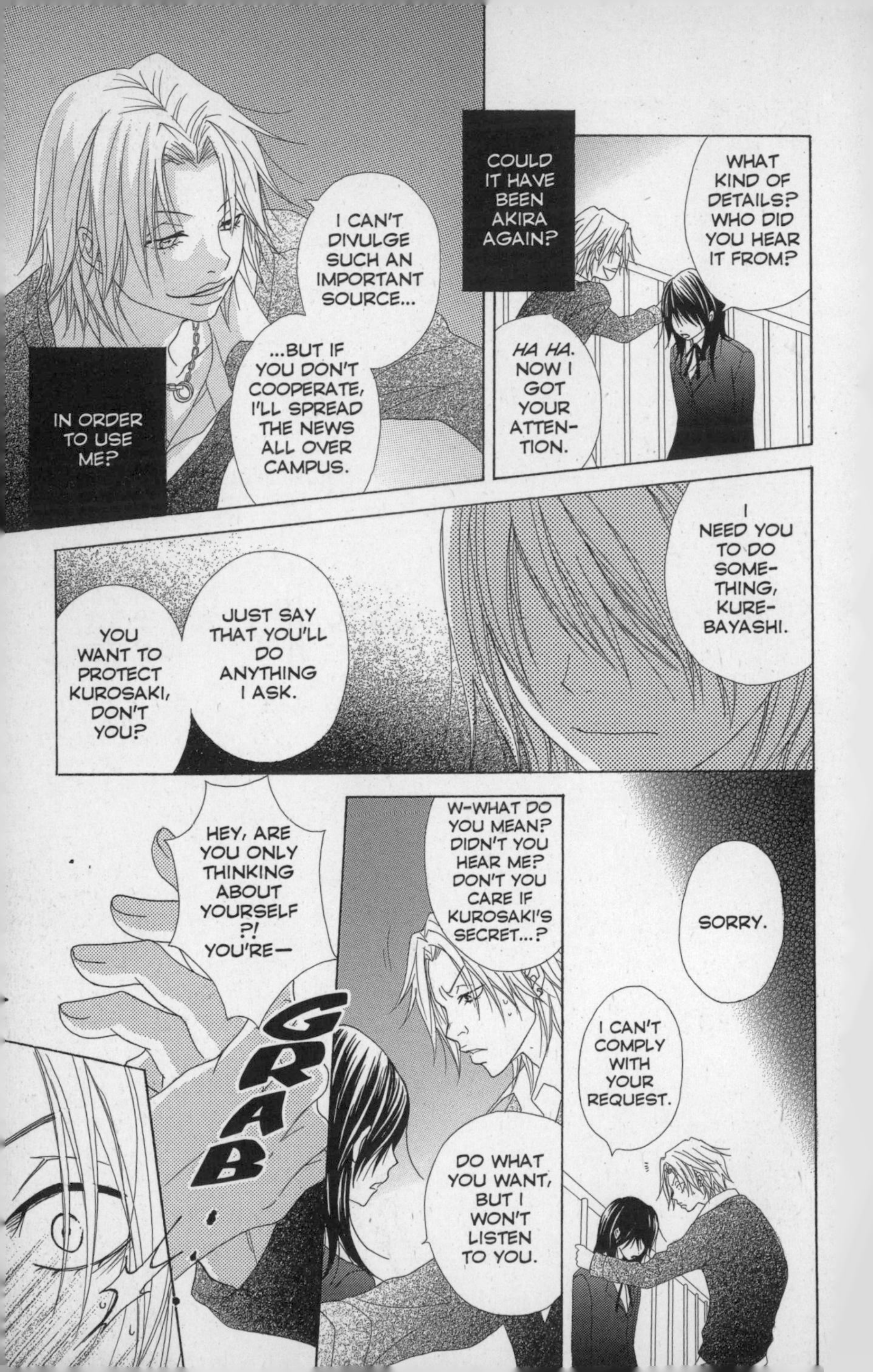
WHAT KIND OF DETAILS? WHO DID YOU HEAR IT FROM?
HA HA. NOW I GOT YOUR ATTEN-TION.
COULD IT HAVE BEEN AKIRA AGAIN?
I CAN'T DIVULGE SUCH AN IMPORTANT SOURCE...
...BUT IF YOU DON'T COOPERATE, I'LL SPREAD THE NEWS ALL OVER CAMPUS.
IN ORDER TO USE ME?
I NEED YOU TO DO SOME-THING, KURE-BAYASHI.
JUST SAY THAT YOU'LL DO ANYTHING I ASK.
YOU WANT TO PROTECT KUROSAKI, DON'T YOU?
SORRY.
I CAN'T COMPLY WITH YOUR REQUEST.
W-WHAT DO YOU MEAN? DIDN'T YOU HEAR ME? DON'T YOU CARE IF KUROSAKI'S SECRET...?
DO WHAT YOU WANT, BUT I WON'T LISTEN TO YOU.
HEY, ARE YOU ONLY THINKING ABOUT YOURSELF ?! YOU'RE—
GRAB

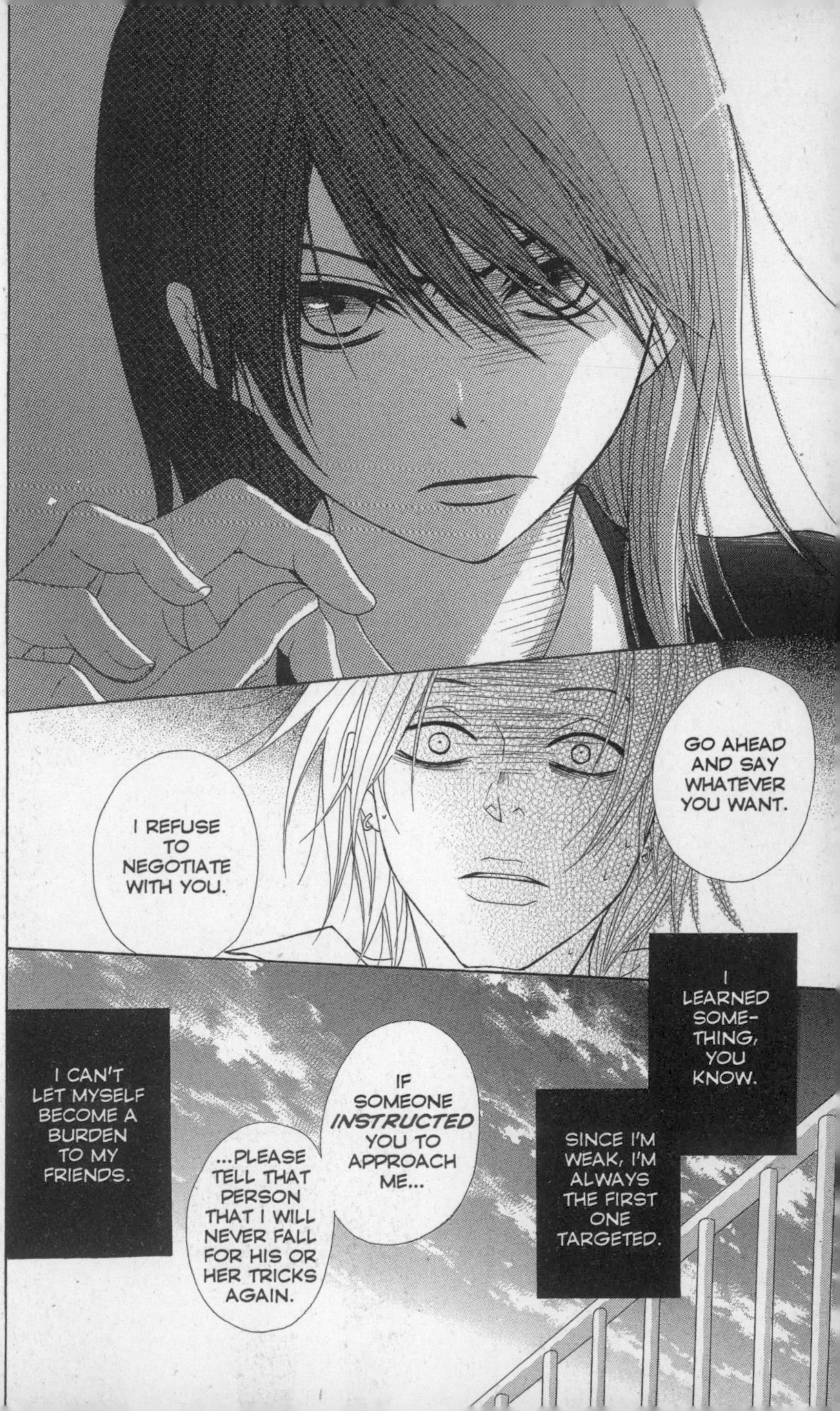
GO AHEAD AND SAY WHATEVER YOU WANT.
I REFUSE TO NEGOTIATE WITH YOU.
I LEARNED SOME-THING, YOU KNOW.
SINCE I'M WEAK, I'M ALWAYS THE FIRST ONE TARGETED.
IF SOMEONE *INSTRUCTED* YOU TO APPROACH ME...
...PLEASE TELL THAT PERSON THAT I WILL NEVER FALL FOR HIS OR HER TRICKS AGAIN.
I CAN'T LET MYSELF BECOME A BURDEN TO MY FRIENDS.

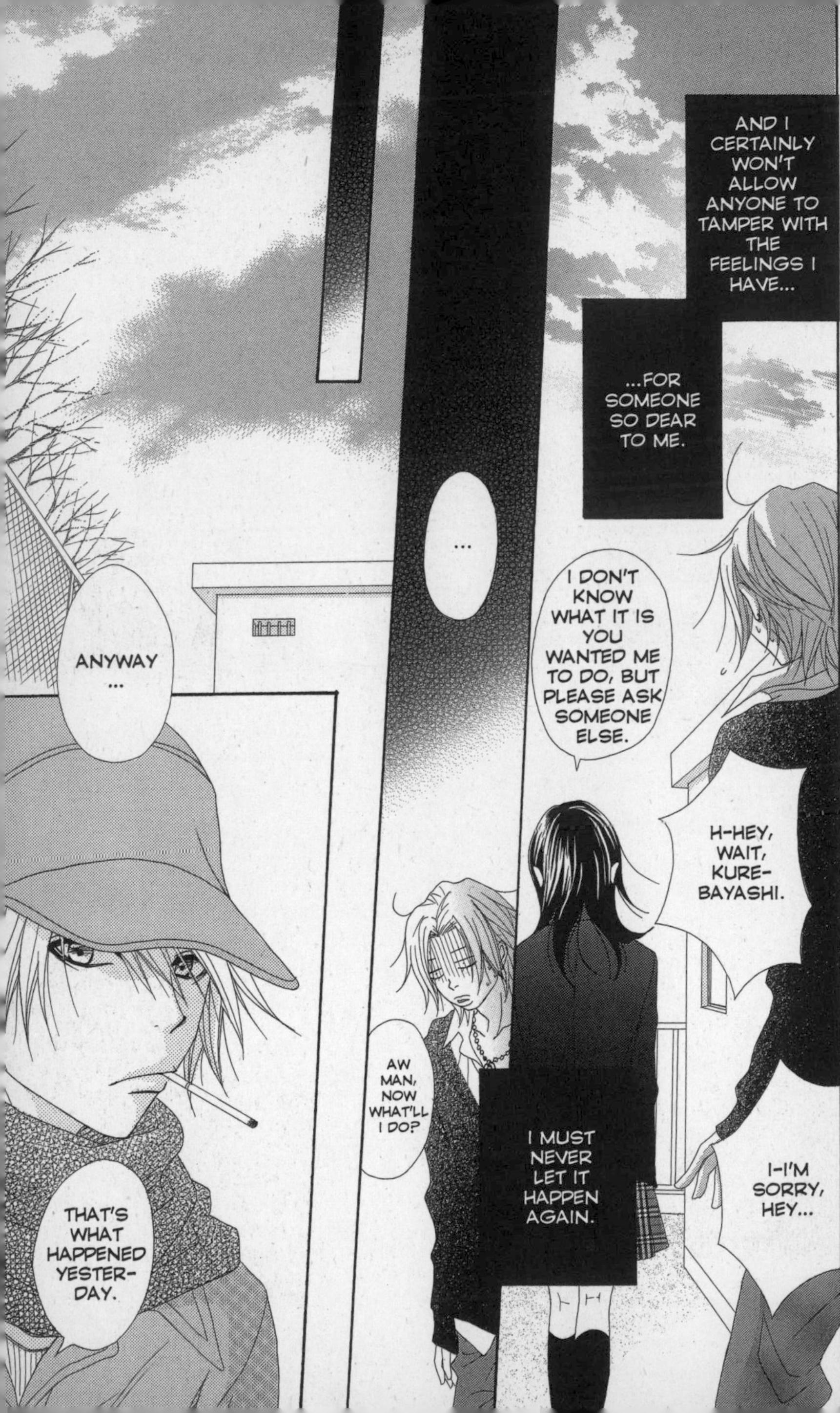
AND I CERTAINLY WON'T ALLOW ANYONE TO TAMPER WITH THE FEELINGS I HAVE...
...FOR SOMEONE SO DEAR TO ME.
I DON'T KNOW WHAT IT IS YOU WANTED ME TO DO, BUT PLEASE ASK SOMEONE ELSE.
H-HEY, WAIT, KURE-BAYASHI.
I-I'M SORRY, HEY...
I MUST NEVER LET IT HAPPEN AGAIN.
...
AW MAN, NOW WHAT'LL I DO?
ANYWAY ...
THAT'S WHAT HAPPENED YESTER-DAY.

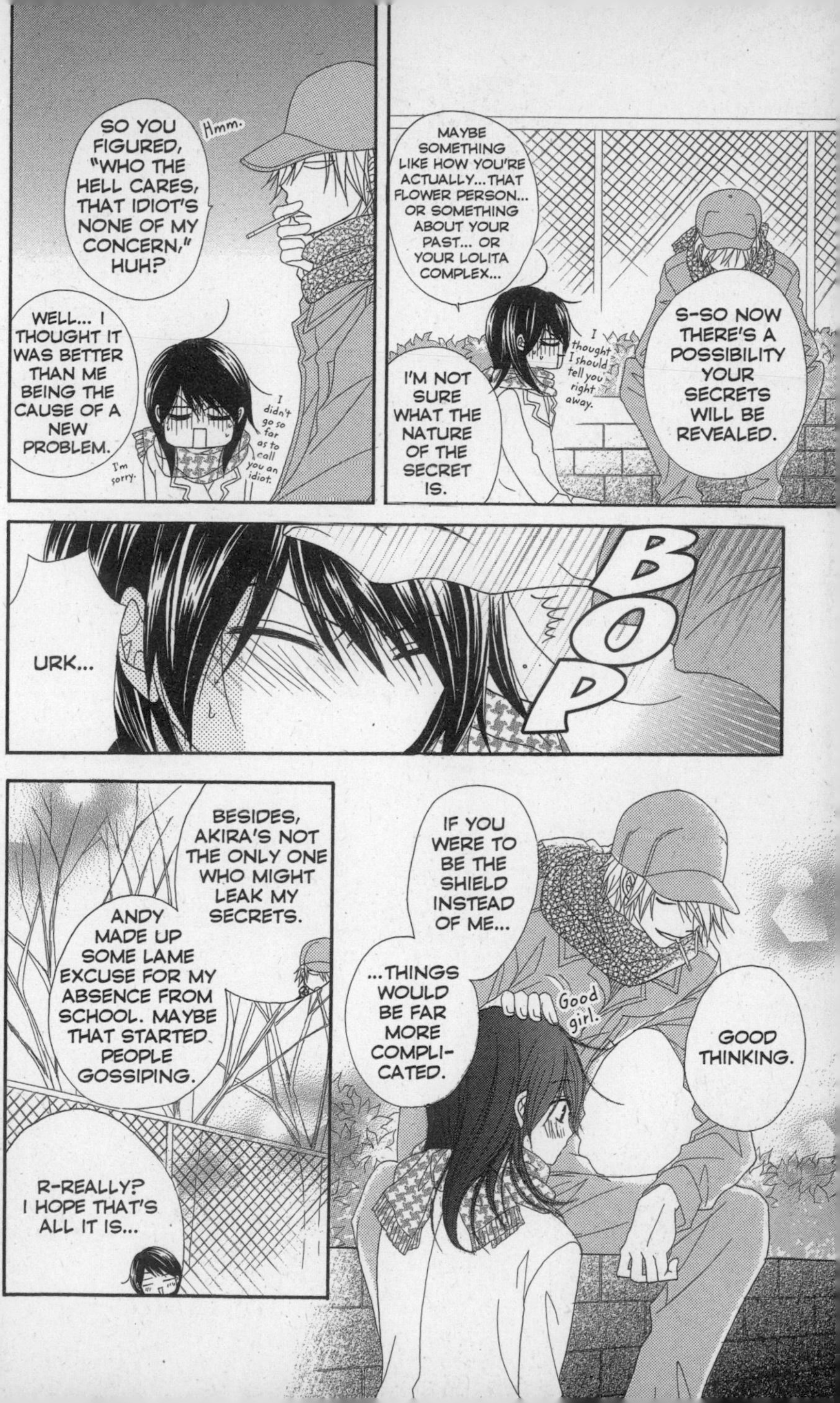
S-SO NOW THERE'S A POSSIBILITY YOUR SECRETS WILL BE REVEALED.
I'M NOT SURE WHAT THE NATURE OF THE SECRET IS.
MAYBE SOMETHING LIKE HOW YOU'RE ACTUALLY...THAT FLOWER PERSON... OR SOMETHING ABOUT YOUR PAST... OR YOUR LOLITA COMPLEX...
I thought I should tell you right away.
SO YOU FIGURED, "WHO THE HELL CARES, THAT IDIOT'S NONE OF MY CONCERN," HUH?
Hmm.
WELL... I THOUGHT IT WAS BETTER THAN ME BEING THE CAUSE OF A NEW PROBLEM.
I didn't go so far as to call you an idiot.
I'm sorry.
BOP
URK...
IF YOU WERE TO BE THE SHIELD INSTEAD OF ME...
...THINGS WOULD BE FAR MORE COMPLICATED.
GOOD THINKING.
Good girl.
BESIDES, AKIRA'S NOT THE ONLY ONE WHO MIGHT LEAK MY SECRETS.
ANDY MADE UP SOME LAME EXCUSE FOR MY ABSENCE FROM SCHOOL. MAYBE THAT STARTED PEOPLE GOSSIPING.
R-REALLY? I HOPE THAT'S ALL IT IS...

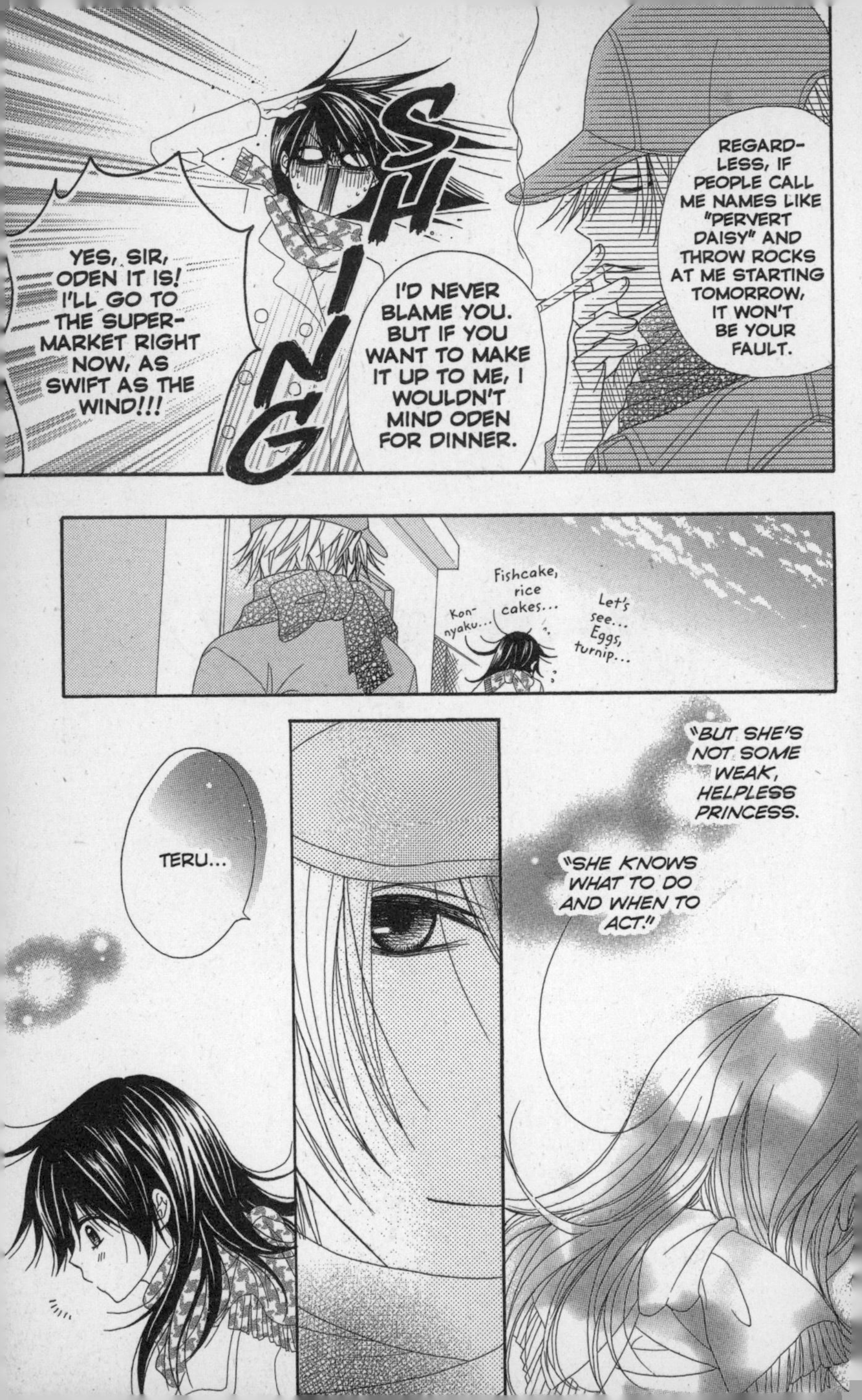
REGARDLESS, IF PEOPLE CALL ME NAMES LIKE "PERVERT DAISY" AND THROW ROCKS AT ME STARTING TOMORROW, IT WON'T BE YOUR FAULT.
I'D NEVER BLAME YOU. BUT IF YOU WANT TO MAKE IT UP TO ME, I WOULDN'T MIND ODEN FOR DINNER.
SHING
YES, SIR, ODEN IT IS! I'LL GO TO THE SUPERMARKET RIGHT NOW, AS SWIFT AS THE WIND!!!
Let's see... Eggs, turnip...
Fishcake, rice cakes...
Kon-nyaku...
"BUT SHE'S NOT SOME WEAK, HELPLESS PRINCESS.
"SHE KNOWS WHAT TO DO AND WHEN TO ACT."
TERU...

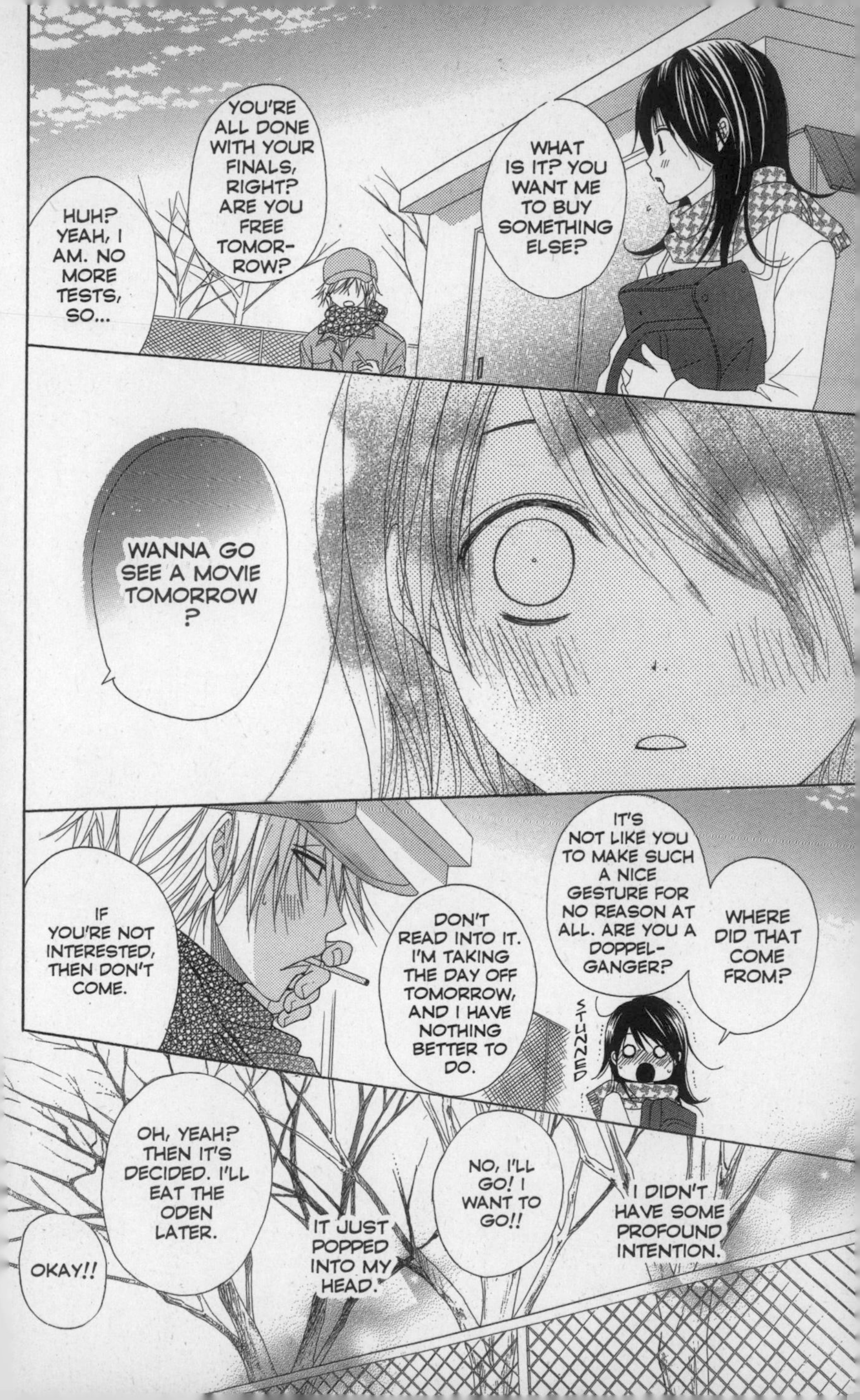
WHAT IS IT? YOU WANT ME TO BUY SOMETHING ELSE?
YOU'RE ALL DONE WITH YOUR FINALS, RIGHT? ARE YOU FREE TOMOR-ROW?
HUH? YEAH, I AM. NO MORE TESTS, SO...
WANNA GO SEE A MOVIE TOMORROW?
WHERE DID THAT COME FROM?
IT'S NOT LIKE YOU TO MAKE SUCH A NICE GESTURE FOR NO REASON AT ALL. ARE YOU A DOPPEL-GANGER?
STUNNED
DON'T READ INTO IT. I'M TAKING THE DAY OFF TOMORROW, AND I HAVE NOTHING BETTER TO DO.
IF YOU'RE NOT INTERESTED, THEN DON'T COME.
I DIDN'T HAVE SOME PROFOUND INTENTION.
NO, I'LL GO! I WANT TO GO!!
IT JUST POPPED INTO MY HEAD.
OH, YEAH? THEN IT'S DECIDED. I'LL EAT THE ODEN LATER.
OKAY!!

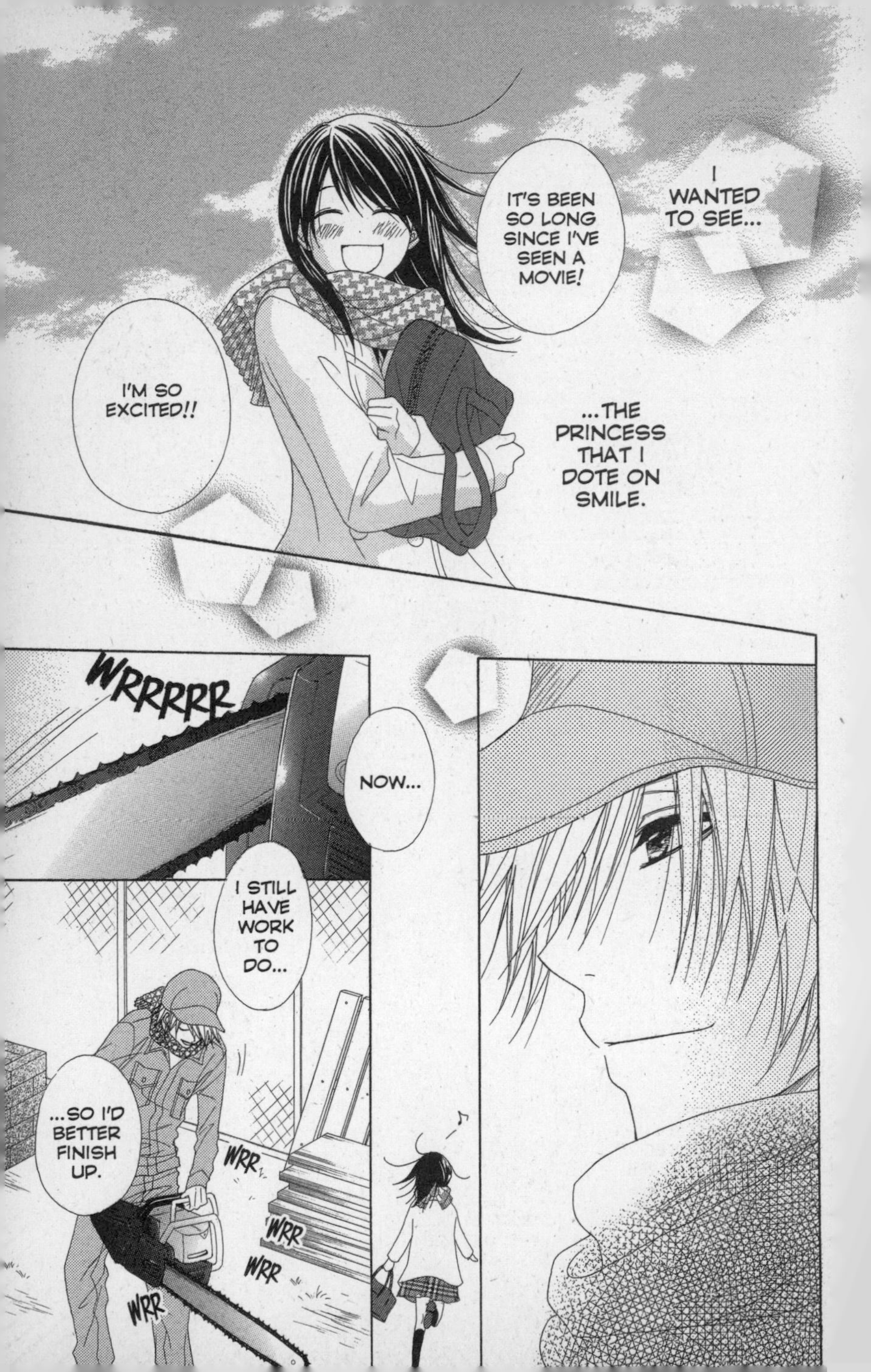
I WANTED TO SEE...
IT'S BEEN SO LONG SINCE I'VE SEEN A MOVIE!
...THE PRINCESS THAT I DOTE ON SMILE.
I'M SO EXCITED!!
NOW...
WRRRRR
I STILL HAVE WORK TO DO...
...SO I'D BETTER FINISH UP.
WRR
WRR
WRR
WRR

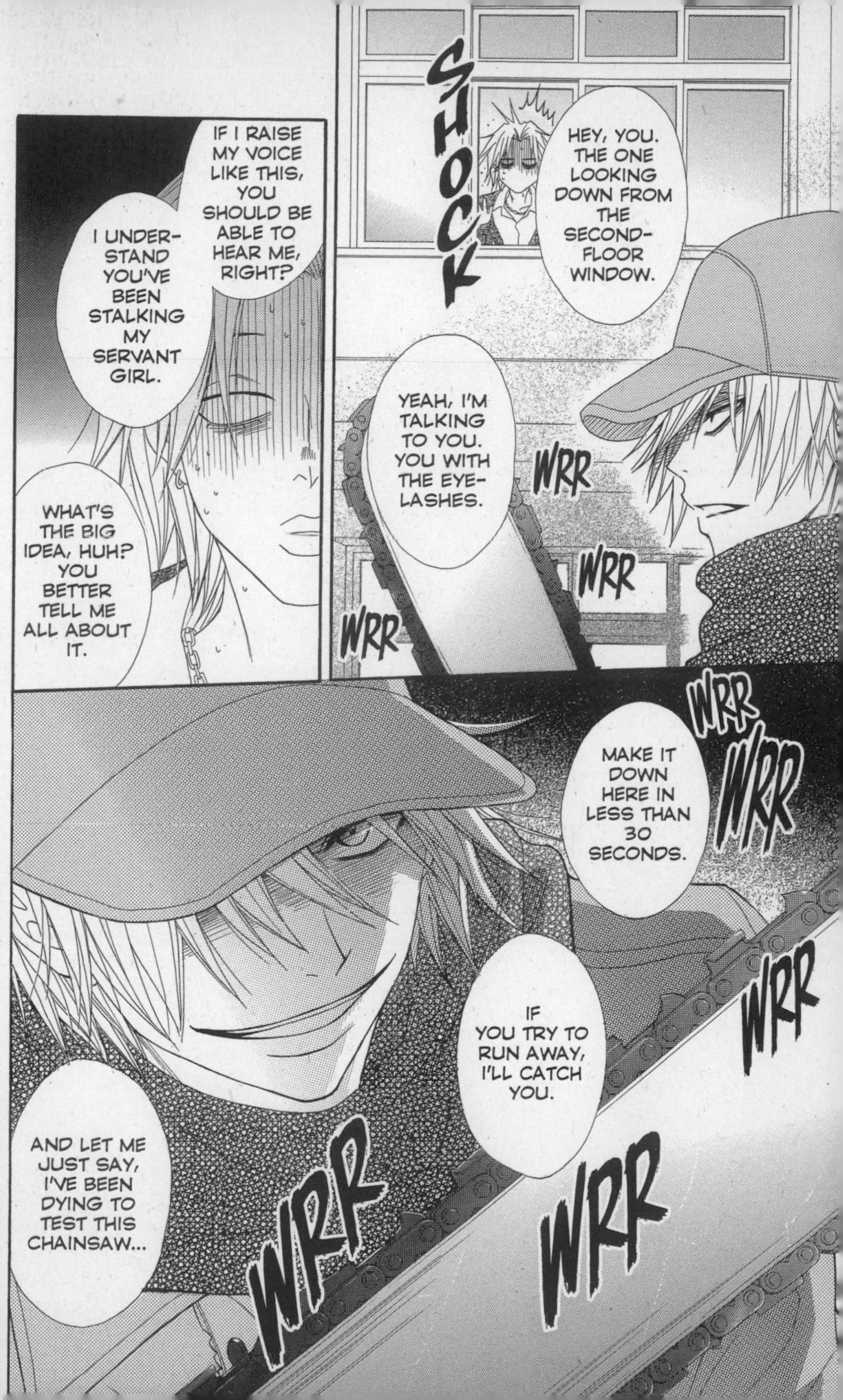
SHOCK
HEY, YOU. THE ONE LOOKING DOWN FROM THE SECOND-FLOOR WINDOW.
YEAH, I'M TALKING TO YOU. YOU WITH THE EYE-LASHES.
WRR
WRR
WRR
IF I RAISE MY VOICE LIKE THIS, YOU SHOULD BE ABLE TO HEAR ME, RIGHT?
I UNDER-STAND YOU'VE BEEN STALKING MY SERVANT GIRL.
WHAT'S THE BIG IDEA, HUH? YOU BETTER TELL ME ALL ABOUT IT.
WRR
WRR
MAKE IT DOWN HERE IN LESS THAN 30 SECONDS.
WRR
IF YOU TRY TO RUN AWAY, I'LL CATCH YOU.
AND LET ME JUST SAY, I'VE BEEN DYING TO TEST THIS CHAINSAW...
WRR
WRR

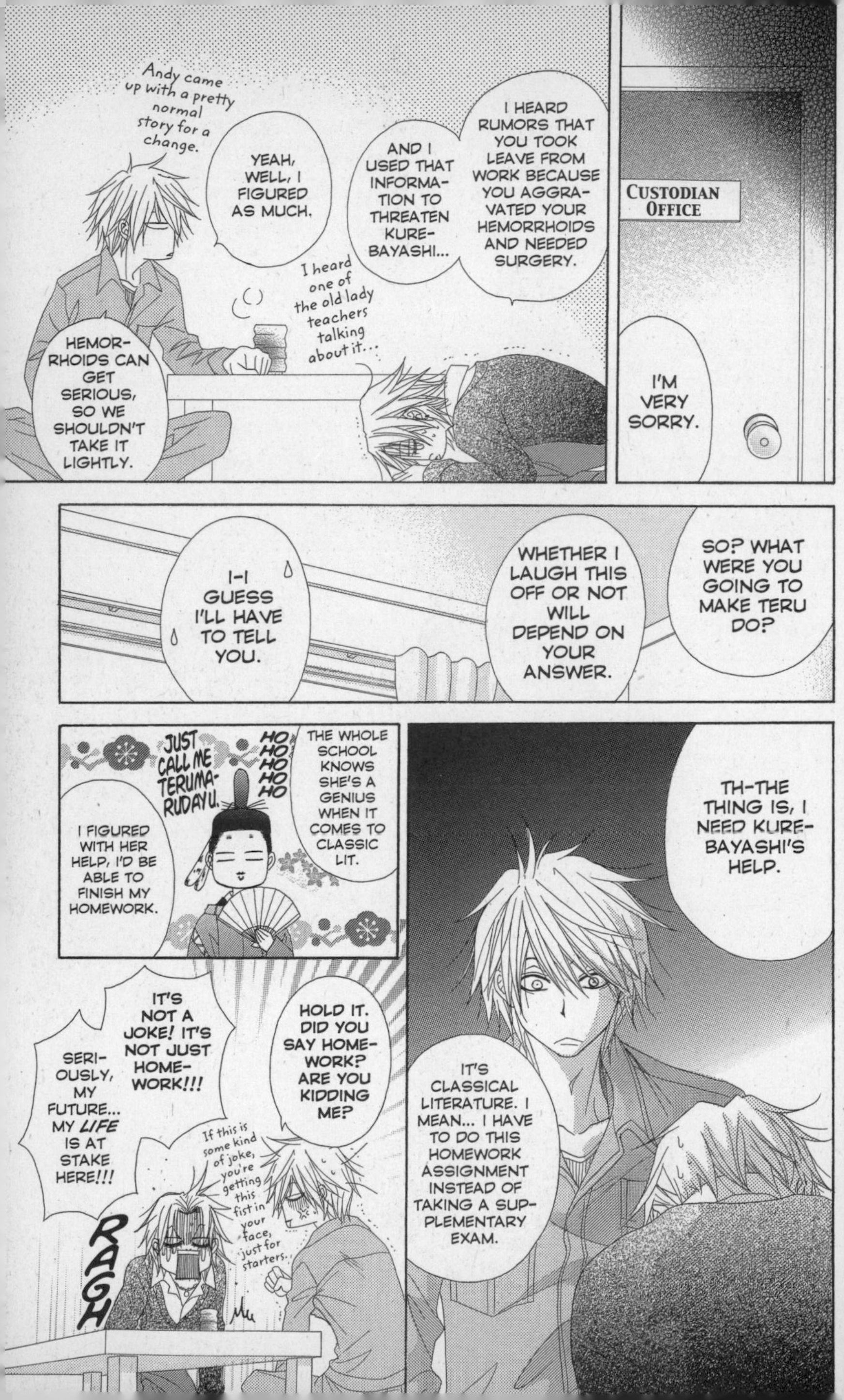
CUSTODIAN OFFICE
I'M VERY SORRY.
I HEARD RUMORS THAT YOU TOOK LEAVE FROM WORK BECAUSE YOU AGGRAVATED YOUR HEMORRHOIDS AND NEEDED SURGERY.
AND I USED THAT INFORMATION TO THREATEN KUREBAYASHI...
YEAH, WELL, I FIGURED AS MUCH.
Andy came up with a pretty normal story for a change.
I heard one of the old lady teachers talking about it...
HEMORRHOIDS CAN GET SERIOUS, SO WE SHOULDN'T TAKE IT LIGHTLY.
SO? WHAT WERE YOU GOING TO MAKE TERU DO?
WHETHER I LAUGH THIS OFF OR NOT WILL DEPEND ON YOUR ANSWER.
I-I GUESS I'LL HAVE TO TELL YOU.
TH-THE THING IS, I NEED KUREBAYASHI'S HELP.
IT'S CLASSICAL LITERATURE. I MEAN... I HAVE TO DO THIS HOMEWORK ASSIGNMENT INSTEAD OF TAKING A SUPPLEMENTARY EXAM.
THE WHOLE SCHOOL KNOWS SHE'S A GENIUS WHEN IT COMES TO CLASSIC LIT.
HOHOHOHOHO
JUST CALL ME TERUMARUDAYU.
I FIGURED WITH HER HELP, I'D BE ABLE TO FINISH MY HOMEWORK.
HOLD IT. DID YOU SAY HOMEWORK? ARE YOU KIDDING ME?
IT'S NOT A JOKE! IT'S NOT JUST HOMEWORK!!!
SERIOUSLY, MY FUTURE... MY *LIFE* IS AT STAKE HERE!!!
If this is some kind of joke, you're getting this fist in your face, just for starters.
RAGH

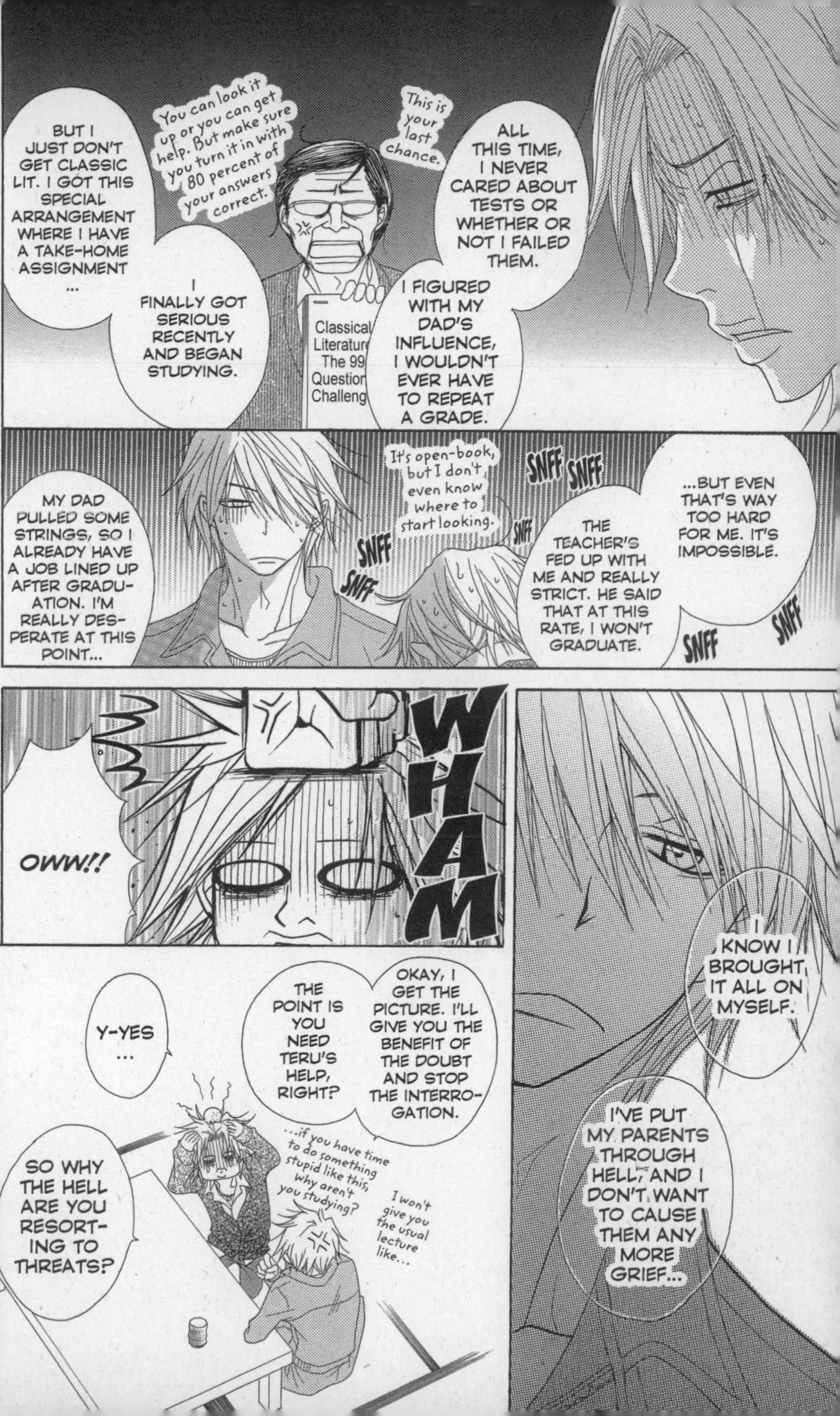
ALL THIS TIME, I NEVER CARED ABOUT TESTS OR WHETHER OR NOT I FAILED THEM.
This is your last chance.
I FIGURED WITH MY DAD'S INFLUENCE, I WOULDN'T EVER HAVE TO REPEAT A GRADE.
You can look it up or you can get help. But make sure you turn it in with 80 percent of your answers correct.
Classical Literature The 99 Question Challeng
BUT I JUST DON'T GET CLASSIC LIT. I GOT THIS SPECIAL ARRANGEMENT WHERE I HAVE A TAKE-HOME ASSIGNMENT ...
I FINALLY GOT SERIOUS RECENTLY AND BEGAN STUDYING.
...BUT EVEN THAT'S WAY TOO HARD FOR ME. IT'S IMPOSSIBLE.
SNFF SNFF
THE TEACHER'S FED UP WITH ME AND REALLY STRICT. HE SAID THAT AT THIS RATE, I WON'T GRADUATE.
SNFF SNFF
It's open-book, but I don't even know where to start looking.
SNFF SNFF SNFF
MY DAD PULLED SOME STRINGS, SO I ALREADY HAVE A JOB LINED UP AFTER GRADUATION. I'M REALLY DESPERATE AT THIS POINT...
I KNOW I BROUGHT IT ALL ON MYSELF.
I'VE PUT MY PARENTS THROUGH HELL, AND I DON'T WANT TO CAUSE THEM ANY MORE GRIEF...
WHAM
OWW!!
OKAY, I GET THE PICTURE. I'LL GIVE YOU THE BENEFIT OF THE DOUBT AND STOP THE INTERROGATION.
THE POINT IS YOU NEED TERU'S HELP, RIGHT?
Y-YES ...
I won't give you the usual lecture like...
...if you have time to do something stupid like this, why aren't you studying?
SO WHY THE HELL ARE YOU RESORTING TO THREATS?

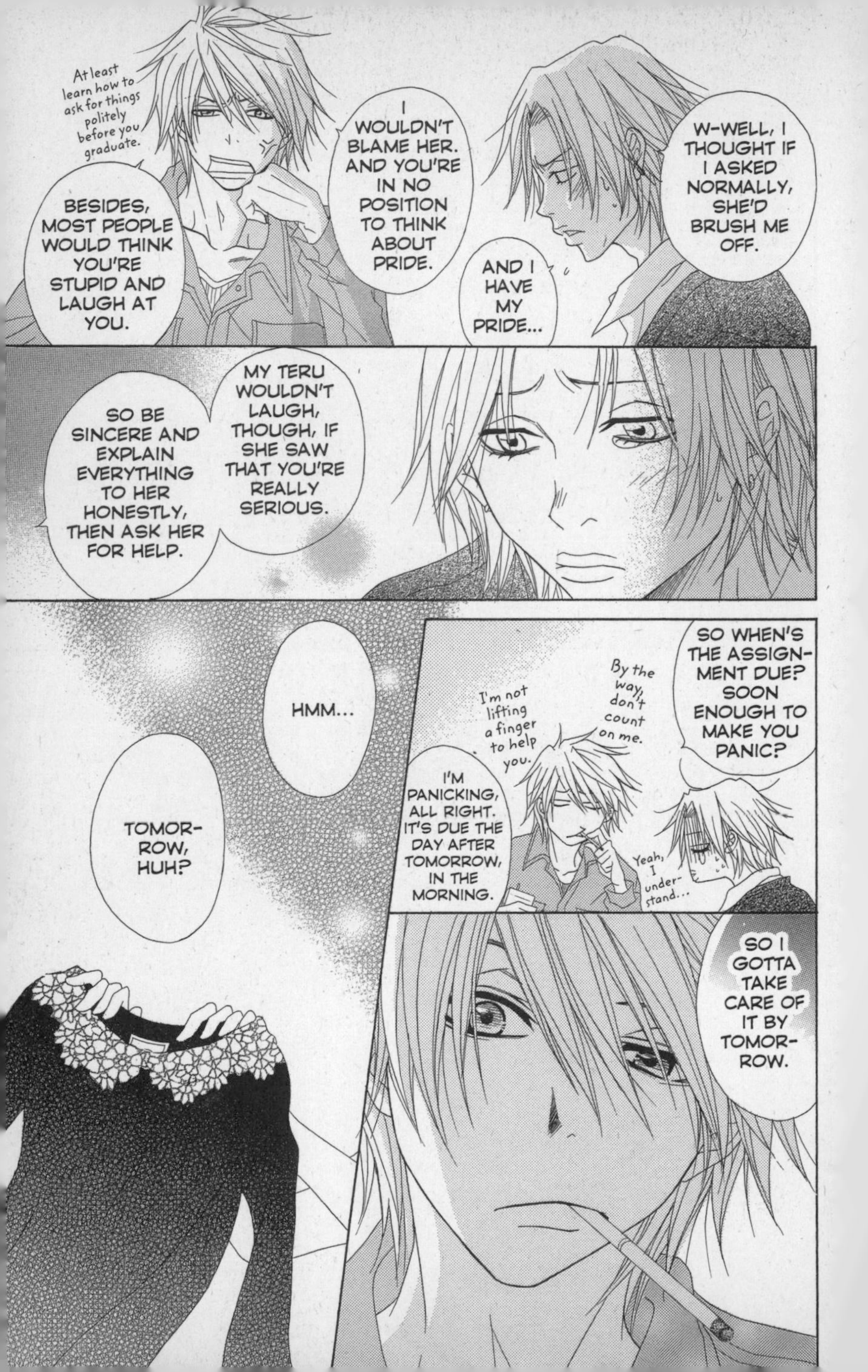
W-WELL, I THOUGHT IF I ASKED NORMALLY, SHE'D BRUSH ME OFF.
AND I HAVE MY PRIDE...
I WOULDN'T BLAME HER. AND YOU'RE IN NO POSITION TO THINK ABOUT PRIDE.
BESIDES, MOST PEOPLE WOULD THINK YOU'RE STUPID AND LAUGH AT YOU.
At least learn how to ask for things politely before you graduate.
MY TERU WOULDN'T LAUGH, THOUGH, IF SHE SAW THAT YOU'RE REALLY SERIOUS.
SO BE SINCERE AND EXPLAIN EVERYTHING TO HER HONESTLY, THEN ASK HER FOR HELP.
SO WHEN'S THE ASSIGNMENT DUE? SOON ENOUGH TO MAKE YOU PANIC?
By the way, don't count on me.
I'm not lifting a finger to help you.
Yeah, I under-stand...
I'M PANICKING, ALL RIGHT. IT'S DUE THE DAY AFTER TOMORROW, IN THE MORNING.
SO I GOTTA TAKE CARE OF IT BY TOMOR-ROW.
HMM...
TOMOR-ROW, HUH?

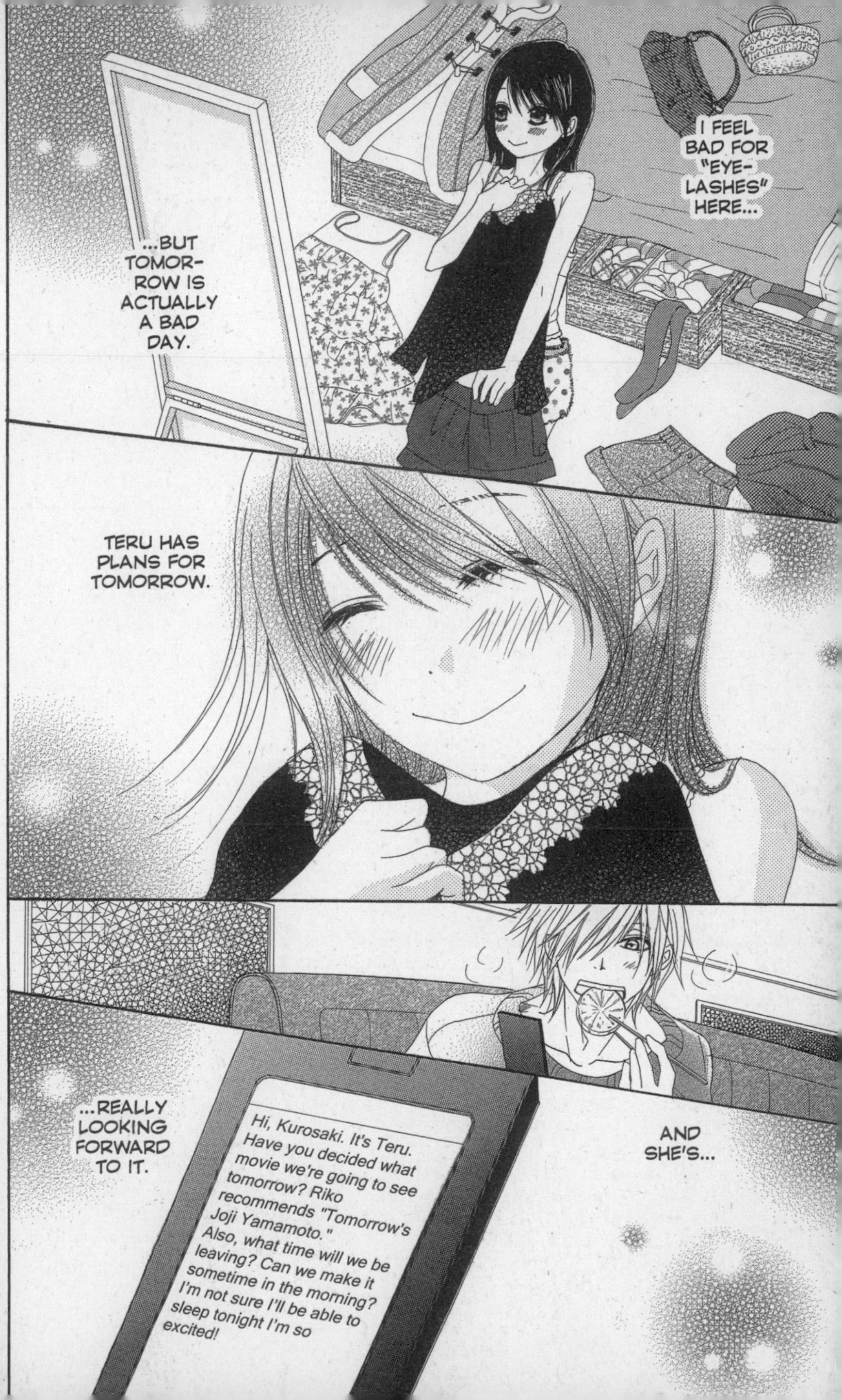
I FEEL BAD FOR "EYE-LASHES" HERE...
...BUT TOMOR-ROW IS ACTUALLY A BAD DAY.
TERU HAS PLANS FOR TOMORROW.
AND SHE'S...
...REALLY LOOKING FORWARD TO IT.
Hi, Kurosaki. It's Teru. Have you decided what movie we're going to see tomorrow? Riko recommends "Tomorrow's Joji Yamamoto." Also, what time will we be leaving? Can we make it sometime in the morning? I'm not sure I'll be able to sleep tonight I'm so excited!

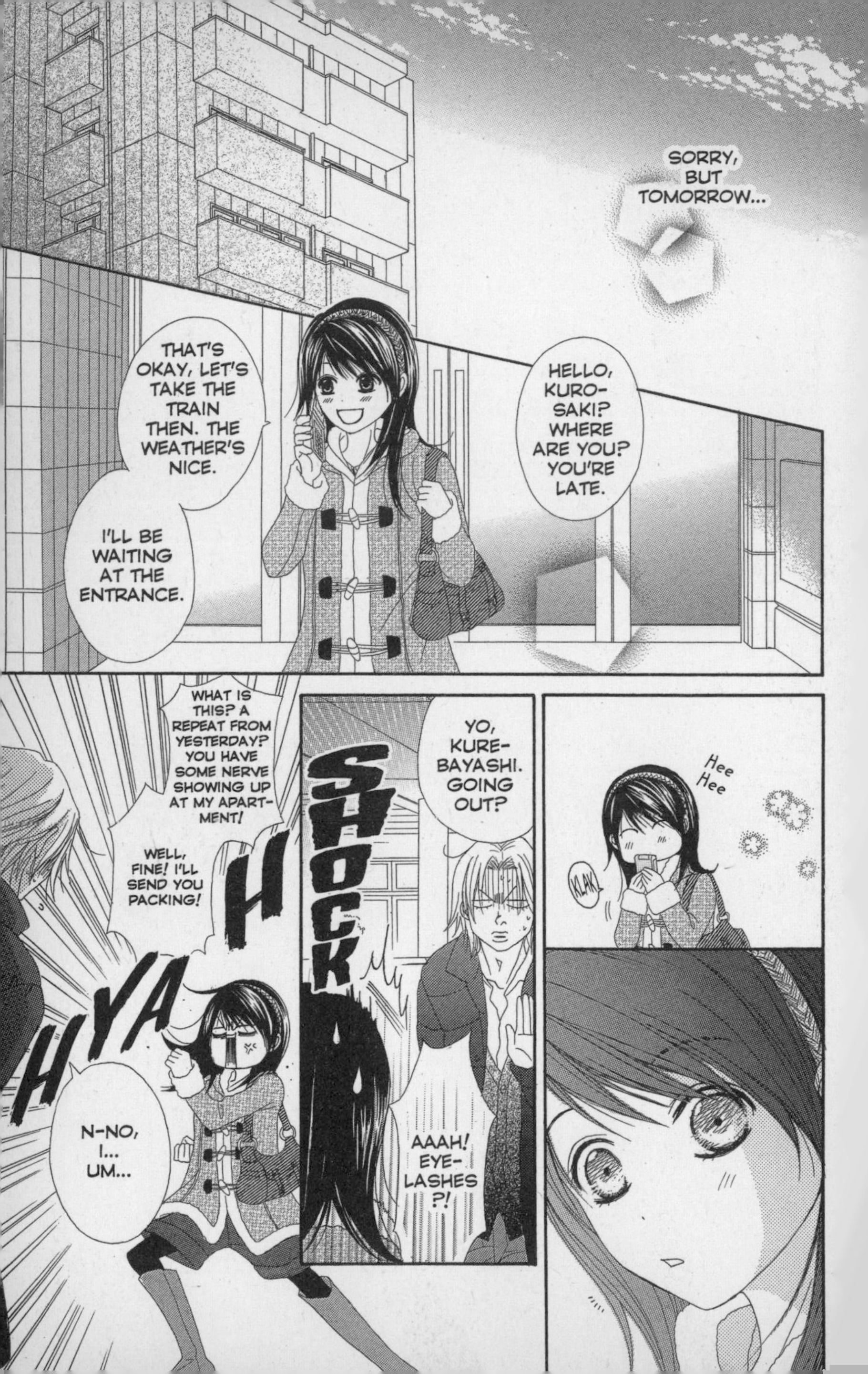
SORRY, BUT TOMORROW...
HELLO, KURO-SAKI? WHERE ARE YOU? YOU'RE LATE.
THAT'S OKAY, LET'S TAKE THE TRAIN THEN. THE WEATHER'S NICE.
I'LL BE WAITING AT THE ENTRANCE.
Hee Hee
KLAK
YO, KURE-BAYASHI. GOING OUT?
SHOCK
AAAH! EYE-LASHES?!
HYAH
WHAT IS THIS? A REPEAT FROM YESTERDAY? YOU HAVE SOME NERVE SHOWING UP AT MY APART-MENT!
WELL, FINE! I'LL SEND YOU PACKING!
N-NO, I... UM...

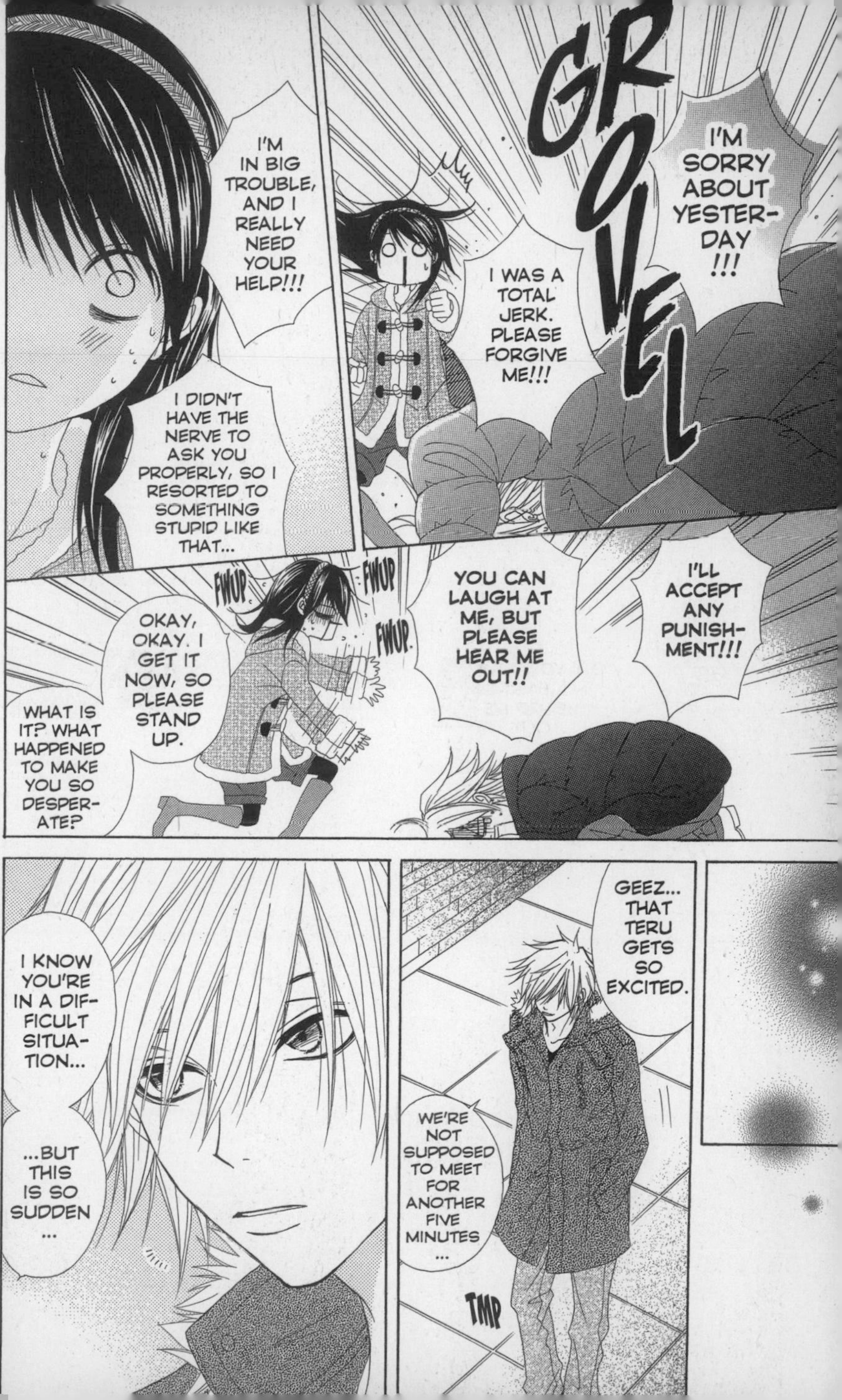
GROVEL
I'M SORRY ABOUT YESTER-DAY!!!
I WAS A TOTAL JERK. PLEASE FORGIVE ME!!!
I'M IN BIG TROUBLE, AND I REALLY NEED YOUR HELP!!!
I DIDN'T HAVE THE NERVE TO ASK YOU PROPERLY, SO I RESORTED TO SOMETHING STUPID LIKE THAT...
I'LL ACCEPT ANY PUNISH-MENT!!!
YOU CAN LAUGH AT ME, BUT PLEASE HEAR ME OUT!!
FWUP
FWUP
FWUP
OKAY, OKAY. I GET IT NOW, SO PLEASE STAND UP.
WHAT IS IT? WHAT HAPPENED TO MAKE YOU SO DESPER-ATE?
GEEZ... THAT TERU GETS SO EXCITED.
WE'RE NOT SUPPOSED TO MEET FOR ANOTHER FIVE MINUTES...
TMP
I KNOW YOU'RE IN A DIF-FICULT SITUA-TION...
...BUT THIS IS SO SUDDEN...

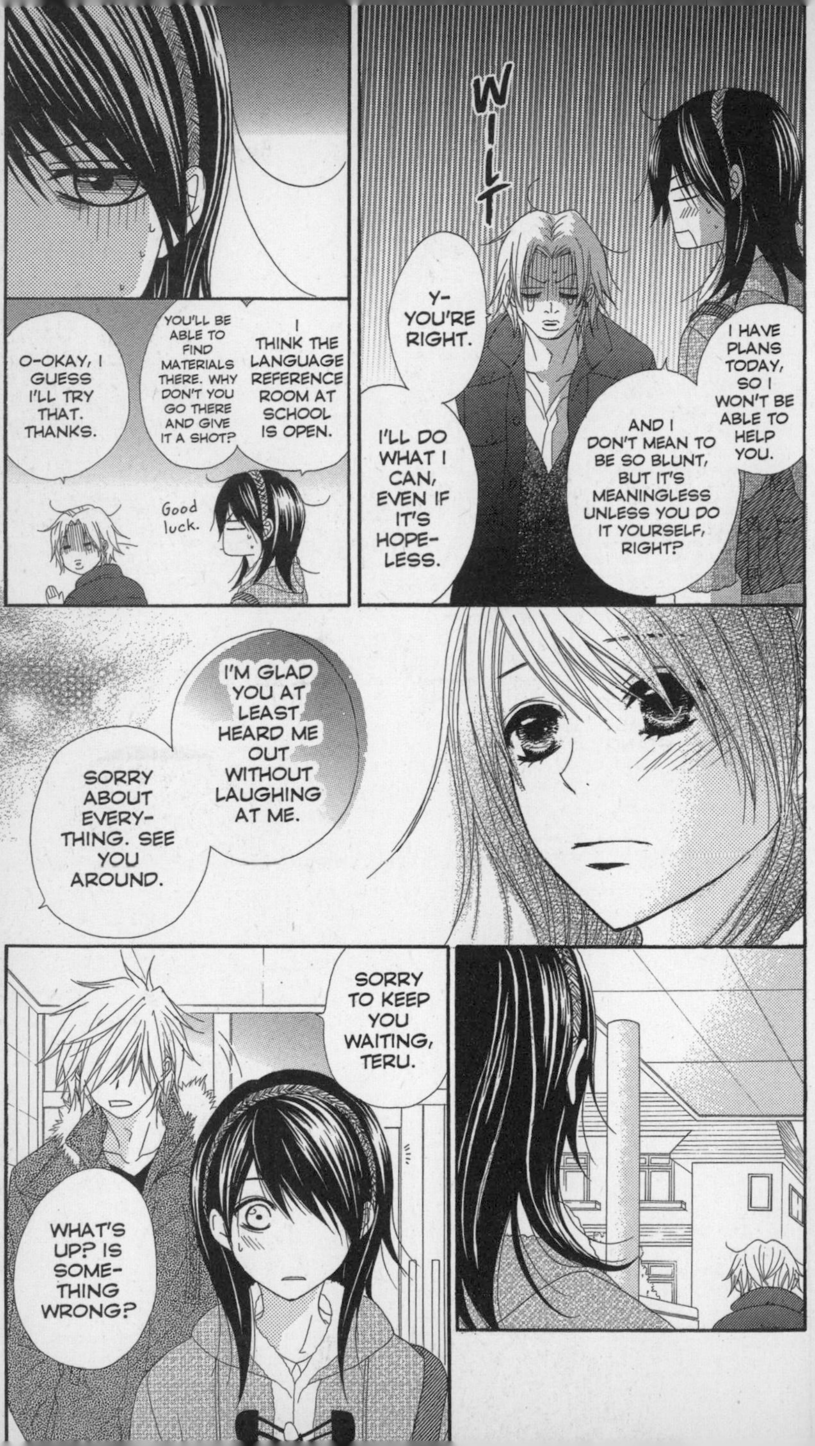
WILT
I HAVE PLANS TODAY, SO I WON'T BE ABLE TO HELP YOU.
AND I DON'T MEAN TO BE SO BLUNT, BUT IT'S MEANINGLESS UNLESS YOU DO IT YOURSELF, RIGHT?
Y-YOU'RE RIGHT.
I'LL DO WHAT I CAN, EVEN IF IT'S HOPE-LESS.
I THINK THE LANGUAGE REFERENCE ROOM AT SCHOOL IS OPEN.
YOU'LL BE ABLE TO FIND MATERIALS THERE. WHY DON'T YOU GO THERE AND GIVE IT A SHOT?
O-OKAY, I GUESS I'LL TRY THAT. THANKS.
Good luck.
I'M GLAD YOU AT LEAST HEARD ME OUT WITHOUT LAUGHING AT ME.
SORRY ABOUT EVERY-THING. SEE YOU AROUND.
SORRY TO KEEP YOU WAITING, TERU.
WHAT'S UP? IS SOME-THING WRONG?

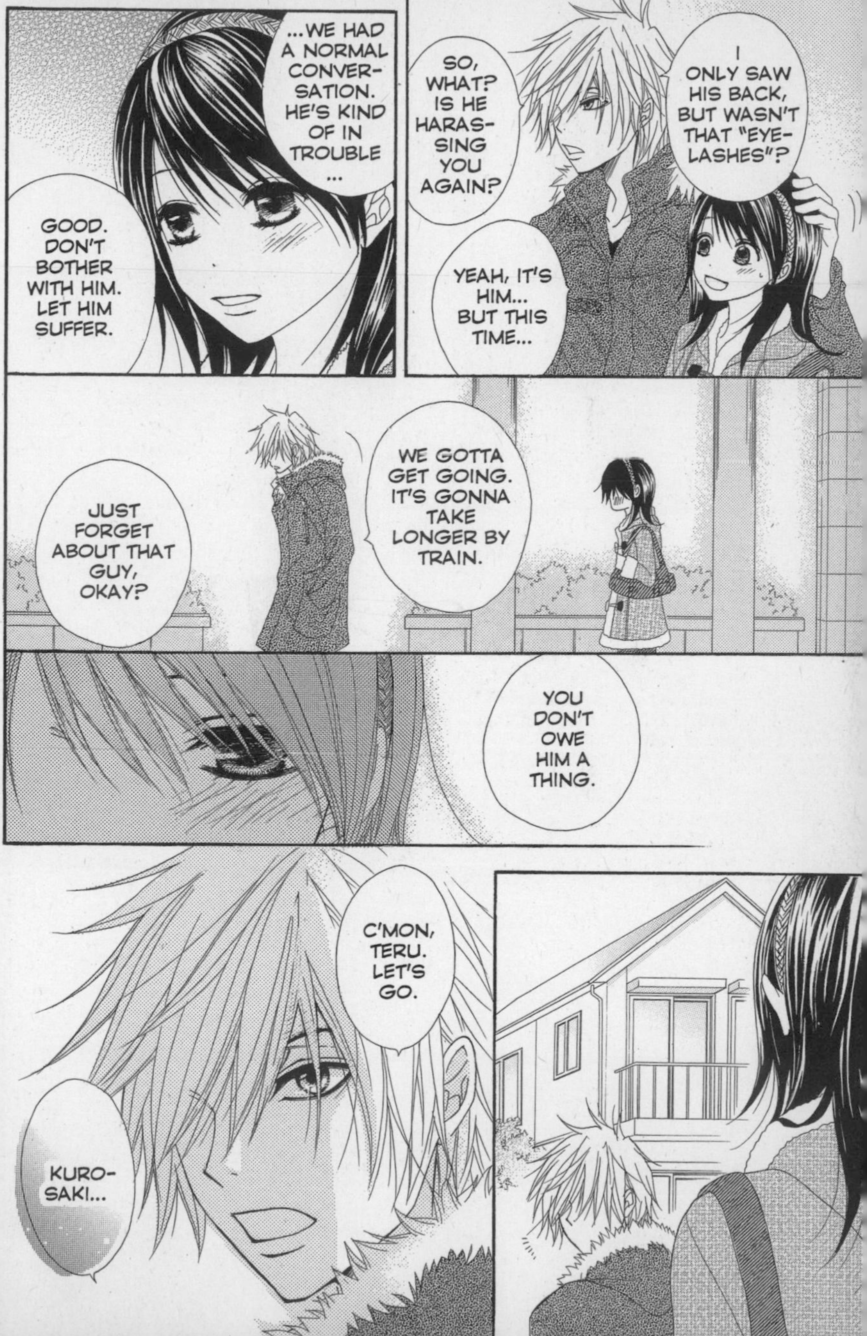
I ONLY SAW HIS BACK, BUT WASN'T THAT "EYE-LASHES"?
SO, WHAT? IS HE HARAS-SING YOU AGAIN?
YEAH, IT'S HIM... BUT THIS TIME...
...WE HAD A NORMAL CONVER-SATION. HE'S KIND OF IN TROUBLE ...
GOOD. DON'T BOTHER WITH HIM. LET HIM SUFFER.
WE GOTTA GET GOING. IT'S GONNA TAKE LONGER BY TRAIN.
JUST FORGET ABOUT THAT GUY, OKAY?
YOU DON'T OWE HIM A THING.
C'MON, TERU. LET'S GO.
KURO-SAKI...

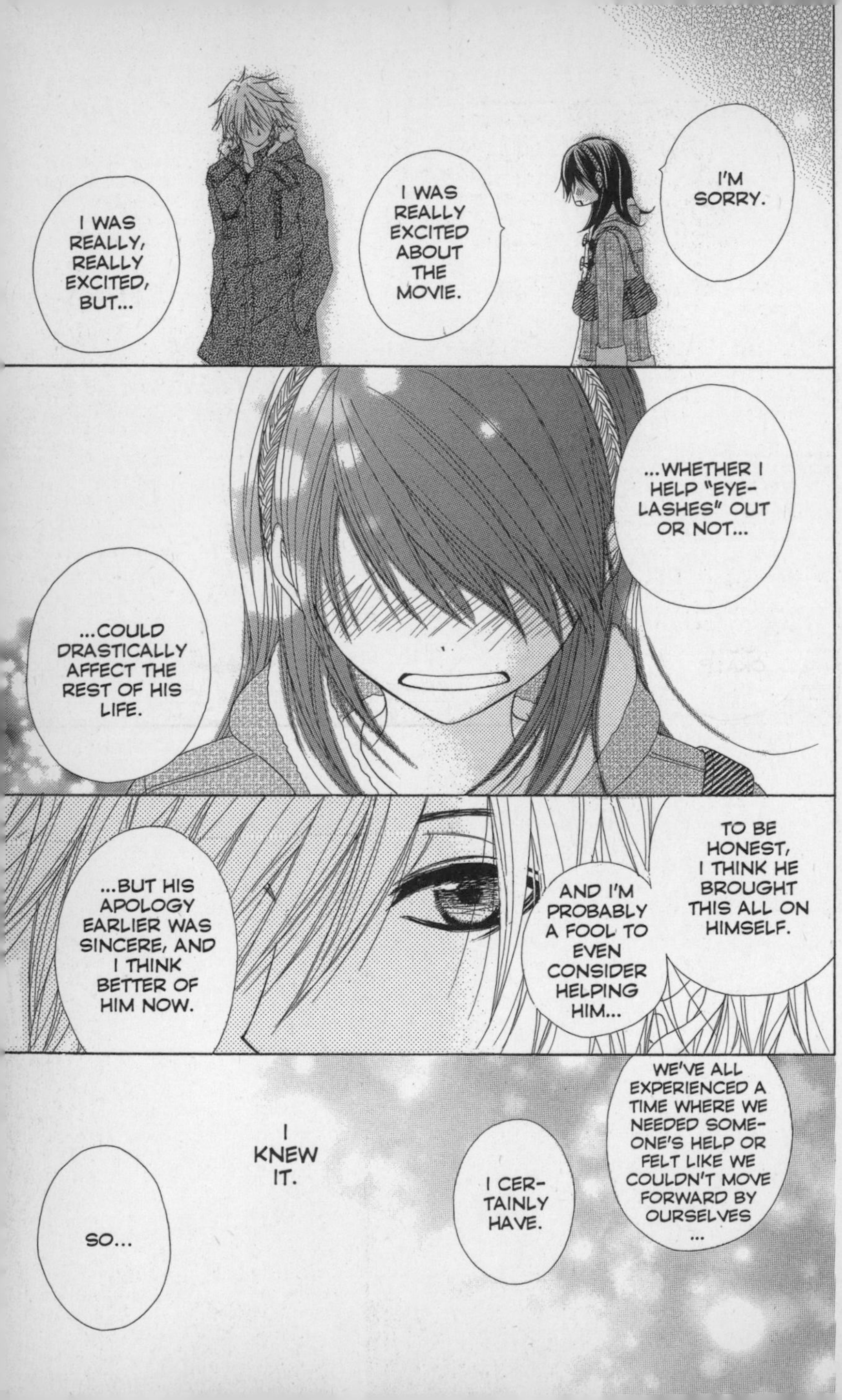
I'M SORRY.
I WAS REALLY EXCITED ABOUT THE MOVIE.
I WAS REALLY, REALLY EXCITED, BUT...
...WHETHER I HELP "EYE-LASHES" OUT OR NOT...
...COULD DRASTICALLY AFFECT THE REST OF HIS LIFE.
TO BE HONEST, I THINK HE BROUGHT THIS ALL ON HIMSELF.
AND I'M PROBABLY A FOOL TO EVEN CONSIDER HELPING HIM...
...BUT HIS APOLOGY EARLIER WAS SINCERE, AND I THINK BETTER OF HIM NOW.
WE'VE ALL EXPERIENCED A TIME WHERE WE NEEDED SOME-ONE'S HELP OR FELT LIKE WE COULDN'T MOVE FORWARD BY OURSELVES...
I CER-TAINLY HAVE.
I KNEW IT.
SO...

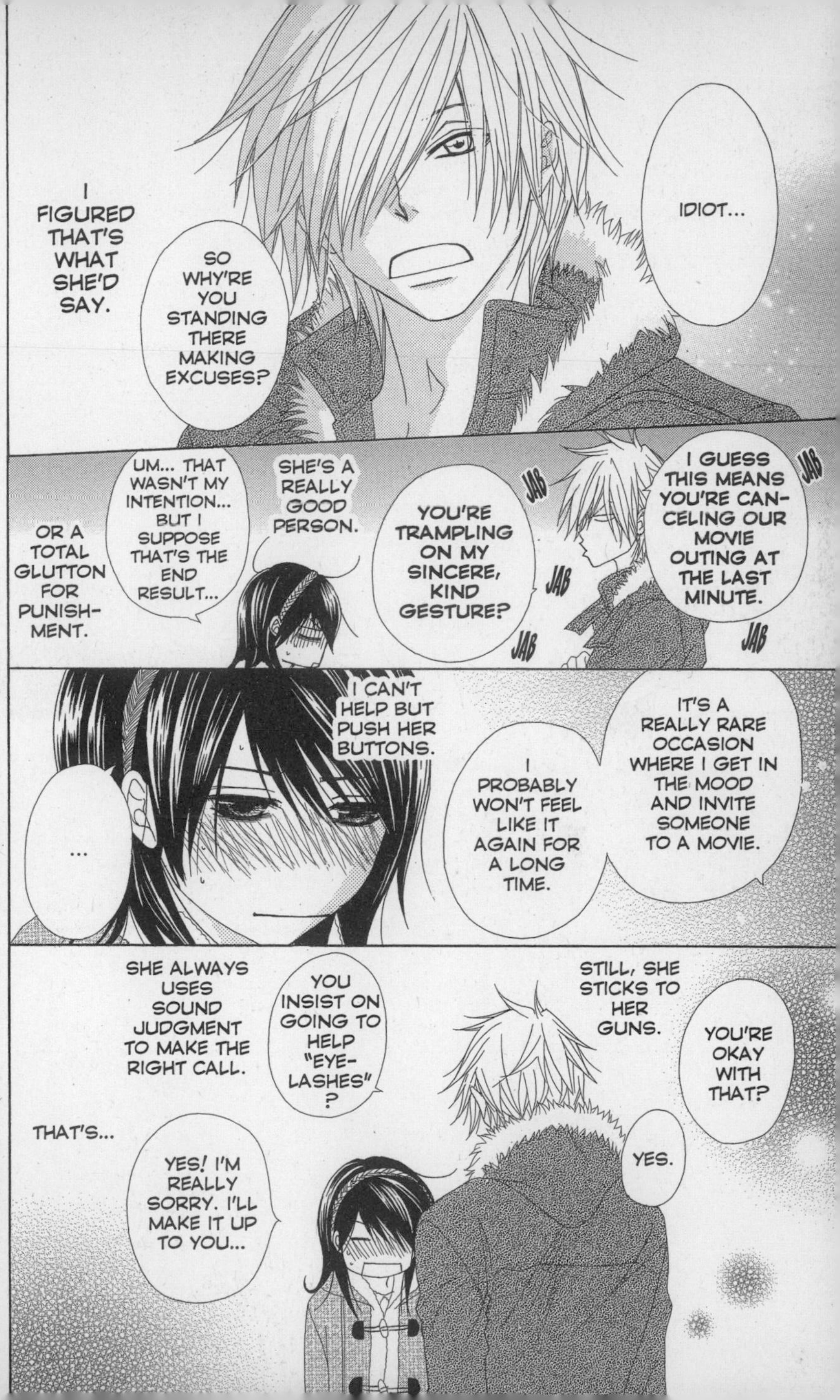
IDIOT...
SO WHY'RE YOU STANDING THERE MAKING EXCUSES?
I FIGURED THAT'S WHAT SHE'D SAY.
JAB
I GUESS THIS MEANS YOU'RE CANCELING OUR MOVIE OUTING AT THE LAST MINUTE.
JAB
JAB
YOU'RE TRAMPLING ON MY SINCERE, KIND GESTURE?
JAB
JAB
SHE'S A REALLY GOOD PERSON.
UM... THAT WASN'T MY INTENTION... BUT I SUPPOSE THAT'S THE END RESULT...
OR A TOTAL GLUTTON FOR PUNISHMENT.
IT'S A REALLY RARE OCCASION WHERE I GET IN THE MOOD AND INVITE SOMEONE TO A MOVIE.
I PROBABLY WON'T FEEL LIKE IT AGAIN FOR A LONG TIME.
I CAN'T HELP BUT PUSH HER BUTTONS.
...
YOU'RE OKAY WITH THAT?
STILL, SHE STICKS TO HER GUNS.
YOU INSIST ON GOING TO HELP "EYELASHES"?
SHE ALWAYS USES SOUND JUDGMENT TO MAKE THE RIGHT CALL.
YES.
YES! I'M REALLY SORRY. I'LL MAKE IT UP TO YOU...
THAT'S...

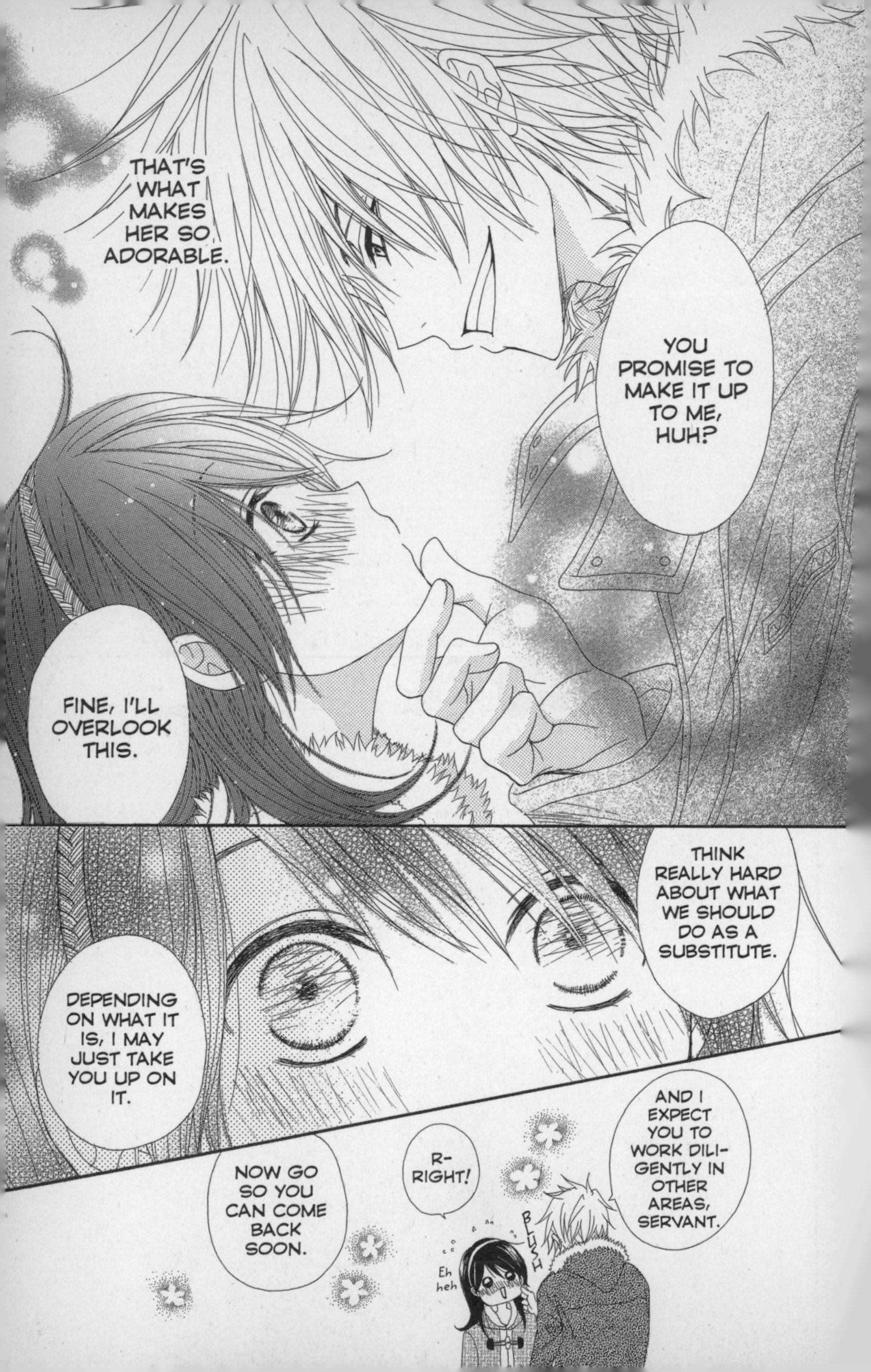
YOU PROMISE TO MAKE IT UP TO ME, HUH?
THAT'S WHAT MAKES HER SO ADORABLE.
FINE, I'LL OVERLOOK THIS.
THINK REALLY HARD ABOUT WHAT WE SHOULD DO AS A SUBSTITUTE.
DEPENDING ON WHAT IT IS, I MAY JUST TAKE YOU UP ON IT.
AND I EXPECT YOU TO WORK DILI-GENTLY IN OTHER AREAS, SERVANT.
BLUSH
R-RIGHT!
Eh heh
NOW GO SO YOU CAN COME BACK SOON.

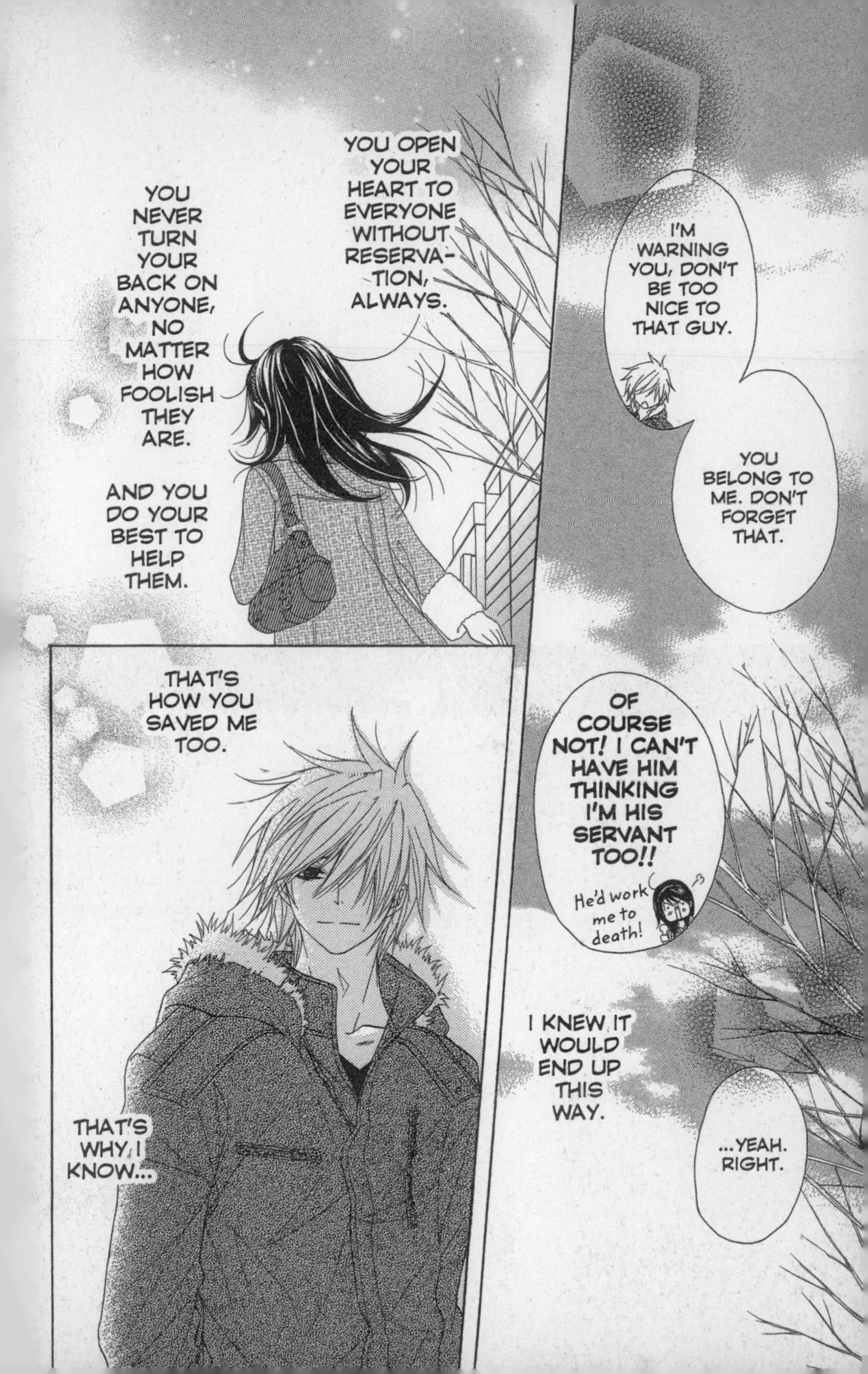

I'M WARNING YOU, DON'T BE TOO NICE TO THAT GUY.
YOU BELONG TO ME. DON'T FORGET THAT.
OF COURSE NOT! I CAN'T HAVE HIM THINKING I'M HIS SERVANT TOO!!
He'd work me to death!
I KNEW IT WOULD END UP THIS WAY.
...YEAH. RIGHT.
YOU OPEN YOUR HEART TO EVERYONE WITHOUT RESERVA-TION, ALWAYS.
YOU NEVER TURN YOUR BACK ON ANYONE, NO MATTER HOW FOOLISH THEY ARE.
AND YOU DO YOUR BEST TO HELP THEM.
THAT'S HOW YOU SAVED ME TOO.
THAT'S WHY I KNOW...

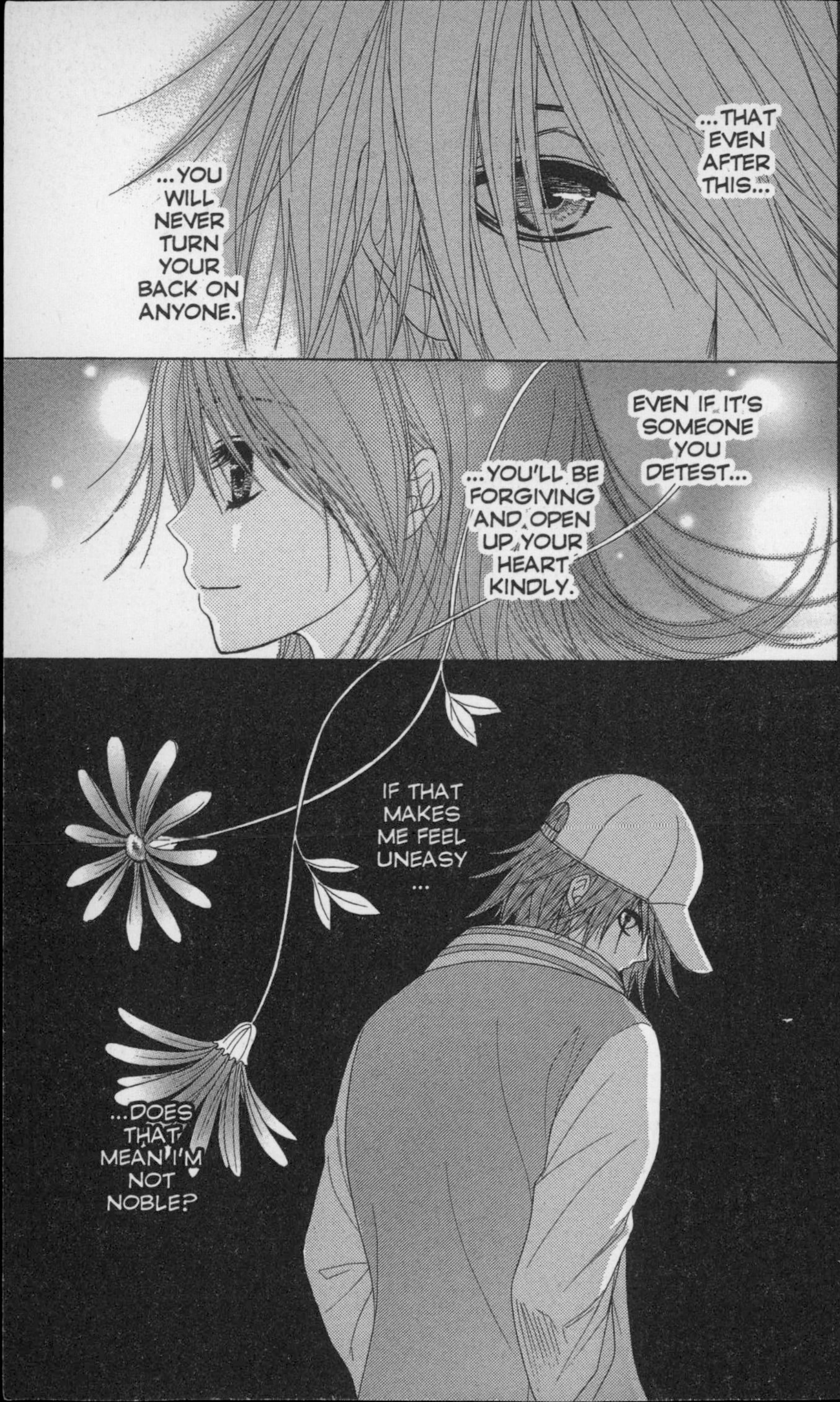
...THAT EVEN AFTER THIS...
...YOU WILL NEVER TURN YOUR BACK ON ANYONE.
EVEN IF IT'S SOMEONE YOU DETEST...
...YOU'LL BE FORGIVING AND OPEN UP YOUR HEART KINDLY.
IF THAT MAKES ME FEEL UNEASY ...
...DOES THAT MEAN I'M NOT NOBLE?

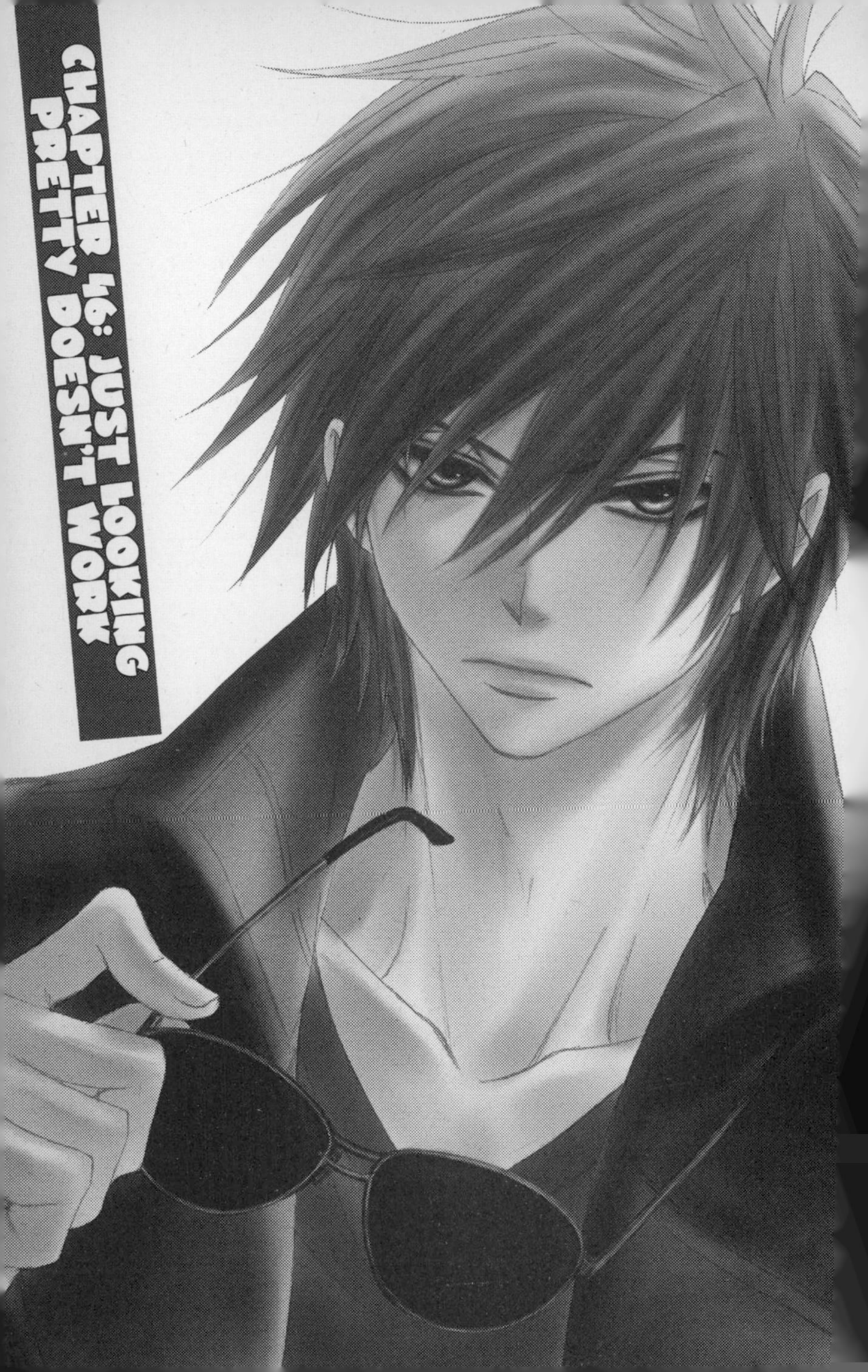
CHAPTER 46: JUST LOOKING
PRETTY DOESN'T WORK

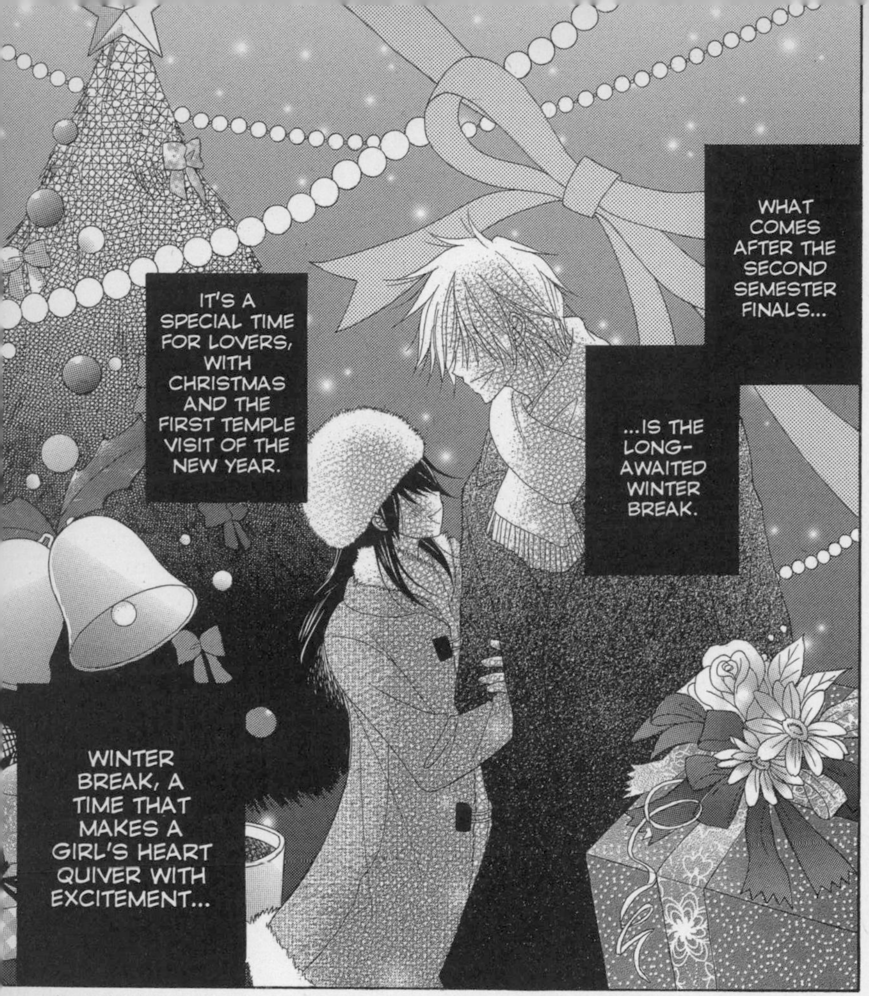
WHAT COMES AFTER THE SECOND SEMESTER FINALS...
...IS THE LONG-AWAITED WINTER BREAK.
IT'S A SPECIAL TIME FOR LOVERS, WITH CHRISTMAS AND THE FIRST TEMPLE VISIT OF THE NEW YEAR.
WINTER BREAK, A TIME THAT MAKES A GIRL'S HEART QUIVER WITH EXCITEMENT...

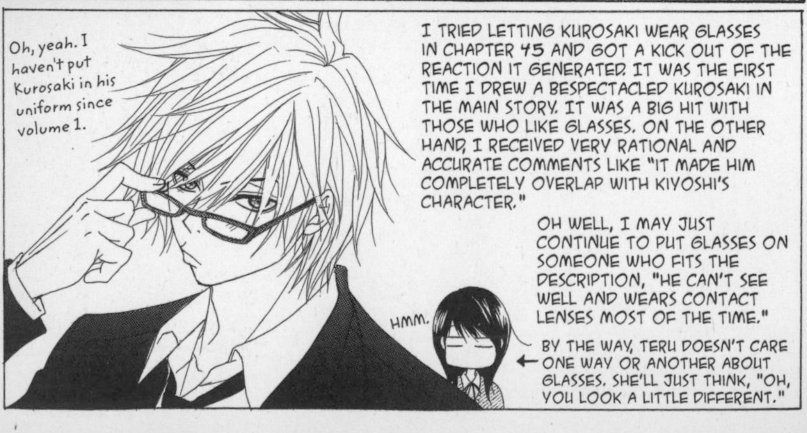
I TRIED LETTING KUROSAKI WEAR GLASSES IN CHAPTER 45 AND GOT A KICK OUT OF THE REACTION IT GENERATED. IT WAS THE FIRST TIME I DREW A BESPECTACLED KUROSAKI IN THE MAIN STORY. IT WAS A BIG HIT WITH THOSE WHO LIKE GLASSES. ON THE OTHER HAND, I RECEIVED VERY RATIONAL AND ACCURATE COMMENTS LIKE "IT MADE HIM COMPLETELY OVERLAP WITH KIYOSHI'S CHARACTER."
OH WELL, I MAY JUST CONTINUE TO PUT GLASSES ON SOMEONE WHO FITS THE DESCRIPTION, "HE CAN'T SEE WELL AND WEARS CONTACT LENSES MOST OF THE TIME."
Oh, yeah. I haven't put Kurosaki in his uniform since volume 1.
BY THE WAY, TERU DOESN'T CARE ONE WAY OR ANOTHER ABOUT GLASSES. SHE'LL JUST THINK, "OH, YOU LOOK A LITTLE DIFFERENT."
HMM.

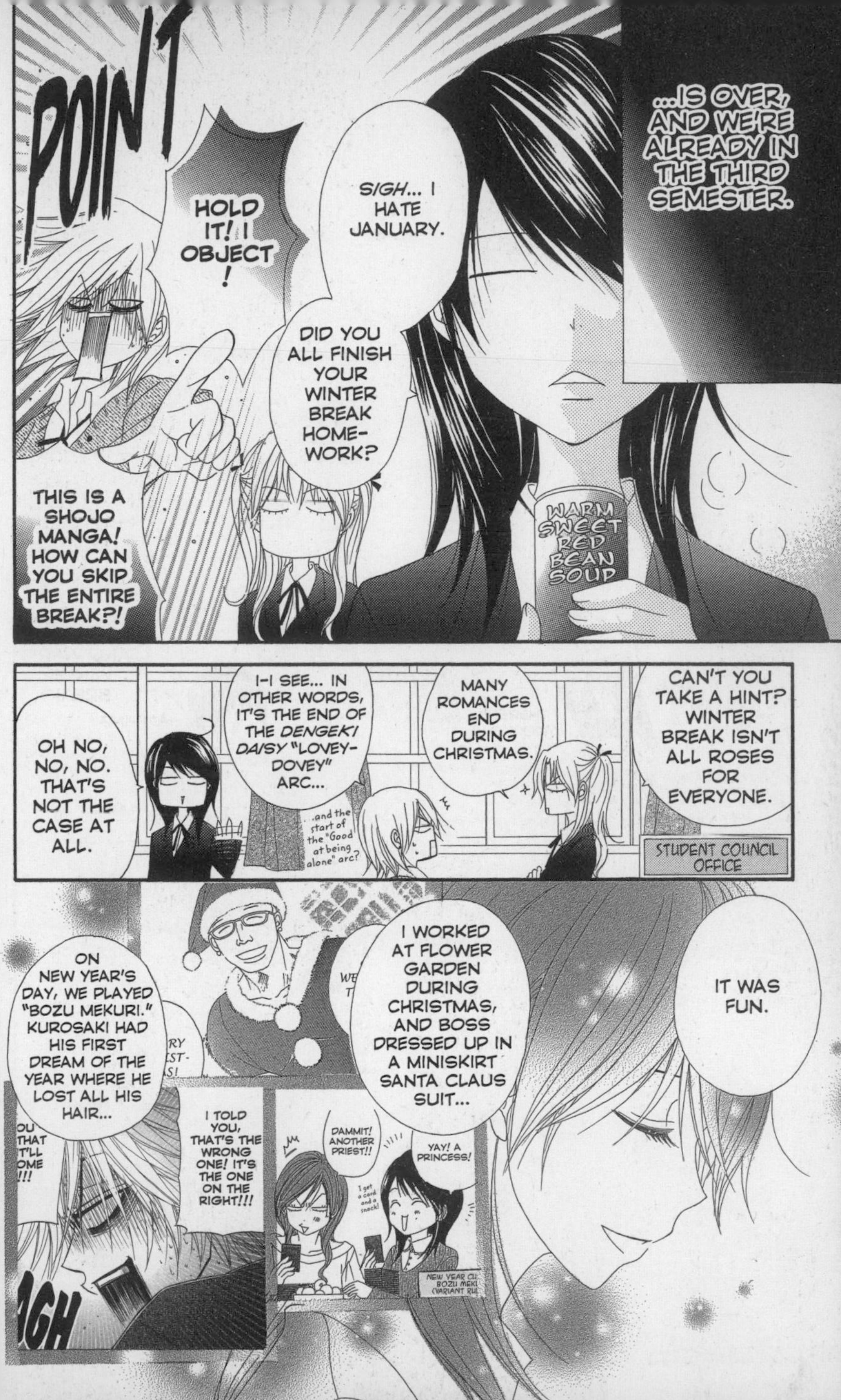
...IS OVER, AND WE'RE ALREADY IN THE THIRD SEMESTER.
SIGH... I HATE JANUARY.
DID YOU ALL FINISH YOUR WINTER BREAK HOME-WORK?
HOLD IT! I OBJECT!
POINT
THIS IS A SHOJO MANGA! HOW CAN YOU SKIP THE ENTIRE BREAK?!
CAN'T YOU TAKE A HINT? WINTER BREAK ISN'T ALL ROSES FOR EVERYONE.
MANY ROMANCES END DURING CHRISTMAS.
I-I SEE... IN OTHER WORDS, IT'S THE END OF THE DENGEKI DAISY "LOVEY-DOVEY" ARC...
...and the start of the "Good at being alone" arc?
OH NO, NO, NO. THAT'S NOT THE CASE AT ALL.
STUDENT COUNCIL OFFICE
IT WAS FUN.
I WORKED AT FLOWER GARDEN DURING CHRISTMAS, AND BOSS DRESSED UP IN A MINISKIRT SANTA CLAUS SUIT...
ON NEW YEAR'S DAY, WE PLAYED "BOZU MEKURI." KUROSAKI HAD HIS FIRST DREAM OF THE YEAR WHERE HE LOST ALL HIS HAIR...
YAY! A PRINCESS!
I get a card and a snack!
DAMMIT! ANOTHER PRIEST!!
I TOLD YOU, THAT'S THE WRONG ONE! IT'S THE ONE ON THE RIGHT!!!

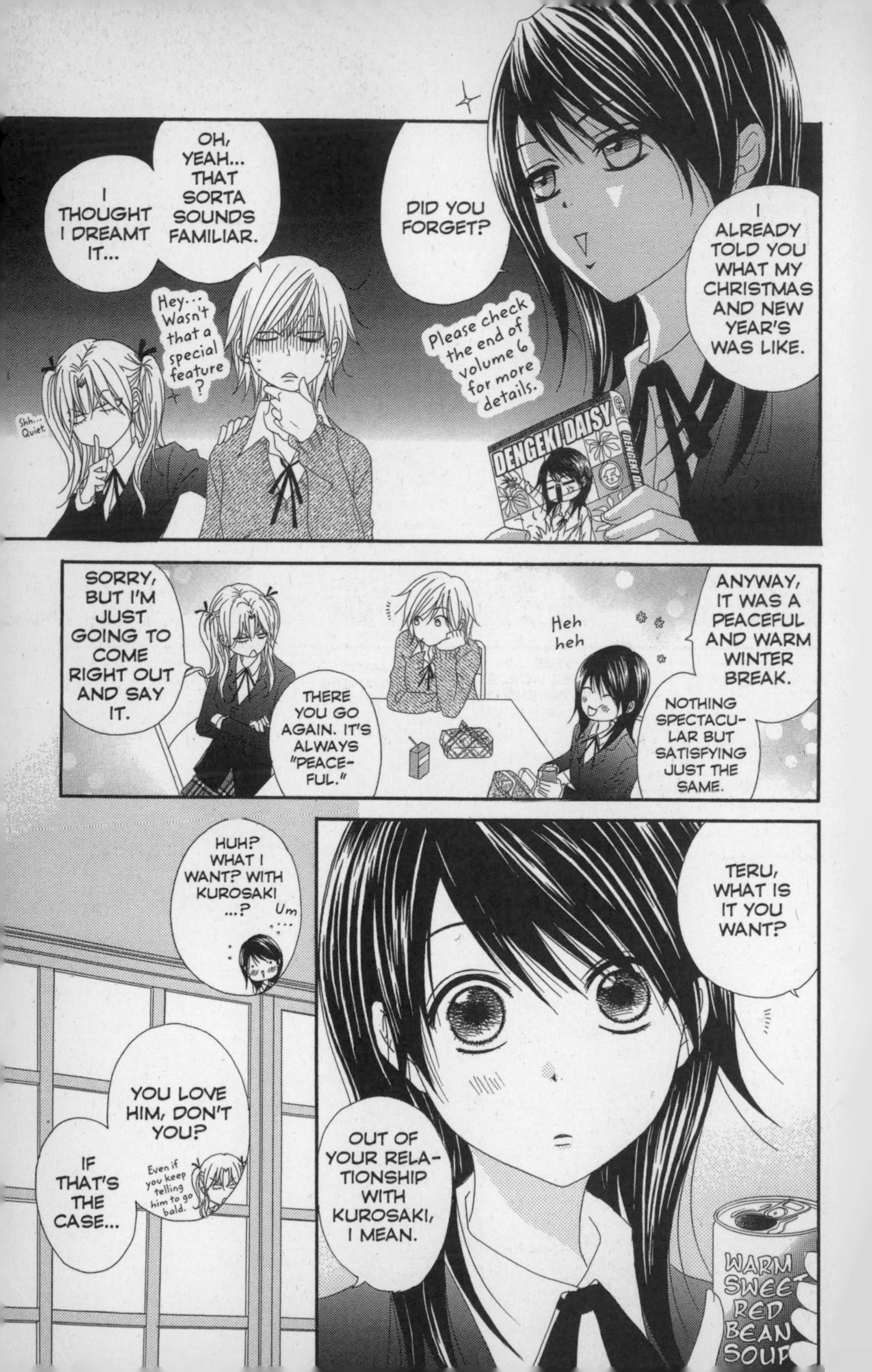
I ALREADY TOLD YOU WHAT MY CHRISTMAS AND NEW YEAR'S WAS LIKE.
DENGEKI DAISY
DID YOU FORGET?
Please check the end of volume 6 for more details.
OH, YEAH... THAT SORTA SOUNDS FAMILIAR.
Hey... Wasn't that a special feature?
I THOUGHT I DREAMT IT...
Shh... Quiet.
ANYWAY, IT WAS A PEACEFUL AND WARM WINTER BREAK.
NOTHING SPECTACULAR BUT SATISFYING JUST THE SAME.
Heh heh
THERE YOU GO AGAIN. IT'S ALWAYS "PEACEFUL."
SORRY, BUT I'M JUST GOING TO COME RIGHT OUT AND SAY IT.
TERU, WHAT IS IT YOU WANT?
OUT OF YOUR RELATIONSHIP WITH KUROSAKI, I MEAN.
WARM SWEET RED BEAN SOUP
HUH? WHAT I WANT? WITH KUROSAKI ...?
Um...
YOU LOVE HIM, DON'T YOU?
IF THAT'S THE CASE...
Even if you keep telling him to go bald.

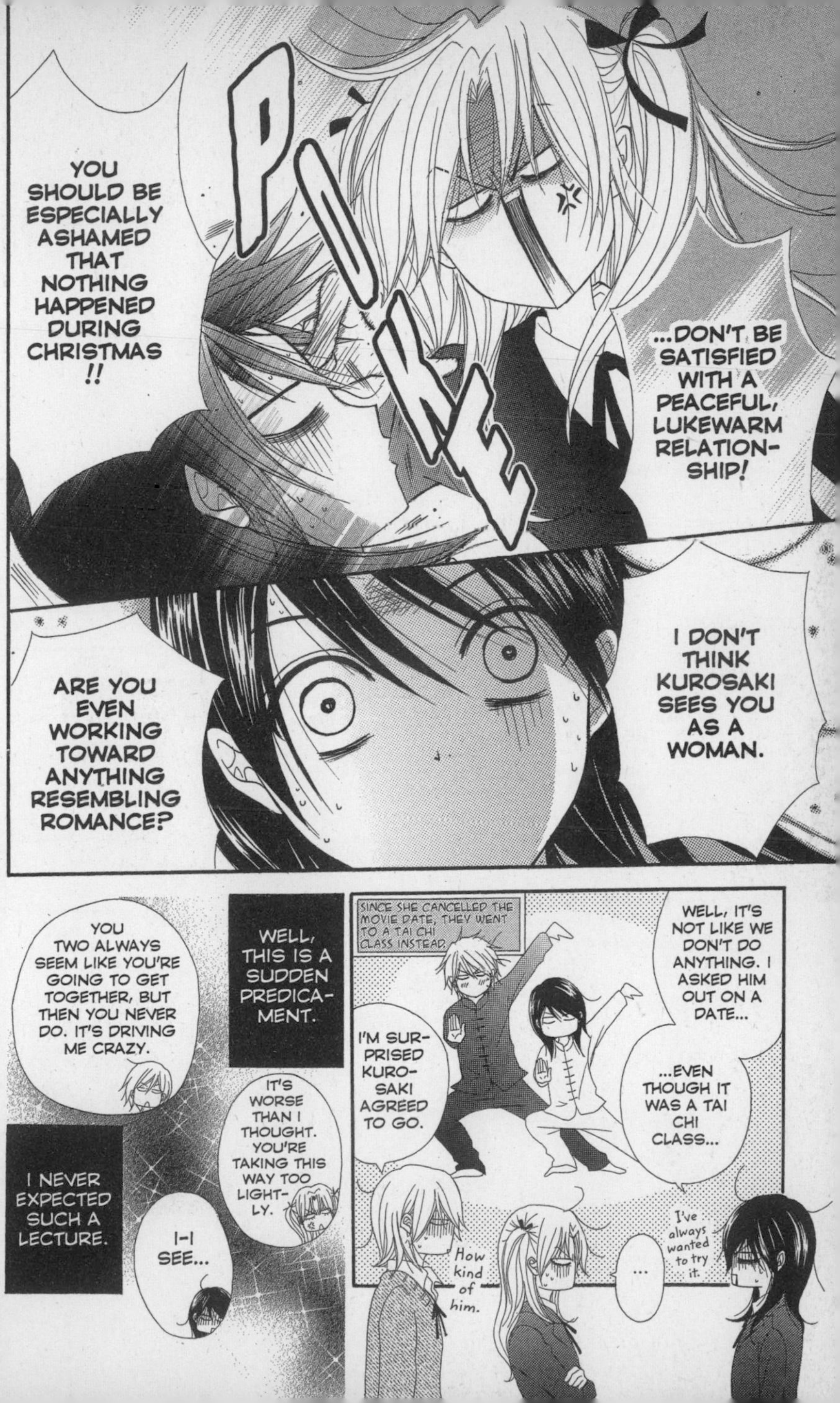
...DON'T BE SATISFIED WITH A PEACEFUL, LUKEWARM RELATION-SHIP!
POKE
YOU SHOULD BE ESPECIALLY ASHAMED THAT NOTHING HAPPENED DURING CHRISTMAS!!
I DON'T THINK KUROSAKI SEES YOU AS A WOMAN.
ARE YOU EVEN WORKING TOWARD ANYTHING RESEMBLING ROMANCE?
WELL, IT'S NOT LIKE WE DON'T DO ANYTHING. I ASKED HIM OUT ON A DATE...
SINCE SHE CANCELLED THE MOVIE DATE, THEY WENT TO A TAI CHI CLASS INSTEAD.
...EVEN THOUGH IT WAS A TAI CHI CLASS...
I'M SUR-PRISED KURO-SAKI AGREED TO GO.
I've always wanted to try it.
...
How kind of him.
WELL, THIS IS A SUDDEN PREDICA-MENT.
YOU TWO ALWAYS SEEM LIKE YOU'RE GOING TO GET TOGETHER, BUT THEN YOU NEVER DO. IT'S DRIVING ME CRAZY.
IT'S WORSE THAN I THOUGHT. YOU'RE TAKING THIS WAY TOO LIGHT-LY.
I NEVER EXPECTED SUCH A LECTURE.
I-I SEE...

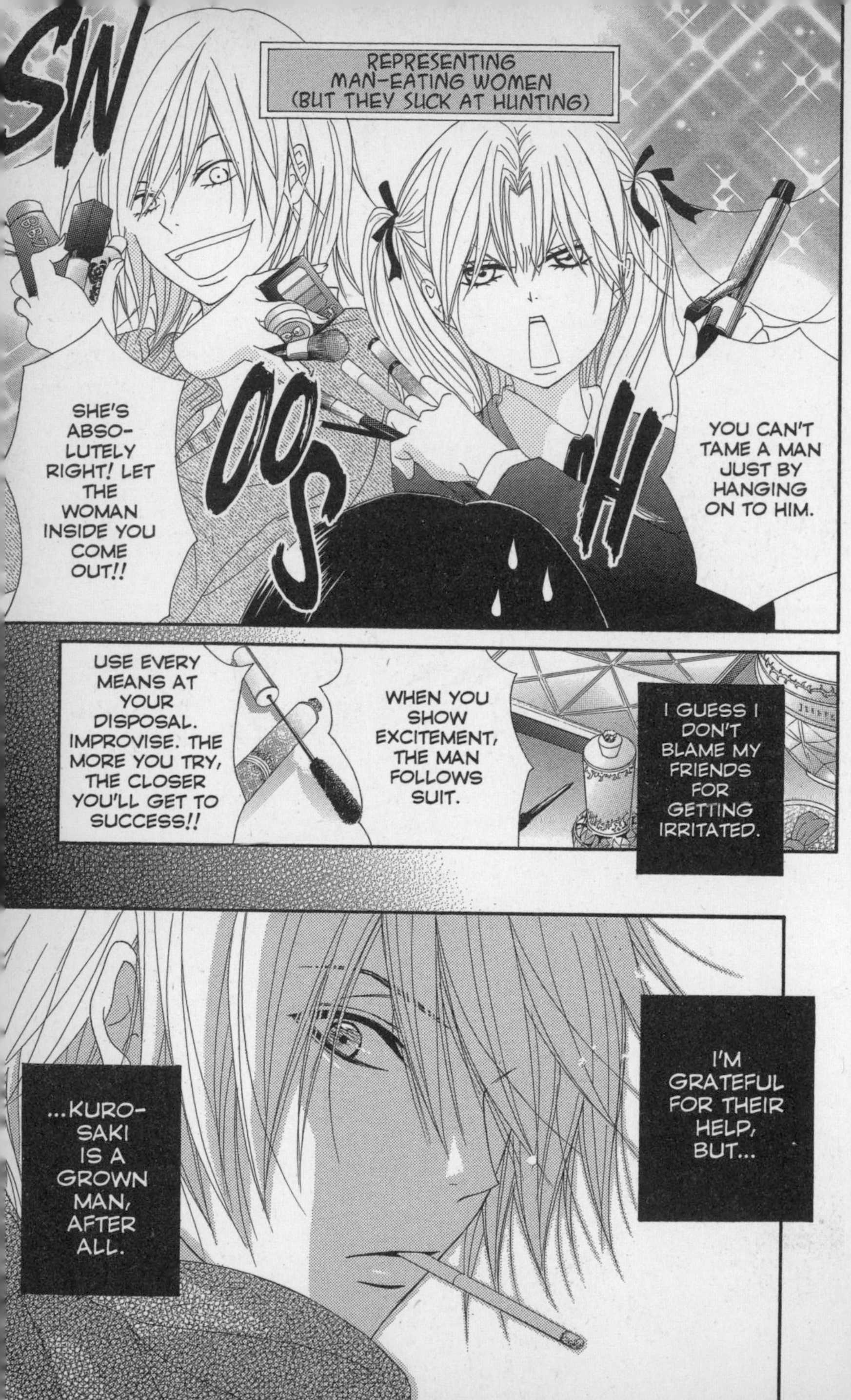
REPRESENTING MAN-EATING WOMEN (BUT THEY SUCK AT HUNTING)
SWOOSH
YOU CAN'T TAME A MAN JUST BY HANGING ON TO HIM.
SHE'S ABSO-LUTELY RIGHT! LET THE WOMAN INSIDE YOU COME OUT!!
I GUESS I DON'T BLAME MY FRIENDS FOR GETTING IRRITATED.
WHEN YOU SHOW EXCITEMENT, THE MAN FOLLOWS SUIT.
USE EVERY MEANS AT YOUR DISPOSAL. IMPROVISE. THE MORE YOU TRY, THE CLOSER YOU'LL GET TO SUCCESS!!
I'M GRATEFUL FOR THEIR HELP, BUT...
...KURO-SAKI IS A GROWN MAN, AFTER ALL.

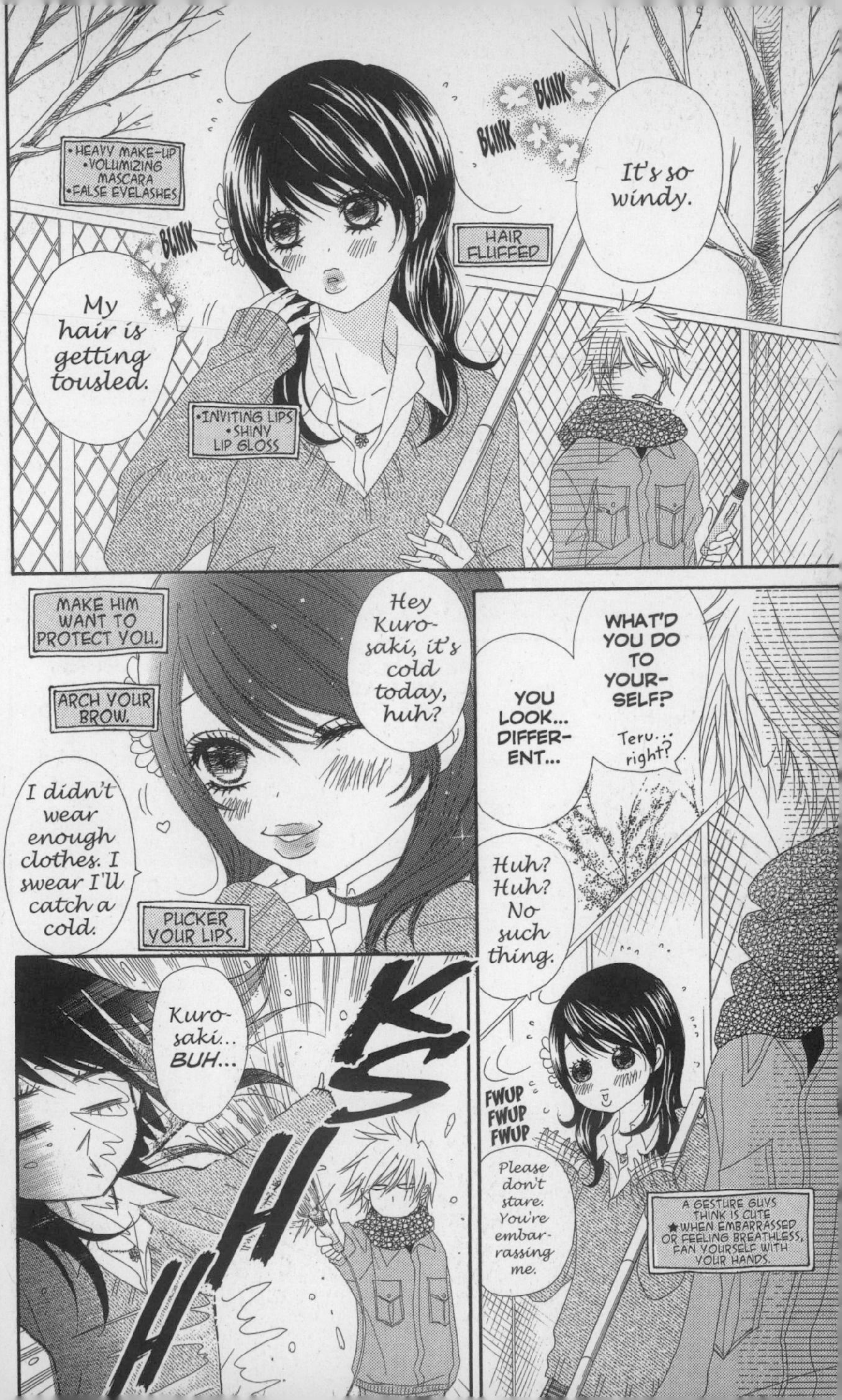
BLINK BLINK
It's so windy.
HAIR FLUFFED
•HEAVY MAKE-UP •VOLUMIZING MASCARA •FALSE EYELASHES
BLINK
My hair is getting tousled.
•INVITING LIPS •SHINY LIP GLOSS
WHAT'D YOU DO TO YOURSELF?
YOU LOOK... DIFFERENT...
Teru... right?
Huh? Huh? No such thing.
FWUP FWUP FWUP
Please don't stare. You're embarrassing me.
A GESTURE GUYS THINK IS CUTE ★WHEN EMBARRASSED OR FEELING BREATHLESS, FAN YOURSELF WITH YOUR HANDS.
MAKE HIM WANT TO PROTECT YOU.
Hey Kurosaki, it's cold today, huh?
ARCH YOUR BROW.
I didn't wear enough clothes. I swear I'll catch a cold.
PUCKER YOUR LIPS.
KSHH
Kurosaki... BUH...

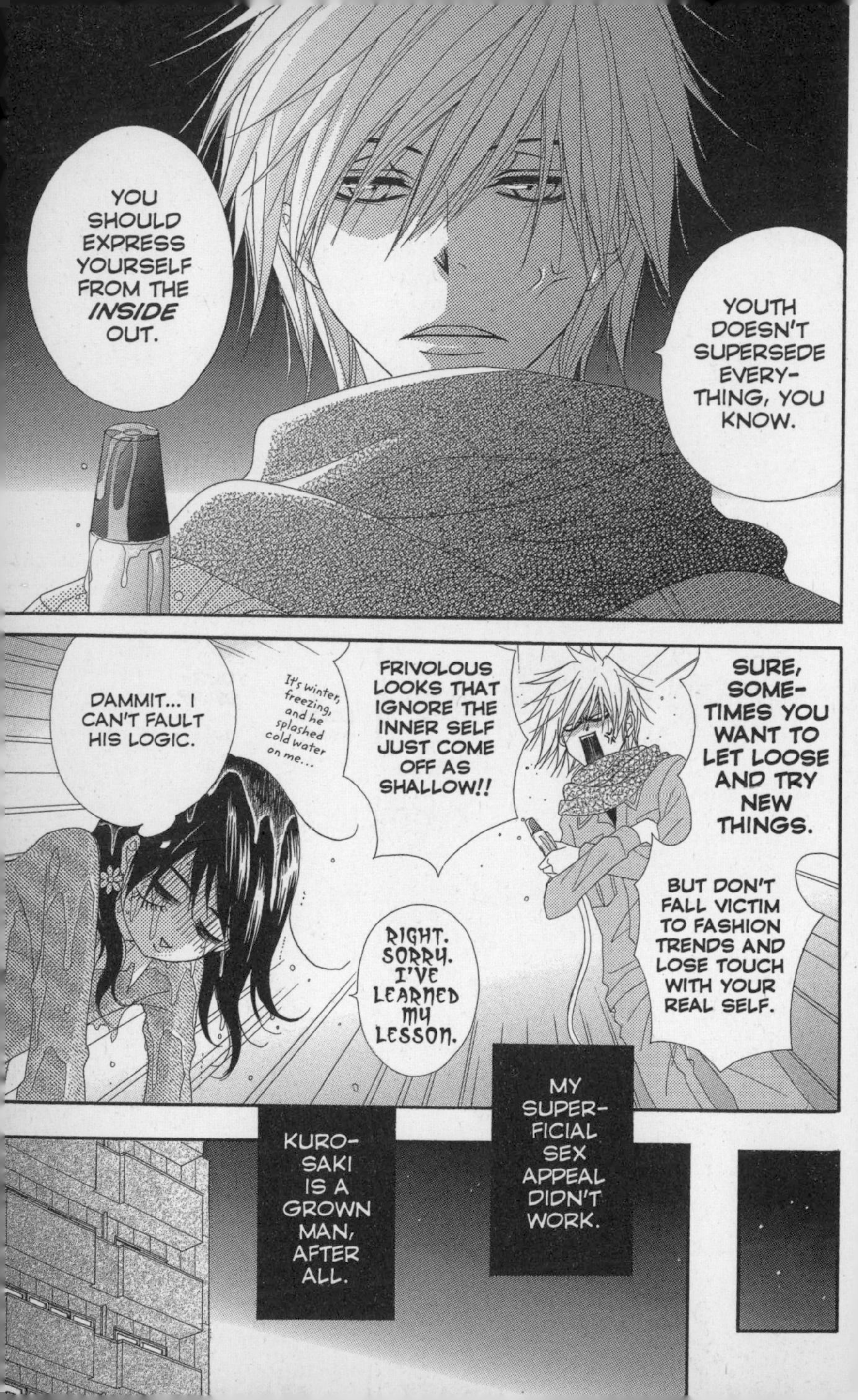
YOUTH DOESN'T SUPERSEDE EVERY-THING, YOU KNOW.
YOU SHOULD EXPRESS YOURSELF FROM THE *INSIDE* OUT.
SURE, SOME-TIMES YOU WANT TO LET LOOSE AND TRY NEW THINGS.
BUT DON'T FALL VICTIM TO FASHION TRENDS AND LOSE TOUCH WITH YOUR REAL SELF.
FRIVOLOUS LOOKS THAT IGNORE THE INNER SELF JUST COME OFF AS SHALLOW!!
It's winter, freezing, and he splashed cold water on me...
RIGHT. SORRY. I'VE LEARNED MY LESSON.
DAMMIT... I CAN'T FAULT HIS LOGIC.
MY SUPER-FICIAL SEX APPEAL DIDN'T WORK.
KURO-SAKI IS A GROWN MAN, AFTER ALL.

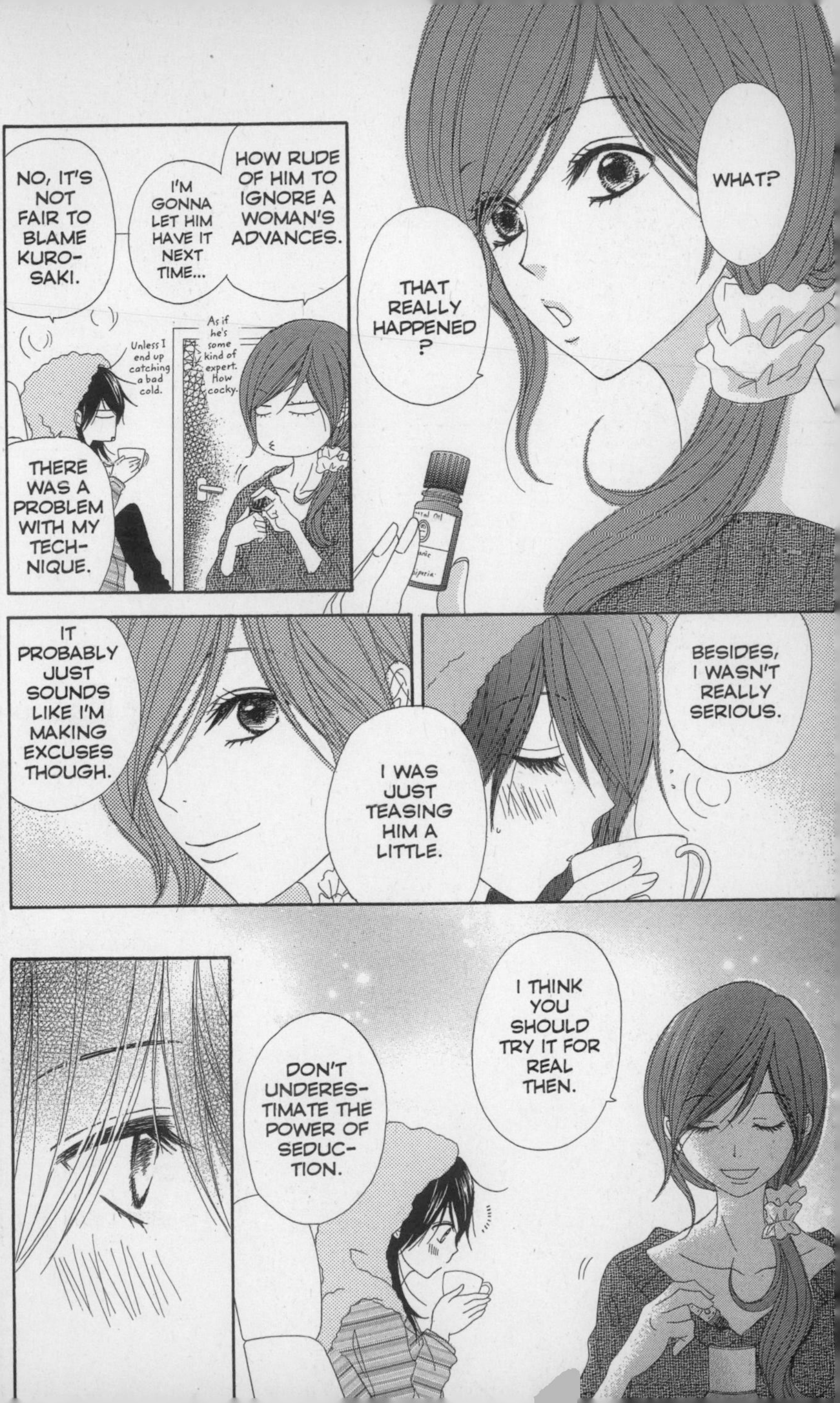
WHAT?
THAT REALLY HAPPENED?
HOW RUDE OF HIM TO IGNORE A WOMAN'S ADVANCES.
I'M GONNA LET HIM HAVE IT NEXT TIME...
NO, IT'S NOT FAIR TO BLAME KURO-SAKI.
As if he's some kind of expert. How cocky.
Unless I end up catching a bad cold.
THERE WAS A PROBLEM WITH MY TECH-NIQUE.
BESIDES, I WASN'T REALLY SERIOUS.
I WAS JUST TEASING HIM A LITTLE.
IT PROBABLY JUST SOUNDS LIKE I'M MAKING EXCUSES THOUGH.
I THINK YOU SHOULD TRY IT FOR REAL THEN.
DON'T UNDERES-TIMATE THE POWER OF SEDUC-TION.

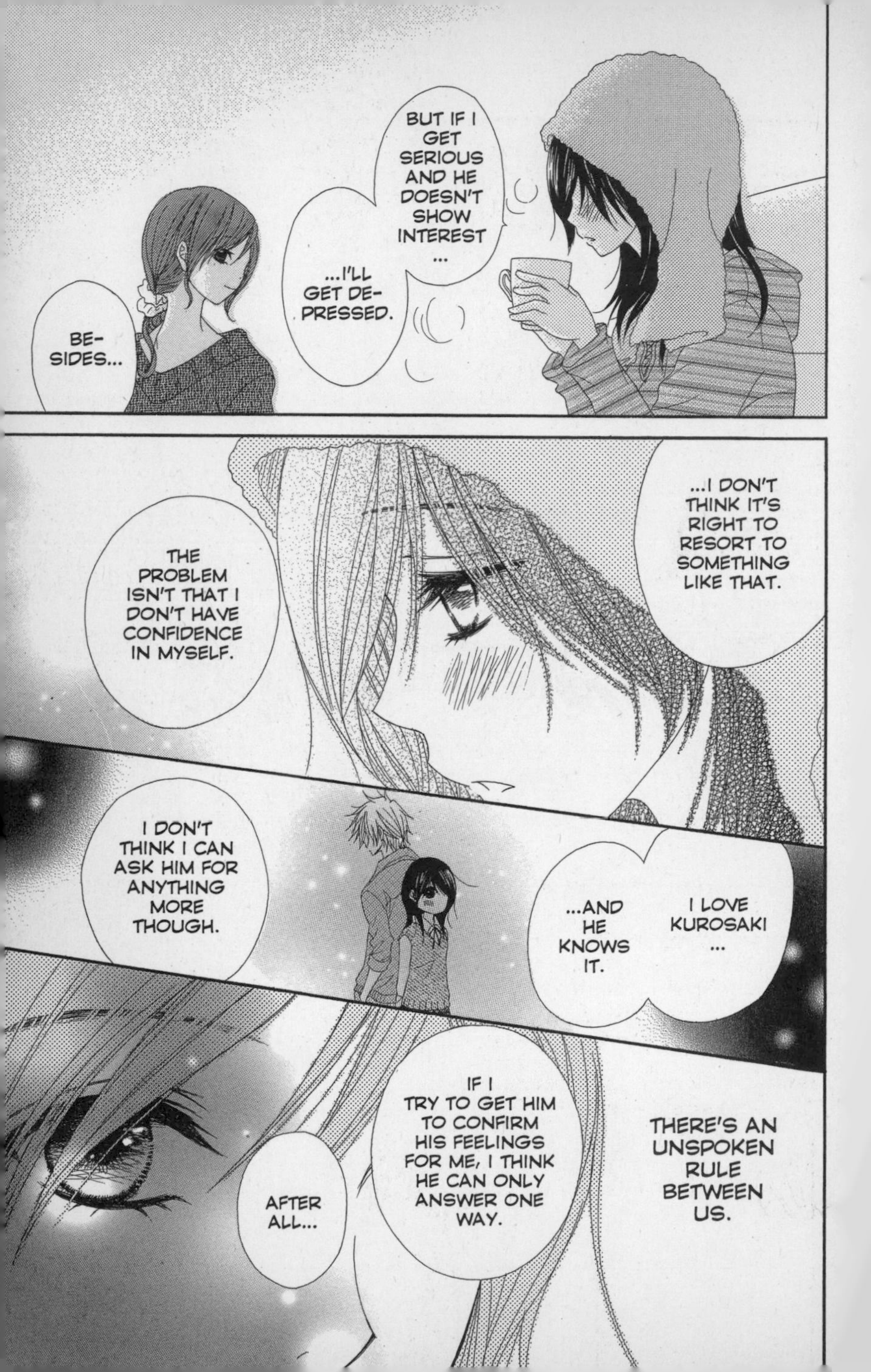
BUT IF I GET SERIOUS AND HE DOESN'T SHOW INTEREST ...
...I'LL GET DE-PRESSED.
BE-SIDES...
...I DON'T THINK IT'S RIGHT TO RESORT TO SOMETHING LIKE THAT.
THE PROBLEM ISN'T THAT I DON'T HAVE CONFIDENCE IN MYSELF.
I LOVE KUROSAKI ...
...AND HE KNOWS IT.
I DON'T THINK I CAN ASK HIM FOR ANYTHING MORE THOUGH.
THERE'S AN UNSPOKEN RULE BETWEEN US.
IF I TRY TO GET HIM TO CONFIRM HIS FEELINGS FOR ME, I THINK HE CAN ONLY ANSWER ONE WAY.
AFTER ALL...

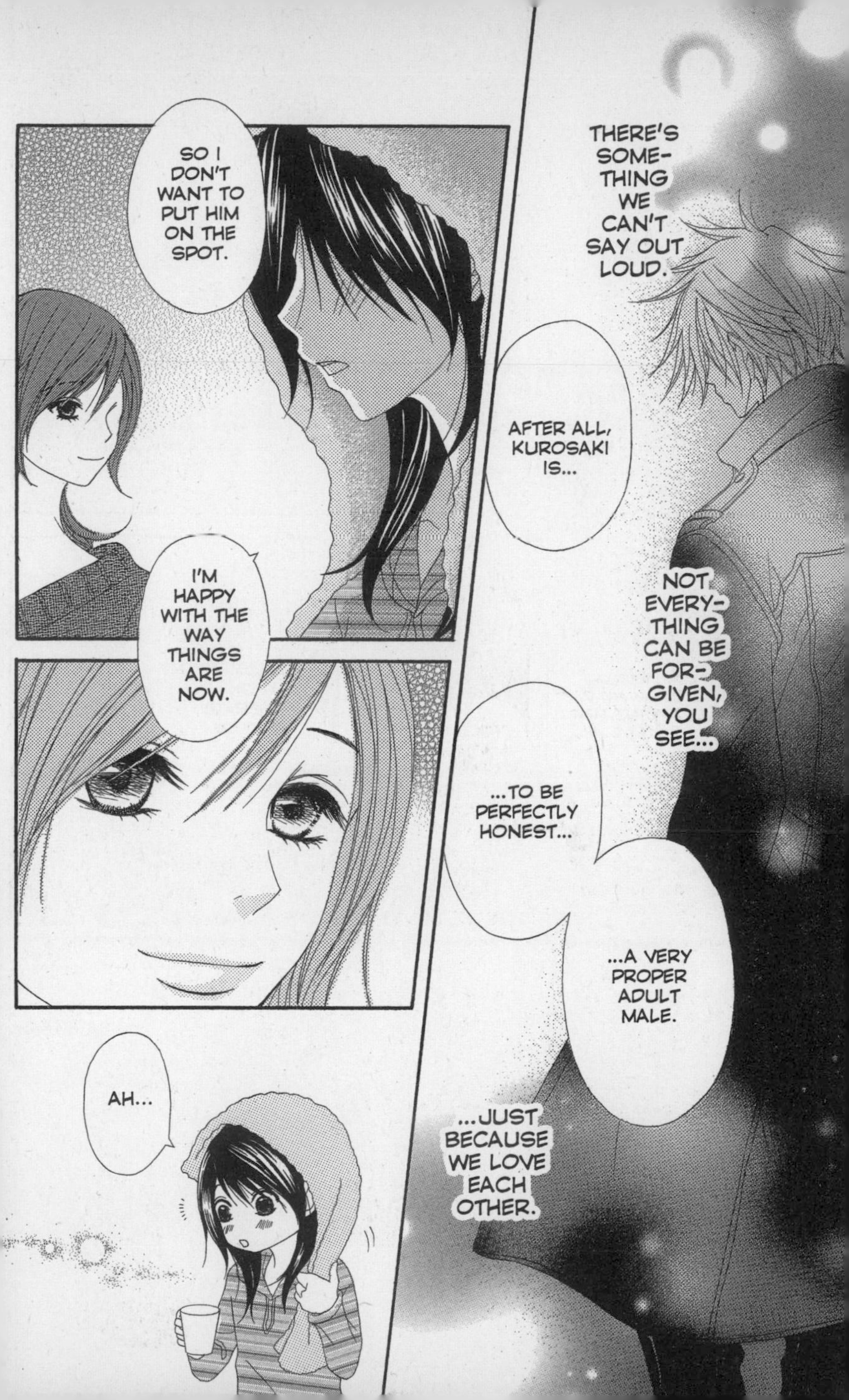
THERE'S SOME-THING WE CAN'T SAY OUT LOUD.
AFTER ALL, KUROSAKI IS...
NOT EVERY-THING CAN BE FOR-GIVEN, YOU SEE...
...TO BE PERFECTLY HONEST...
...A VERY PROPER ADULT MALE.
...JUST BECAUSE WE LOVE EACH OTHER.
SO I DON'T WANT TO PUT HIM ON THE SPOT.
I'M HAPPY WITH THE WAY THINGS ARE NOW.
AH...

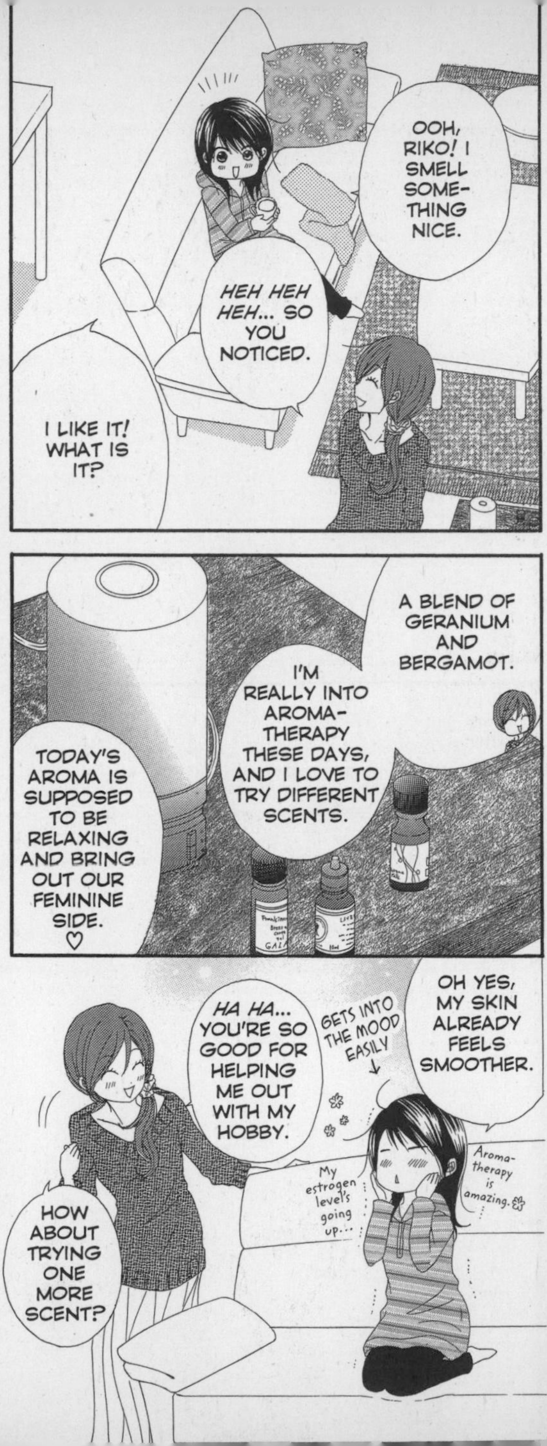
OOH, RIKO! I SMELL SOME-THING NICE.
HEH HEH HEH... SO YOU NOTICED.
I LIKE IT! WHAT IS IT?
A BLEND OF GERANIUM AND BERGAMOT.
I'M REALLY INTO AROMA-THERAPY THESE DAYS, AND I LOVE TO TRY DIFFERENT SCENTS.
TODAY'S AROMA IS SUPPOSED TO BE RELAXING AND BRING OUT OUR FEMININE SIDE. ♡
OH YES, MY SKIN ALREADY FEELS SMOOTHER.
Aroma-therapy is amazing.
GETS INTO THE MOOD EASILY
My estrogen level's going up...
HA HA... YOU'RE SO GOOD FOR HELPING ME OUT WITH MY HOBBY.
HOW ABOUT TRYING ONE MORE SCENT?

DENGEKI DAISY QUESTION CORNER

BALDLY ASK!! ②

Q.

IF THERE ARE TOMATOES IN HIS SALAD, DOES KUROSAKI LEAVE THEM UNEATEN? OR DOES HE FORCE HIMSELF TO EAT THEM? DOES BOSS ADD TOMATOES KNOWINGLY?

(C.I., AICHI PREFECTURE)

WHAT DO KUROSAKI AND COMPANY LIKE TO EAT? ALTHOUGH, I THINK KUROSAKI'S FAVORITE IS TERU...

(S. AND MANY OTHERS, AICHI PREFECTURE)

A.

THERE WERE MANY INQUIRIES ABOUT THE FOOD LIKES AND DISLIKES OF THE CHARACTERS. FIRST OF ALL, TERU ISN'T PARTICULAR. RIKO LOVES MEAT. ANDY LIKES JAPANESE CUISINE. SOICHIRO'S PREFERENCES ARE MENTIONED IN THE MAIN STORY. AND, AS FOR KUROSAKI... ~~HIS FAVORITE IS TERU KUREBAYASHI.~~ HE SEEMS TO LIKE CHILDREN'S STAPLES LIKE OMELET RICE AND *HANBAAGU*. BOSS IS TRYING TO CORRECT KUROSAKI'S UNBALANCED DIET BY USING LOTS OF CARROTS AND TOMATOES AND MAKING HIM EAT THEM. KUROSAKI SECRETLY TRIES NOT TO EAT THEM, BUT WHEN HE'S CAUGHT IN THE ACT, HE GETS IT FROM BOSS, SO HE FORCES HIMSELF TO EAT THEM THROUGH TEARS.

Q.

DOES KUROSAKI REALLY WORK TERU TO THE BONE? OR DOES HE JUST WANT TO KEEP HER CLOSE TO HIM?

(R.I., IBARAKI PREFECTURE)

A.

SHHH. PLEASE DON'T ASK.

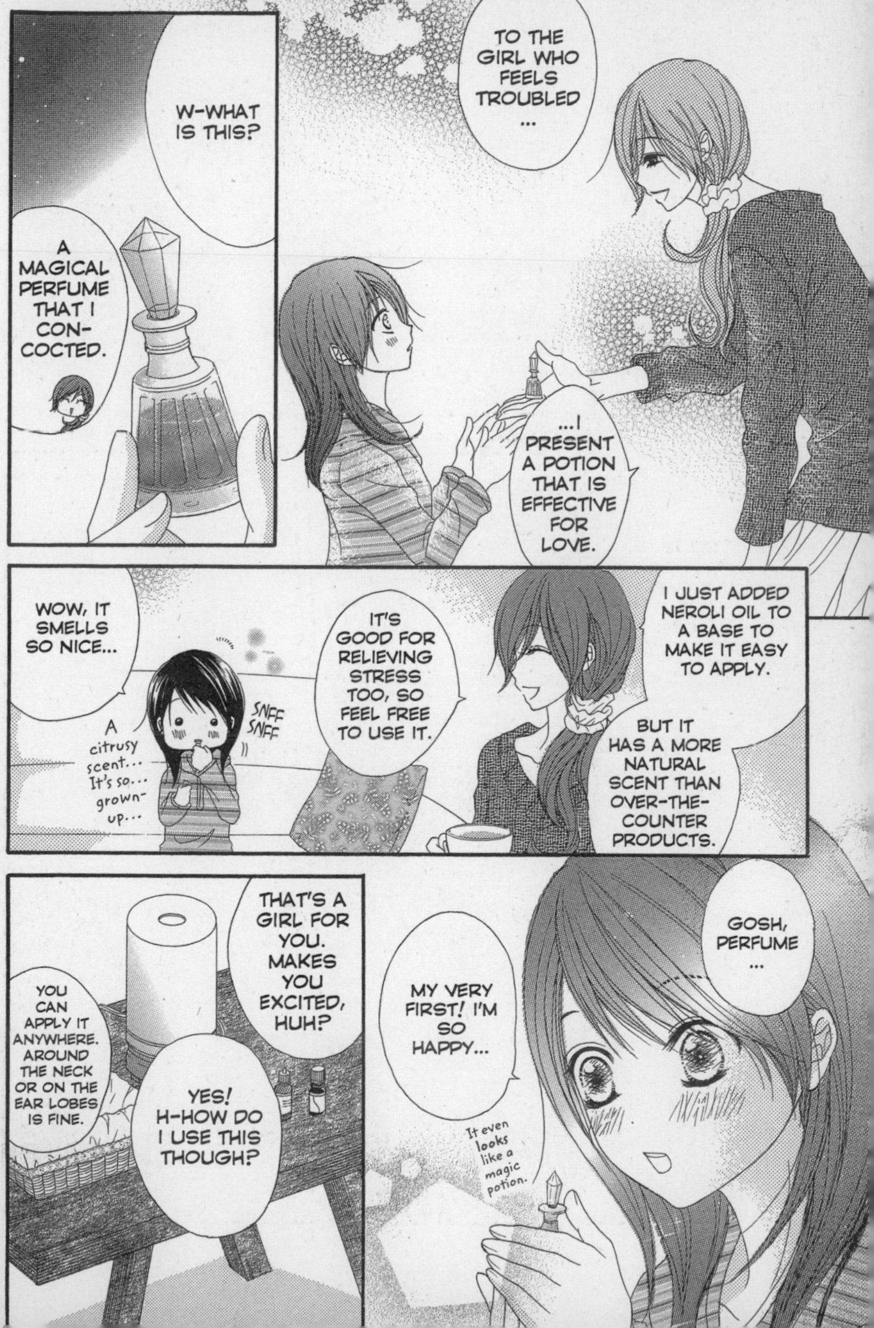
TO THE GIRL WHO FEELS TROUBLED ...
...I PRESENT A POTION THAT IS EFFECTIVE FOR LOVE.
W-WHAT IS THIS?
A MAGICAL PERFUME THAT I CONCOCTED.
I JUST ADDED NEROLI OIL TO A BASE TO MAKE IT EASY TO APPLY.
BUT IT HAS A MORE NATURAL SCENT THAN OVER-THE-COUNTER PRODUCTS.
IT'S GOOD FOR RELIEVING STRESS TOO, SO FEEL FREE TO USE IT.
WOW, IT SMELLS SO NICE...
SNFF SNFF
A citrusy scent... It's so... grown-up...
GOSH, PERFUME ...
MY VERY FIRST! I'M SO HAPPY...
It even looks like a magic potion.
THAT'S A GIRL FOR YOU. MAKES YOU EXCITED, HUH?
YES! H-HOW DO I USE THIS THOUGH?
YOU CAN APPLY IT ANYWHERE. AROUND THE NECK OR ON THE EAR LOBES IS FINE.

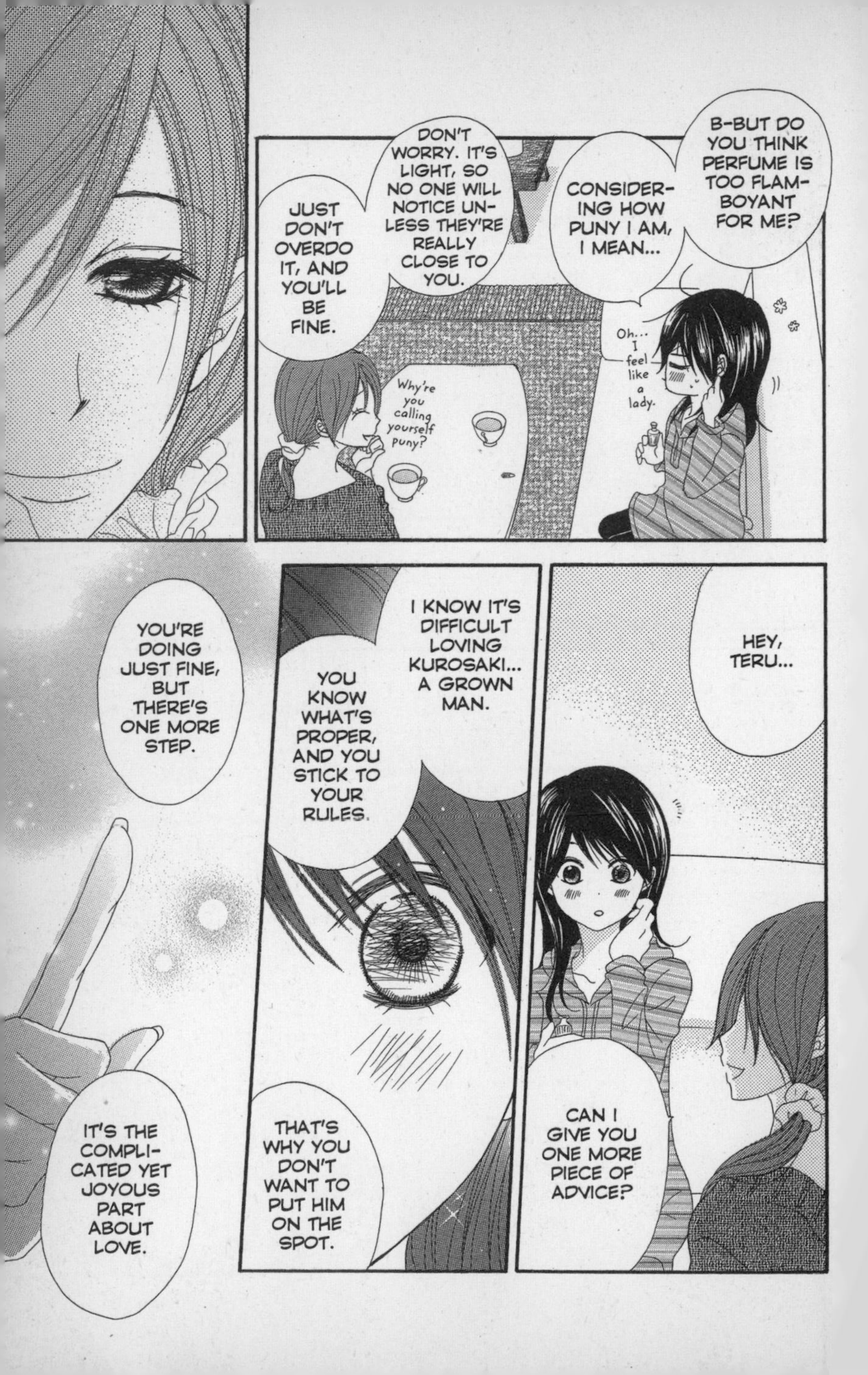
B-BUT DO YOU THINK PERFUME IS TOO FLAMBOYANT FOR ME?
CONSIDERING HOW PUNY I AM, I MEAN...
Oh... I feel like a lady.
DON'T WORRY. IT'S LIGHT, SO NO ONE WILL NOTICE UNLESS THEY'RE REALLY CLOSE TO YOU.
JUST DON'T OVERDO IT, AND YOU'LL BE FINE.
Why're you calling yourself puny?
HEY, TERU...
CAN I GIVE YOU ONE MORE PIECE OF ADVICE?
I KNOW IT'S DIFFICULT LOVING KUROSAKI... A GROWN MAN.
YOU KNOW WHAT'S PROPER, AND YOU STICK TO YOUR RULES.
THAT'S WHY YOU DON'T WANT TO PUT HIM ON THE SPOT.
YOU'RE DOING JUST FINE, BUT THERE'S ONE MORE STEP.
IT'S THE COMPLICATED YET JOYOUS PART ABOUT LOVE.

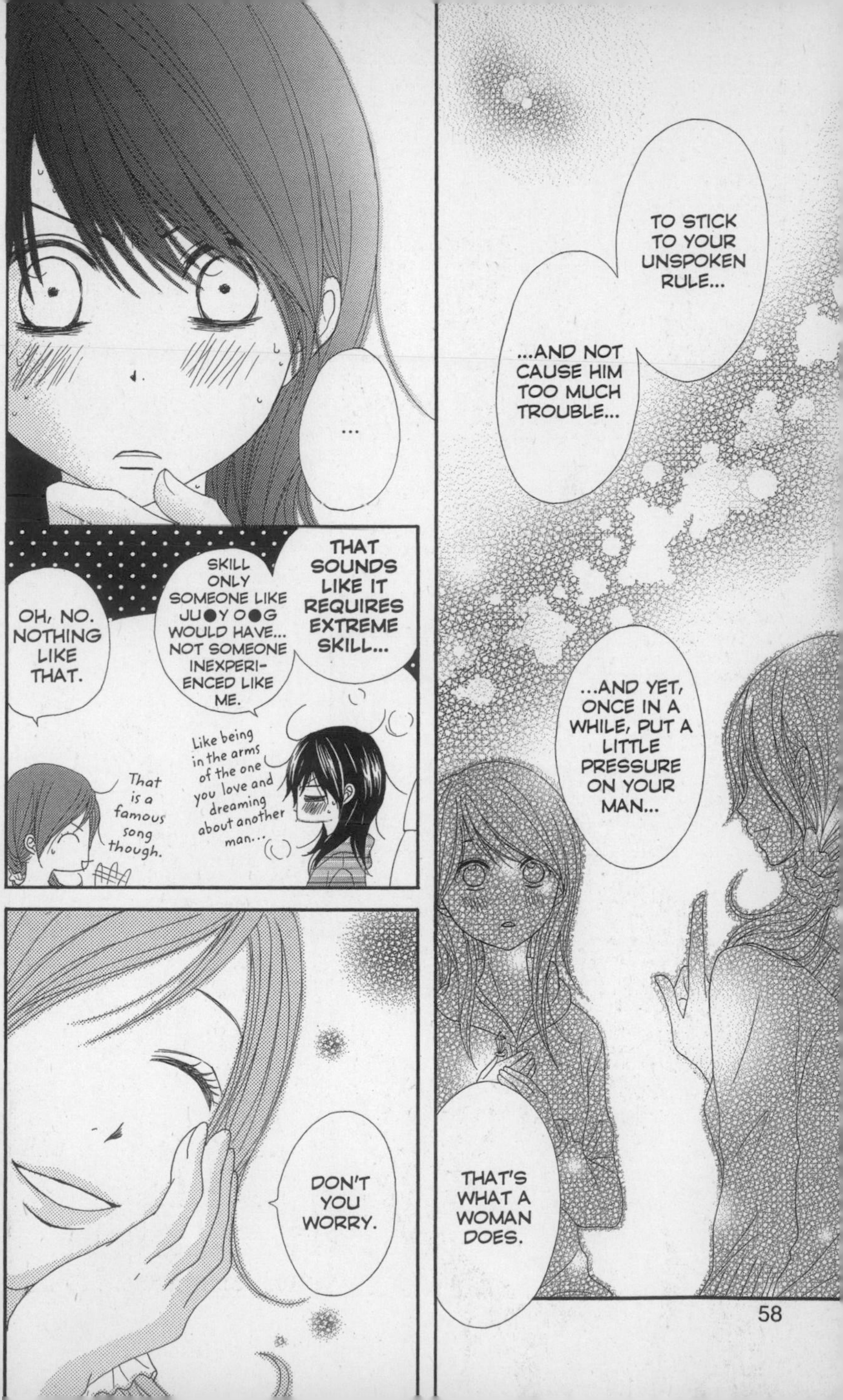
TO STICK TO YOUR UNSPOKEN RULE...
...AND NOT CAUSE HIM TOO MUCH TROUBLE...
...AND YET, ONCE IN A WHILE, PUT A LITTLE PRESSURE ON YOUR MAN...
THAT'S WHAT A WOMAN DOES.
...
THAT SOUNDS LIKE IT REQUIRES EXTREME SKILL...
SKILL ONLY SOMEONE LIKE JU●Y O●G WOULD HAVE... NOT SOMEONE INEXPERIENCED LIKE ME.
OH, NO. NOTHING LIKE THAT.
Like being in the arms of the one you love and dreaming about another man...
That is a famous song though.
DON'T YOU WORRY.

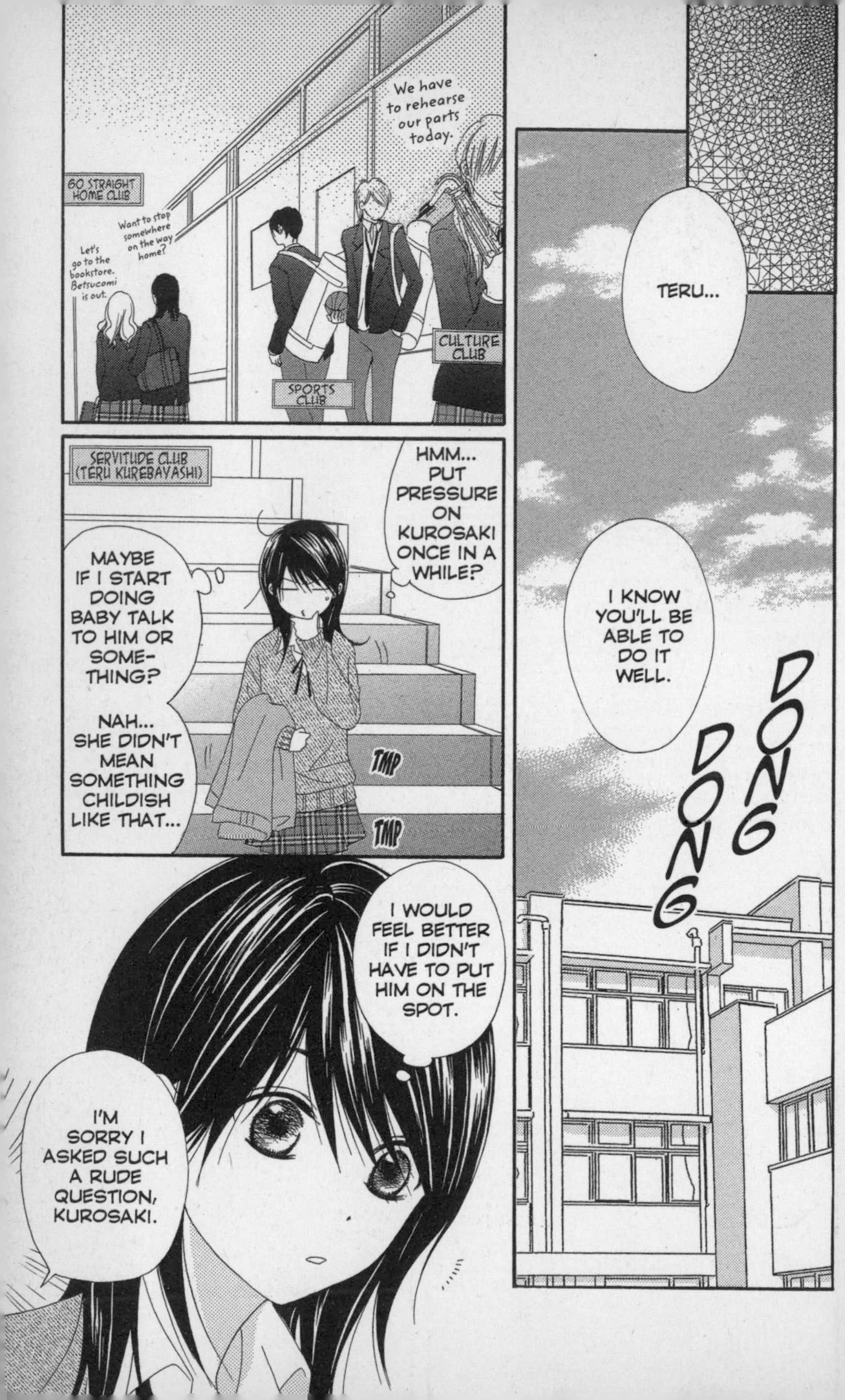

TERU...
I KNOW YOU'LL BE ABLE TO DO IT WELL.
DONG DONG
We have to rehearse our parts today.
CULTURE CLUB
SPORTS CLUB
GO STRAIGHT HOME CLUB
Want to stop somewhere on the way home?
Let's go to the bookstore. Betsucomi is out.
HMM... PUT PRESSURE ON KUROSAKI ONCE IN A WHILE?
SERVITUDE CLUB (TERU KUREBAYASHI)
MAYBE IF I START DOING BABY TALK TO HIM OR SOME-THING?
NAH... SHE DIDN'T MEAN SOMETHING CHILDISH LIKE THAT...
TMP
TMP
I WOULD FEEL BETTER IF I DIDN'T HAVE TO PUT HIM ON THE SPOT.
I'M SORRY I ASKED SUCH A RUDE QUESTION, KUROSAKI.

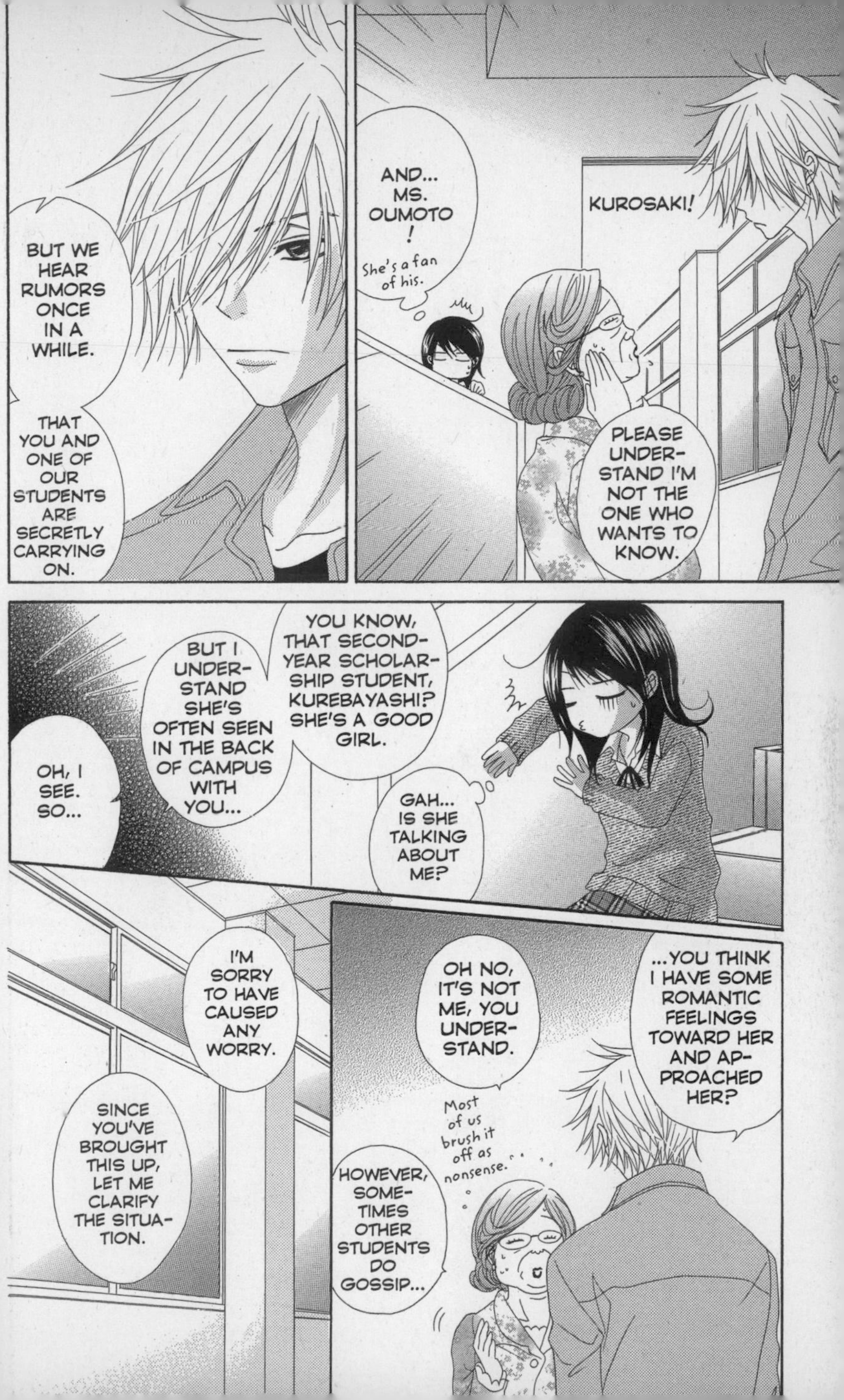
KUROSAKI!
AND... MS. OUMOTO!
She's a fan of his.
PLEASE UNDERSTAND I'M NOT THE ONE WHO WANTS TO KNOW.
BUT WE HEAR RUMORS ONCE IN A WHILE.
THAT YOU AND ONE OF OUR STUDENTS ARE SECRETLY CARRYING ON.
YOU KNOW, THAT SECOND-YEAR SCHOLARSHIP STUDENT, KUREBAYASHI? SHE'S A GOOD GIRL.
BUT I UNDERSTAND SHE'S OFTEN SEEN IN THE BACK OF CAMPUS WITH YOU...
GAH... IS SHE TALKING ABOUT ME?
OH, I SEE. SO...
...YOU THINK I HAVE SOME ROMANTIC FEELINGS TOWARD HER AND APPROACHED HER?
OH NO, IT'S NOT ME, YOU UNDERSTAND.
Most of us brush it off as nonsense.
HOWEVER, SOMETIMES OTHER STUDENTS DO GOSSIP...
I'M SORRY TO HAVE CAUSED ANY WORRY.
SINCE YOU'VE BROUGHT THIS UP, LET ME CLARIFY THE SITUATION.

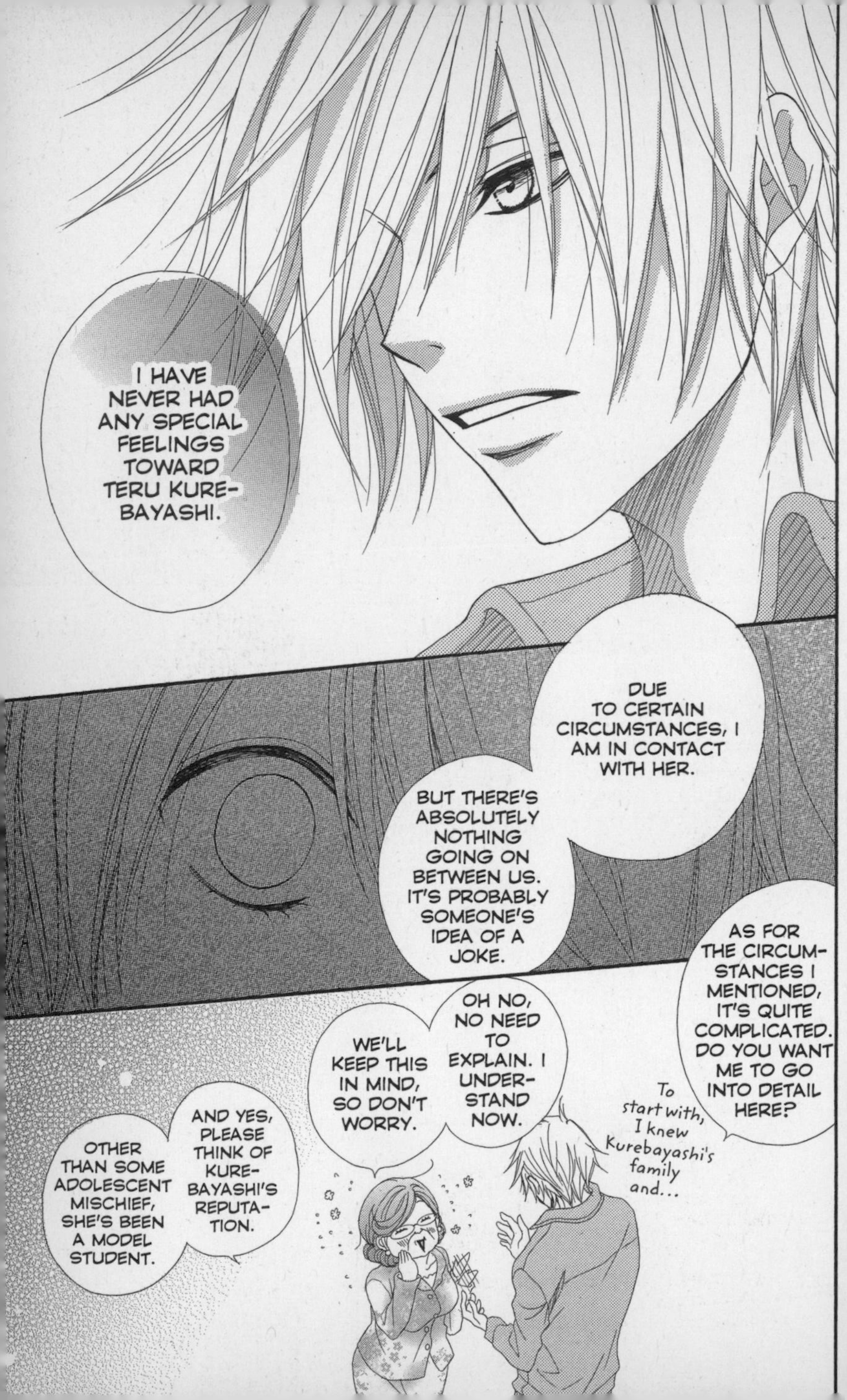
I HAVE NEVER HAD ANY SPECIAL FEELINGS TOWARD TERU KURE-BAYASHI.
DUE TO CERTAIN CIRCUMSTANCES, I AM IN CONTACT WITH HER.
BUT THERE'S ABSOLUTELY NOTHING GOING ON BETWEEN US. IT'S PROBABLY SOMEONE'S IDEA OF A JOKE.
AS FOR THE CIRCUM-STANCES I MENTIONED, IT'S QUITE COMPLICATED. DO YOU WANT ME TO GO INTO DETAIL HERE?
To start with, I knew Kurebayashi's family and...
OH NO, NO NEED TO EXPLAIN. I UNDER-STAND NOW.
WE'LL KEEP THIS IN MIND, SO DON'T WORRY.
AND YES, PLEASE THINK OF KURE-BAYASHI'S REPUTA-TION.
OTHER THAN SOME ADOLESCENT MISCHIEF, SHE'S BEEN A MODEL STUDENT.

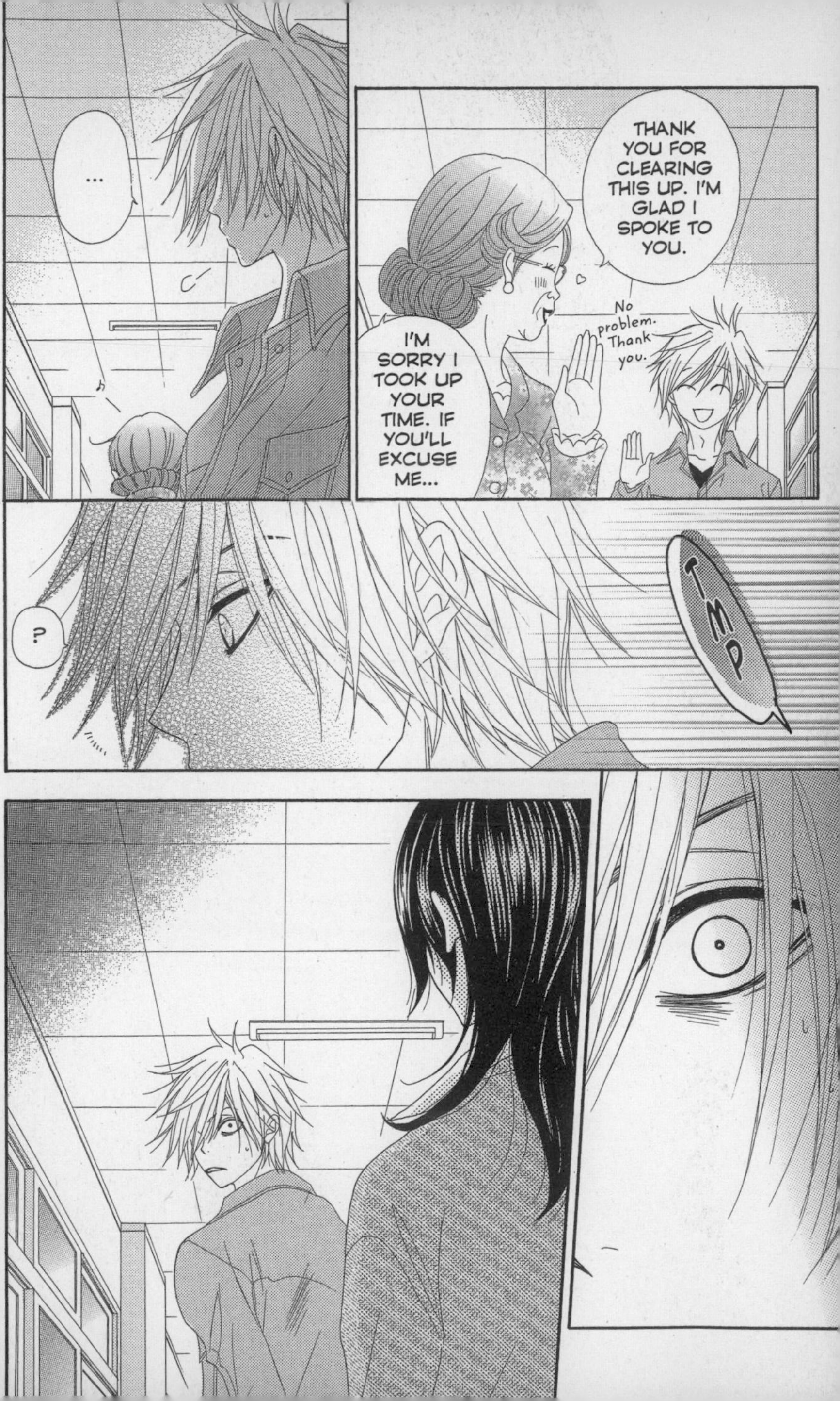
THANK YOU FOR CLEARING THIS UP. I'M GLAD I SPOKE TO YOU.
No problem. Thank you.
I'M SORRY I TOOK UP YOUR TIME. IF YOU'LL EXCUSE ME...
...
TMP
?

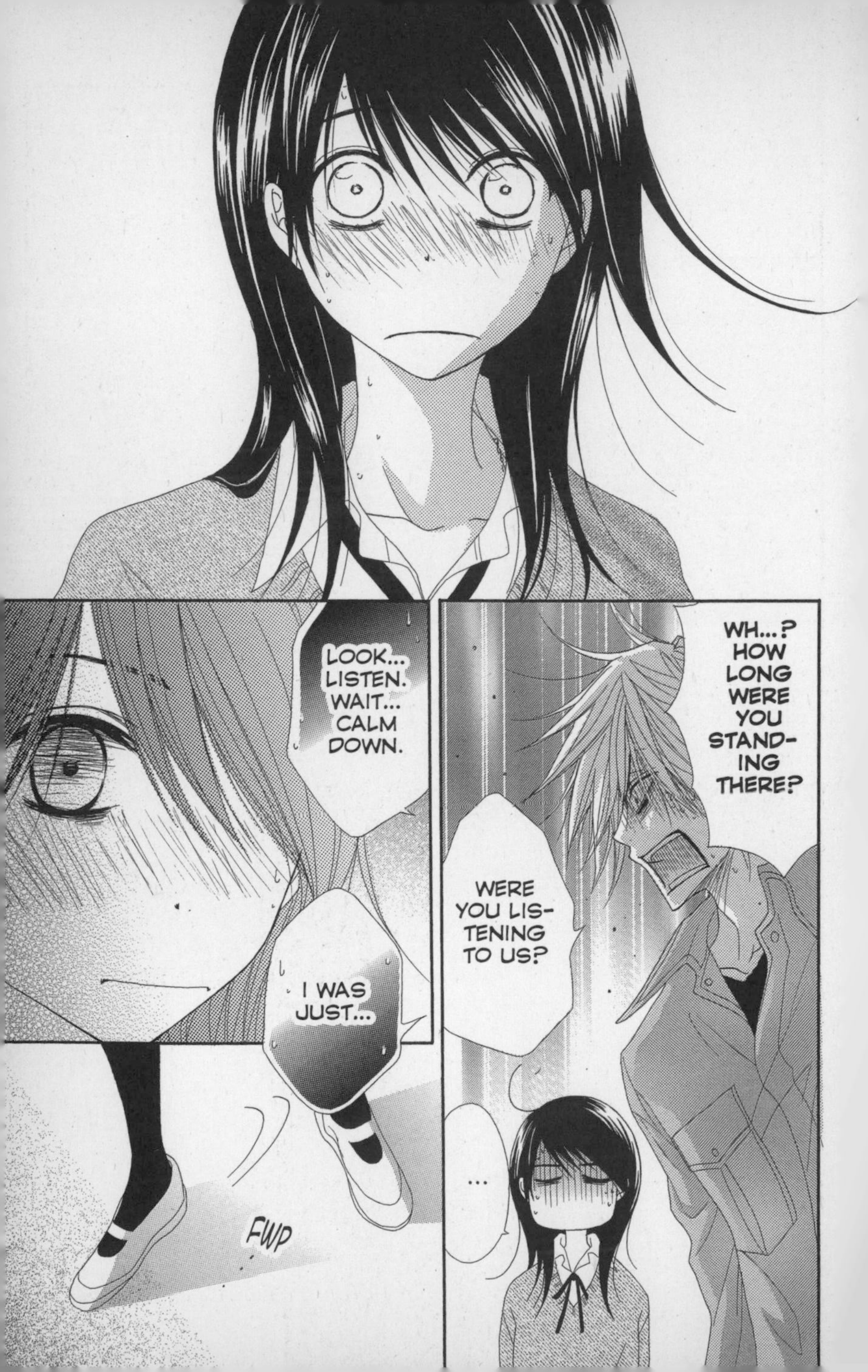
WH...? HOW LONG WERE YOU STAND-ING THERE?
WERE YOU LIS-TENING TO US?
...
LOOK... LISTEN. WAIT... CALM DOWN.
I WAS JUST...
FWP

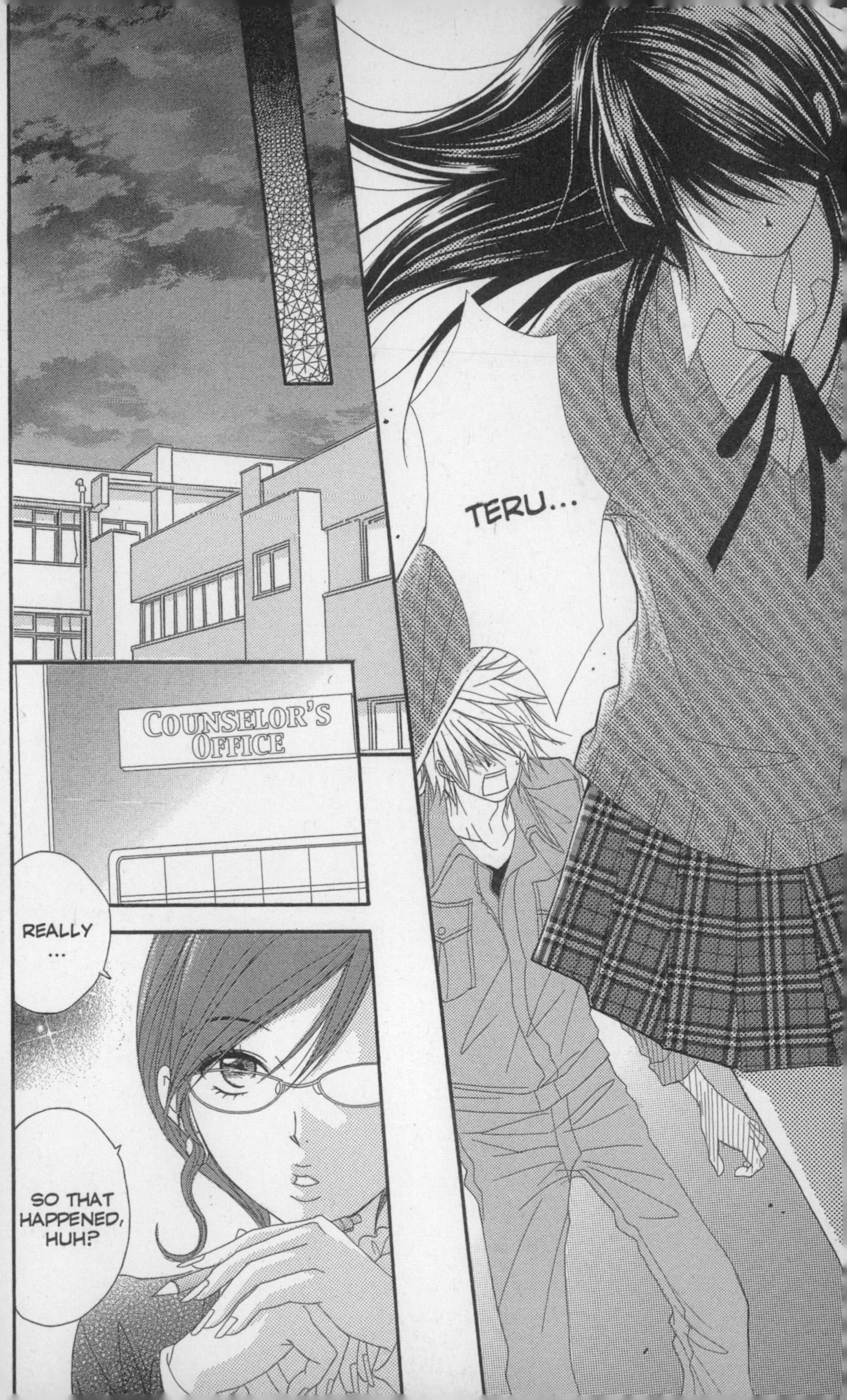
TERU...
COUNSELOR'S OFFICE
REALLY ...
SO THAT HAPPENED, HUH?

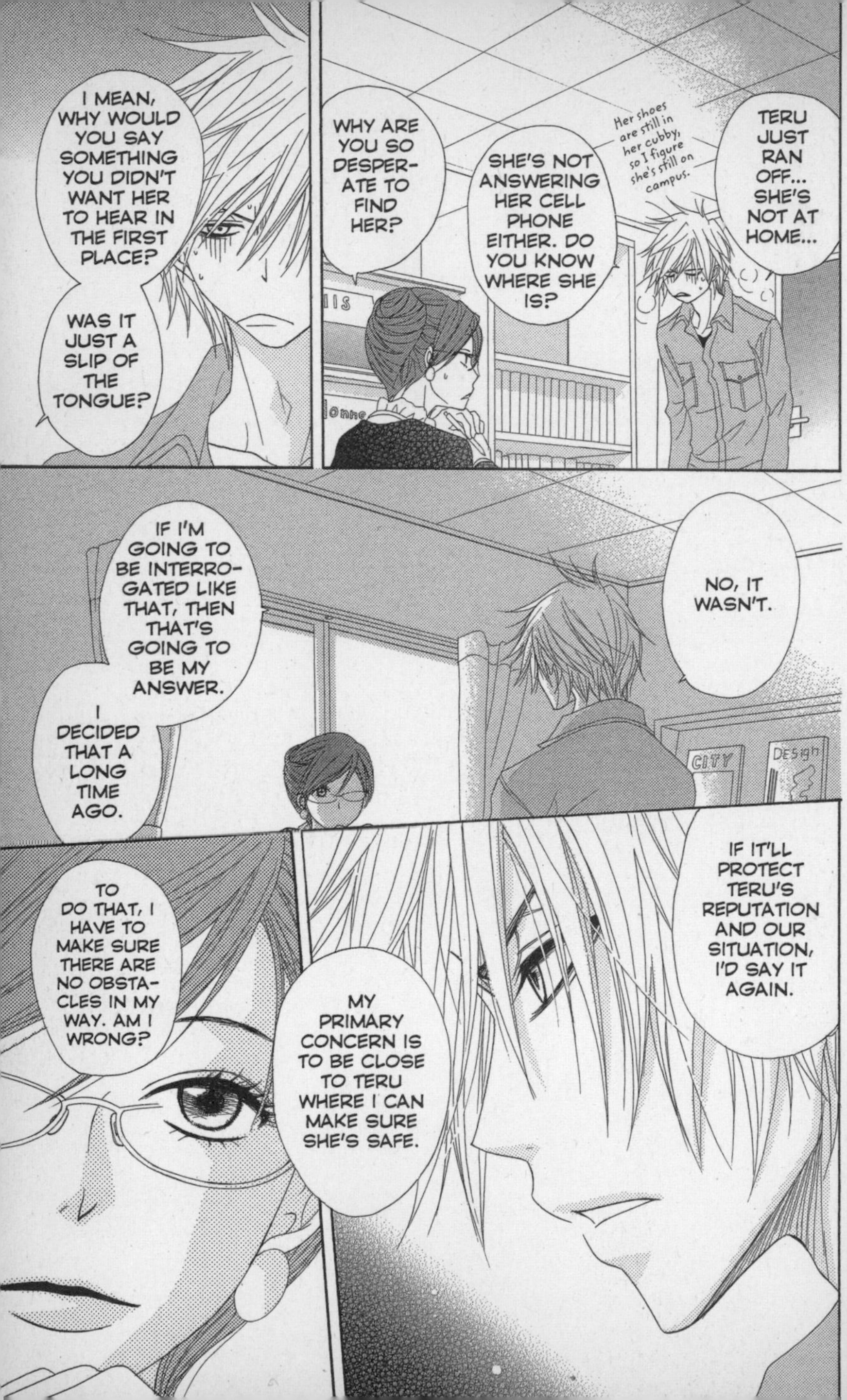
TERU JUST RAN OFF... SHE'S NOT AT HOME...
Her shoes are still in her cubby, so I figure she's still on campus.
SHE'S NOT ANSWERING HER CELL PHONE EITHER. DO YOU KNOW WHERE SHE IS?
WHY ARE YOU SO DESPERATE TO FIND HER?
I MEAN, WHY WOULD YOU SAY SOMETHING YOU DIDN'T WANT HER TO HEAR IN THE FIRST PLACE?
WAS IT JUST A SLIP OF THE TONGUE?
NO, IT WASN'T.
IF I'M GOING TO BE INTERROGATED LIKE THAT, THEN THAT'S GOING TO BE MY ANSWER.
I DECIDED THAT A LONG TIME AGO.
IF IT'LL PROTECT TERU'S REPUTATION AND OUR SITUATION, I'D SAY IT AGAIN.
MY PRIMARY CONCERN IS TO BE CLOSE TO TERU WHERE I CAN MAKE SURE SHE'S SAFE.
TO DO THAT, I HAVE TO MAKE SURE THERE ARE NO OBSTACLES IN MY WAY. AM I WRONG?

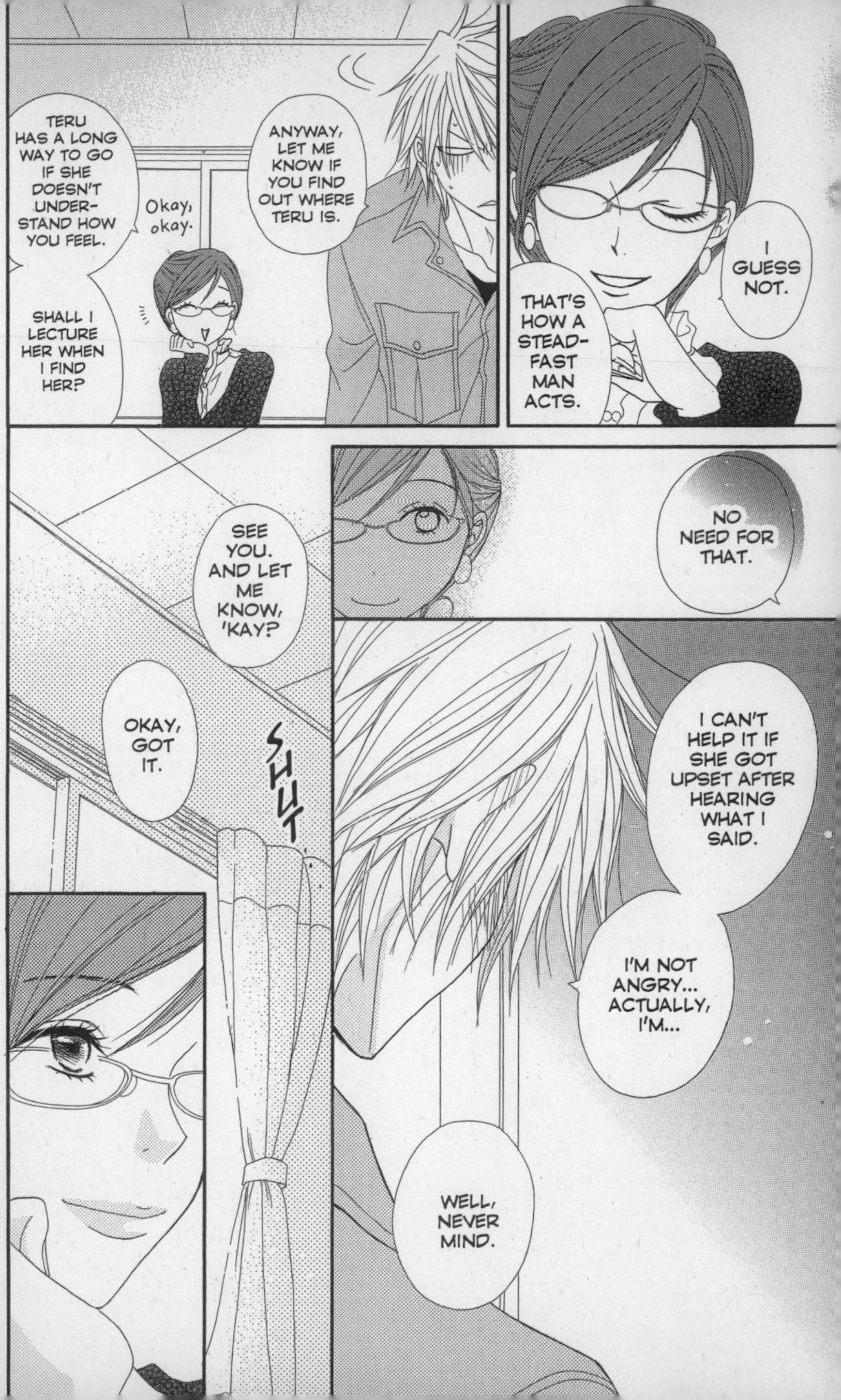

I GUESS NOT.
THAT'S HOW A STEAD-FAST MAN ACTS.
ANYWAY, LET ME KNOW IF YOU FIND OUT WHERE TERU IS.
Okay, okay.
TERU HAS A LONG WAY TO GO IF SHE DOESN'T UNDER-STAND HOW YOU FEEL.
SHALL I LECTURE HER WHEN I FIND HER?
NO NEED FOR THAT.
I CAN'T HELP IT IF SHE GOT UPSET AFTER HEARING WHAT I SAID.
I'M NOT ANGRY... ACTUALLY, I'M...
WELL, NEVER MIND.
SEE YOU. AND LET ME KNOW, 'KAY?
OKAY, GOT IT.
SHUT

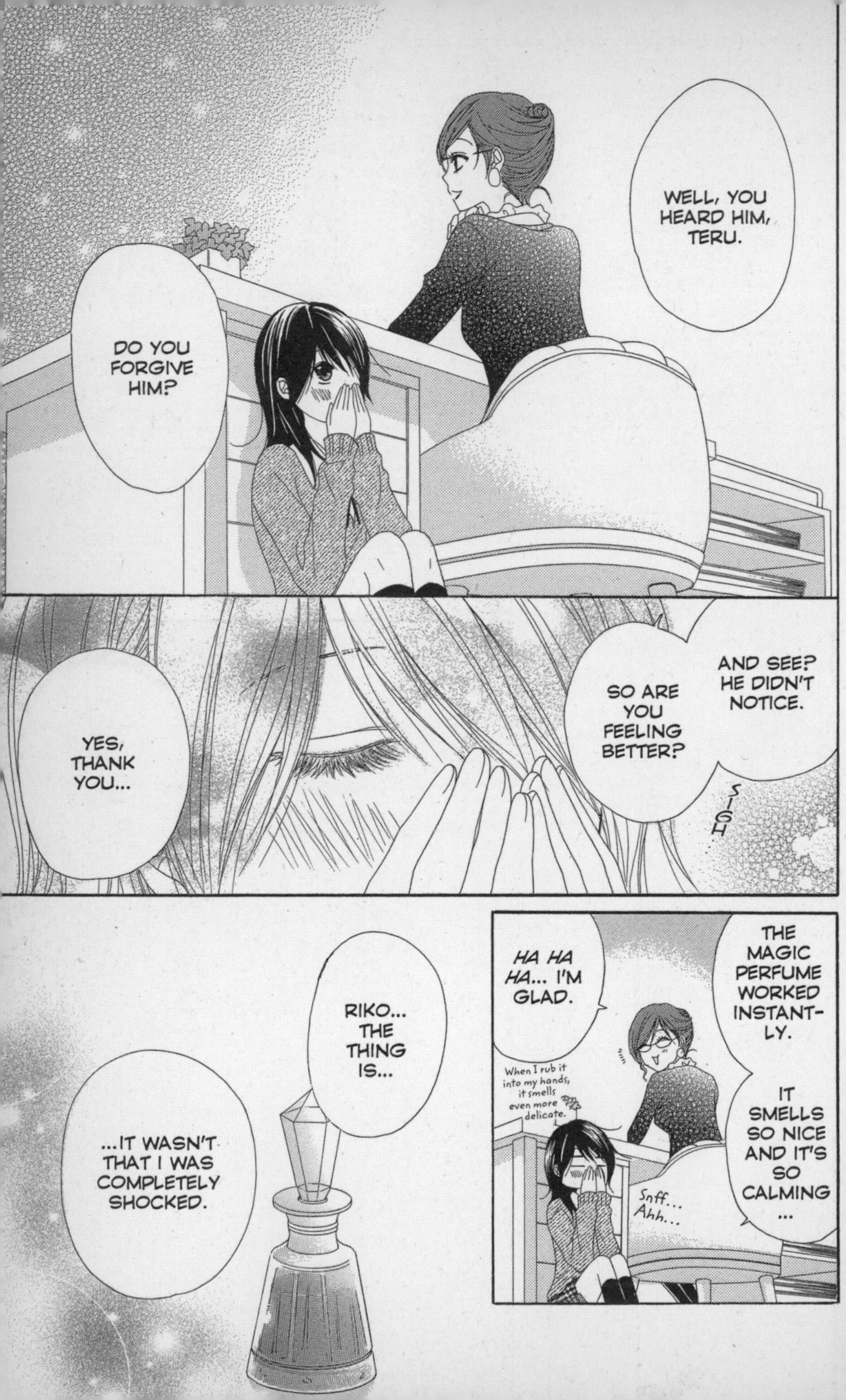
WELL, YOU HEARD HIM, TERU.
DO YOU FORGIVE HIM?
AND SEE? HE DIDN'T NOTICE.
SO ARE YOU FEELING BETTER?
SIGH
YES, THANK YOU...
THE MAGIC PERFUME WORKED INSTANT-LY.
HA HA HA... I'M GLAD.
IT SMELLS SO NICE AND IT'S SO CALMING...
When I rub it into my hands, it smells even more delicate.
Snff... Ahh...
RIKO... THE THING IS...
...IT WASN'T THAT I WAS COMPLETELY SHOCKED.

KUROSAKI ISN'T WRONG.

IF HE'S PRESSED ABOUT HIS RELATIONSHIP WITH ME...

...I UNDERSTAND WHY HE'D HAVE TO REPLY THE WAY HE DID.

I UNDERSTAND... IN MY HEAD.

BUT HEARING IT PUT SO BLUNTLY MADE MY HEART FEEL FUNNY.

SOMETHING TOLD ME NOT TO ACT AS IF NOTHING HAPPENED.

SEEING KUROSAKI PANIC MADE ME FEEL LIKE I SHOULD ACT UPSET.

SO I DECIDED TO RUN OFF JUST LIKE THEY DO IN SHOJO MANGA.

AH, THE AGE-OLD TRICK OF TURNING SUDDENLY AND RUNNING OFF WHEN HE CALLS YOUR NAME...

Women do that these days.

I JUST TURNED UP THE HEAT ON HIM, DIDN'T I?

HEH HEH. YOU SURE DID.

BUT IT'S ALL RIGHT. HE WASN'T MAD.

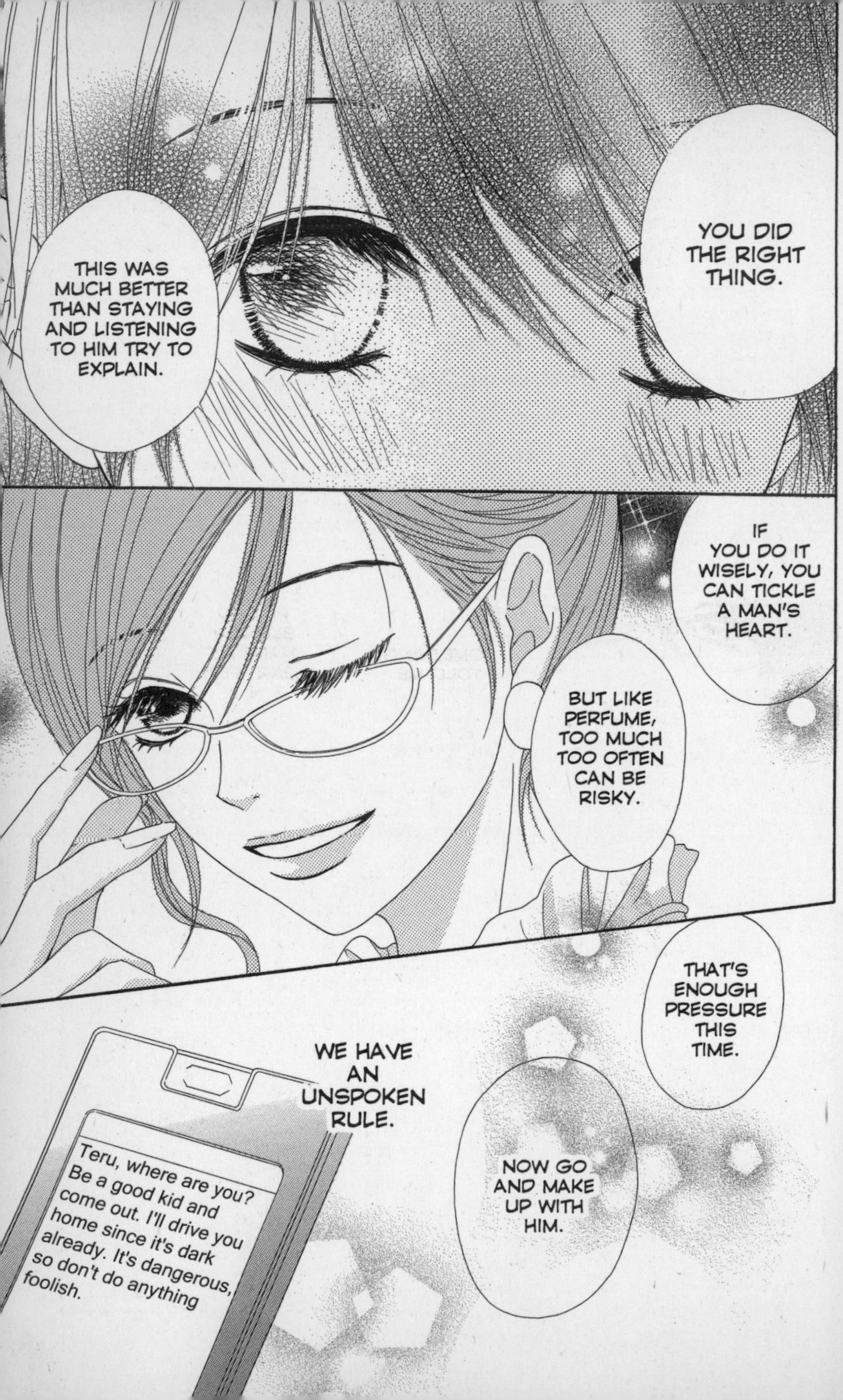
YOU DID THE RIGHT THING.
THIS WAS MUCH BETTER THAN STAYING AND LISTENING TO HIM TRY TO EXPLAIN.
IF YOU DO IT WISELY, YOU CAN TICKLE A MAN'S HEART.
BUT LIKE PERFUME, TOO MUCH TOO OFTEN CAN BE RISKY.
THAT'S ENOUGH PRESSURE THIS TIME.
WE HAVE AN UNSPOKEN RULE.
NOW GO AND MAKE UP WITH HIM.
Teru, where are you? Be a good kid and come out. I'll drive you home since it's dark already. It's dangerous, so don't do anything foolish.

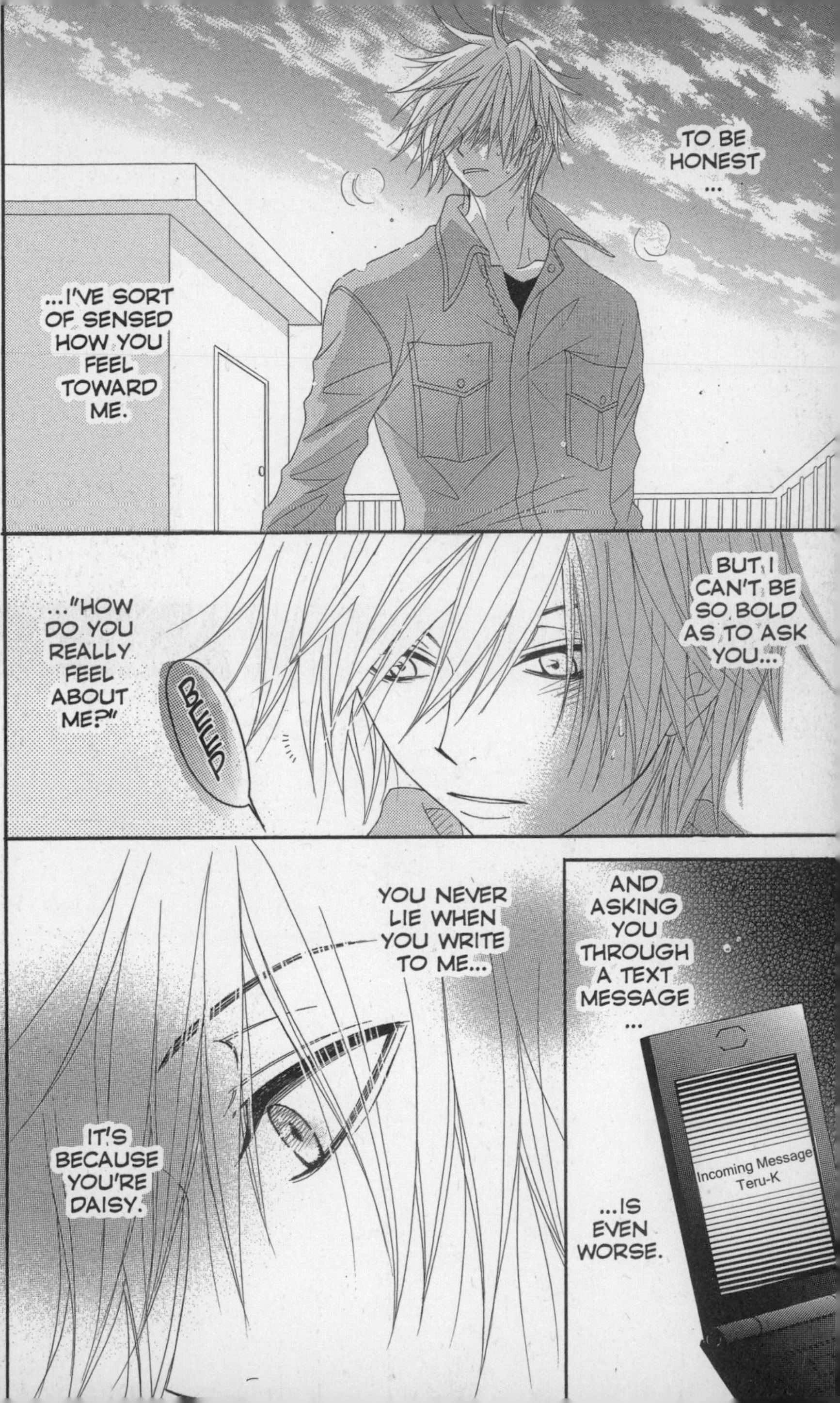
TO BE HONEST ...
...I'VE SORT OF SENSED HOW YOU FEEL TOWARD ME.
BUT I CAN'T BE SO BOLD AS TO ASK YOU...
BLINK
..."HOW DO YOU REALLY FEEL ABOUT ME?"
AND ASKING YOU THROUGH A TEXT MESSAGE ...
Incoming Message
Teru-K
...IS EVEN WORSE.
YOU NEVER LIE WHEN YOU WRITE TO ME...
IT'S BECAUSE YOU'RE DAISY.

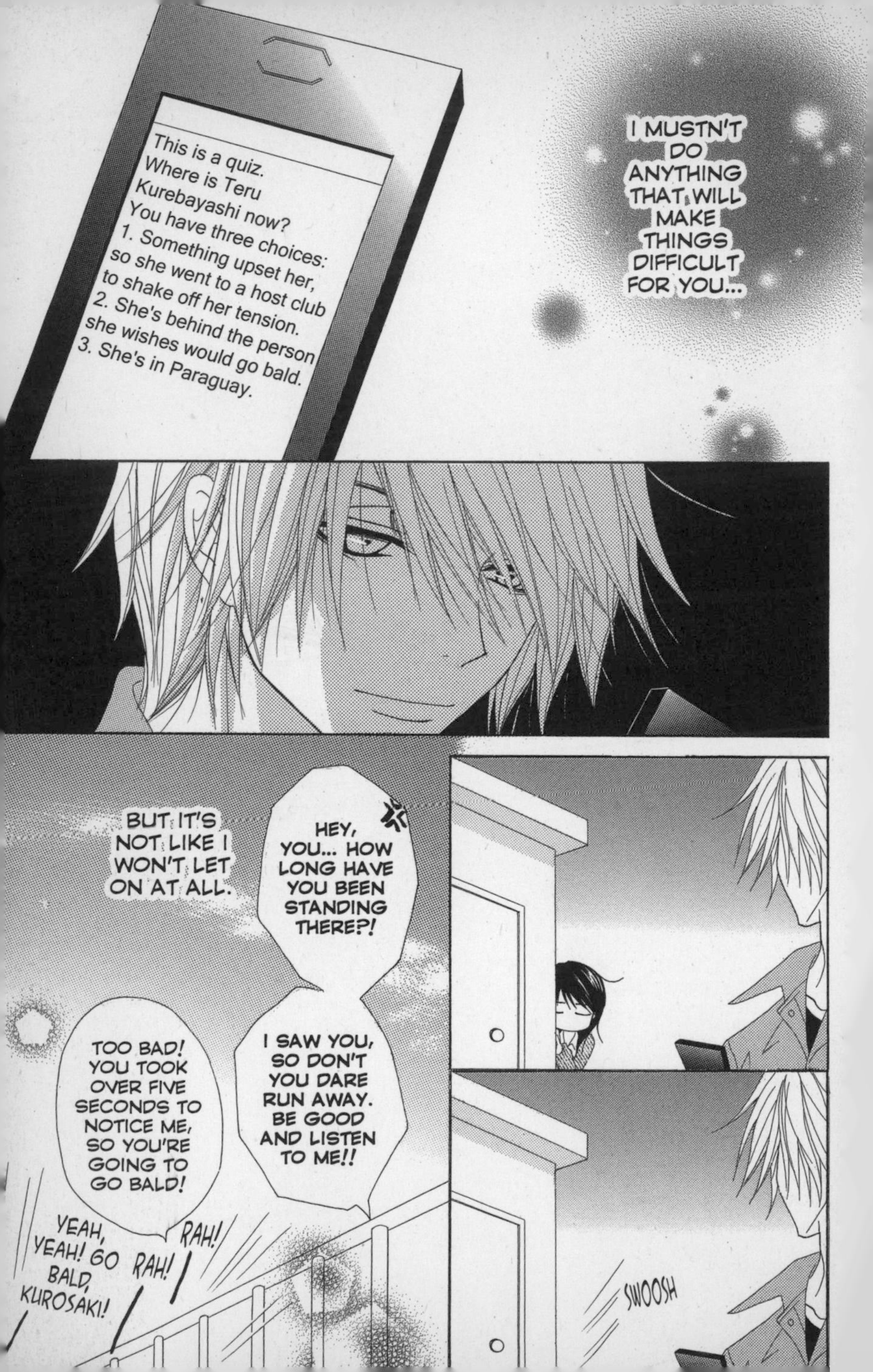
I MUSTN'T DO ANYTHING THAT WILL MAKE THINGS DIFFICULT FOR YOU...
This is a quiz. Where is Teru Kurebayashi now? You have three choices: 1. Something upset her, so she went to a host club to shake off her tension. 2. She's behind the person she wishes would go bald. 3. She's in Paraguay.
SWOOSH
BUT IT'S NOT LIKE I WON'T LET ON AT ALL.
HEY, YOU... HOW LONG HAVE YOU BEEN STANDING THERE?!
I SAW YOU, SO DON'T YOU DARE RUN AWAY. BE GOOD AND LISTEN TO ME!!
TOO BAD! YOU TOOK OVER FIVE SECONDS TO NOTICE ME, SO YOU'RE GOING TO GO BALD!
RAH! RAH!
YEAH, YEAH! GO BALD, KUROSAKI!

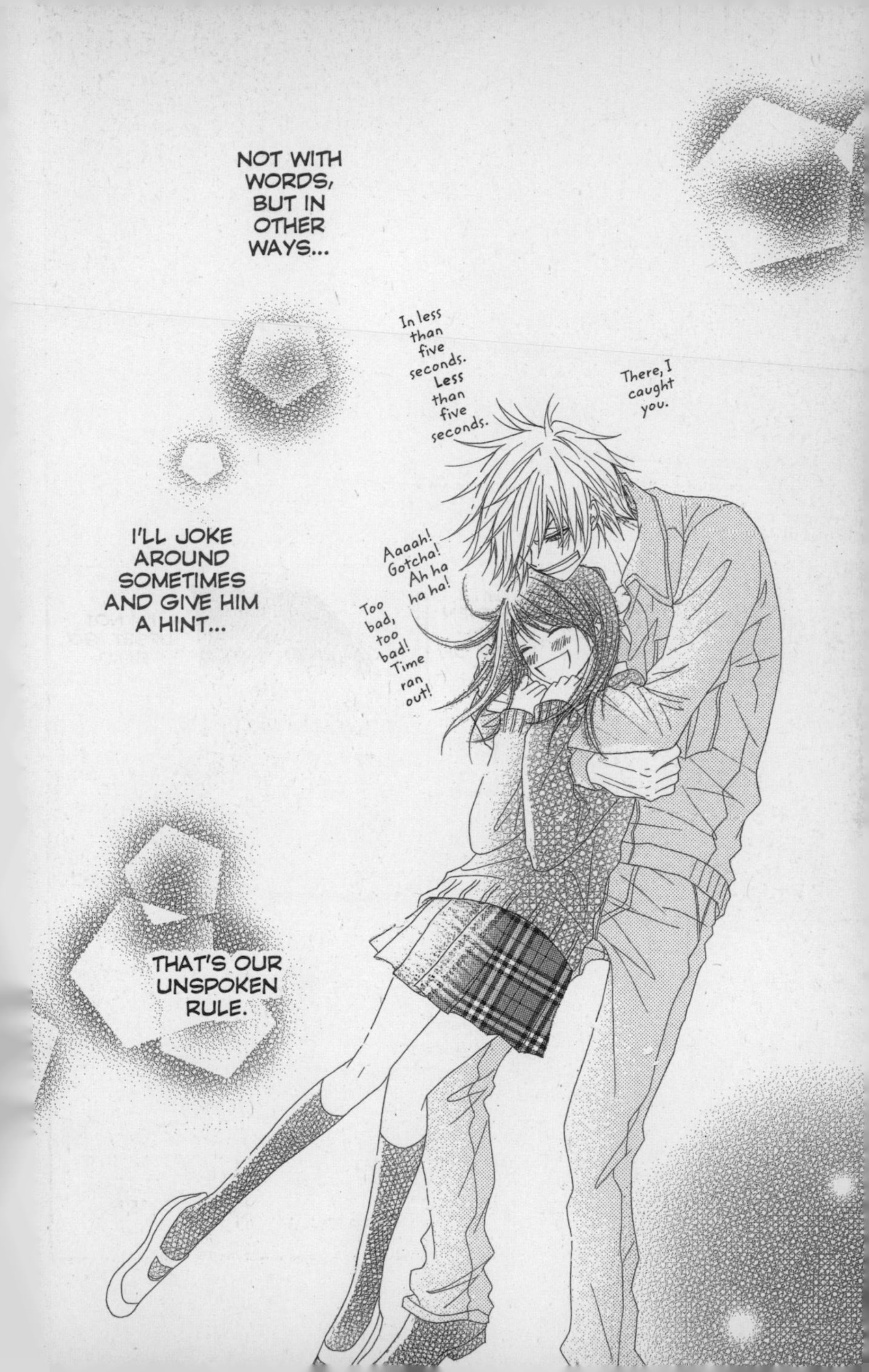
NOT WITH WORDS, BUT IN OTHER WAYS...
There, I caught you.
In less than five seconds. Less than five seconds.
Aaaah! Gotcha! Ah ha ha ha!
Too bad, too bad! Time ran out!
I'LL JOKE AROUND SOMETIMES AND GIVE HIM A HINT...
THAT'S OUR UNSPOKEN RULE.

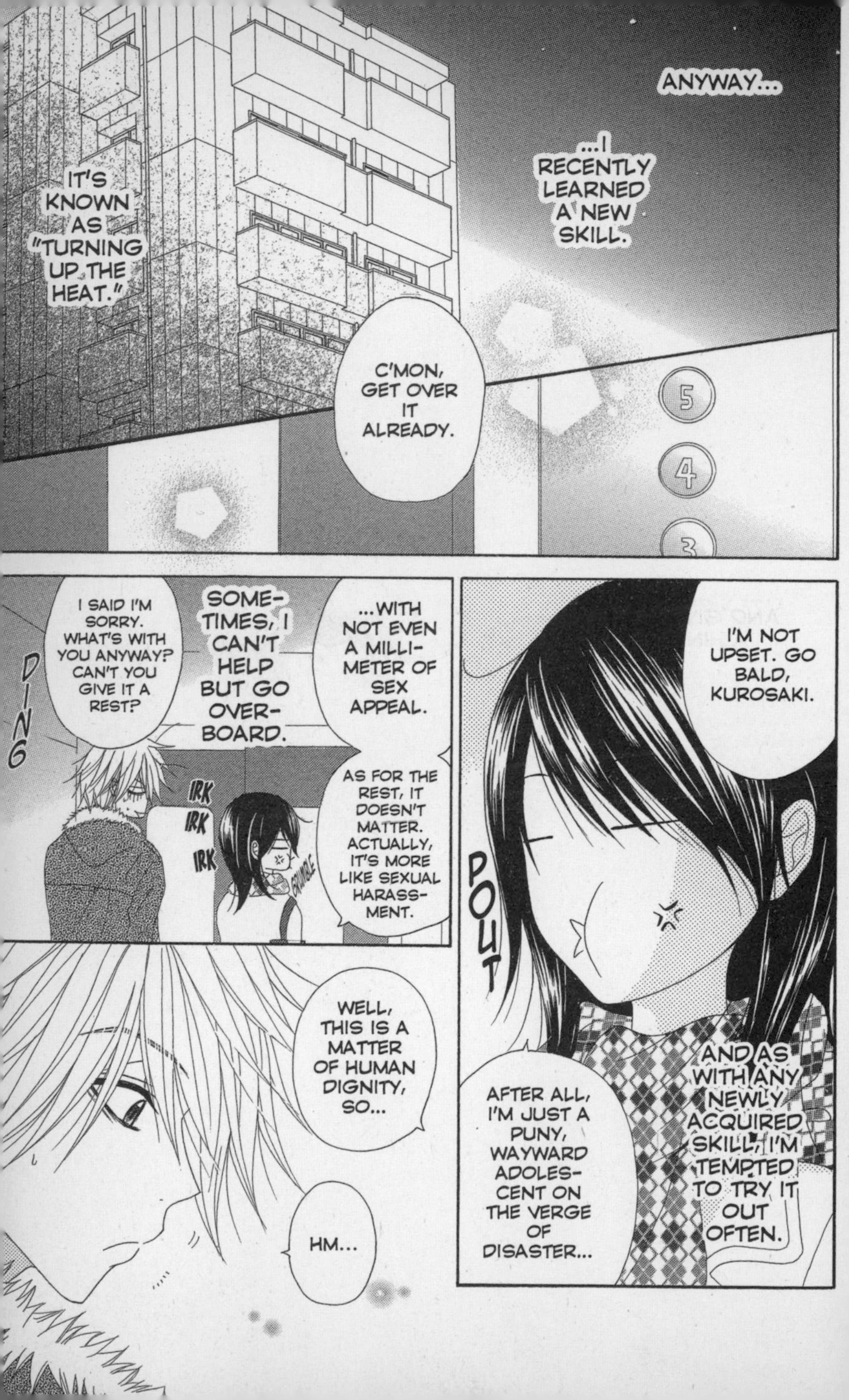
ANYWAY...
...I RECENTLY LEARNED A NEW SKILL.
IT'S KNOWN AS "TURNING UP THE HEAT."
C'MON, GET OVER IT ALREADY.
5
4
3
I'M NOT UPSET. GO BALD, KUROSAKI.
POUT
AND AS WITH ANY NEWLY ACQUIRED SKILL, I'M TEMPTED TO TRY IT OUT OFTEN.
AFTER ALL, I'M JUST A PUNY, WAYWARD ADOLESCENT ON THE VERGE OF DISASTER...
...WITH NOT EVEN A MILLIMETER OF SEX APPEAL.
AS FOR THE REST, IT DOESN'T MATTER. ACTUALLY, IT'S MORE LIKE SEXUAL HARASSMENT.
SOMETIMES, I CAN'T HELP BUT GO OVERBOARD.
I SAID I'M SORRY. WHAT'S WITH YOU ANYWAY? CAN'T YOU GIVE IT A REST?
DING
IRK
IRK
IRK
GRUMBLE
WELL, THIS IS A MATTER OF HUMAN DIGNITY, SO...
HM...

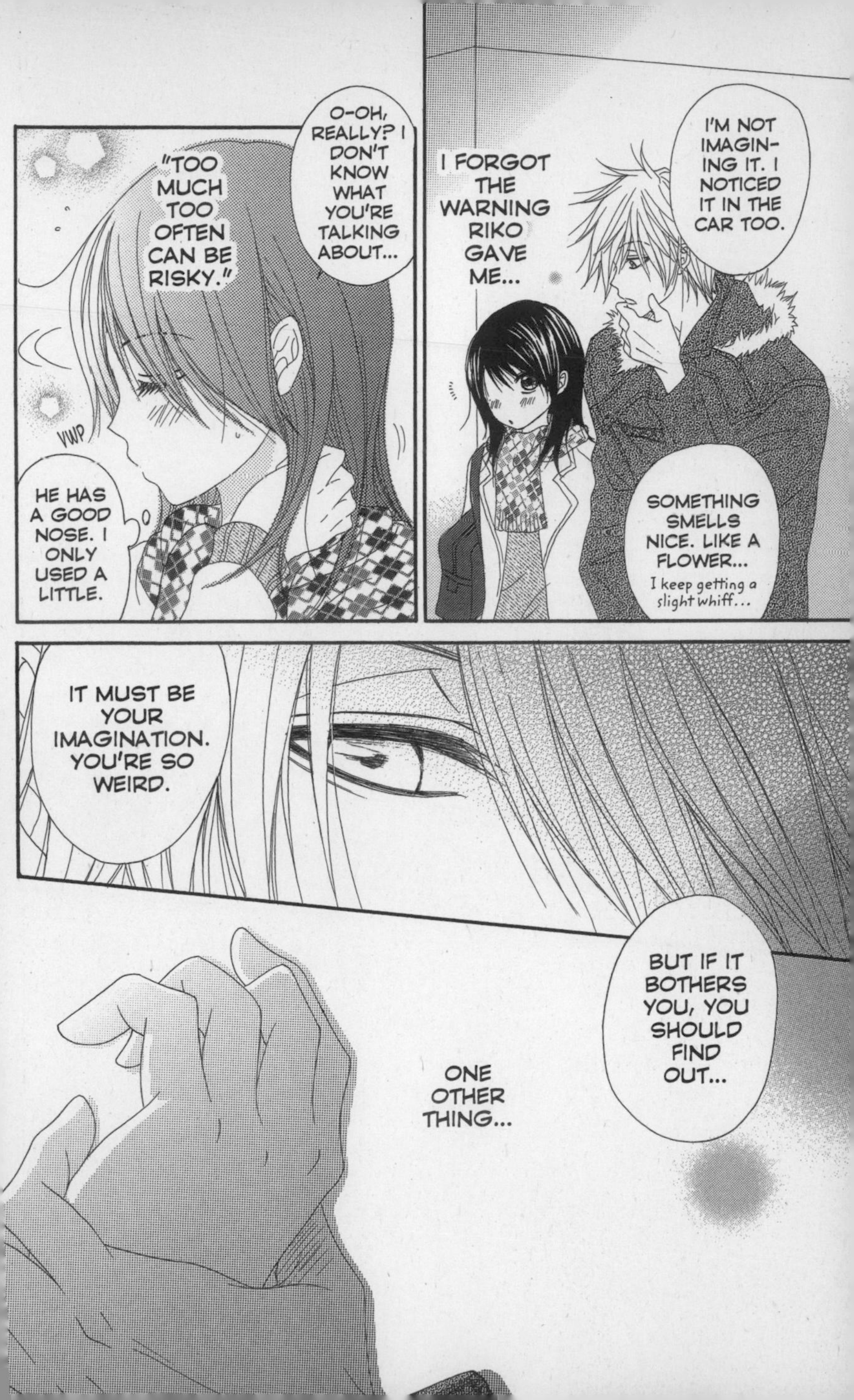
I'M NOT IMAGINING IT. I NOTICED IT IN THE CAR TOO.
I FORGOT THE WARNING RIKO GAVE ME...
SOMETHING SMELLS NICE. LIKE A FLOWER...
I keep getting a slight whiff...
O-OH, REALLY? I DON'T KNOW WHAT YOU'RE TALKING ABOUT...
"TOO MUCH TOO OFTEN CAN BE RISKY."
VWP
HE HAS A GOOD NOSE. I ONLY USED A LITTLE.
IT MUST BE YOUR IMAGINATION. YOU'RE SO WEIRD.
BUT IF IT BOTHERS YOU, YOU SHOULD FIND OUT...
ONE OTHER THING...

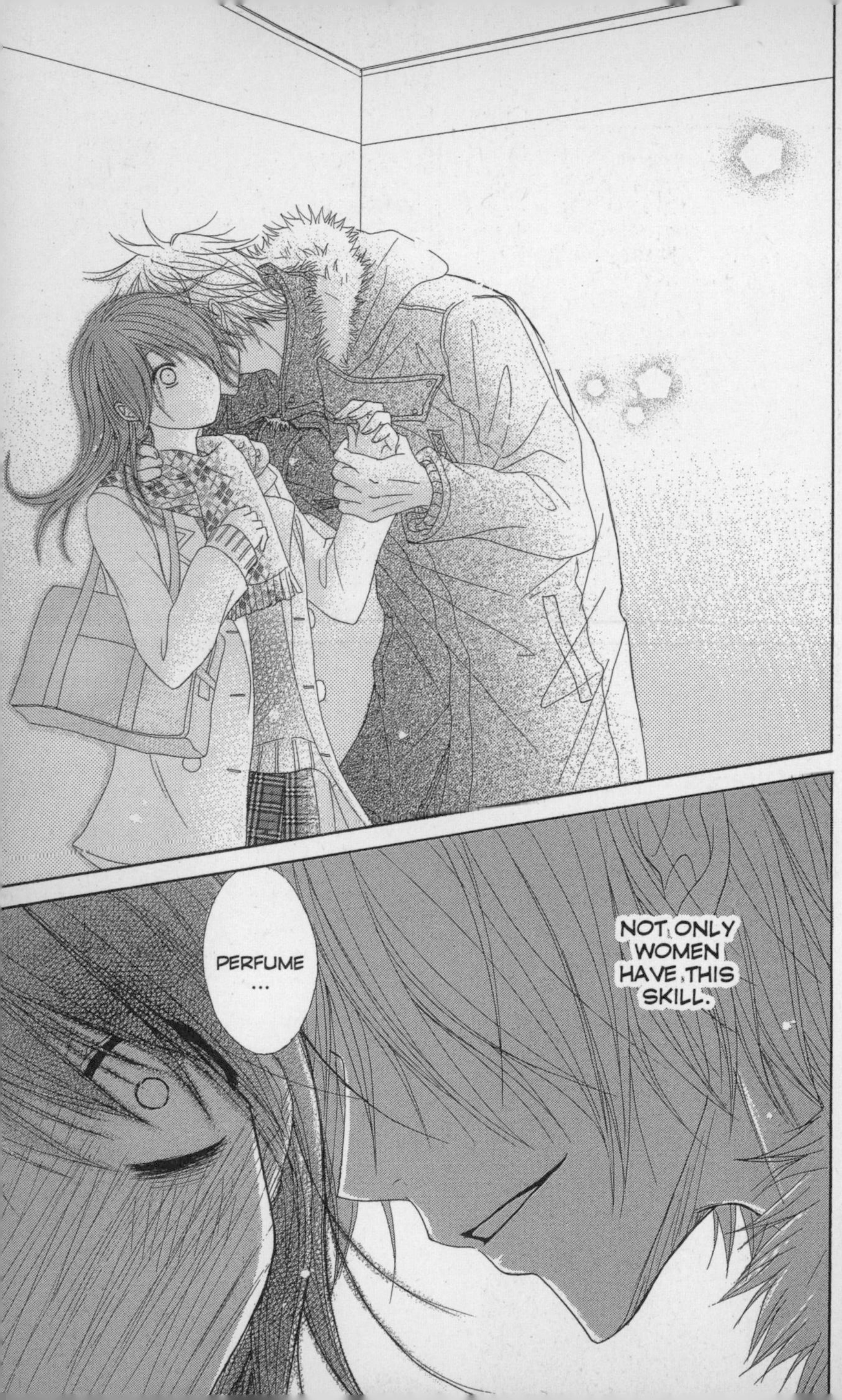
NOT ONLY WOMEN HAVE THIS SKILL.
PERFUME ...

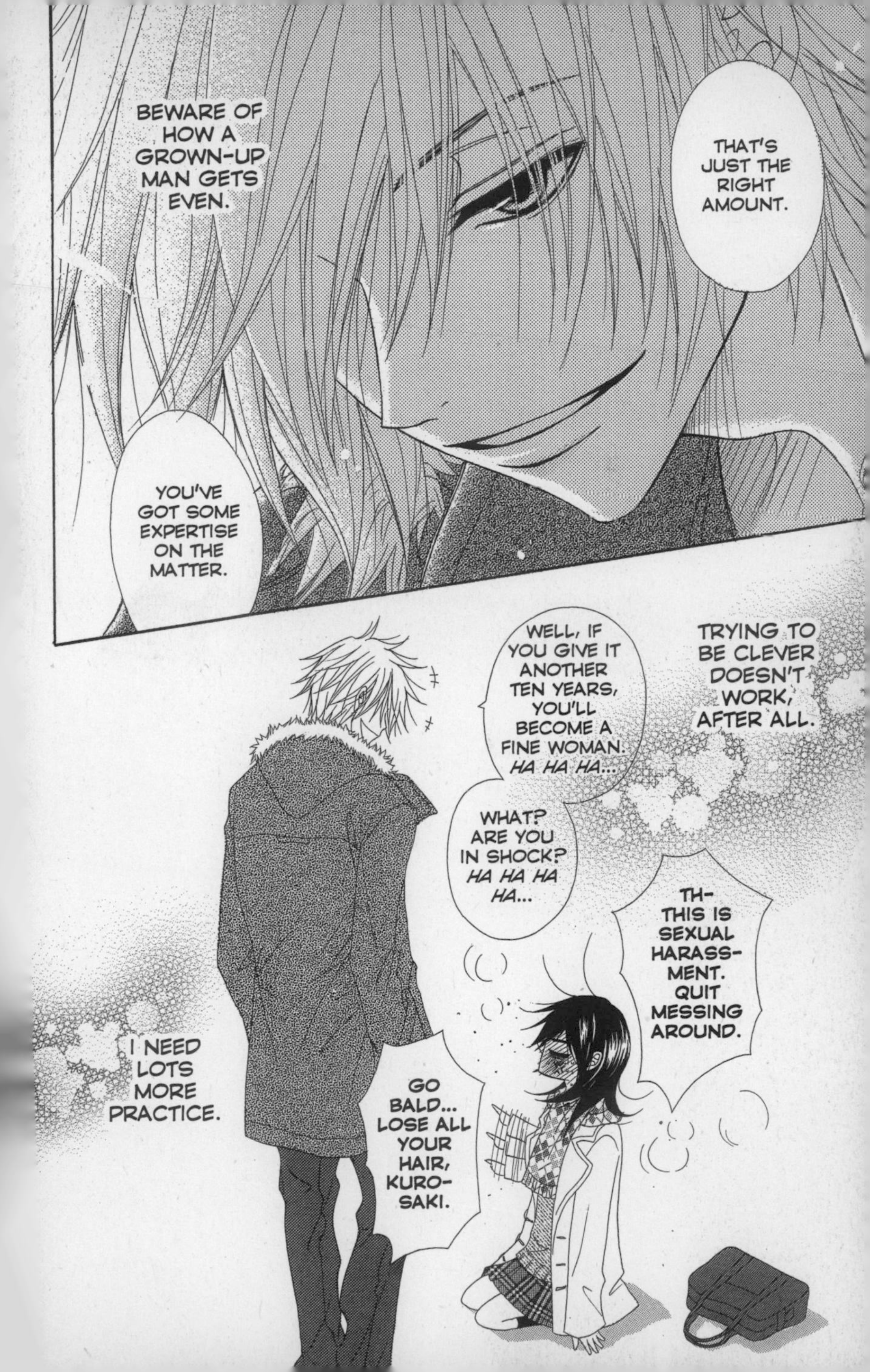
THAT'S JUST THE RIGHT AMOUNT.
BEWARE OF HOW A GROWN-UP MAN GETS EVEN.
YOU'VE GOT SOME EXPERTISE ON THE MATTER.
TRYING TO BE CLEVER DOESN'T WORK, AFTER ALL.
WELL, IF YOU GIVE IT ANOTHER TEN YEARS, YOU'LL BECOME A FINE WOMAN. *HA HA HA...*
WHAT? ARE YOU IN SHOCK? *HA HA HA HA...*
TH- THIS IS SEXUAL HARASS-MENT. QUIT MESSING AROUND.
GO BALD... LOSE ALL YOUR HAIR, KURO-SAKI.
I NEED LOTS MORE PRACTICE.

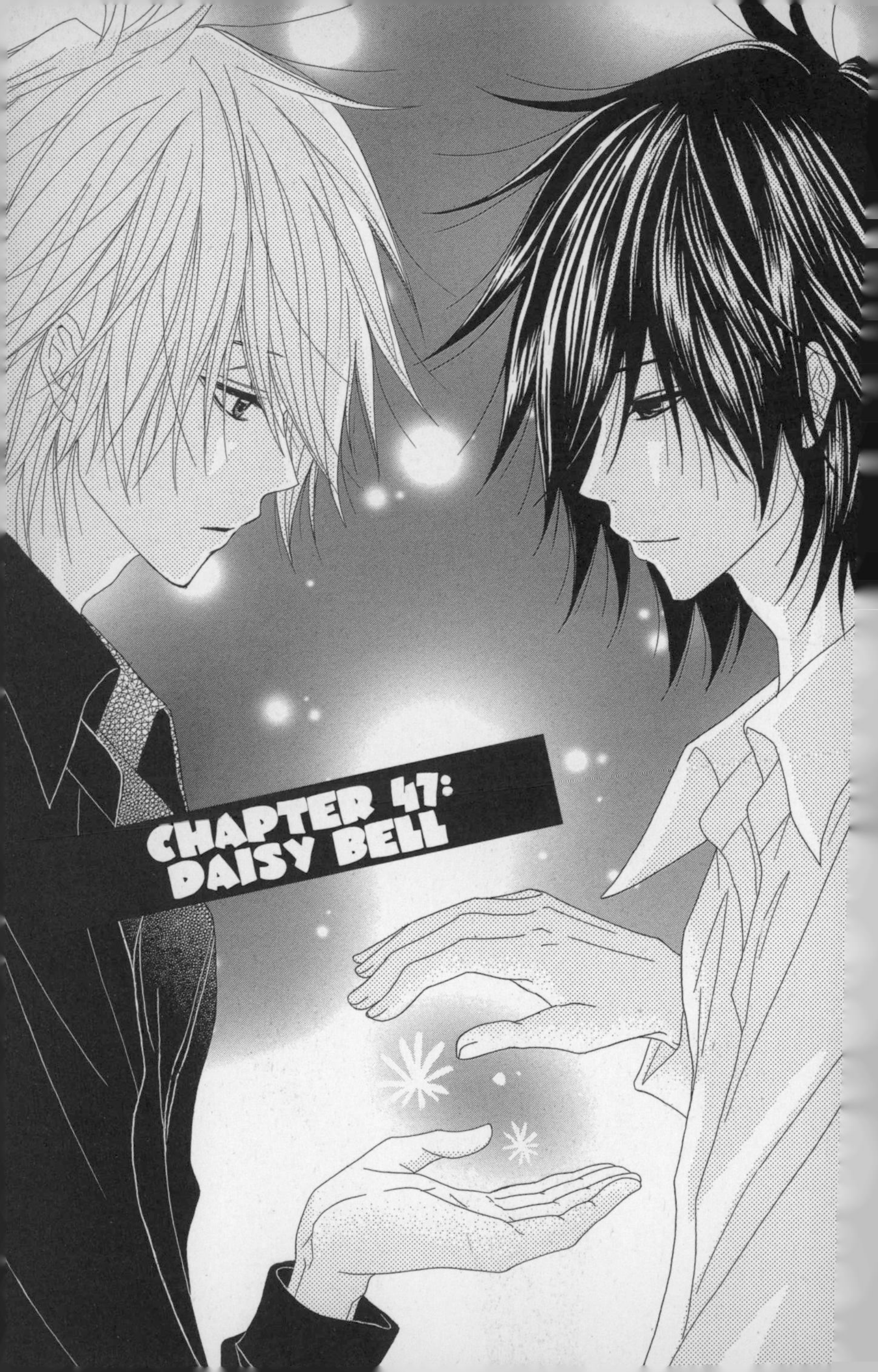
CHAPTER 47:
DAISY BELL

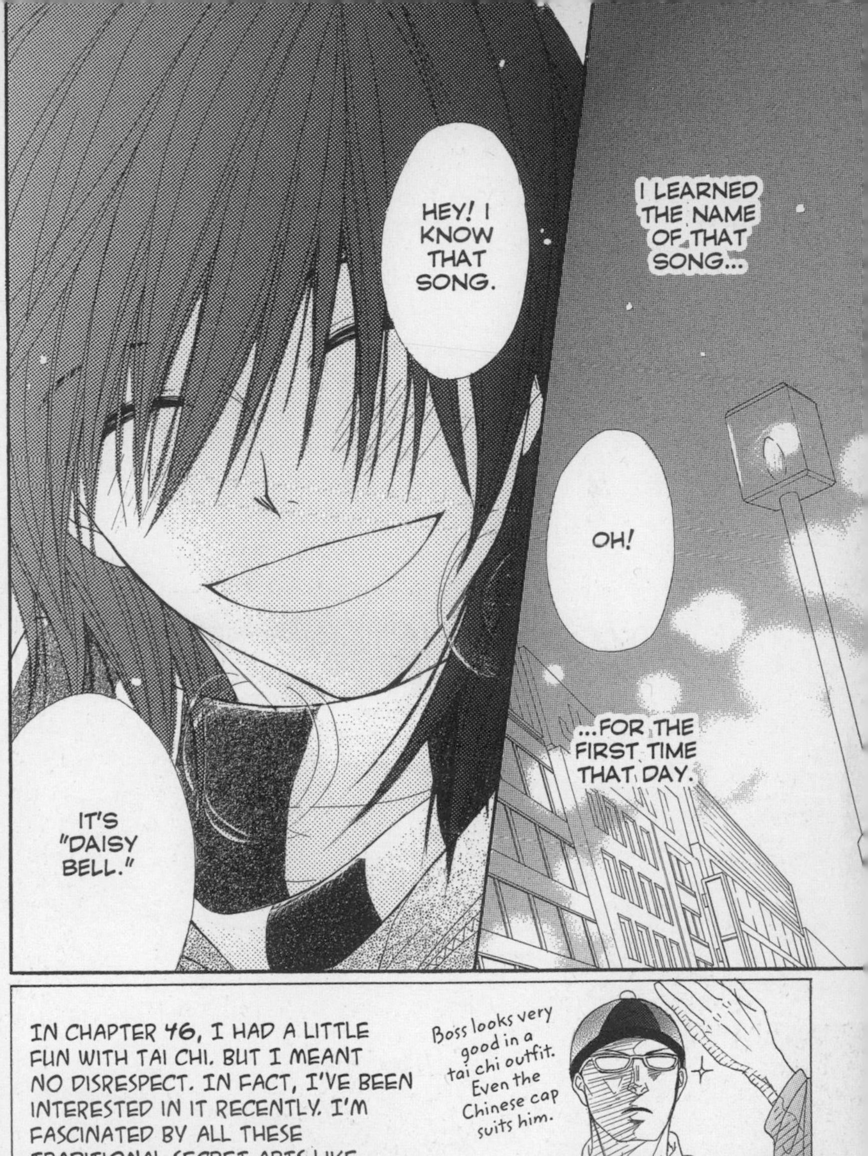
I LEARNED THE NAME OF THAT SONG...
HEY! I KNOW THAT SONG.
OH!
...FOR THE FIRST TIME THAT DAY.
IT'S "DAISY BELL."

IN CHAPTER 46, I HAD A LITTLE FUN WITH TAI CHI. BUT I MEANT NO DISRESPECT. IN FACT, I'VE BEEN INTERESTED IN IT RECENTLY. I'M FASCINATED BY ALL THESE TRADITIONAL SECRET ARTS LIKE TAI CHI, YOGA, AND RADIO CALISTHENICS, WHICH SEEM TO BE GOOD FOR YOUR HEALTH. MY BODY'S IN BAD SHAPE.

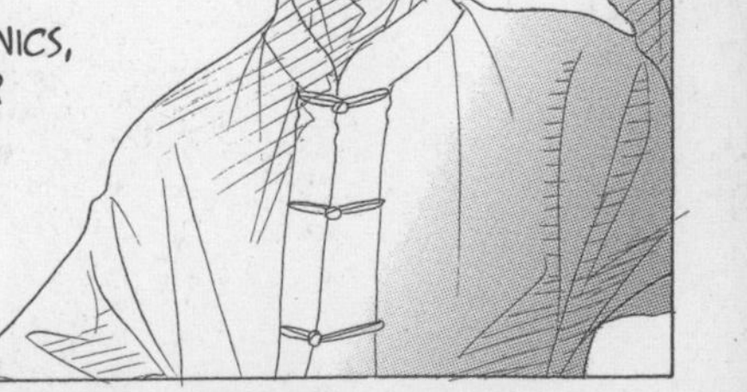
Boss looks very good in a tai chi outfit. Even the Chinese cap suits him.

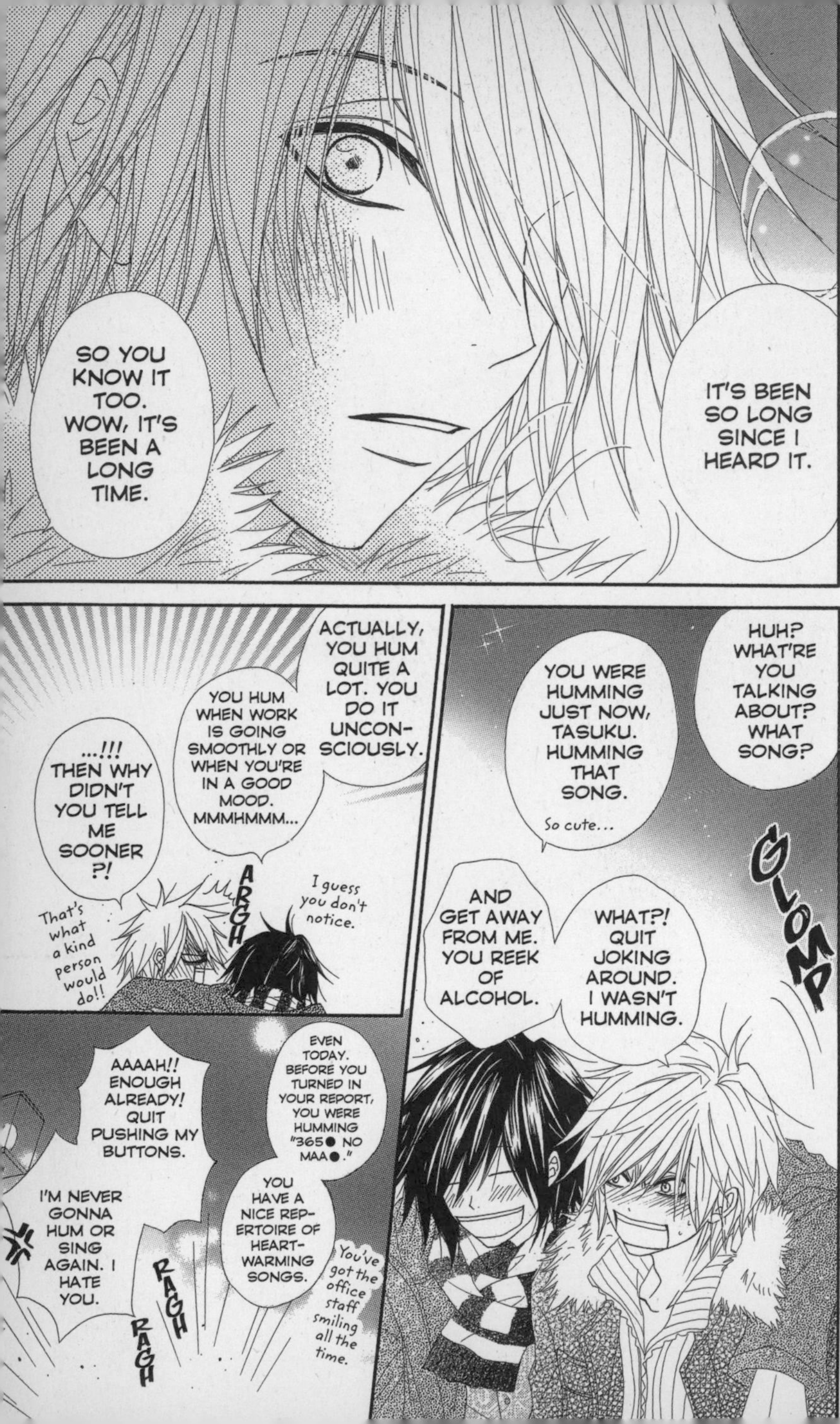
IT'S BEEN SO LONG SINCE I HEARD IT.
SO YOU KNOW IT TOO. WOW, IT'S BEEN A LONG TIME.
HUH? WHAT'RE YOU TALKING ABOUT? WHAT SONG?
YOU WERE HUMMING JUST NOW, TASUKU. HUMMING THAT SONG.
So cute...
GLOMP
WHAT?! QUIT JOKING AROUND. I WASN'T HUMMING.
AND GET AWAY FROM ME. YOU REEK OF ALCOHOL.
ACTUALLY, YOU HUM QUITE A LOT. YOU DO IT UNCONSCIOUSLY.
YOU HUM WHEN WORK IS GOING SMOOTHLY OR WHEN YOU'RE IN A GOOD MOOD. MMMHMMM...
I guess you don't notice.
ARGH
...!!! THEN WHY DIDN'T YOU TELL ME SOONER?!
That's what a kind person would do!!
EVEN TODAY. BEFORE YOU TURNED IN YOUR REPORT, YOU WERE HUMMING "365● NO MAA●."
YOU HAVE A NICE REPERTOIRE OF HEART-WARMING SONGS.
You've got the office staff smiling all the time.
AAAAH!! ENOUGH ALREADY! QUIT PUSHING MY BUTTONS.
I'M NEVER GONNA HUM OR SING AGAIN. I HATE YOU.
RAGH
RAGH

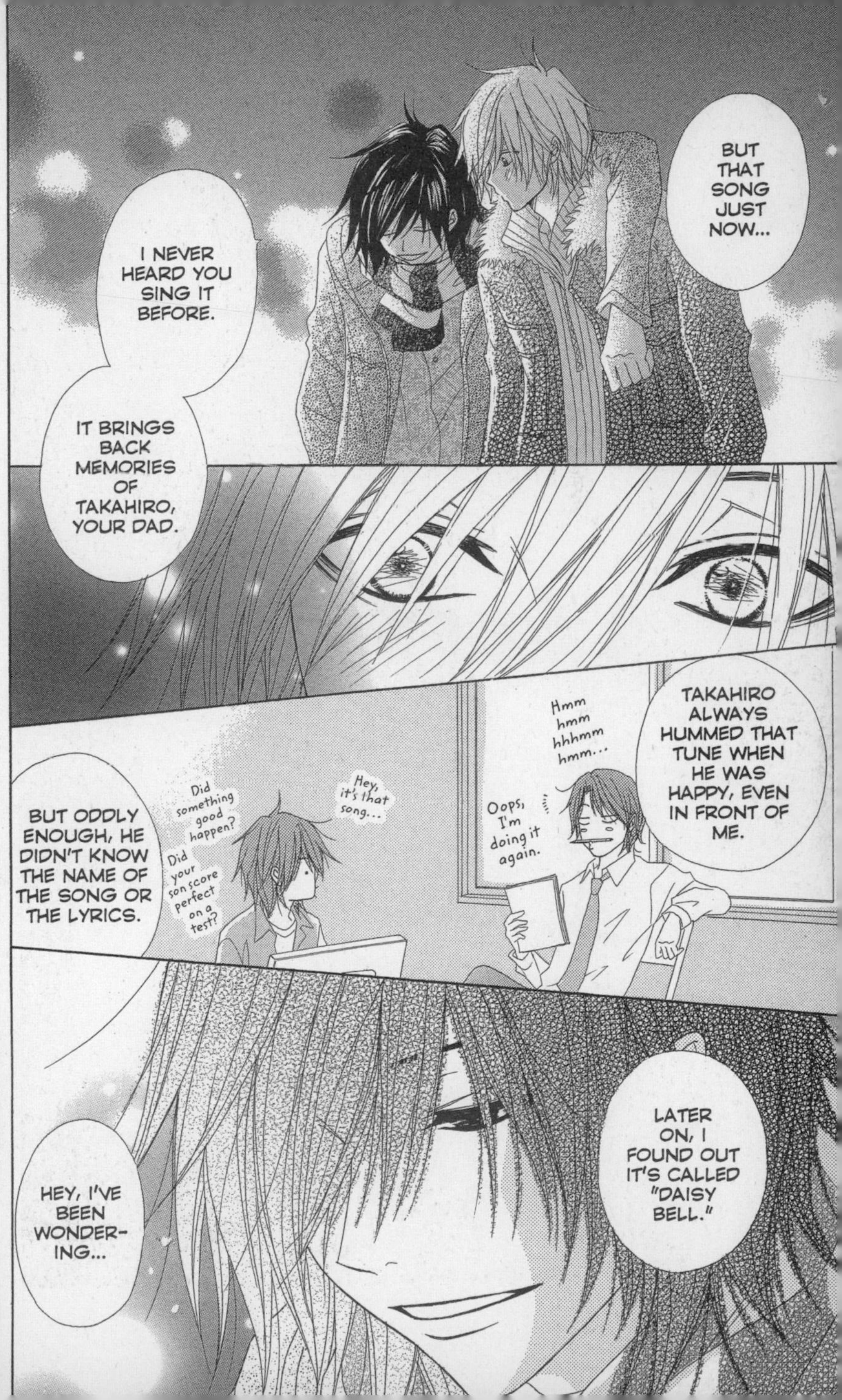
BUT THAT SONG JUST NOW...
I NEVER HEARD YOU SING IT BEFORE.
IT BRINGS BACK MEMORIES OF TAKAHIRO, YOUR DAD.
TAKAHIRO ALWAYS HUMMED THAT TUNE WHEN HE WAS HAPPY, EVEN IN FRONT OF ME.
Hmm hmm hhhmm hmm...
Oops, I'm doing it again.
Hey, it's that song...
Did something good happen?
Did your son score perfect on a test?
BUT ODDLY ENOUGH, HE DIDN'T KNOW THE NAME OF THE SONG OR THE LYRICS.
LATER ON, I FOUND OUT IT'S CALLED "DAISY BELL."
HEY, I'VE BEEN WONDERING...

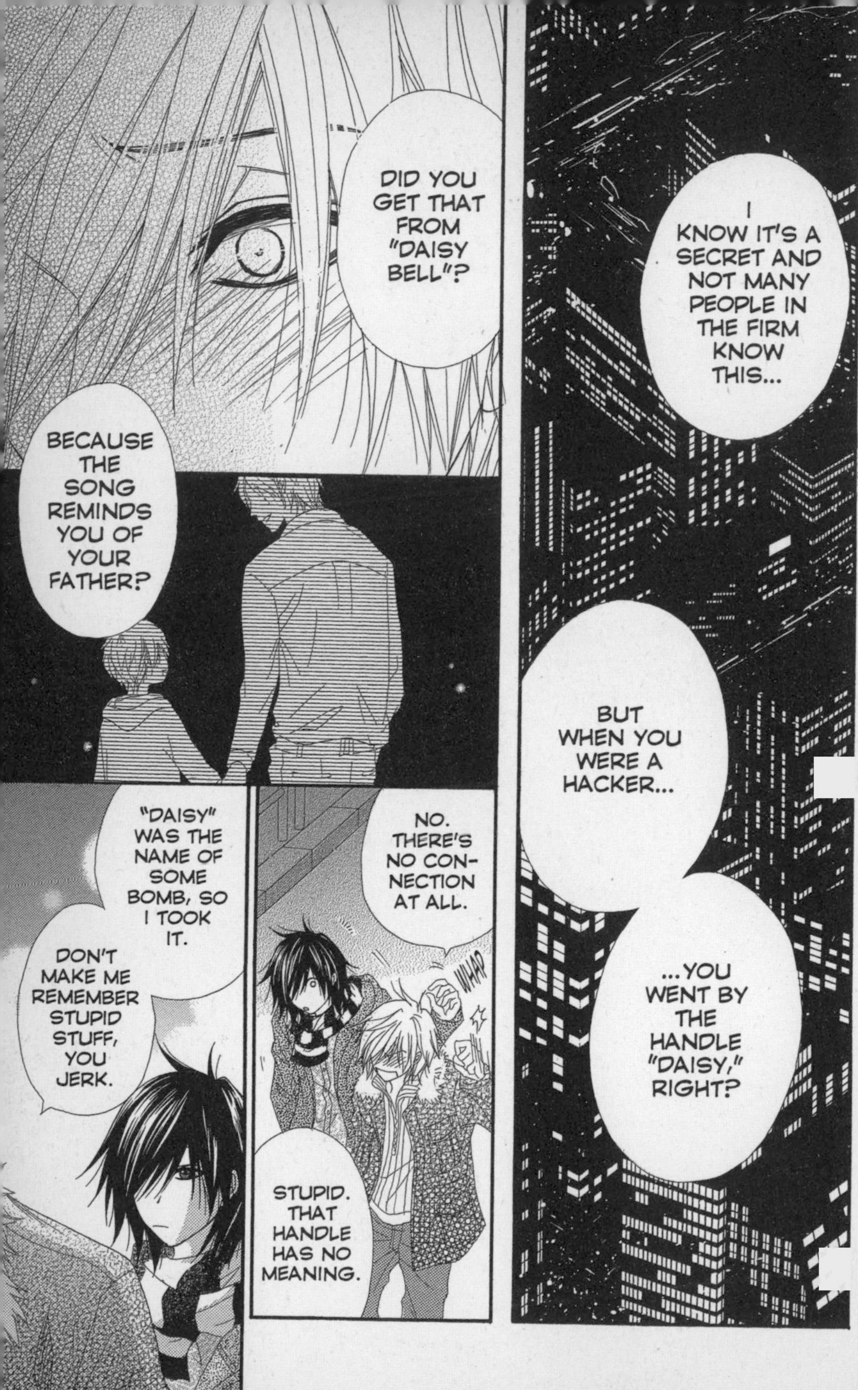
I KNOW IT'S A SECRET AND NOT MANY PEOPLE IN THE FIRM KNOW THIS...
BUT WHEN YOU WERE A HACKER...
...YOU WENT BY THE HANDLE "DAISY," RIGHT?
DID YOU GET THAT FROM "DAISY BELL"?
BECAUSE THE SONG REMINDS YOU OF YOUR FATHER?
NO. THERE'S NO CON-NECTION AT ALL.
WHAP
STUPID. THAT HANDLE HAS NO MEANING.
"DAISY" WAS THE NAME OF SOME BOMB, SO I TOOK IT.
DON'T MAKE ME REMEMBER STUPID STUFF, YOU JERK.

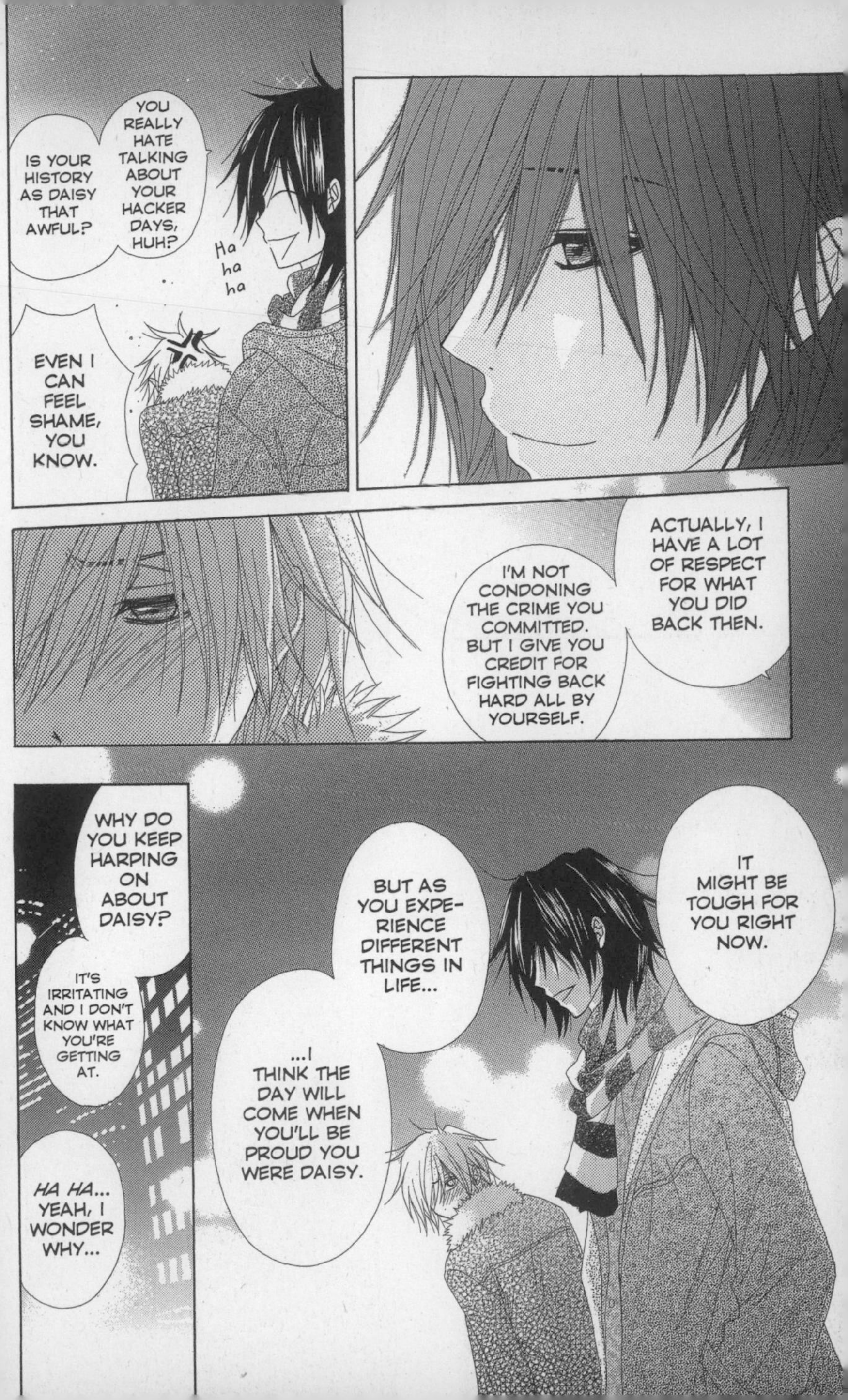
YOU REALLY HATE TALKING ABOUT YOUR HACKER DAYS, HUH?
IS YOUR HISTORY AS DAISY THAT AWFUL?
Ha ha ha
EVEN I CAN FEEL SHAME, YOU KNOW.
ACTUALLY, I HAVE A LOT OF RESPECT FOR WHAT YOU DID BACK THEN.
I'M NOT CONDONING THE CRIME YOU COMMITTED. BUT I GIVE YOU CREDIT FOR FIGHTING BACK HARD ALL BY YOURSELF.
IT MIGHT BE TOUGH FOR YOU RIGHT NOW.
BUT AS YOU EXPE-RIENCE DIFFERENT THINGS IN LIFE...
...I THINK THE DAY WILL COME WHEN YOU'LL BE PROUD YOU WERE DAISY.
WHY DO YOU KEEP HARPING ON ABOUT DAISY?
IT'S IRRITATING AND I DON'T KNOW WHAT YOU'RE GETTING AT.
HA HA... YEAH, I WONDER WHY...

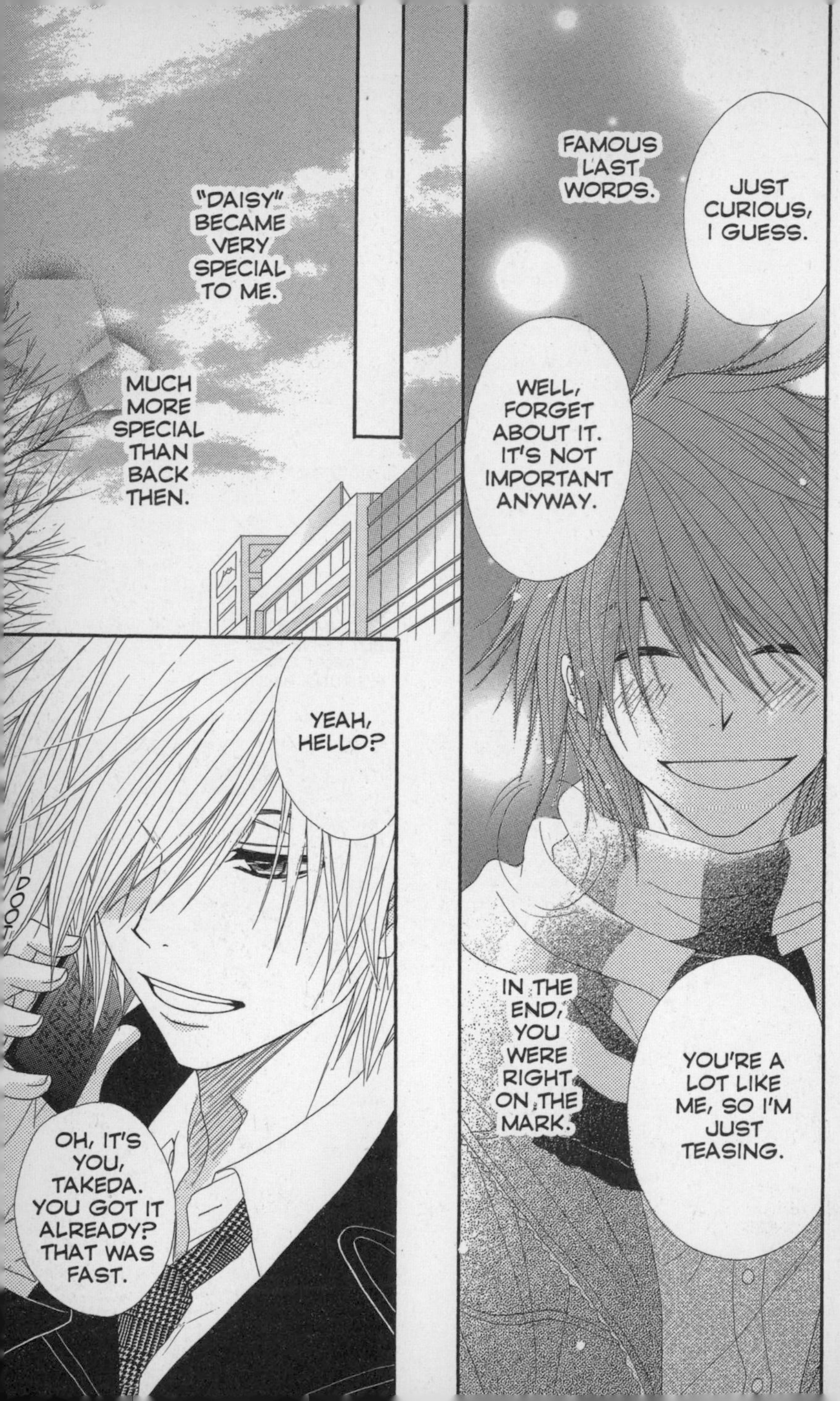
JUST CURIOUS, I GUESS.
FAMOUS LAST WORDS.
WELL, FORGET ABOUT IT. IT'S NOT IMPORTANT ANYWAY.
YOU'RE A LOT LIKE ME, SO I'M JUST TEASING.
IN THE END, YOU WERE RIGHT ON THE MARK.
"DAISY" BECAME VERY SPECIAL TO ME.
MUCH MORE SPECIAL THAN BACK THEN.
YEAH, HELLO?
DOOT
OH, IT'S YOU, TAKEDA. YOU GOT IT ALREADY? THAT WAS FAST.

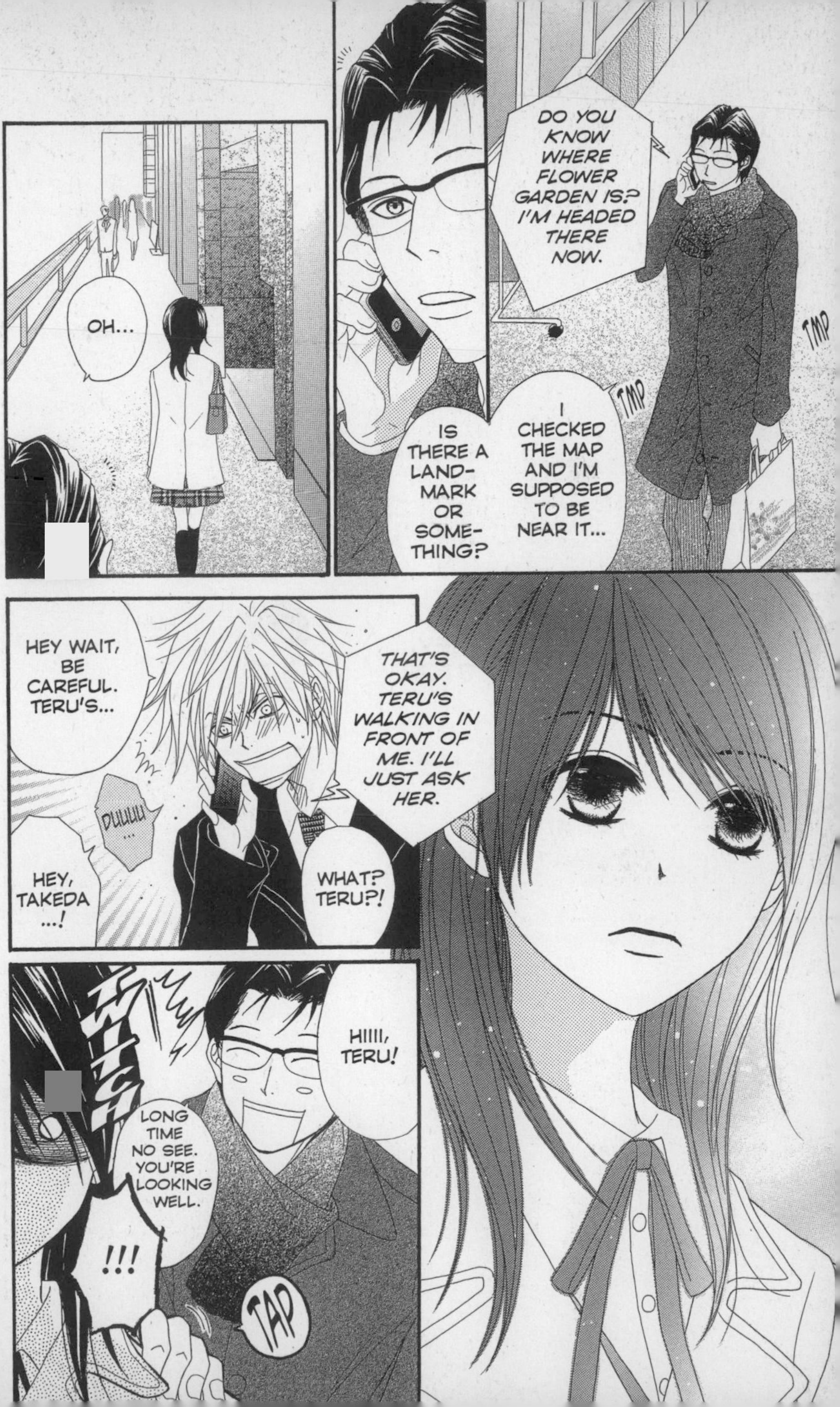
DO YOU KNOW WHERE FLOWER GARDEN IS? I'M HEADED THERE NOW.
TMP
TMP
I CHECKED THE MAP AND I'M SUPPOSED TO BE NEAR IT...
IS THERE A LANDMARK OR SOMETHING?
OH...
THAT'S OKAY. TERU'S WALKING IN FRONT OF ME. I'LL JUST ASK HER.
HEY WAIT, BE CAREFUL. TERU'S...
WHAT? TERU?!
DUUUU...
HEY, TAKEDA ...!
HIIII, TERU!
TWITCH
LONG TIME NO SEE. YOU'RE LOOKING WELL.
!!!
TAP

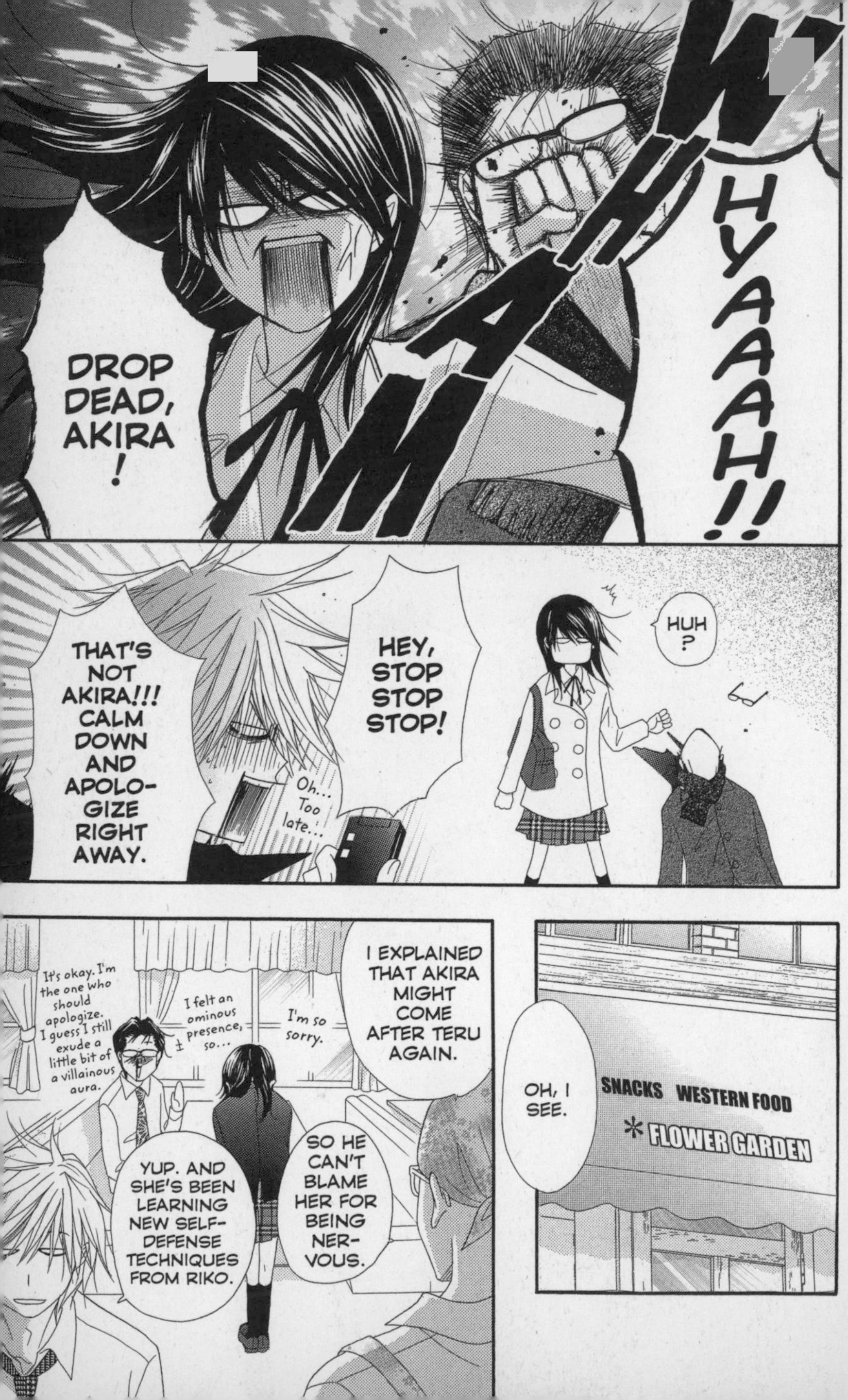
WHAM
HYAAAH!!
DROP DEAD, AKIRA!
HUH?
HEY, STOP STOP STOP!
Oh... Too late...
THAT'S NOT AKIRA!!! CALM DOWN AND APOLOGIZE RIGHT AWAY.
SNACKS WESTERN FOOD
* FLOWER GARDEN
OH, I SEE.
I EXPLAINED THAT AKIRA MIGHT COME AFTER TERU AGAIN.
I'm so sorry.
I felt an ominous presence, so...
It's okay. I'm the one who should apologize. I guess I still exude a little bit of a villainous aura.
SO HE CAN'T BLAME HER FOR BEING NERVOUS.
YUP. AND SHE'S BEEN LEARNING NEW SELF-DEFENSE TECHNIQUES FROM RIKO.

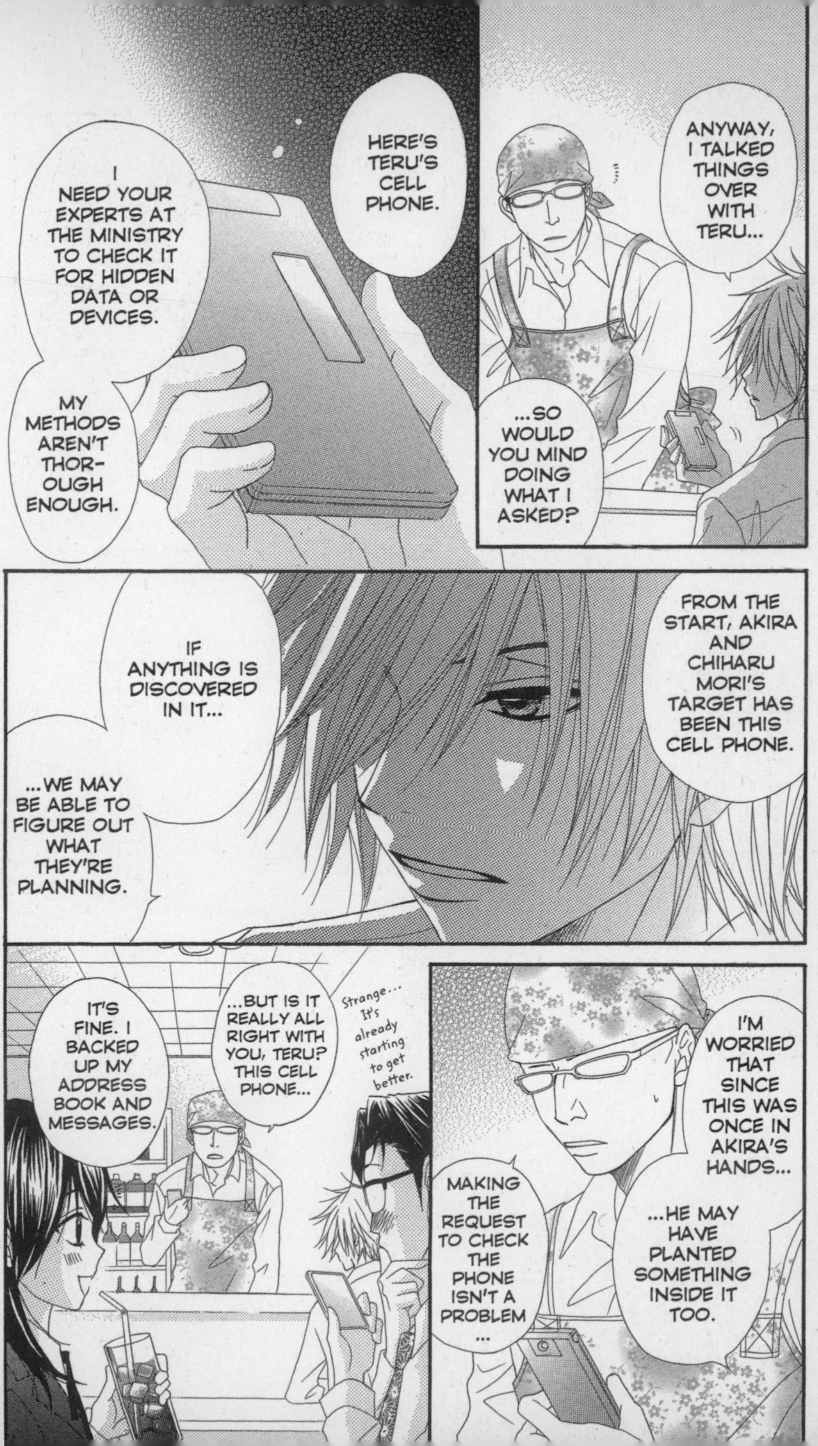
ANYWAY, I TALKED THINGS OVER WITH TERU...
...SO WOULD YOU MIND DOING WHAT I ASKED?
HERE'S TERU'S CELL PHONE.
I NEED YOUR EXPERTS AT THE MINISTRY TO CHECK IT FOR HIDDEN DATA OR DEVICES.
MY METHODS AREN'T THOR-OUGH ENOUGH.
FROM THE START, AKIRA AND CHIHARU MORI'S TARGET HAS BEEN THIS CELL PHONE.
IF ANYTHING IS DISCOVERED IN IT...
...WE MAY BE ABLE TO FIGURE OUT WHAT THEY'RE PLANNING.
I'M WORRIED THAT SINCE THIS WAS ONCE IN AKIRA'S HANDS...
...HE MAY HAVE PLANTED SOMETHING INSIDE IT TOO.
MAKING THE REQUEST TO CHECK THE PHONE ISN'T A PROBLEM ...
Strange... It's already starting to get better.
...BUT IS IT REALLY ALL RIGHT WITH YOU, TERU? THIS CELL PHONE...
IT'S FINE. I BACKED UP MY ADDRESS BOOK AND MESSAGES.

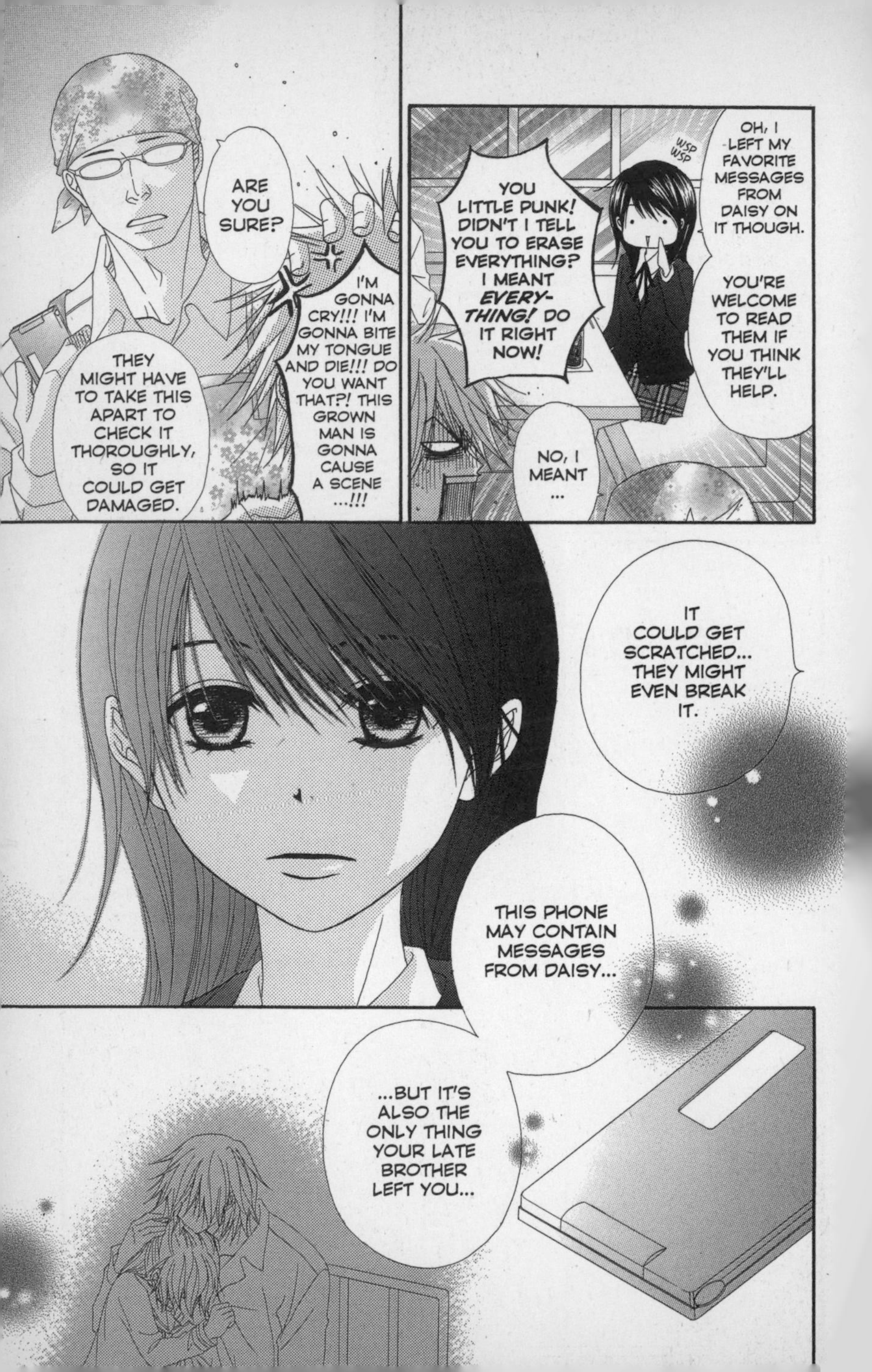
WSP WSP
OH, I LEFT MY FAVORITE MESSAGES FROM DAISY ON IT THOUGH.
YOU'RE WELCOME TO READ THEM IF YOU THINK THEY'LL HELP.
YOU LITTLE PUNK! DIDN'T I TELL YOU TO ERASE EVERYTHING? I MEANT ***EVERY-THING!*** DO IT RIGHT NOW!
NO, I MEANT ...
ARE YOU SURE?
I'M GONNA CRY!!! I'M GONNA BITE MY TONGUE AND DIE!!! DO YOU WANT THAT?! THIS GROWN MAN IS GONNA CAUSE A SCENE ...!!!
THEY MIGHT HAVE TO TAKE THIS APART TO CHECK IT THOROUGHLY, SO IT COULD GET DAMAGED.
IT COULD GET SCRATCHED... THEY MIGHT EVEN BREAK IT.
THIS PHONE MAY CONTAIN MESSAGES FROM DAISY...
...BUT IT'S ALSO THE ONLY THING YOUR LATE BROTHER LEFT YOU...

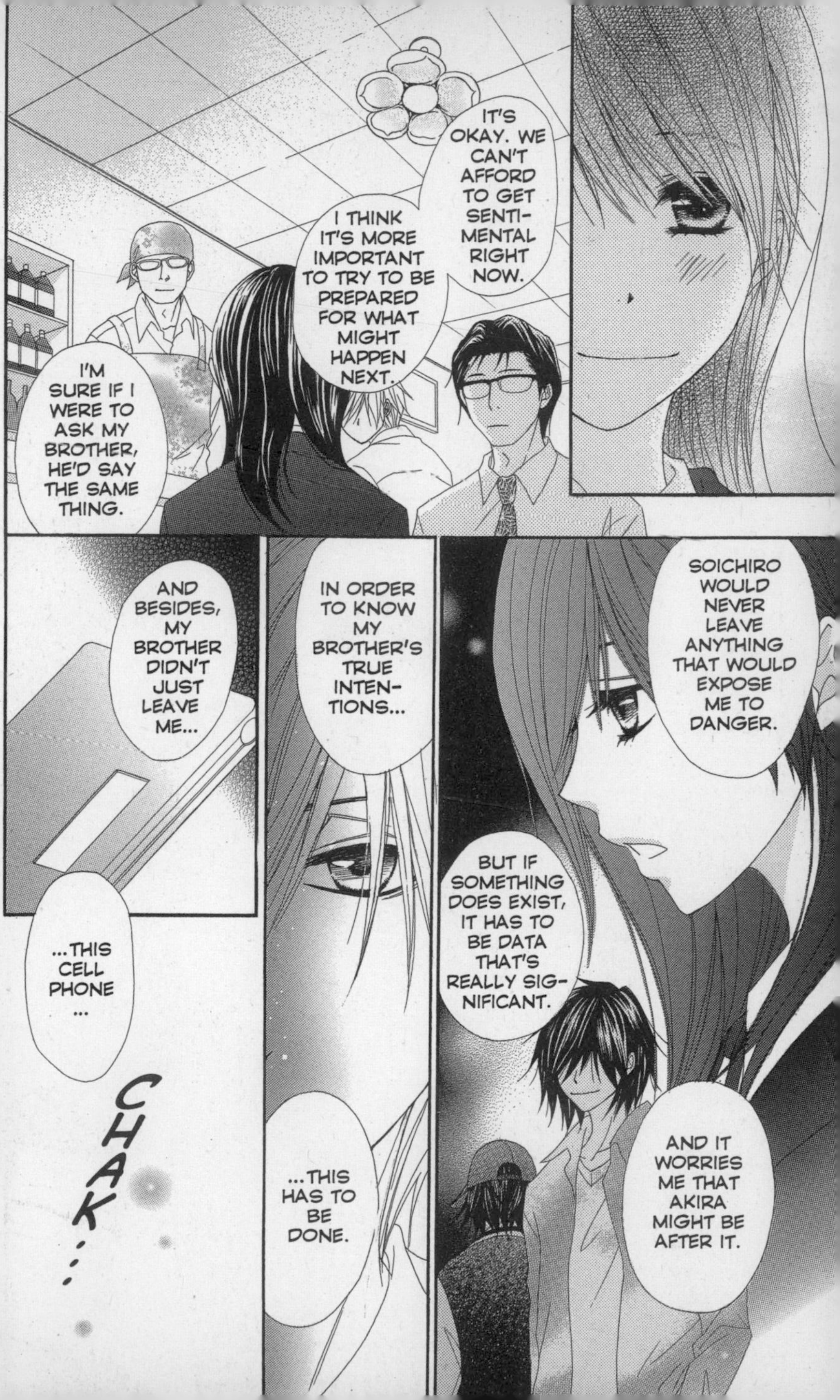
IT'S OKAY. WE CAN'T AFFORD TO GET SENTIMENTAL RIGHT NOW.
I THINK IT'S MORE IMPORTANT TO TRY TO BE PREPARED FOR WHAT MIGHT HAPPEN NEXT.
I'M SURE IF I WERE TO ASK MY BROTHER, HE'D SAY THE SAME THING.
SOICHIRO WOULD NEVER LEAVE ANYTHING THAT WOULD EXPOSE ME TO DANGER.
BUT IF SOMETHING DOES EXIST, IT HAS TO BE DATA THAT'S REALLY SIGNIFICANT.
AND IT WORRIES ME THAT AKIRA MIGHT BE AFTER IT.
IN ORDER TO KNOW MY BROTHER'S TRUE INTENTIONS...
...THIS HAS TO BE DONE.
AND BESIDES, MY BROTHER DIDN'T JUST LEAVE ME...
...THIS CELL PHONE ...
CHAK...

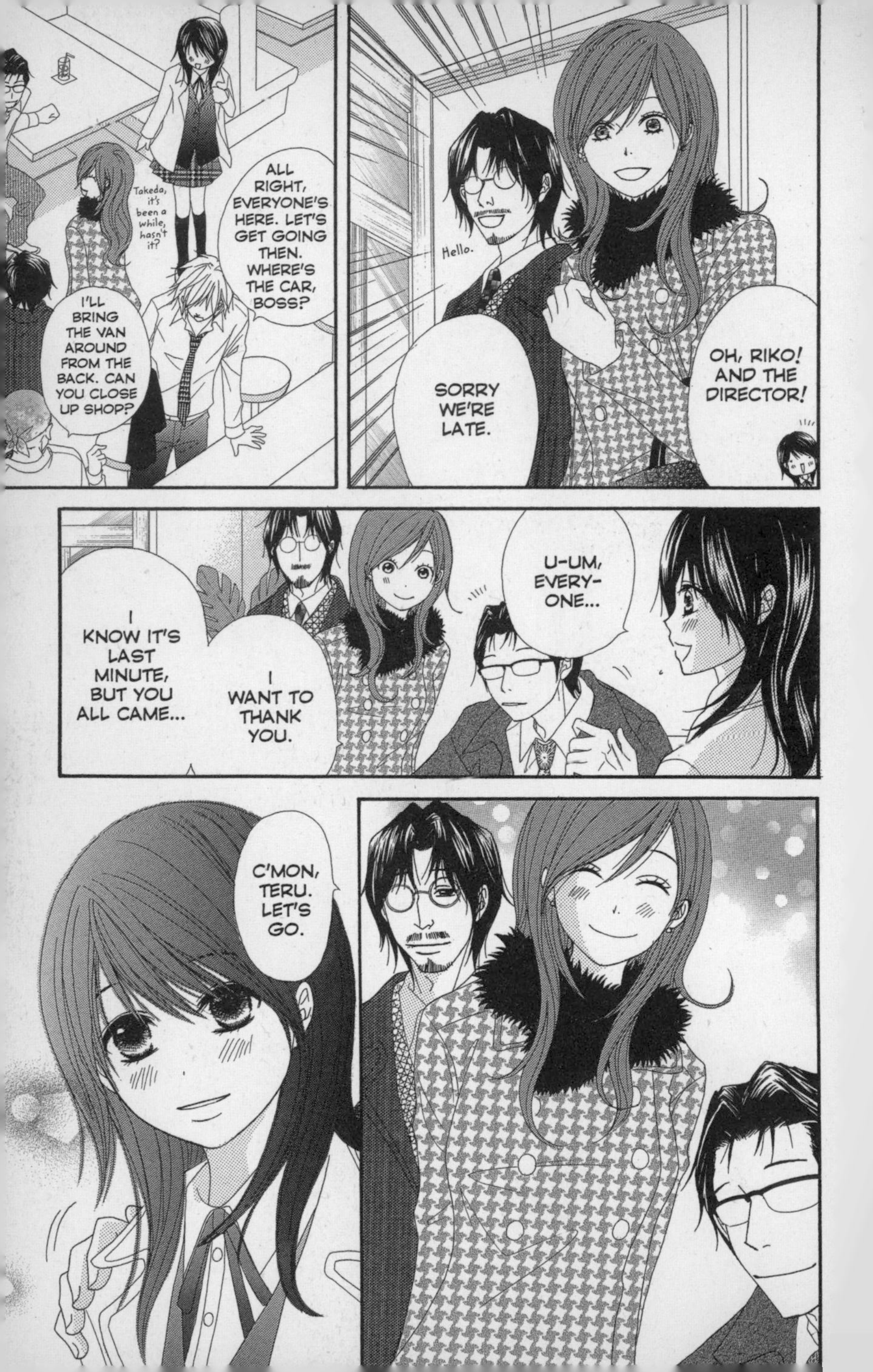
OH, RIKO! AND THE DIRECTOR!
SORRY WE'RE LATE.
Hello.
ALL RIGHT, EVERYONE'S HERE. LET'S GET GOING THEN. WHERE'S THE CAR, BOSS?
Takeda, it's been a while, hasn't it?
I'LL BRING THE VAN AROUND FROM THE BACK. CAN YOU CLOSE UP SHOP?
U-UM, EVERYONE...
I KNOW IT'S LAST MINUTE, BUT YOU ALL CAME...
I WANT TO THANK YOU.
C'MON, TERU. LET'S GO.

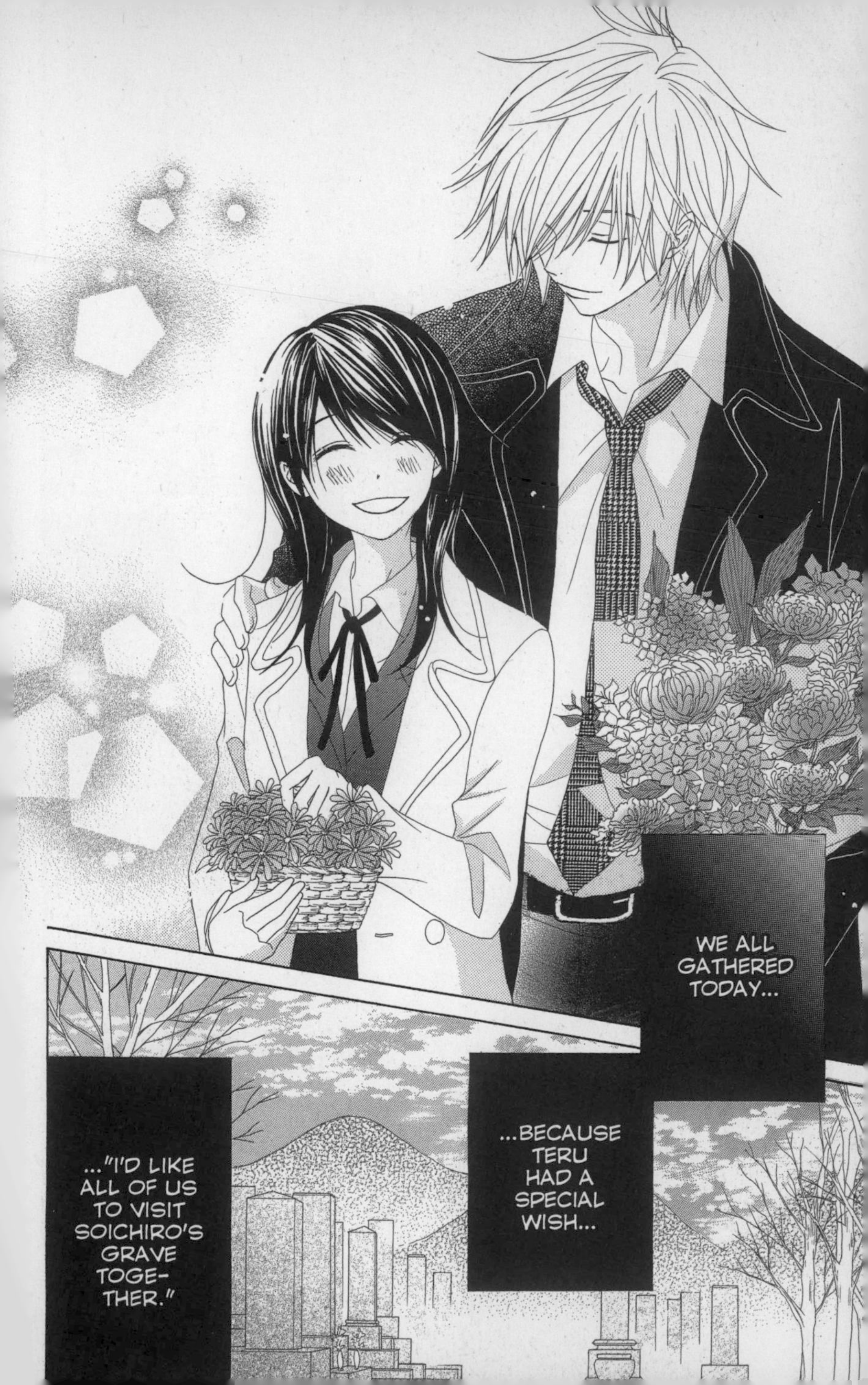
WE ALL GATHERED TODAY...
...BECAUSE TERU HAD A SPECIAL WISH...
..."I'D LIKE ALL OF US TO VISIT SOICHIRO'S GRAVE TOGE- THER."

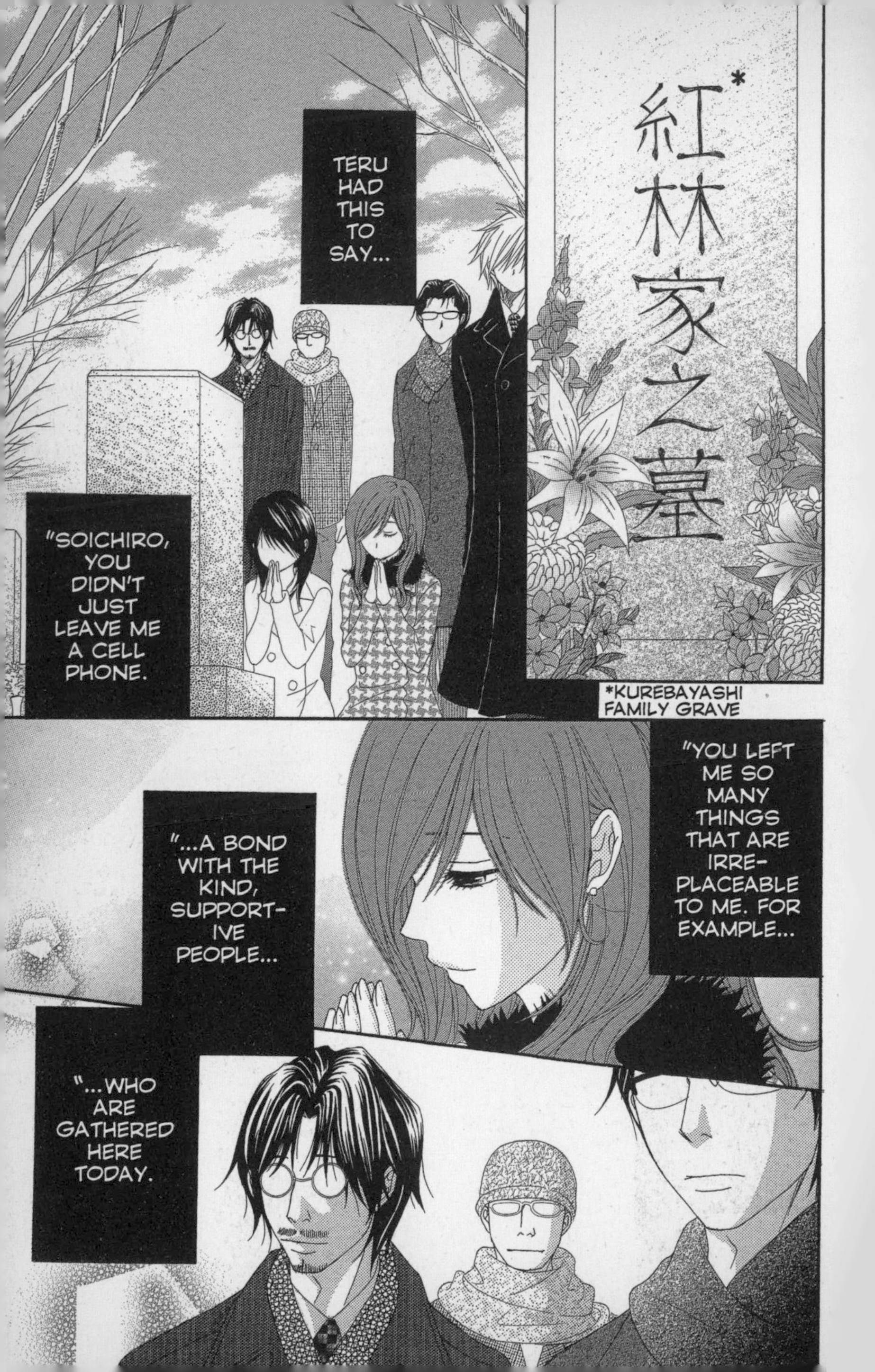
紅林家之墓*
*KUREBAYASHI FAMILY GRAVE
TERU HAD THIS TO SAY...
"SOICHIRO, YOU DIDN'T JUST LEAVE ME A CELL PHONE.
"YOU LEFT ME SO MANY THINGS THAT ARE IRRE-PLACEABLE TO ME. FOR EXAMPLE...
"...A BOND WITH THE KIND, SUPPORT-IVE PEOPLE...
"...WHO ARE GATHERED HERE TODAY.

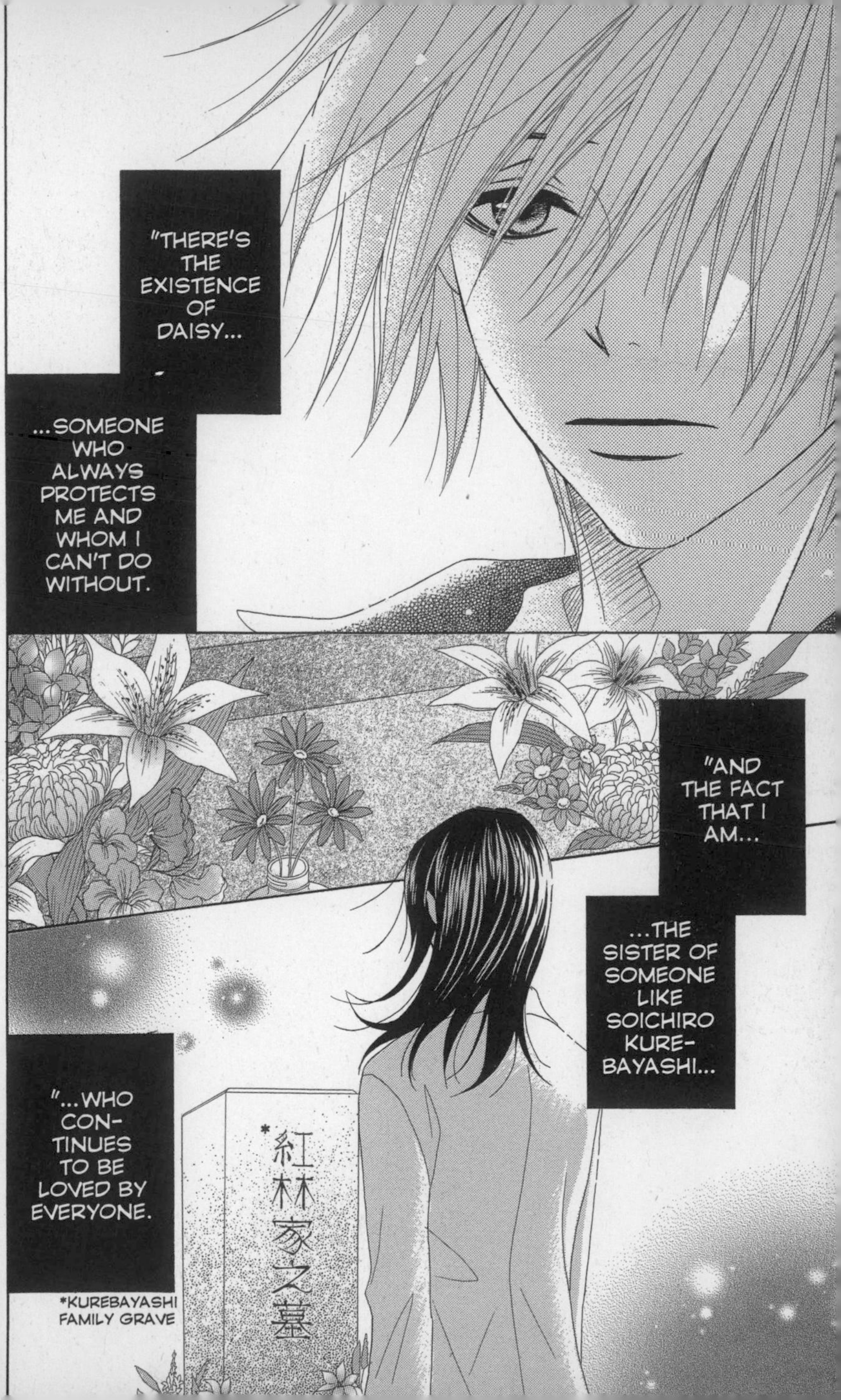
"THERE'S THE EXISTENCE OF DAISY...
...SOMEONE WHO ALWAYS PROTECTS ME AND WHOM I CAN'T DO WITHOUT.
"AND THE FACT THAT I AM...
...THE SISTER OF SOMEONE LIKE SOICHIRO KURE-BAYASHI...
"...WHO CON-TINUES TO BE LOVED BY EVERYONE.
*紅林家之墓
*KUREBAYASHI FAMILY GRAVE

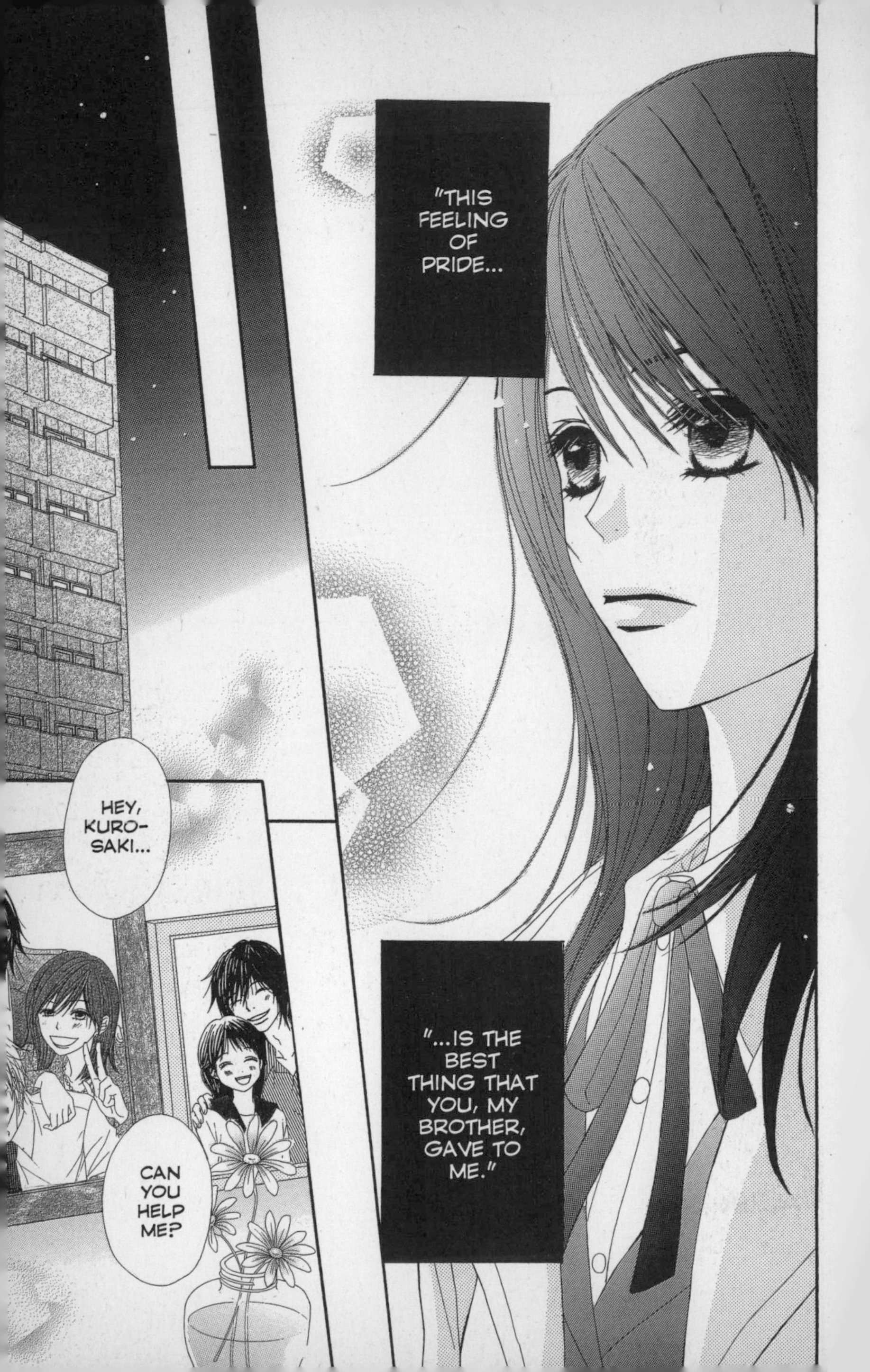
"THIS FEELING OF PRIDE...
"...IS THE BEST THING THAT YOU, MY BROTHER, GAVE TO ME."
HEY, KURO-SAKI...
CAN YOU HELP ME?

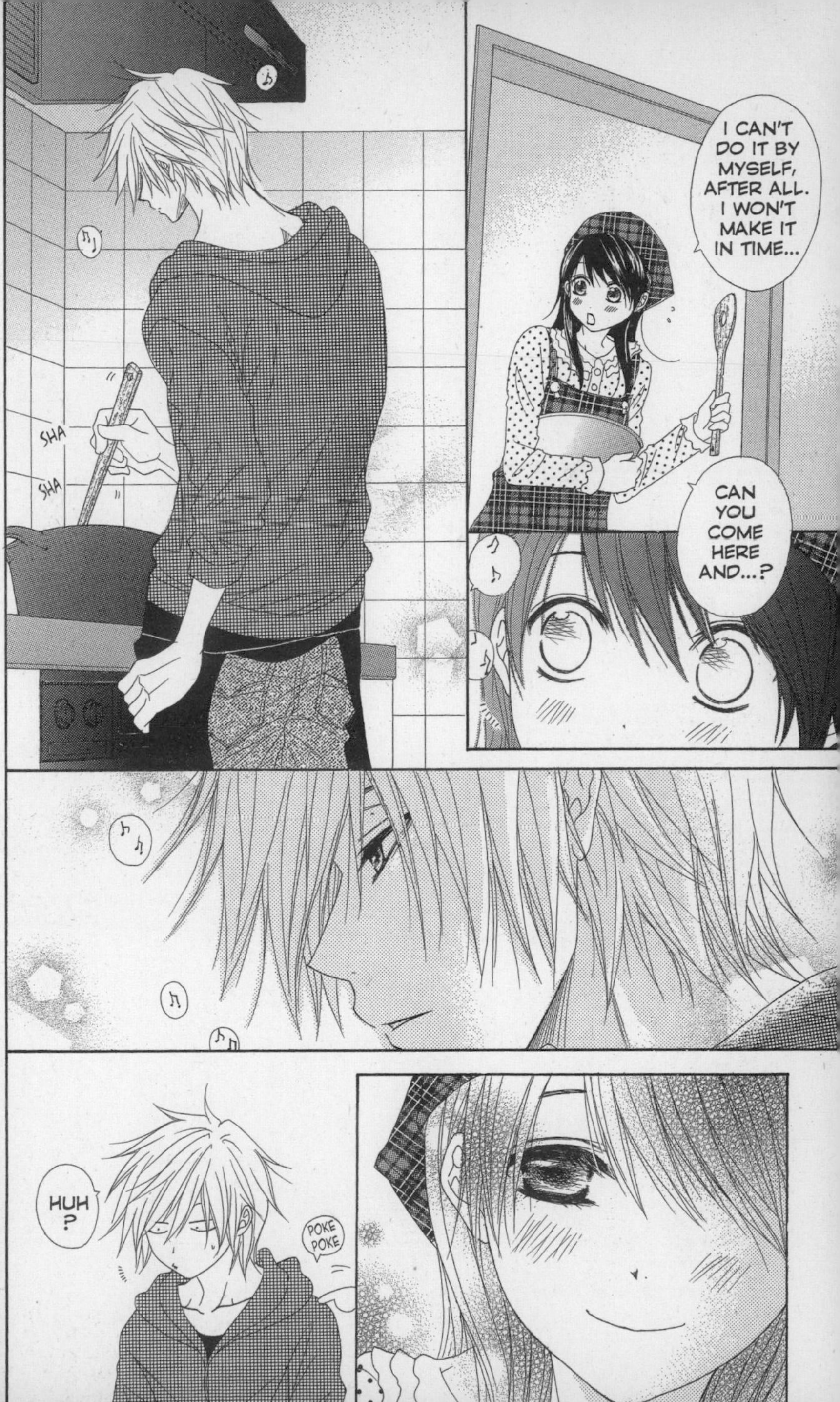
I CAN'T DO IT BY MYSELF, AFTER ALL. I WON'T MAKE IT IN TIME...
CAN YOU COME HERE AND...?
SHA
SHA
HUH?
POKE POKE

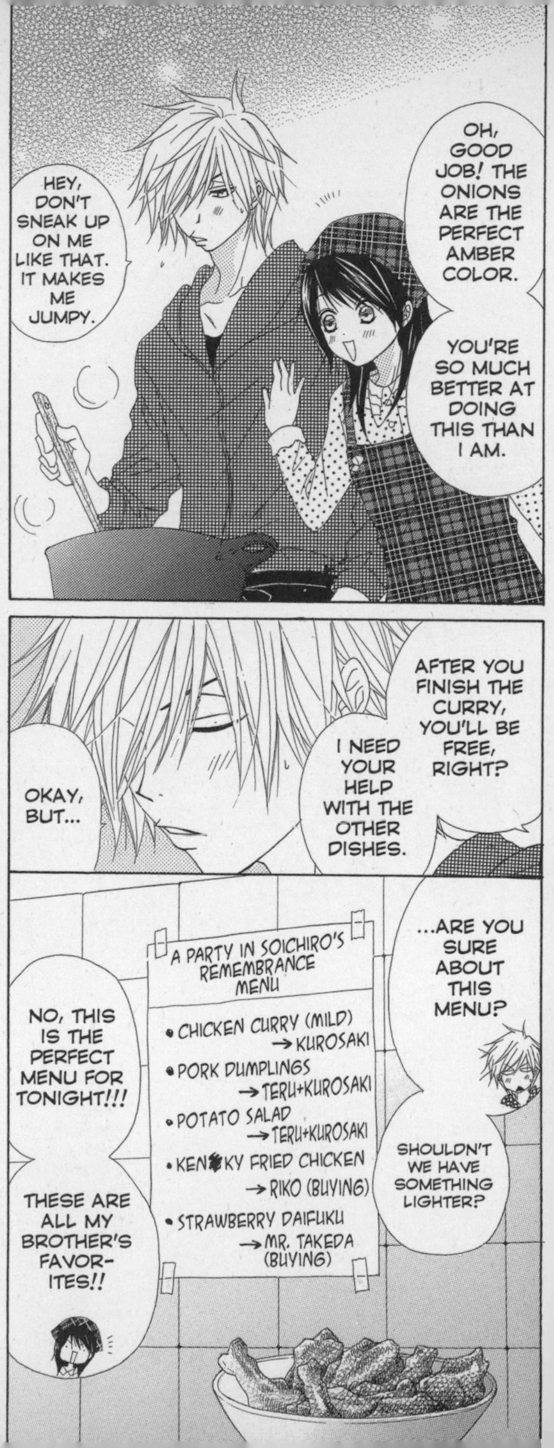
OH, GOOD JOB! THE ONIONS ARE THE PERFECT AMBER COLOR.
YOU'RE SO MUCH BETTER AT DOING THIS THAN I AM.
HEY, DON'T SNEAK UP ON ME LIKE THAT. IT MAKES ME JUMPY.
AFTER YOU FINISH THE CURRY, YOU'LL BE FREE, RIGHT?
I NEED YOUR HELP WITH THE OTHER DISHES.
OKAY, BUT...
...ARE YOU SURE ABOUT THIS MENU?
SHOULDN'T WE HAVE SOMETHING LIGHTER?
A PARTY IN SOICHIRO'S REMEMBRANCE MENU
• CHICKEN CURRY (MILD) → KUROSAKI
• PORK DUMPLINGS → TERU+KUROSAKI
• POTATO SALAD → TERU+KUROSAKI
• KEN✱KY FRIED CHICKEN → RIKO (BUYING)
• STRAWBERRY DAIFUKU → MR. TAKEDA (BUYING)
NO, THIS IS THE PERFECT MENU FOR TONIGHT!!!
THESE ARE ALL MY BROTHER'S FAVOR-ITES!!

DENGEKI DAISY QUESTION CORNER

BALDLY ASK!!

③

Q.
DOES KUROSAKI'S PILLOW HAVE THAT "OLD MAN SMELL"?
(NUHACHIKUWA, HYOGO PREFECTURE)

A.
IT'S ONLY NATURAL TO ASSUME SO. HOWEVER, HE'S QUITE NERVOUS ABOUT LOSING HIS HAIR AND IS EXTREMELY DILIGENT ABOUT KEEPING HIS PILLOW CLEAN. FOR EXAMPLE, HE WRAPS A TOWEL AROUND HIS PILLOW AND CHANGES IT EVERY DAY.

Q.
IN VOLUME 7 WHEN KUROSAKI UNDRESSED CHIHARU, WASN'T IT HARD FOR HIM TO RESIST TEMPTION? DID HE HAVE TO REMOVE HER UNDERWEAR AS WELL?
(C.K. AND OTHERS, KAGAWA PREFECTURE)

IN VOLUME 6 WHEN KUROSAKI RESCUED TERU, HOW MUCH DID HE UNDRESS HER? DID HE REMOVE HER UNDIES, TOO? I CAN'T SLEEP AT NIGHT THINKING ABOUT IT!!
(AMEN☆HIRATA, KANAGAWA PREFECTURE)

A.
GEE, NOW THAT YOU READERS BRING IT UP, IT SEEMS AS THOUGH KUROSAKI DOES NOTHING BUT UNDRESS WOMEN. HE TOOK CHIHARU'S CLOTHES SO THAT SHE "COULDN'T RUN AWAY," SO IT WAS NECESSARY TO REMOVE HER UNDERWEAR, TOO. HE WAS TOTALLY DISINTERESTED IN CHIHARU'S BREASTS AND STAYED COOL. IN CONTRAST, HE WAS SO NERVOUS DURING THE TIME HE RESCUED TERU THAT HE CAN'T REMEMBER HOW FAR HE WENT IN UNDRESSING HER. HE'S PITIFUL, REALLY.

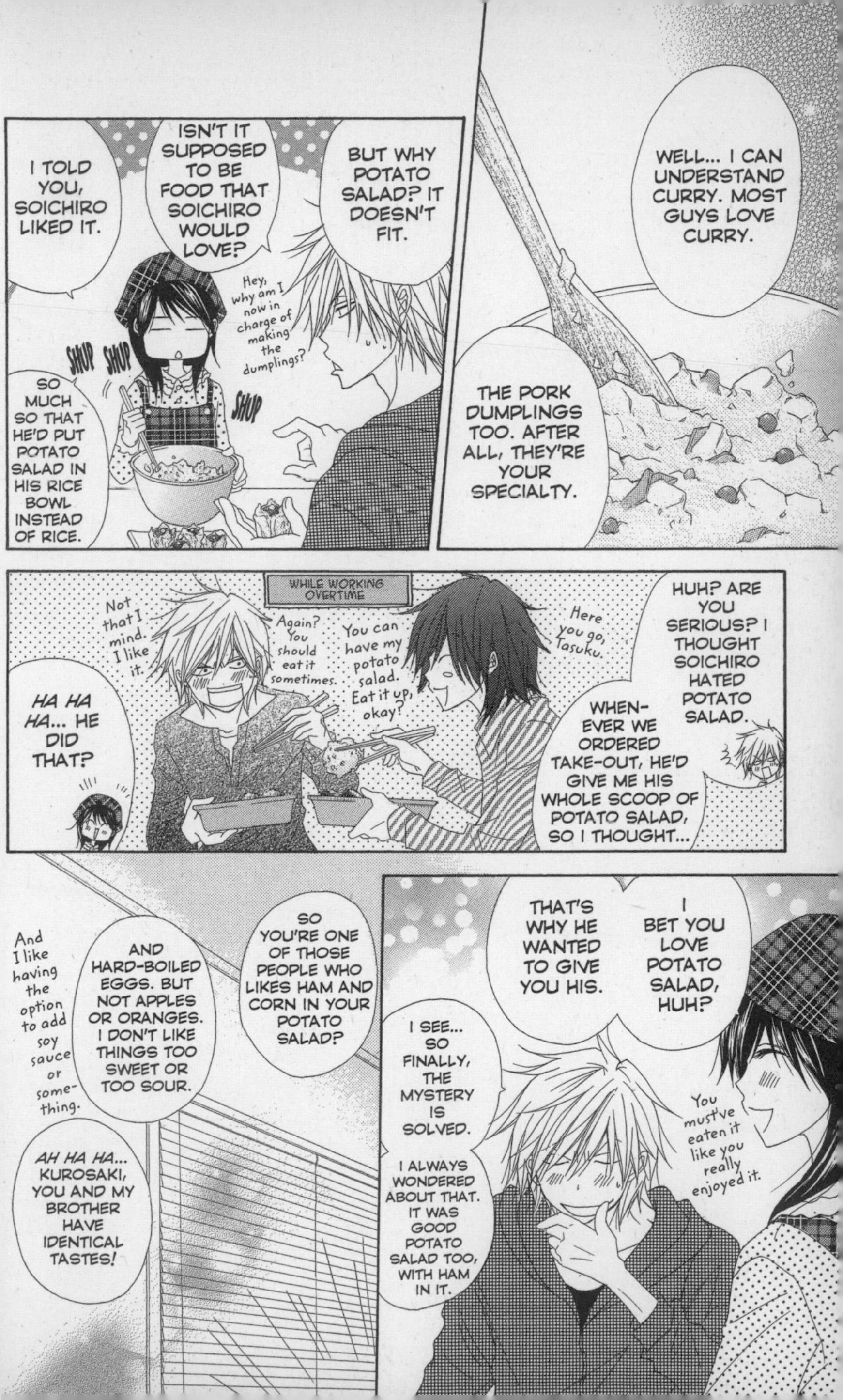

WELL... I CAN UNDERSTAND CURRY. MOST GUYS LOVE CURRY.
THE PORK DUMPLINGS TOO. AFTER ALL, THEY'RE YOUR SPECIALTY.
BUT WHY POTATO SALAD? IT DOESN'T FIT.
ISN'T IT SUPPOSED TO BE FOOD THAT SOICHIRO WOULD LOVE?
I TOLD YOU, SOICHIRO LIKED IT.
Hey, why am I now in charge of making the dumplings?
SHUP SHUP
SO MUCH SO THAT HE'D PUT POTATO SALAD IN HIS RICE BOWL INSTEAD OF RICE.
SHUP
HUH? ARE YOU SERIOUS? I THOUGHT SOICHIRO HATED POTATO SALAD.
WHEN-EVER WE ORDERED TAKE-OUT, HE'D GIVE ME HIS WHOLE SCOOP OF POTATO SALAD, SO I THOUGHT...
WHILE WORKING OVERTIME
Here you go, Tasuku.
You can have my potato salad. Eat it up, okay?
Again? You should eat it sometimes.
Not that I mind. I like it.
HA HA HA... HE DID THAT?
I BET YOU LOVE POTATO SALAD, HUH?
THAT'S WHY HE WANTED TO GIVE YOU HIS.
You must've eaten it like you really enjoyed it.
I SEE... SO FINALLY, THE MYSTERY IS SOLVED.
I ALWAYS WONDERED ABOUT THAT. IT WAS GOOD POTATO SALAD TOO, WITH HAM IN IT.
SO YOU'RE ONE OF THOSE PEOPLE WHO LIKES HAM AND CORN IN YOUR POTATO SALAD?
AND HARD-BOILED EGGS. BUT NOT APPLES OR ORANGES. I DON'T LIKE THINGS TOO SWEET OR TOO SOUR.
And I like having the option to add soy sauce or some-thing.
AH HA HA... KUROSAKI, YOU AND MY BROTHER HAVE IDENTICAL TASTES!

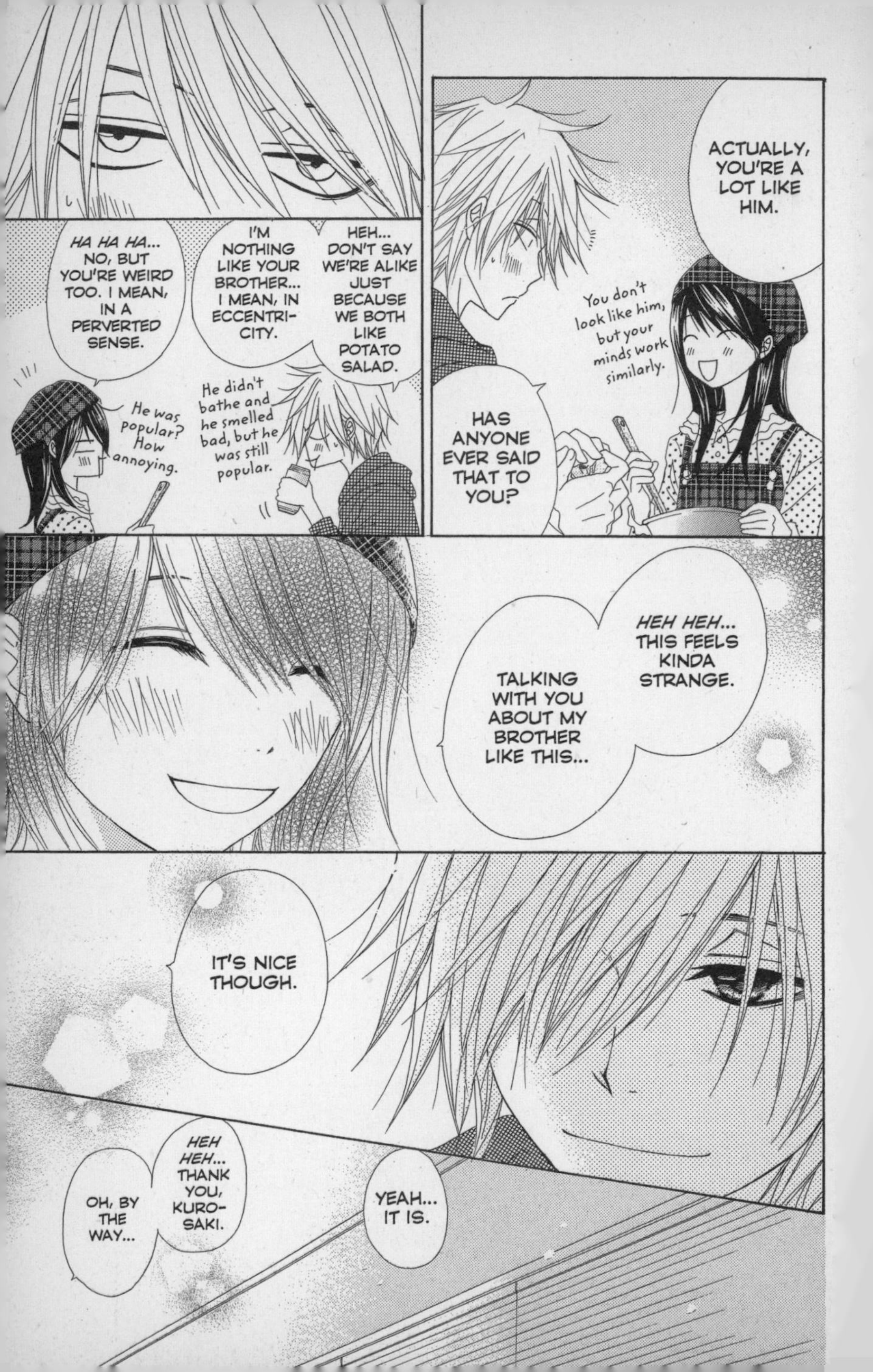
ACTUALLY, YOU'RE A LOT LIKE HIM.
You don't look like him, but your minds work similarly.
HAS ANYONE EVER SAID THAT TO YOU?
HEH... DON'T SAY WE'RE ALIKE JUST BECAUSE WE BOTH LIKE POTATO SALAD.
I'M NOTHING LIKE YOUR BROTHER... I MEAN, IN ECCENTRI-CITY.
HA HA HA... NO, BUT YOU'RE WEIRD TOO. I MEAN, IN A PERVERTED SENSE.
He didn't bathe and he smelled bad, but he was still popular.
He was popular? How annoying.
HEH HEH... THIS FEELS KINDA STRANGE.
TALKING WITH YOU ABOUT MY BROTHER LIKE THIS...
IT'S NICE THOUGH.
YEAH... IT IS.
HEH HEH... THANK YOU, KURO-SAKI.
OH, BY THE WAY...

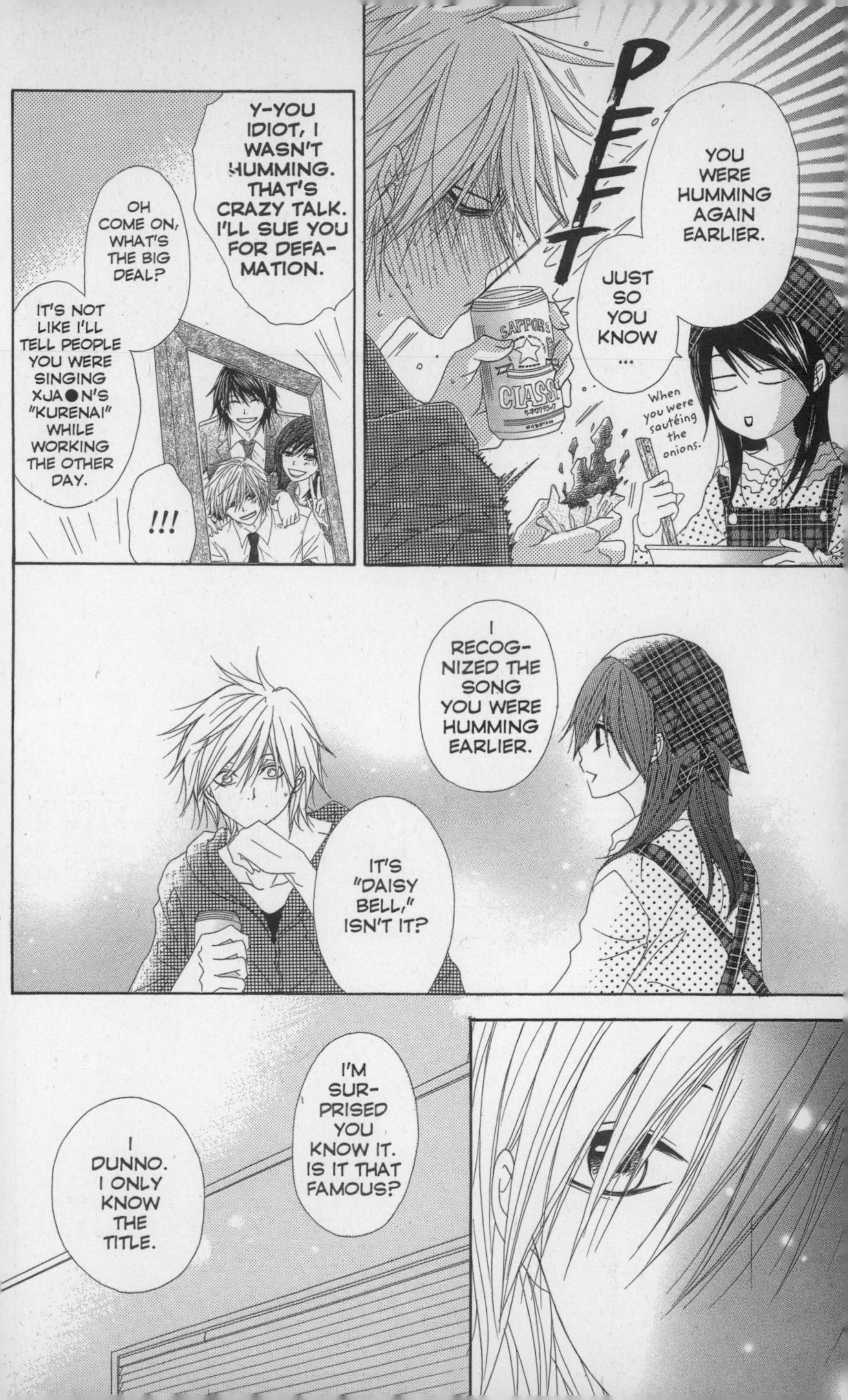
PFFT
YOU WERE HUMMING AGAIN EARLIER.
JUST SO YOU KNOW...
When you were sautéing the onions.
Y-YOU IDIOT, I WASN'T HUMMING. THAT'S CRAZY TALK. I'LL SUE YOU FOR DEFAMATION.
OH COME ON, WHAT'S THE BIG DEAL?
IT'S NOT LIKE I'LL TELL PEOPLE YOU WERE SINGING XJA●N'S "KURENAI" WHILE WORKING THE OTHER DAY.
!!!
I RECOGNIZED THE SONG YOU WERE HUMMING EARLIER.
IT'S "DAISY BELL," ISN'T IT?
I'M SURPRISED YOU KNOW IT. IS IT THAT FAMOUS?
I DUNNO. I ONLY KNOW THE TITLE.

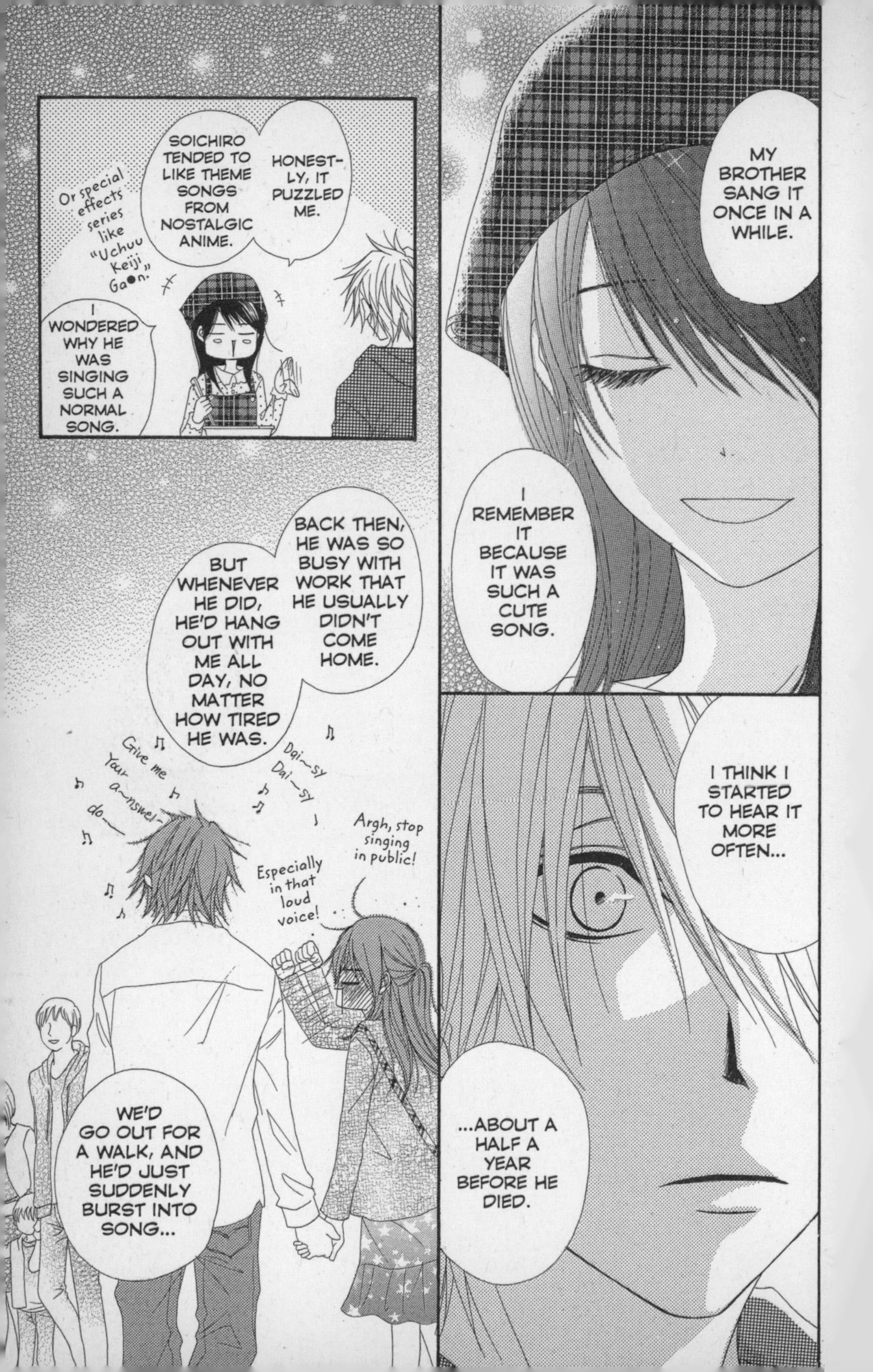
MY BROTHER SANG IT ONCE IN A WHILE.
I REMEMBER IT BECAUSE IT WAS SUCH A CUTE SONG.
SOICHIRO TENDED TO LIKE THEME SONGS FROM NOSTALGIC ANIME.
HONESTLY, IT PUZZLED ME.
Or special effects series like "Uchuu Keiji Ga●n."
I WONDERED WHY HE WAS SINGING SUCH A NORMAL SONG.
BACK THEN, HE WAS SO BUSY WITH WORK THAT HE USUALLY DIDN'T COME HOME.
BUT WHENEVER HE DID, HE'D HANG OUT WITH ME ALL DAY, NO MATTER HOW TIRED HE WAS.
Dai~sy Dai~sy
Give me Your a~nswer do~
Argh, stop singing in public!
Especially in that loud voice!
WE'D GO OUT FOR A WALK, AND HE'D JUST SUDDENLY BURST INTO SONG...
I THINK I STARTED TO HEAR IT MORE OFTEN...
...ABOUT A HALF A YEAR BEFORE HE DIED.

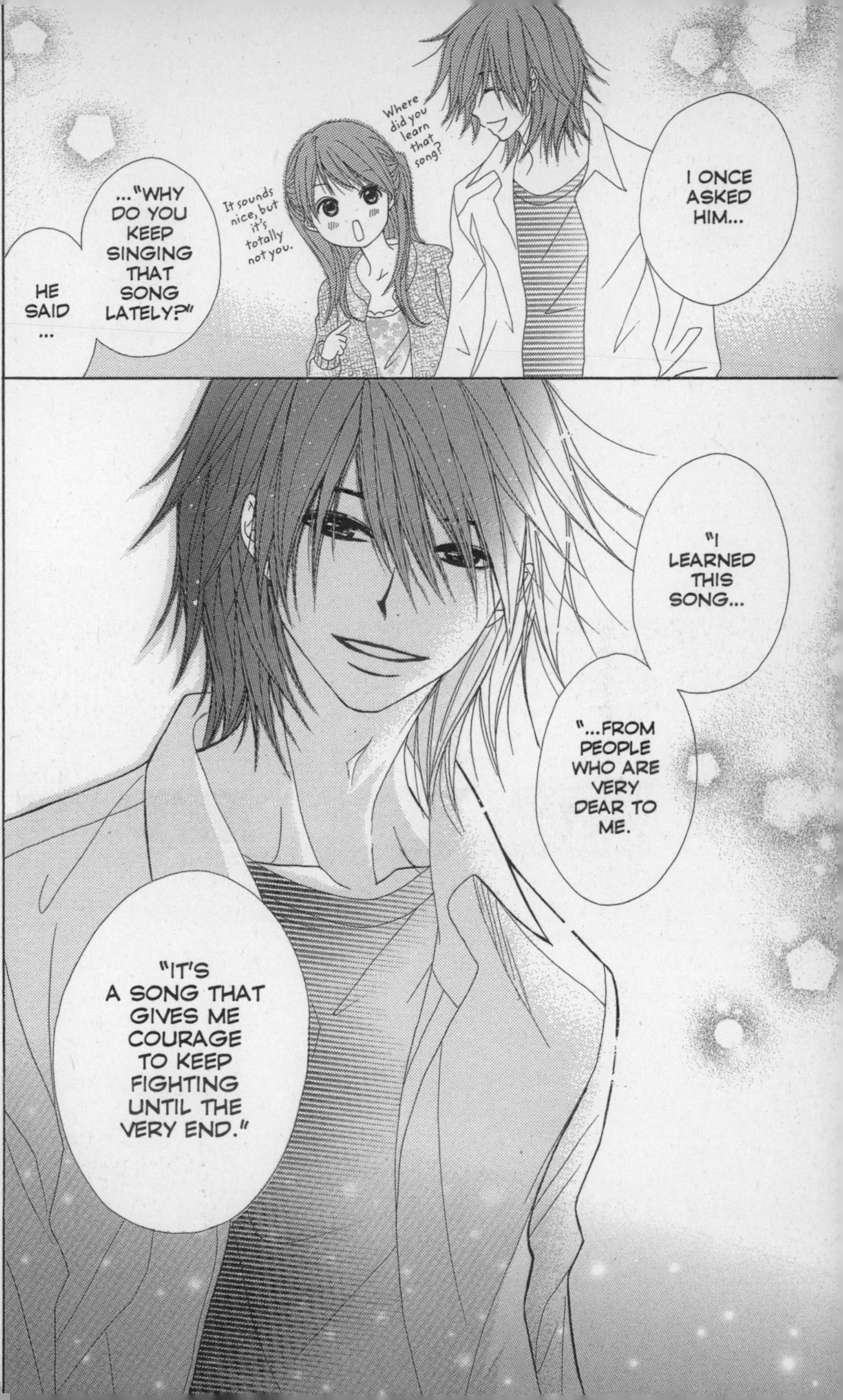
I ONCE ASKED HIM...
Where did you learn that song?
It sounds nice, but it's totally not you.
..."WHY DO YOU KEEP SINGING THAT SONG LATELY?"
HE SAID...
"I LEARNED THIS SONG...
"...FROM PEOPLE WHO ARE VERY DEAR TO ME.
"IT'S A SONG THAT GIVES ME COURAGE TO KEEP FIGHTING UNTIL THE VERY END."

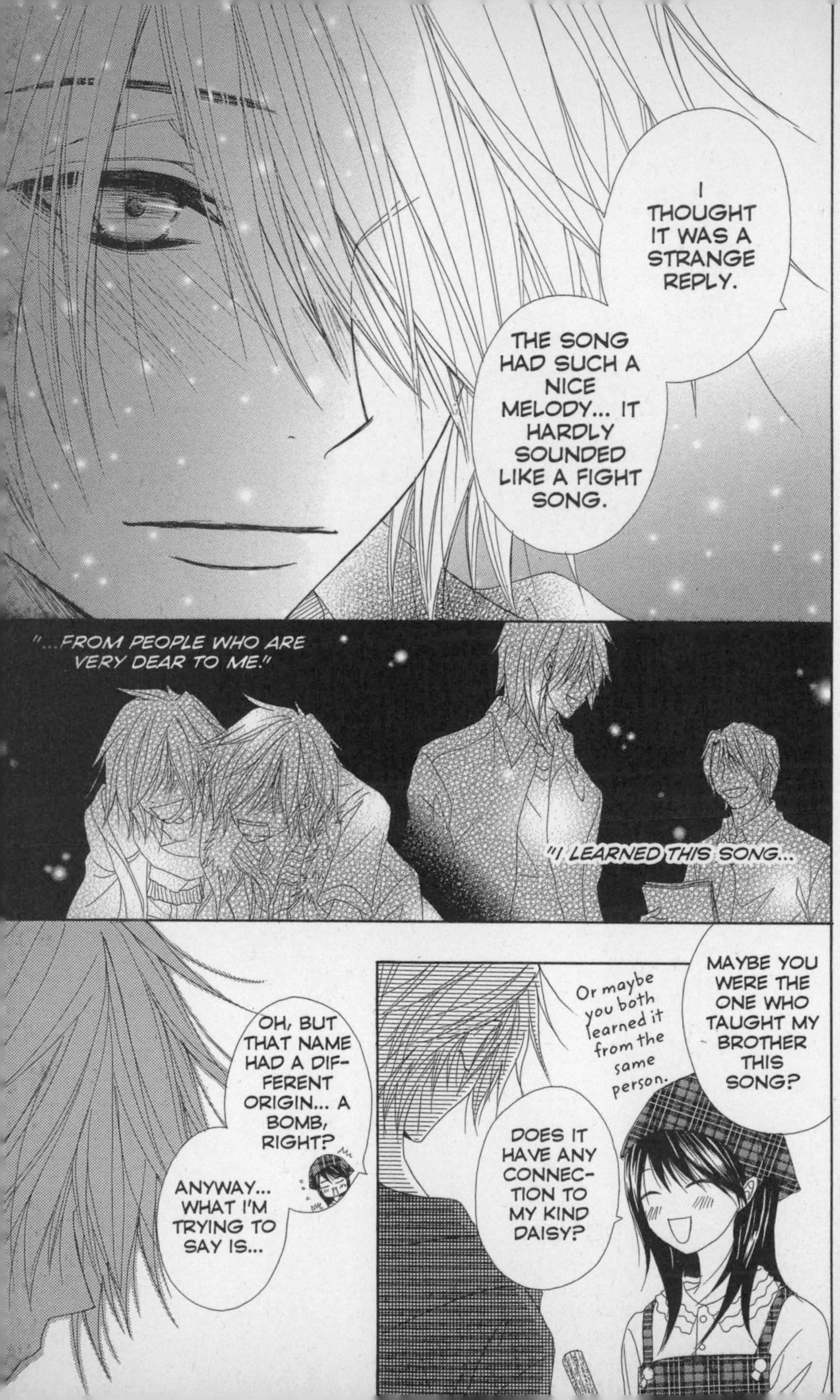
I THOUGHT IT WAS A STRANGE REPLY.
THE SONG HAD SUCH A NICE MELODY... IT HARDLY SOUNDED LIKE A FIGHT SONG.
"I LEARNED THIS SONG...
"...FROM PEOPLE WHO ARE VERY DEAR TO ME."
MAYBE YOU WERE THE ONE WHO TAUGHT MY BROTHER THIS SONG?
Or maybe you both learned it from the same person.
DOES IT HAVE ANY CONNECTION TO MY KIND DAISY?
OH, BUT THAT NAME HAD A DIF-FERENT ORIGIN... A BOMB, RIGHT?
ANYWAY... WHAT I'M TRYING TO SAY IS...

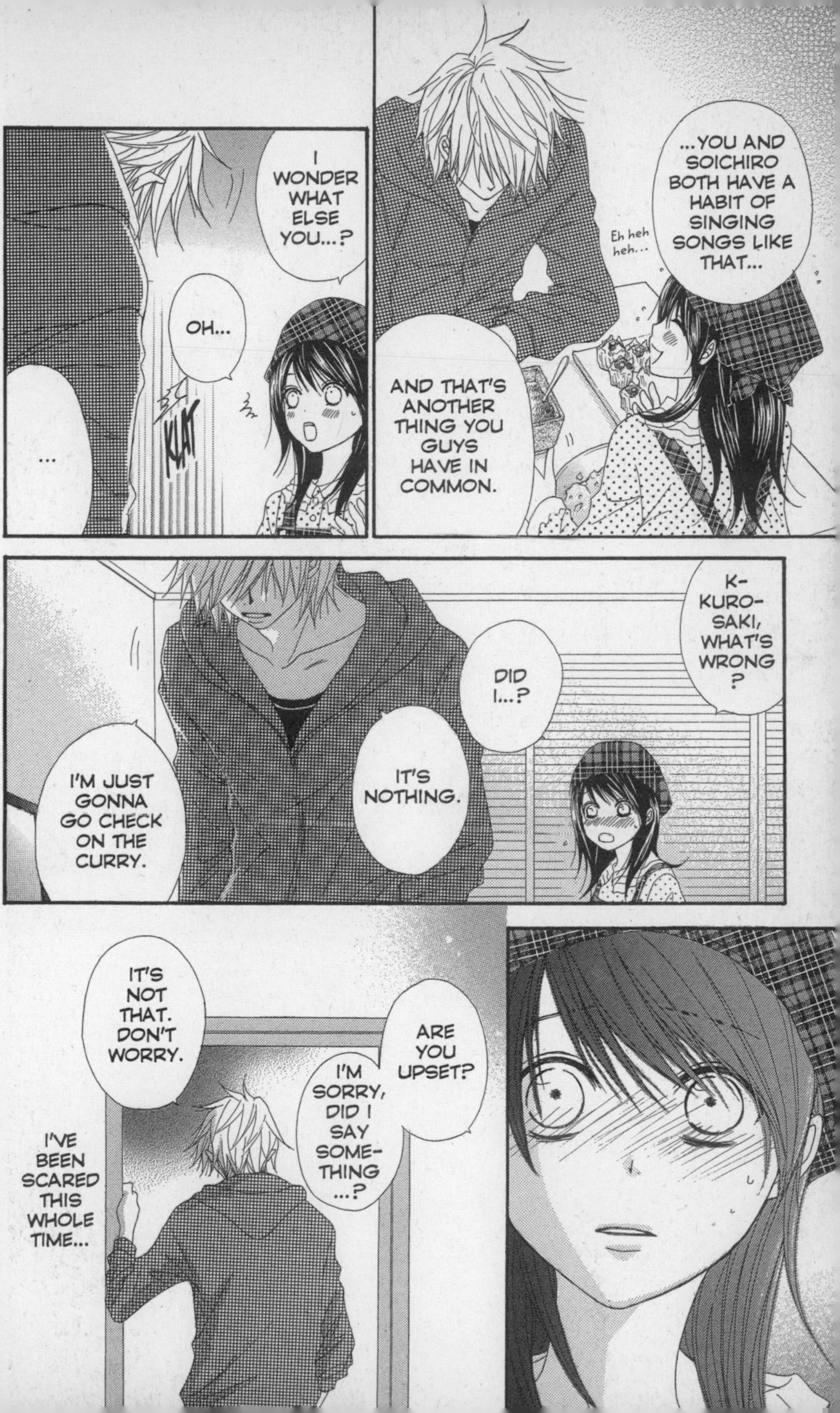
...YOU AND SOICHIRO BOTH HAVE A HABIT OF SINGING SONGS LIKE THAT...
Eh heh heh...
AND THAT'S ANOTHER THING YOU GUYS HAVE IN COMMON.
I WONDER WHAT ELSE YOU...?
OH...
KLAT
...
K-KUROSAKI, WHAT'S WRONG?
DID I...?
IT'S NOTHING.
I'M JUST GONNA GO CHECK ON THE CURRY.
ARE YOU UPSET?
I'M SORRY, DID I SAY SOMETHING...?
IT'S NOT THAT. DON'T WORRY.
I'VE BEEN SCARED THIS WHOLE TIME...

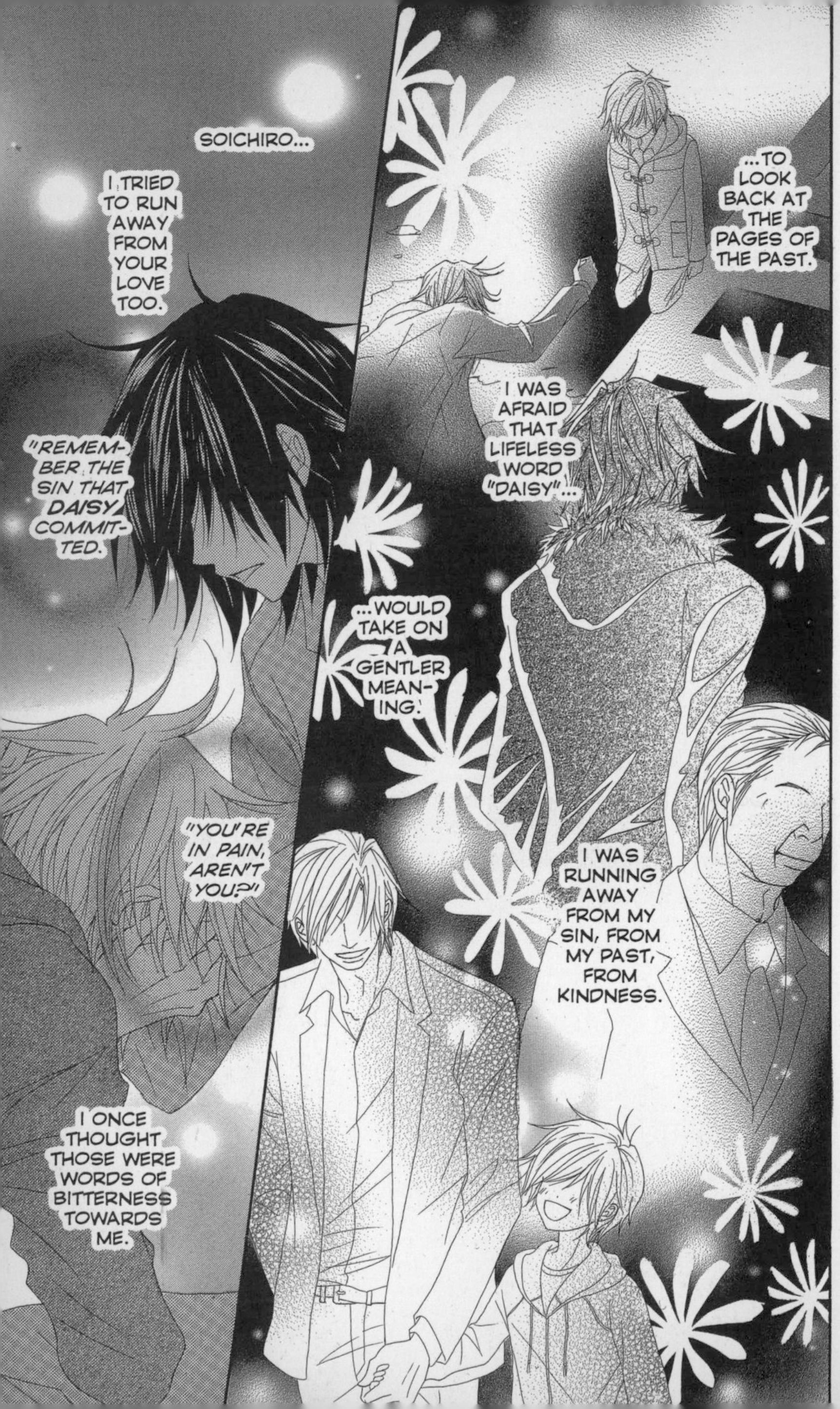
...TO LOOK BACK AT THE PAGES OF THE PAST.
I WAS AFRAID THAT LIFELESS WORD "DAISY"...
...WOULD TAKE ON A GENTLER MEANING.
I WAS RUNNING AWAY FROM MY SIN, FROM MY PAST, FROM KINDNESS.
SOICHIRO...
I TRIED TO RUN AWAY FROM YOUR LOVE TOO.
"REMEMBER THE SIN THAT DAISY COMMITTED.
"YOU'RE IN PAIN, AREN'T YOU?"
I ONCE THOUGHT THOSE WERE WORDS OF BITTERNESS TOWARDS ME.

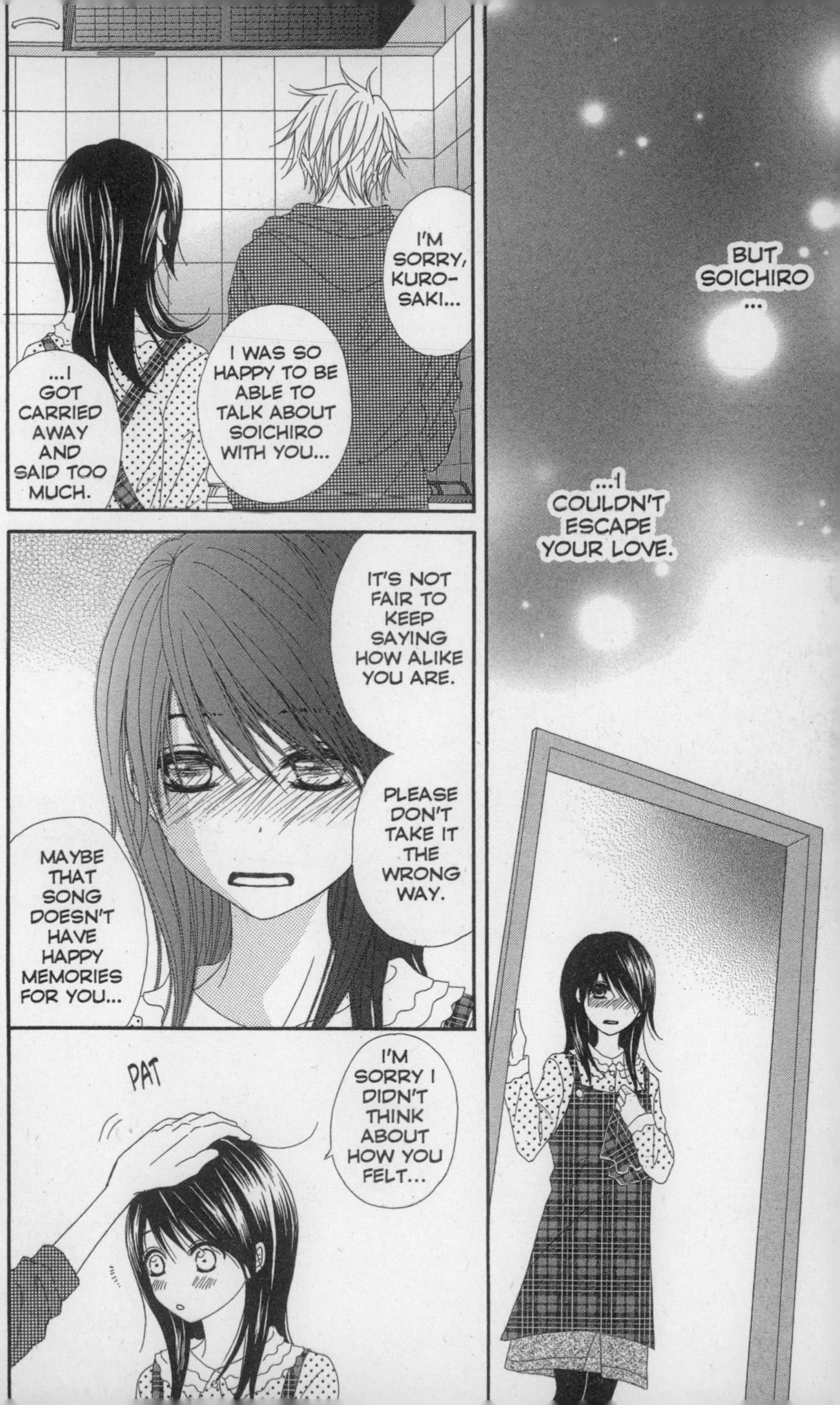
BUT SOICHIRO ...
...I COULDN'T ESCAPE YOUR LOVE.
I'M SORRY, KURO-SAKI...
I WAS SO HAPPY TO BE ABLE TO TALK ABOUT SOICHIRO WITH YOU...
...I GOT CARRIED AWAY AND SAID TOO MUCH.
IT'S NOT FAIR TO KEEP SAYING HOW ALIKE YOU ARE.
PLEASE DON'T TAKE IT THE WRONG WAY.
MAYBE THAT SONG DOESN'T HAVE HAPPY MEMORIES FOR YOU...
I'M SORRY I DIDN'T THINK ABOUT HOW YOU FELT...
PAT

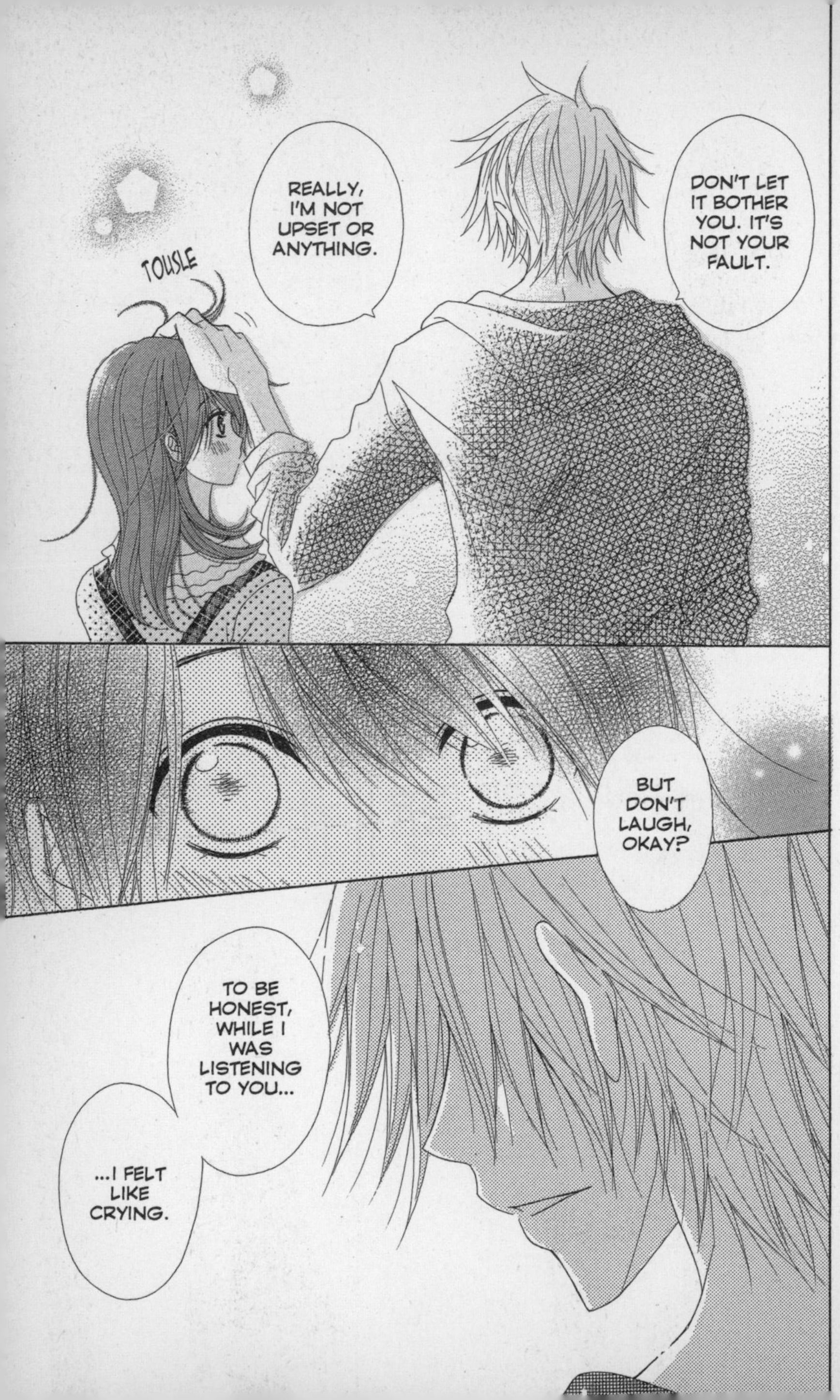
DON'T LET IT BOTHER YOU. IT'S NOT YOUR FAULT.
REALLY, I'M NOT UPSET OR ANYTHING.
TOUSLE
BUT DON'T LAUGH, OKAY?
TO BE HONEST, WHILE I WAS LISTENING TO YOU...
...I FELT LIKE CRYING.

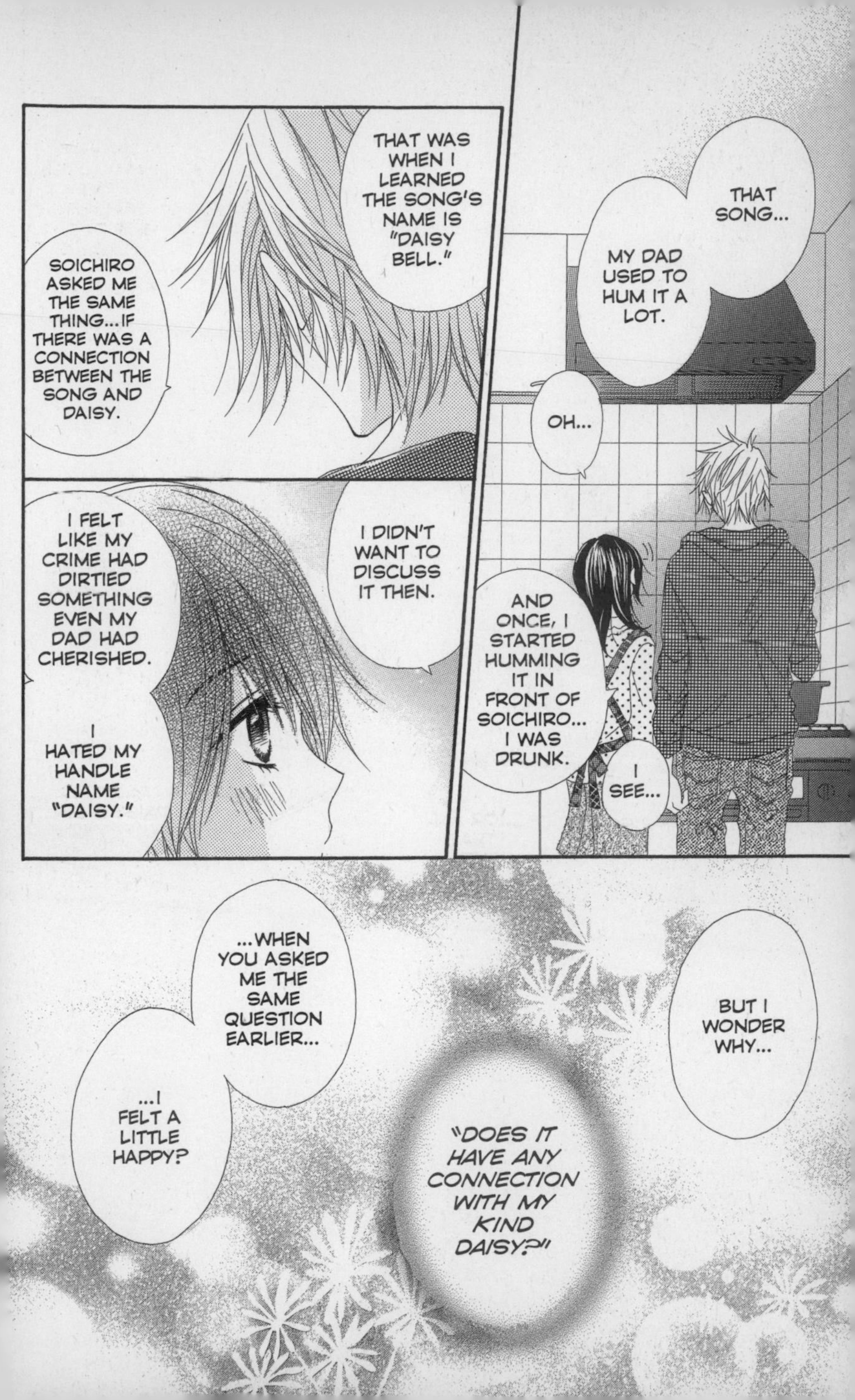
THAT SONG...
MY DAD USED TO HUM IT A LOT.
OH...
AND ONCE, I STARTED HUMMING IT IN FRONT OF SOICHIRO... I WAS DRUNK.
I SEE...
THAT WAS WHEN I LEARNED THE SONG'S NAME IS "DAISY BELL."
SOICHIRO ASKED ME THE SAME THING...IF THERE WAS A CONNECTION BETWEEN THE SONG AND DAISY.
I DIDN'T WANT TO DISCUSS IT THEN.
I FELT LIKE MY CRIME HAD DIRTIED SOMETHING EVEN MY DAD HAD CHERISHED.
I HATED MY HANDLE NAME "DAISY."
BUT I WONDER WHY...
"DOES IT HAVE ANY CONNECTION WITH MY KIND DAISY?"
...WHEN YOU ASKED ME THE SAME QUESTION EARLIER...
...I FELT A LITTLE HAPPY?

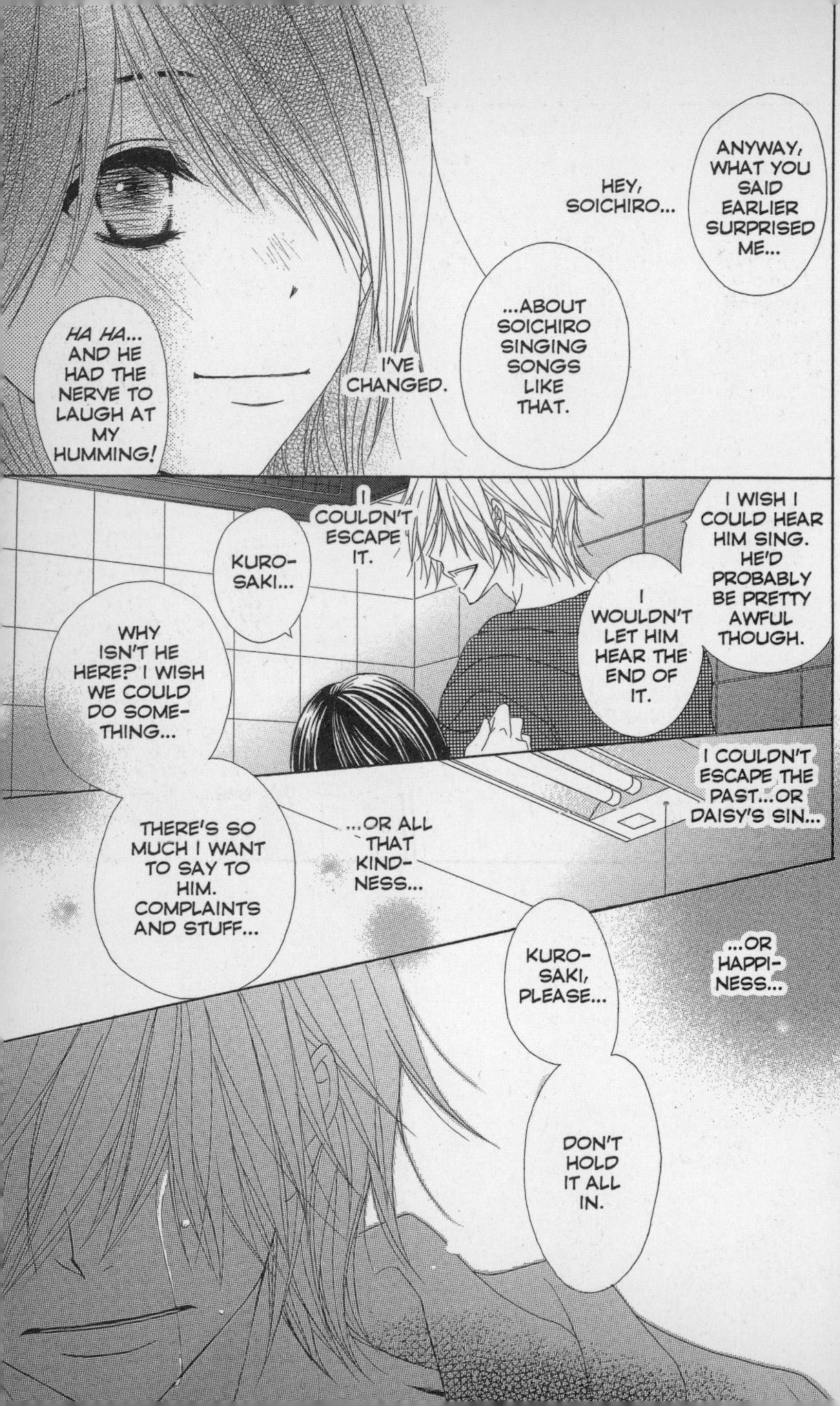
ANYWAY, WHAT YOU SAID EARLIER SURPRISED ME...
HEY, SOICHIRO...
...ABOUT SOICHIRO SINGING SONGS LIKE THAT.
I'VE CHANGED.
HA HA... AND HE HAD THE NERVE TO LAUGH AT MY HUMMING!
I WISH I COULD HEAR HIM SING. HE'D PROBABLY BE PRETTY AWFUL THOUGH.
I WOULDN'T LET HIM HEAR THE END OF IT.
I COULDN'T ESCAPE IT.
KURO-SAKI...
WHY ISN'T HE HERE? I WISH WE COULD DO SOME-THING...
I COULDN'T ESCAPE THE PAST...OR DAISY'S SIN...
...OR ALL THAT KINDNESS...
THERE'S SO MUCH I WANT TO SAY TO HIM. COMPLAINTS AND STUFF...
...OR HAPPINESS...
KURO-SAKI, PLEASE...
DON'T HOLD IT ALL IN.

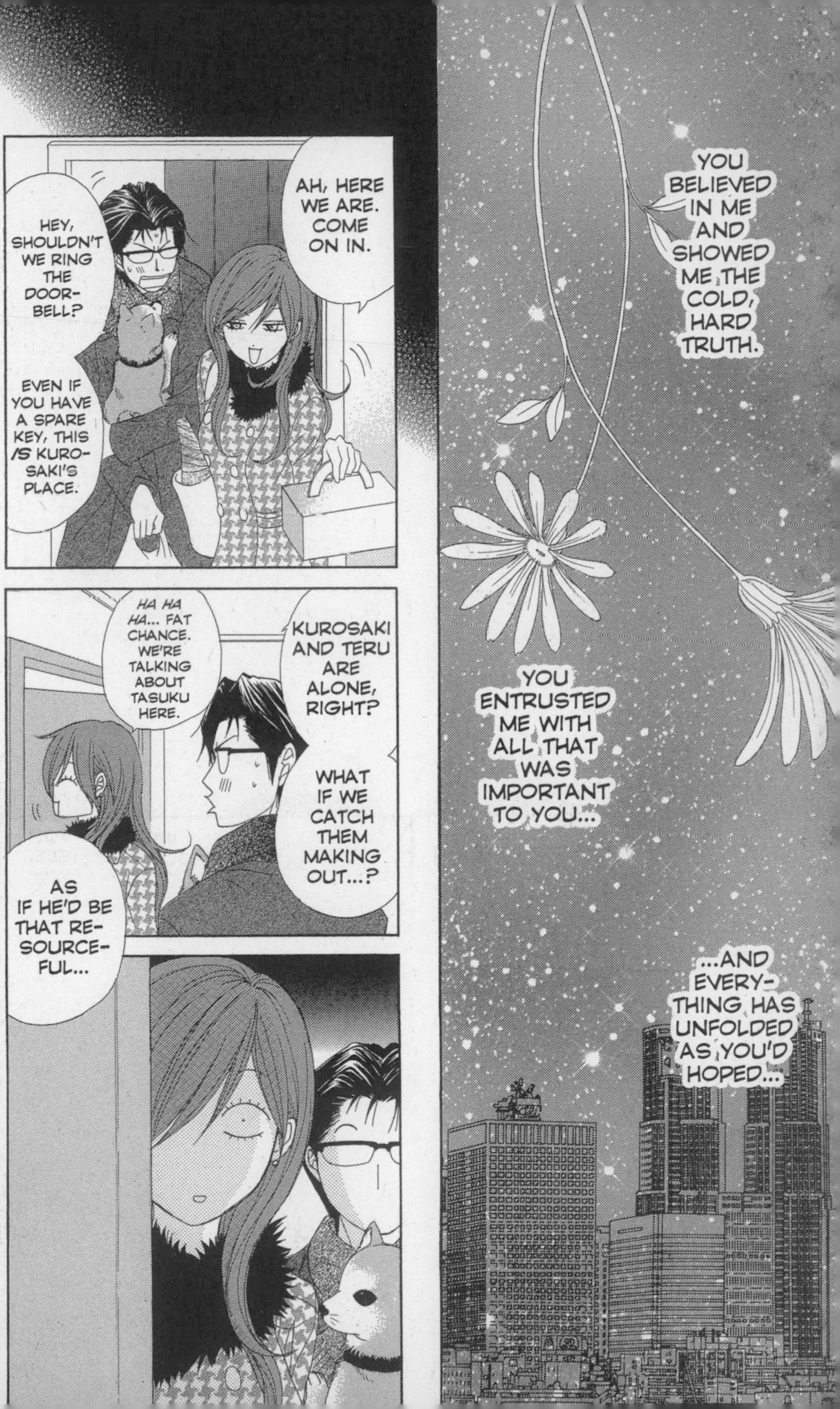
YOU BELIEVED IN ME AND SHOWED ME THE COLD, HARD TRUTH.
YOU ENTRUSTED ME WITH ALL THAT WAS IMPORTANT TO YOU...
...AND EVERY-THING HAS UNFOLDED AS YOU'D HOPED...
AH, HERE WE ARE. COME ON IN.
HEY, SHOULDN'T WE RING THE DOOR-BELL?
EVEN IF YOU HAVE A SPARE KEY, THIS *IS* KURO-SAKI'S PLACE.
KUROSAKI AND TERU ARE ALONE, RIGHT?
HA HA HA... FAT CHANCE. WE'RE TALKING ABOUT TASUKU HERE.
WHAT IF WE CATCH THEM MAKING OUT...?
AS IF HE'D BE THAT RE-SOURCE-FUL...

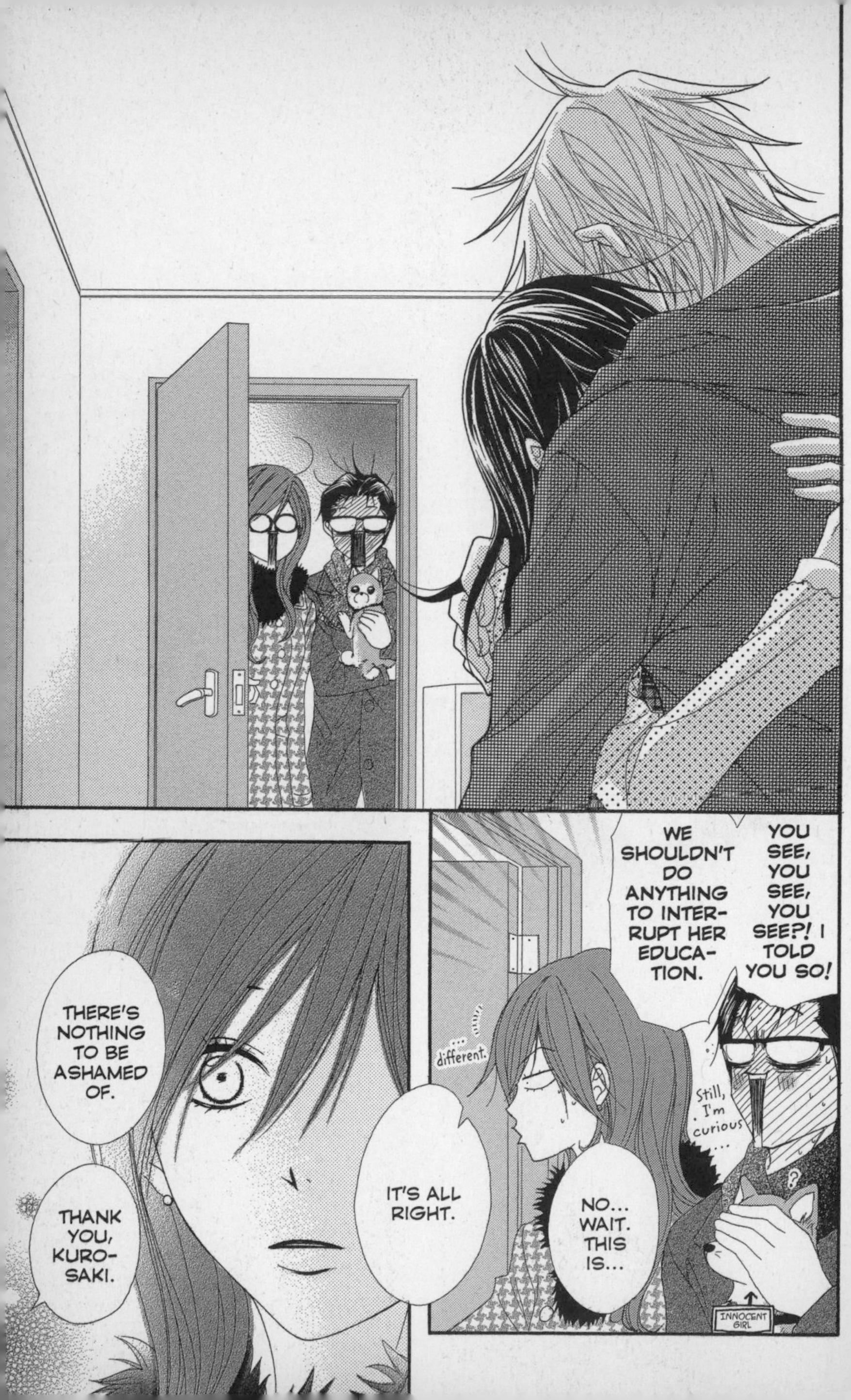
YOU SEE, YOU SEE, YOU SEE?! I TOLD YOU SO!
WE SHOULDN'T DO ANYTHING TO INTER-RUPT HER EDUCA-TION.
Still, I'm curious...
...different.
NO... WAIT. THIS IS...
INNOCENT GIRL
THERE'S NOTHING TO BE ASHAMED OF.
IT'S ALL RIGHT.
THANK YOU, KURO-SAKI.

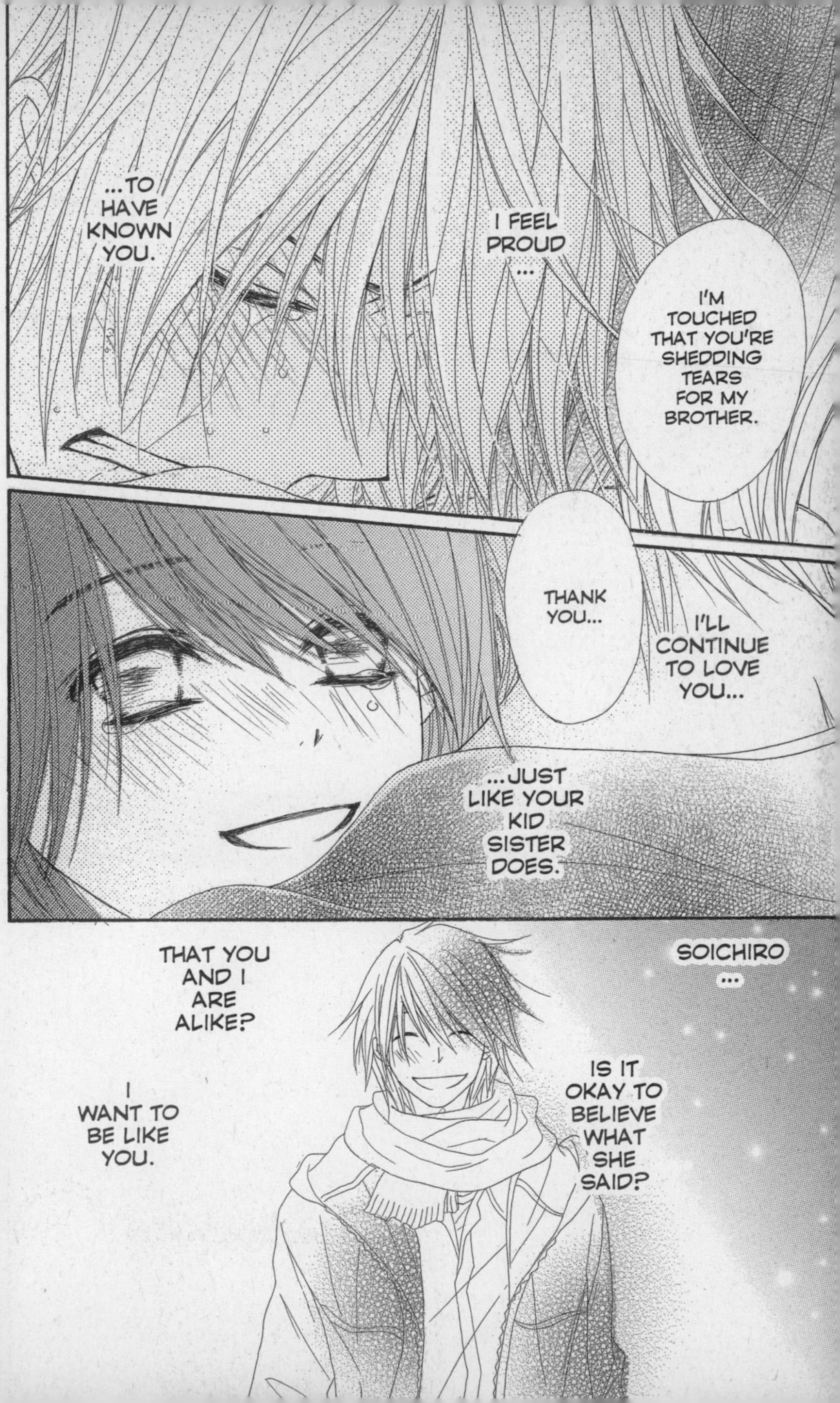
I'M TOUCHED THAT YOU'RE SHEDDING TEARS FOR MY BROTHER.
I FEEL PROUD...
...TO HAVE KNOWN YOU.
THANK YOU...
I'LL CONTINUE TO LOVE YOU...
...JUST LIKE YOUR KID SISTER DOES.
SOICHIRO...
IS IT OKAY TO BELIEVE WHAT SHE SAID?
THAT YOU AND I ARE ALIKE?
I WANT TO BE LIKE YOU.

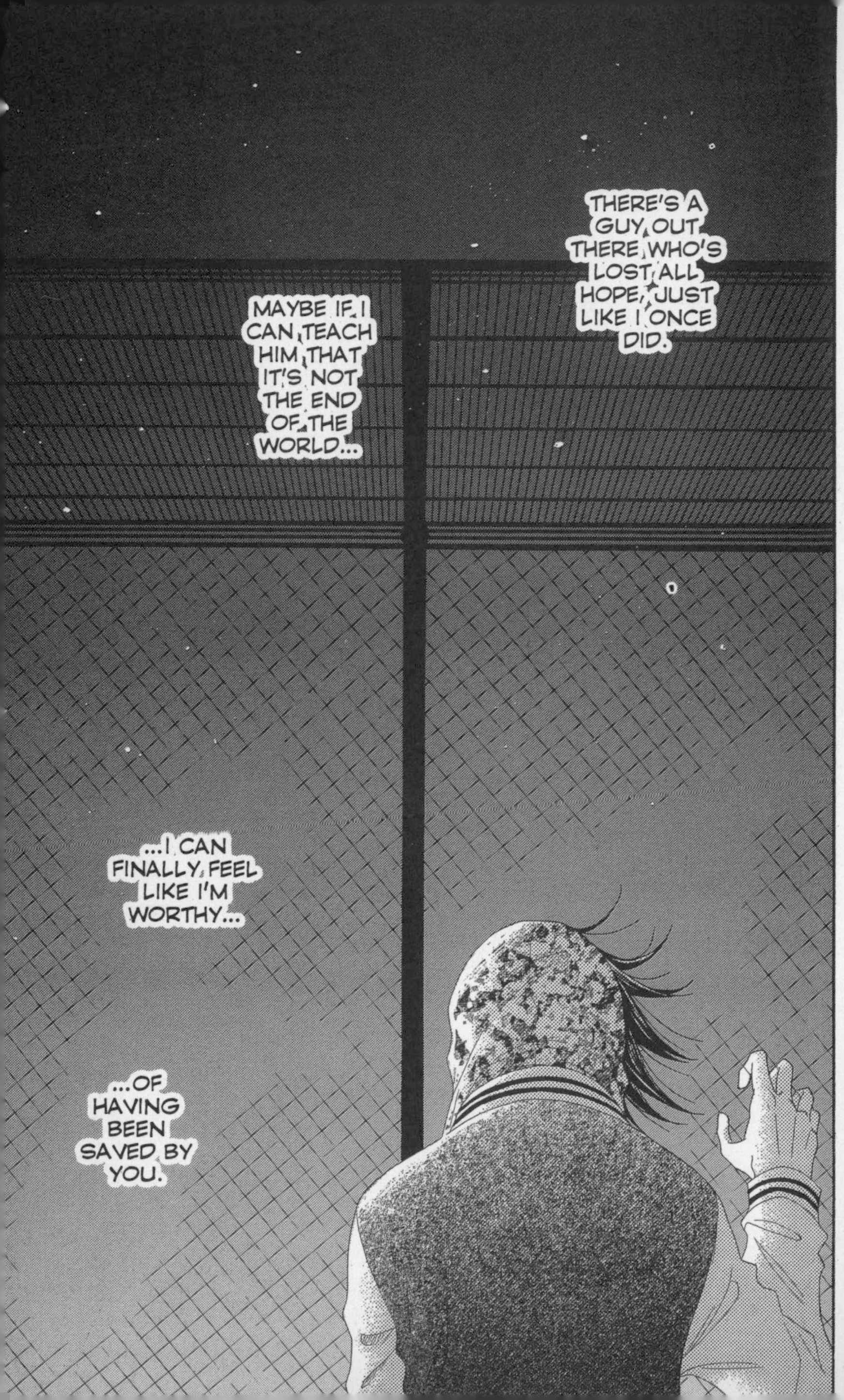
THERE'S A GUY OUT THERE WHO'S LOST ALL HOPE, JUST LIKE I ONCE DID.
MAYBE IF I CAN TEACH HIM THAT IT'S NOT THE END OF THE WORLD...
...I CAN FINALLY FEEL LIKE I'M WORTHY...
...OF HAVING BEEN SAVED BY YOU.

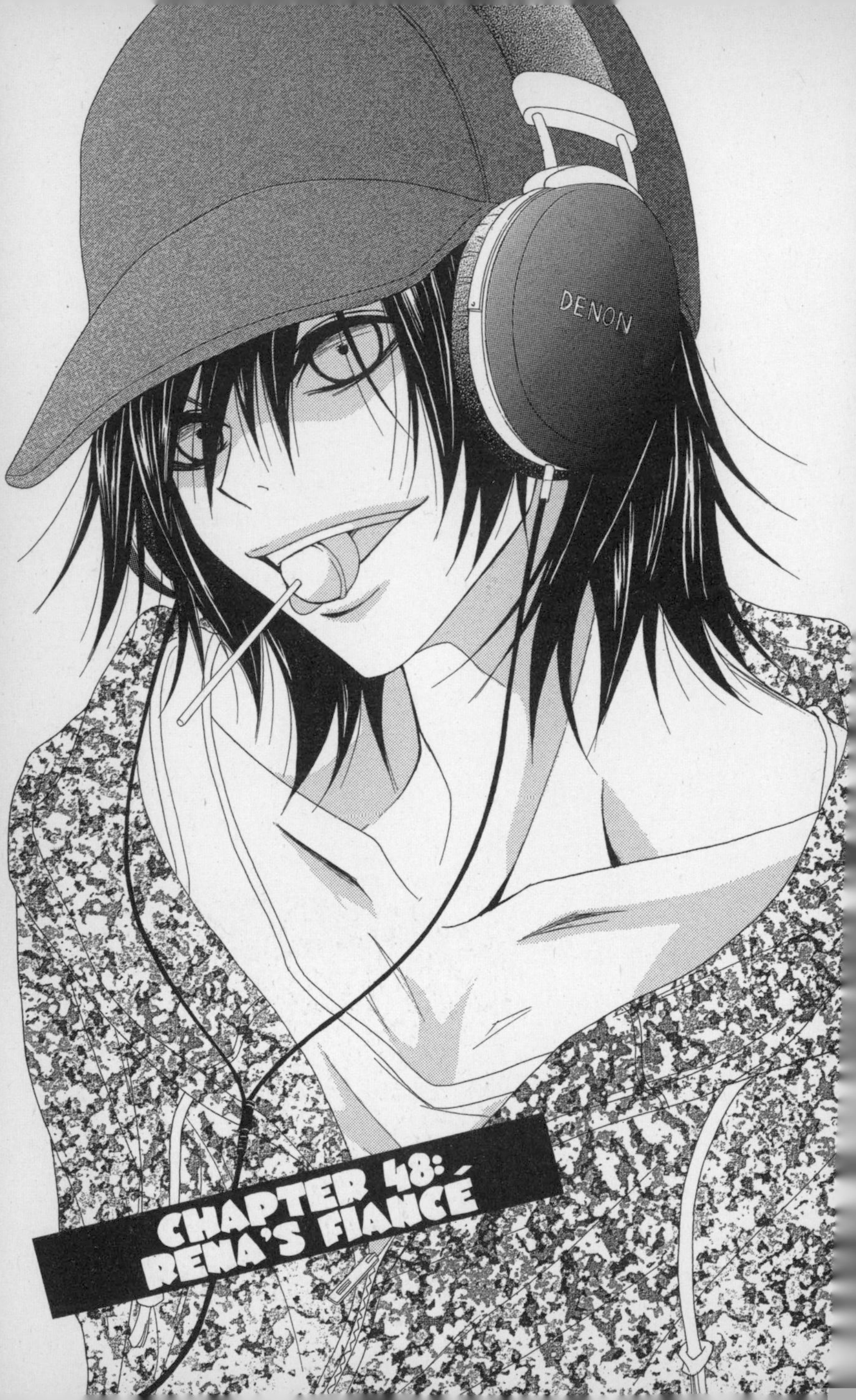
DENON
CHAPTER 48:
RENA'S FIANCÉ

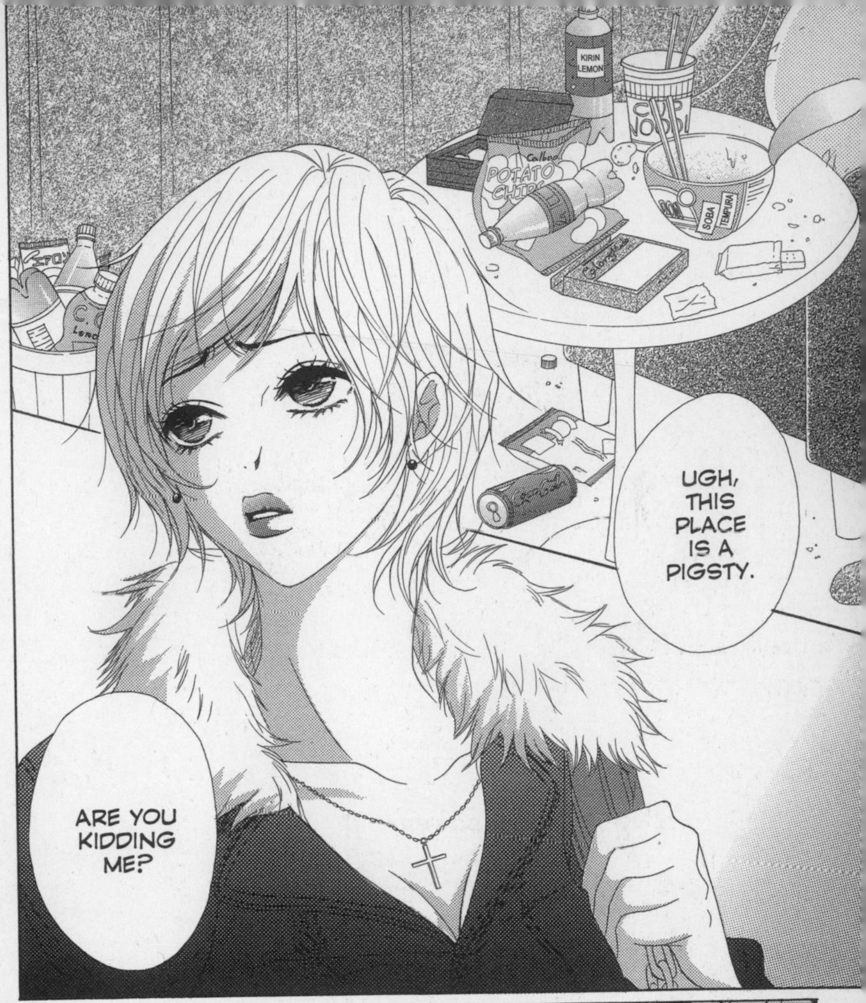
UGH, THIS PLACE IS A PIGSTY.
ARE YOU KIDDING ME?

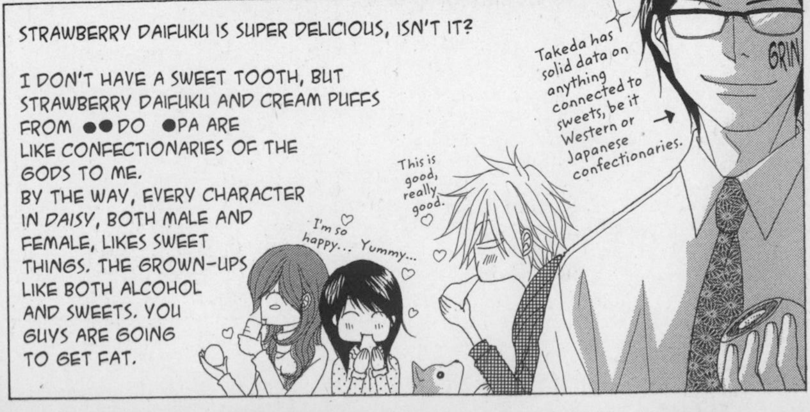
GRIN
Takeda has solid data on anything connected to sweets, be it Western or Japanese confectionaries. →
STRAWBERRY DAIFUKU IS SUPER DELICIOUS, ISN'T IT?
I DON'T HAVE A SWEET TOOTH, BUT STRAWBERRY DAIFUKU AND CREAM PUFFS FROM ●●DO ●PA ARE LIKE CONFECTIONARIES OF THE GODS TO ME.
BY THE WAY, EVERY CHARACTER IN *DAISY*, BOTH MALE AND FEMALE, LIKES SWEET THINGS. THE GROWN-UPS LIKE BOTH ALCOHOL AND SWEETS. YOU GUYS ARE GOING TO GET FAT.
This is good, really good.
I'm so happy... Yummy...

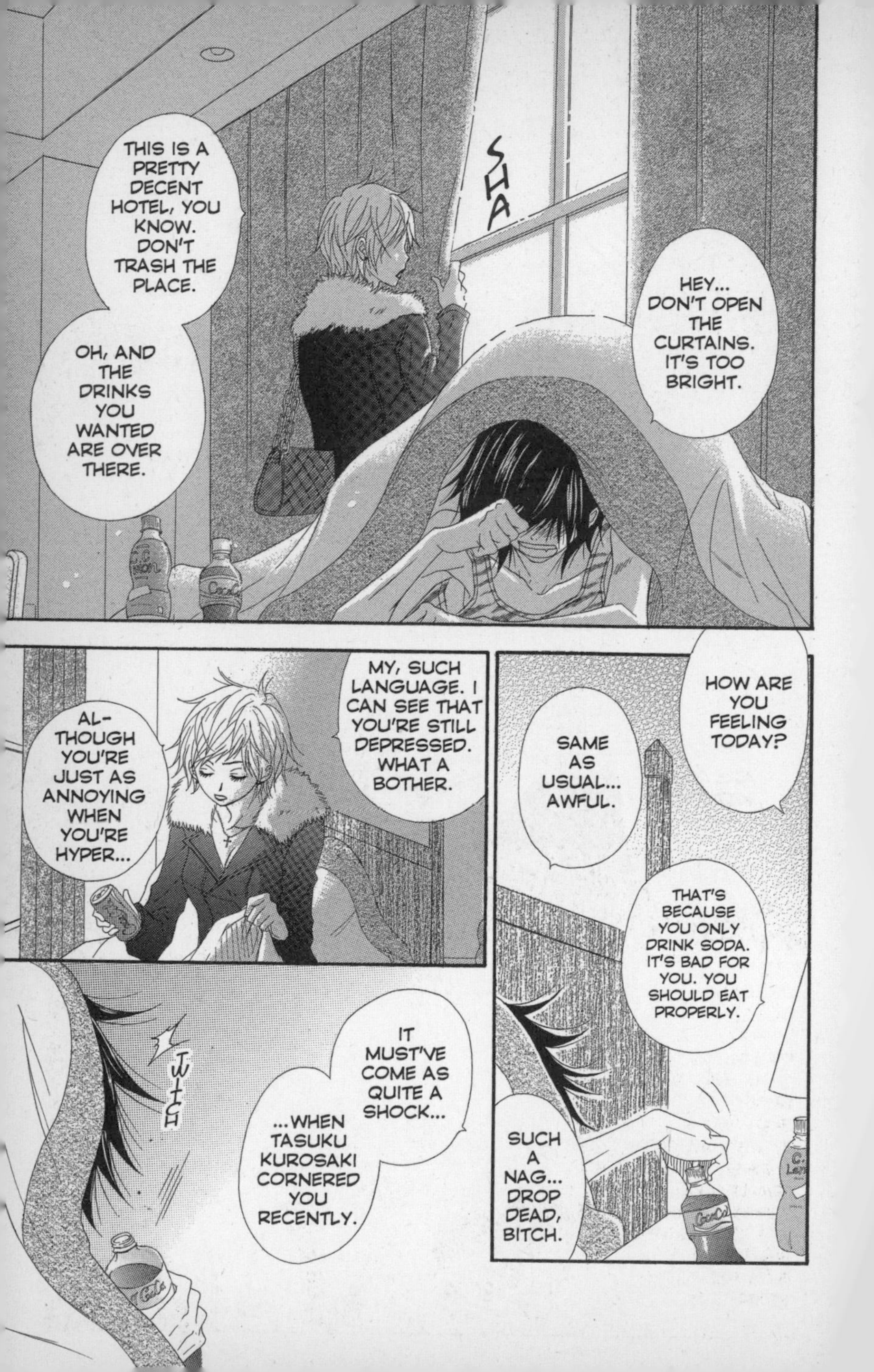
SHA
HEY... DON'T OPEN THE CURTAINS. IT'S TOO BRIGHT.
THIS IS A PRETTY DECENT HOTEL, YOU KNOW. DON'T TRASH THE PLACE.
OH, AND THE DRINKS YOU WANTED ARE OVER THERE.
HOW ARE YOU FEELING TODAY?
SAME AS USUAL... AWFUL.
THAT'S BECAUSE YOU ONLY DRINK SODA. IT'S BAD FOR YOU. YOU SHOULD EAT PROPERLY.
SUCH A NAG... DROP DEAD, BITCH.
MY, SUCH LANGUAGE. I CAN SEE THAT YOU'RE STILL DEPRESSED. WHAT A BOTHER.
AL-THOUGH YOU'RE JUST AS ANNOYING WHEN YOU'RE HYPER...
IT MUST'VE COME AS QUITE A SHOCK...
...WHEN TASUKU KUROSAKI CORNERED YOU RECENTLY.
TWITCH

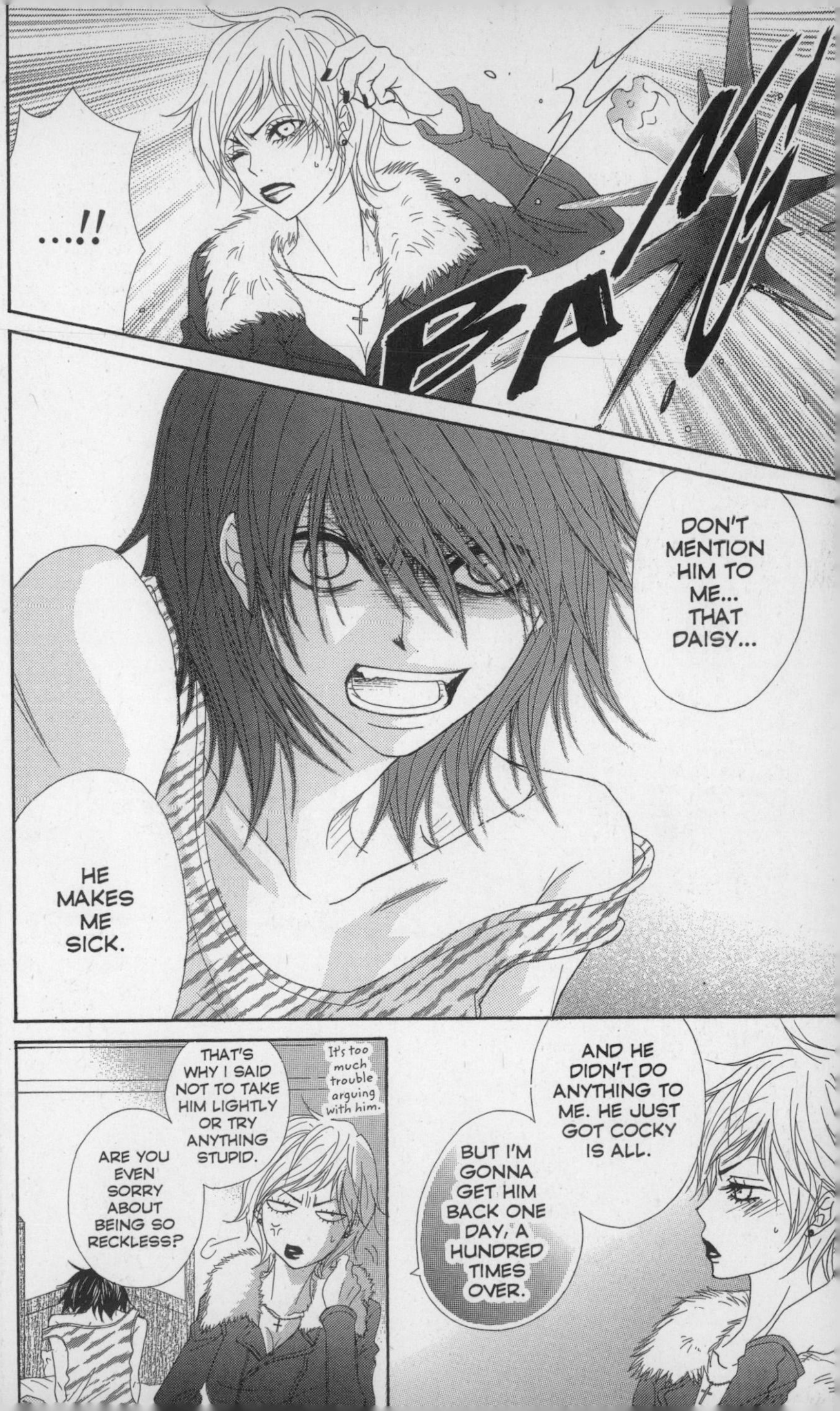
...!!
BAM
DON'T MENTION HIM TO ME... THAT DAISY...
HE MAKES ME SICK.
AND HE DIDN'T DO ANYTHING TO ME. HE JUST GOT COCKY IS ALL.
BUT I'M GONNA GET HIM BACK ONE DAY, A HUNDRED TIMES OVER.
It's too much trouble arguing with him.
THAT'S WHY I SAID NOT TO TAKE HIM LIGHTLY OR TRY ANYTHING STUPID.
ARE YOU EVEN SORRY ABOUT BEING SO RECKLESS?

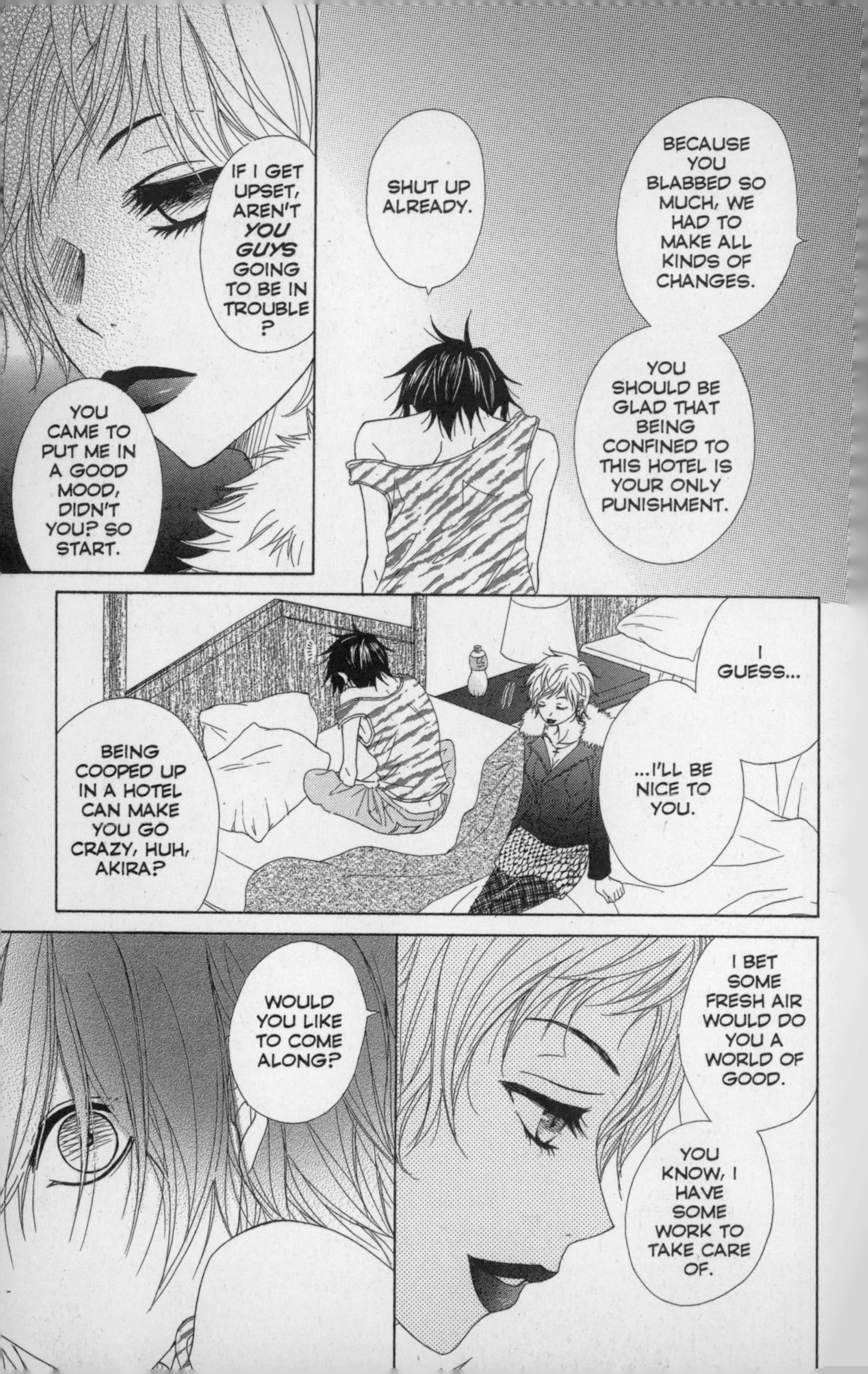
BECAUSE YOU BLABBED SO MUCH, WE HAD TO MAKE ALL KINDS OF CHANGES.
YOU SHOULD BE GLAD THAT BEING CONFINED TO THIS HOTEL IS YOUR ONLY PUNISHMENT.
SHUT UP ALREADY.
IF I GET UPSET, AREN'T *YOU GUYS* GOING TO BE IN TROUBLE?
YOU CAME TO PUT ME IN A GOOD MOOD, DIDN'T YOU? SO START.
I GUESS...
...I'LL BE NICE TO YOU.
BEING COOPED UP IN A HOTEL CAN MAKE YOU GO CRAZY, HUH, AKIRA?
I BET SOME FRESH AIR WOULD DO YOU A WORLD OF GOOD.
YOU KNOW, I HAVE SOME WORK TO TAKE CARE OF.
WOULD YOU LIKE TO COME ALONG?

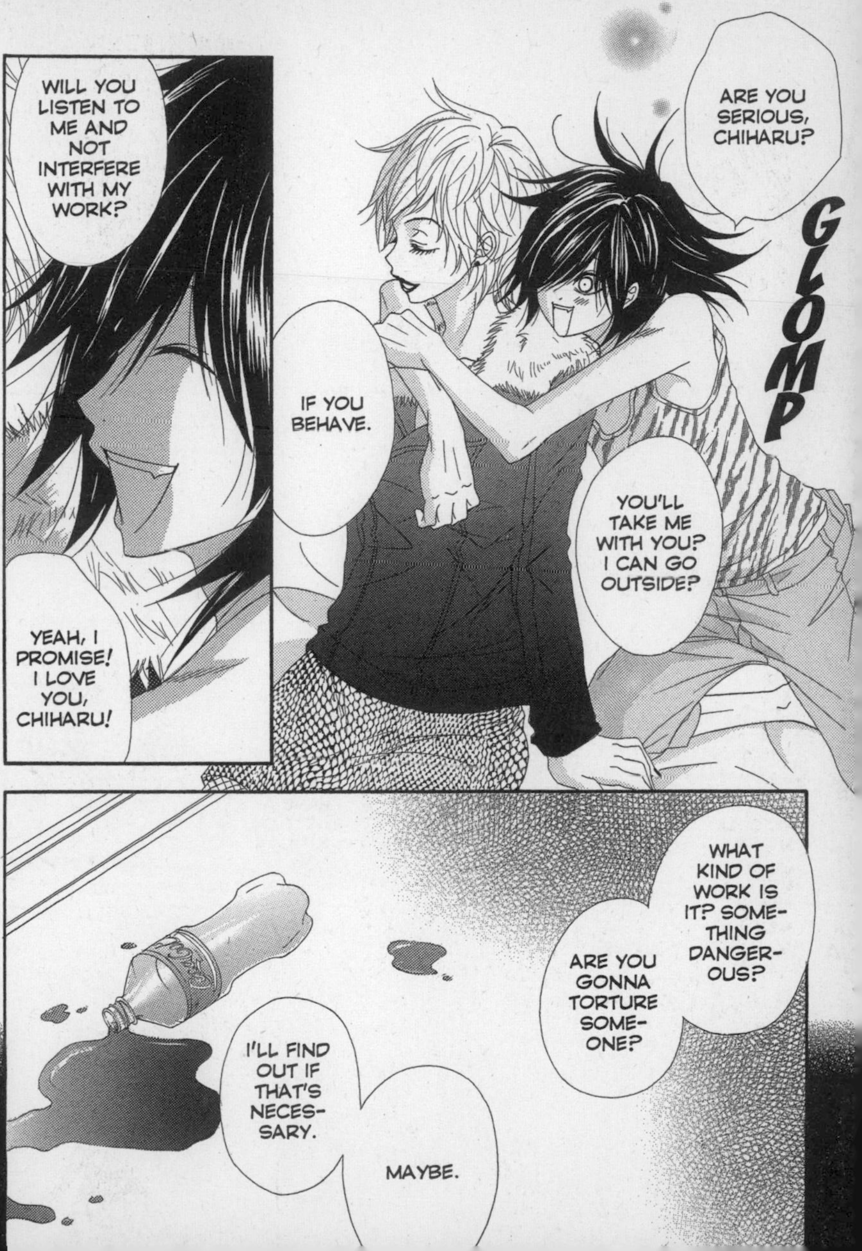
ARE YOU SERIOUS, CHIHARU?
GLOMP
YOU'LL TAKE ME WITH YOU? I CAN GO OUTSIDE?
IF YOU BEHAVE.
WILL YOU LISTEN TO ME AND NOT INTERFERE WITH MY WORK?
YEAH, I PROMISE! I LOVE YOU, CHIHARU!
WHAT KIND OF WORK IS IT? SOME-THING DANGER-OUS?
ARE YOU GONNA TORTURE SOME-ONE?
I'LL FIND OUT IF THAT'S NECES-SARY.
MAYBE.

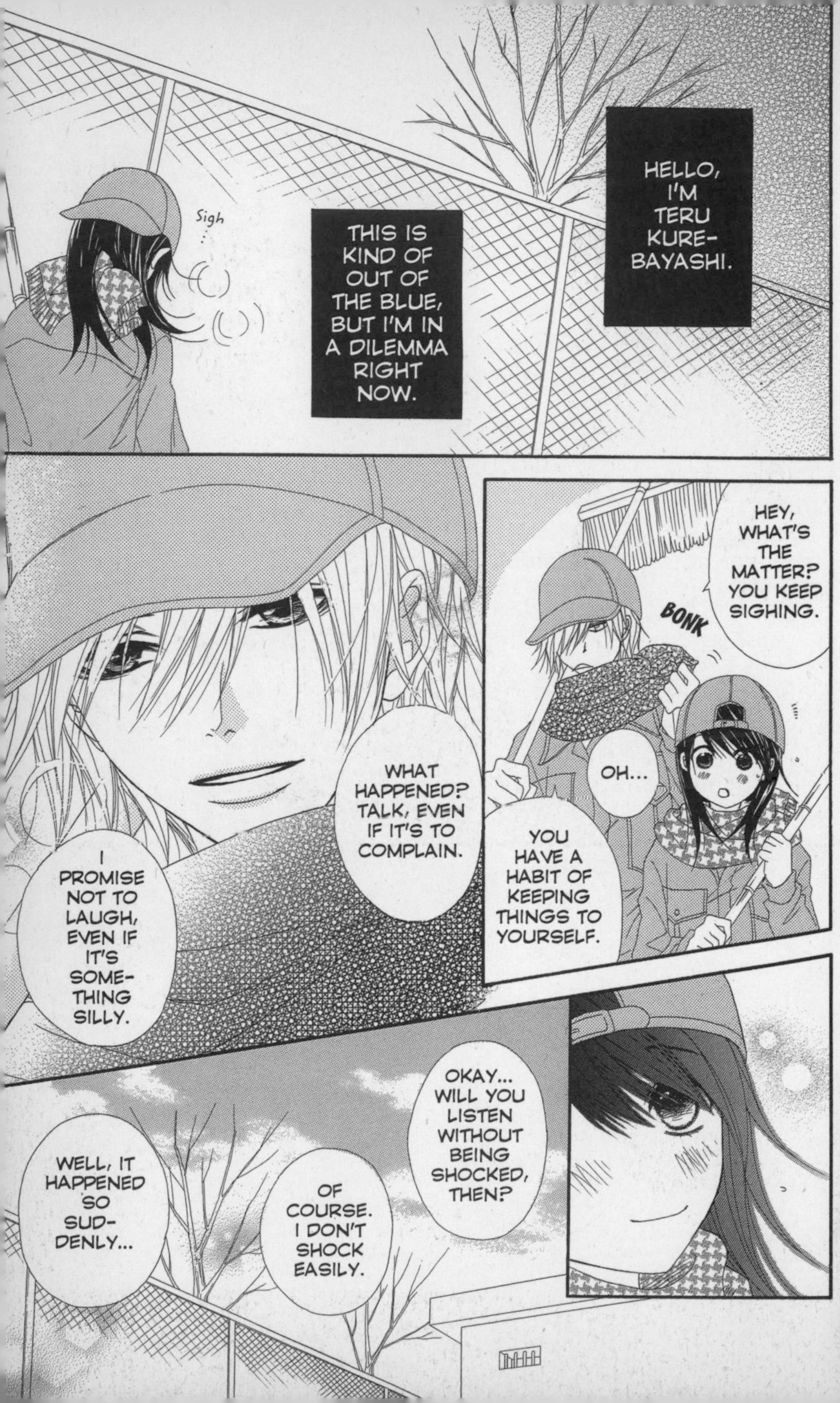
HELLO, I'M TERU KURE-BAYASHI.
THIS IS KIND OF OUT OF THE BLUE, BUT I'M IN A DILEMMA RIGHT NOW.
Sigh...
HEY, WHAT'S THE MATTER? YOU KEEP SIGHING.
BONK
OH...
YOU HAVE A HABIT OF KEEPING THINGS TO YOURSELF.
WHAT HAPPENED? TALK, EVEN IF IT'S TO COMPLAIN.
I PROMISE NOT TO LAUGH, EVEN IF IT'S SOME-THING SILLY.
OKAY... WILL YOU LISTEN WITHOUT BEING SHOCKED, THEN?
OF COURSE. I DON'T SHOCK EASILY.
WELL, IT HAPPENED SO SUD-DENLY...

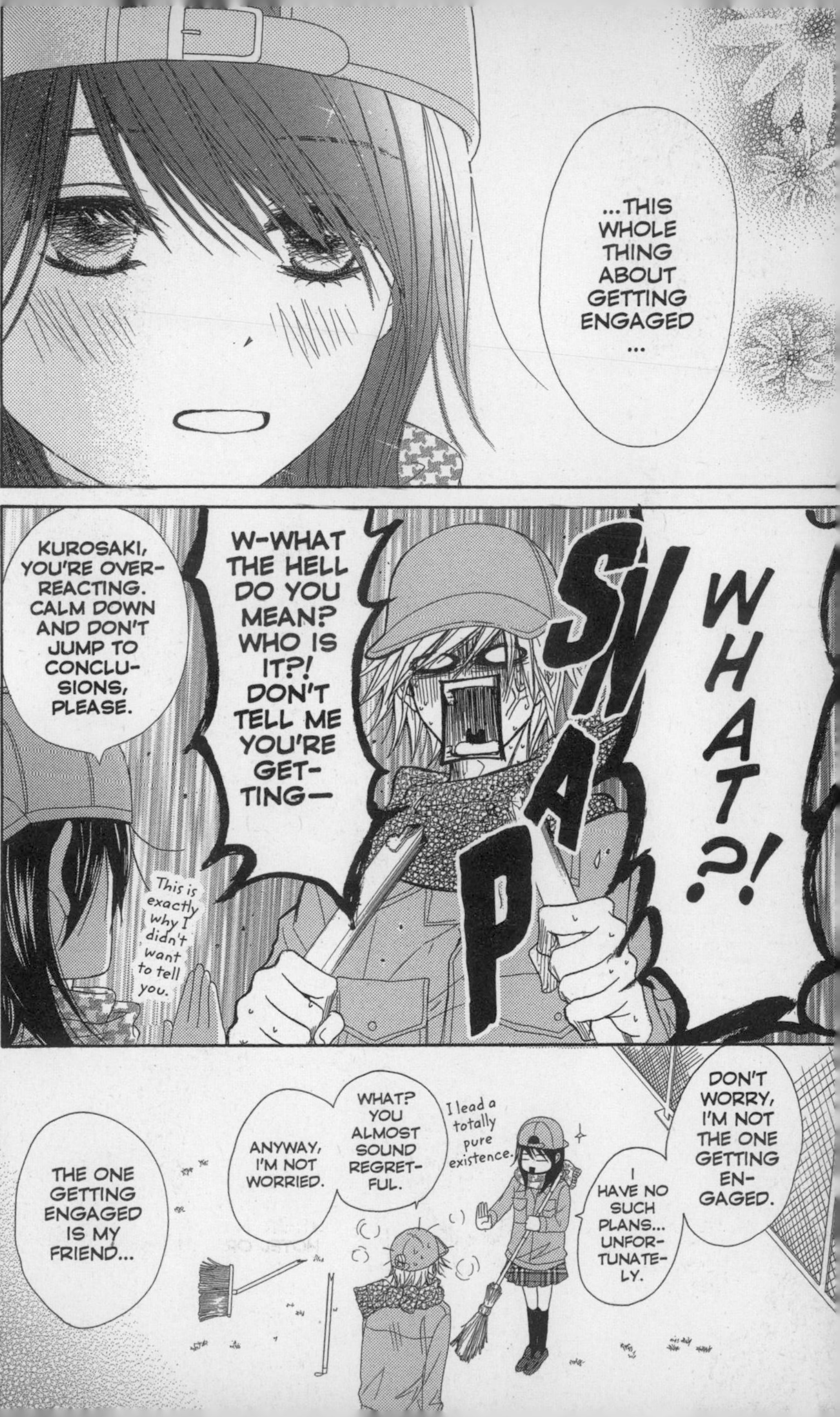
...THIS WHOLE THING ABOUT GETTING ENGAGED ...
WHAT?!
SNAP
W-WHAT THE HELL DO YOU MEAN? WHO IS IT?! DON'T TELL ME YOU'RE GET-TING—
KUROSAKI, YOU'RE OVER-REACTING. CALM DOWN AND DON'T JUMP TO CONCLU-SIONS, PLEASE.
This is exactly why I didn't want to tell you.
DON'T WORRY, I'M NOT THE ONE GETTING EN-GAGED.
I HAVE NO SUCH PLANS... UNFOR-TUNATE-LY.
I lead a totally pure existence.
WHAT? YOU ALMOST SOUND REGRET-FUL.
ANYWAY, I'M NOT WORRIED.
THE ONE GETTING ENGAGED IS MY FRIEND...

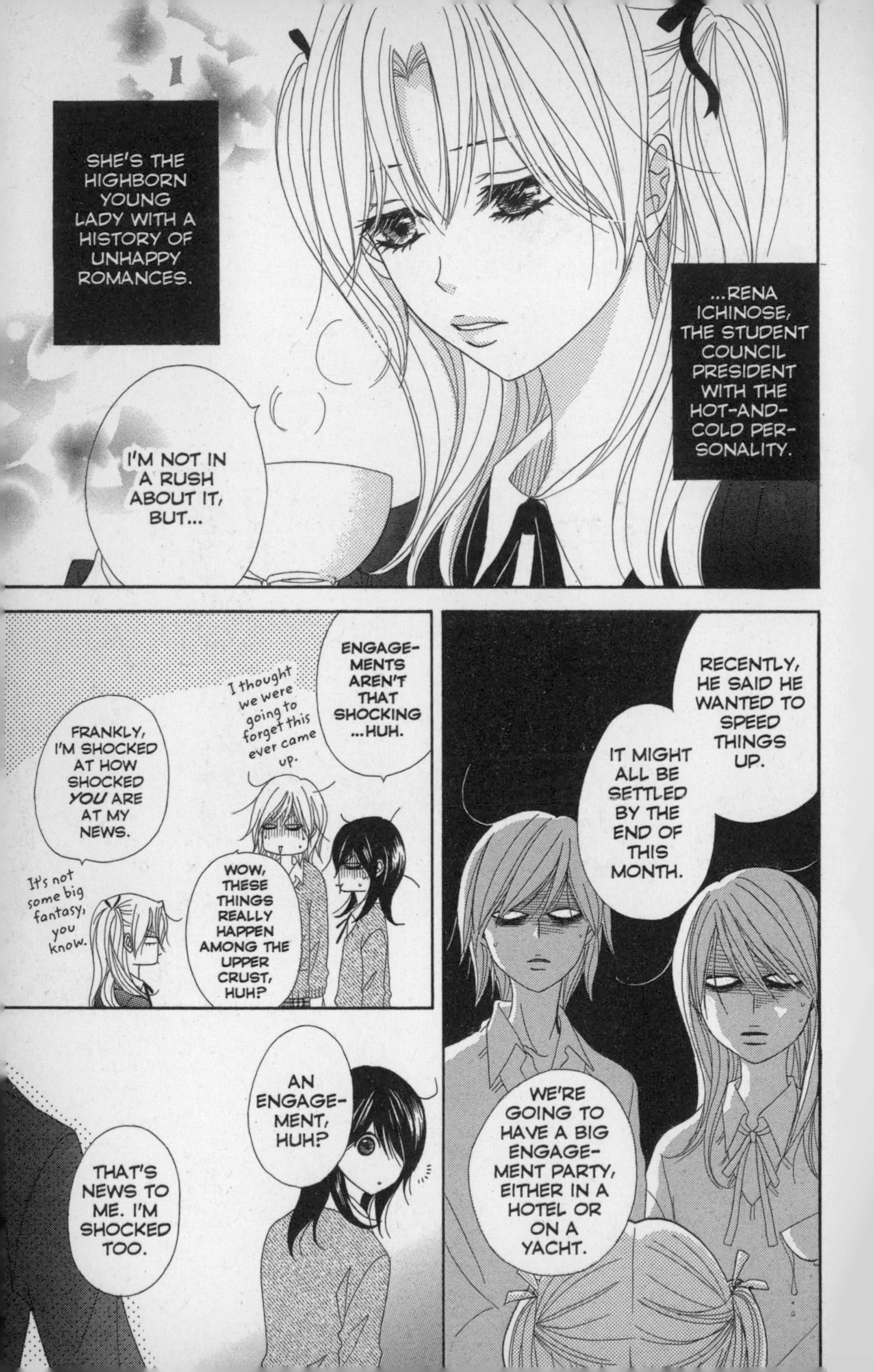
...RENA ICHINOSE, THE STUDENT COUNCIL PRESIDENT WITH THE HOT-AND-COLD PERSONALITY.
SHE'S THE HIGHBORN YOUNG LADY WITH A HISTORY OF UNHAPPY ROMANCES.
I'M NOT IN A RUSH ABOUT IT, BUT...
RECENTLY, HE SAID HE WANTED TO SPEED THINGS UP.
IT MIGHT ALL BE SETTLED BY THE END OF THIS MONTH.
WE'RE GOING TO HAVE A BIG ENGAGEMENT PARTY, EITHER IN A HOTEL OR ON A YACHT.
ENGAGEMENTS AREN'T THAT SHOCKING ...HUH.
I thought we were going to forget this ever came up.
FRANKLY, I'M SHOCKED AT HOW SHOCKED *YOU* ARE AT MY NEWS.
WOW, THESE THINGS REALLY HAPPEN AMONG THE UPPER CRUST, HUH?
It's not some big fantasy, you know.
AN ENGAGEMENT, HUH?
THAT'S NEWS TO ME. I'M SHOCKED TOO.

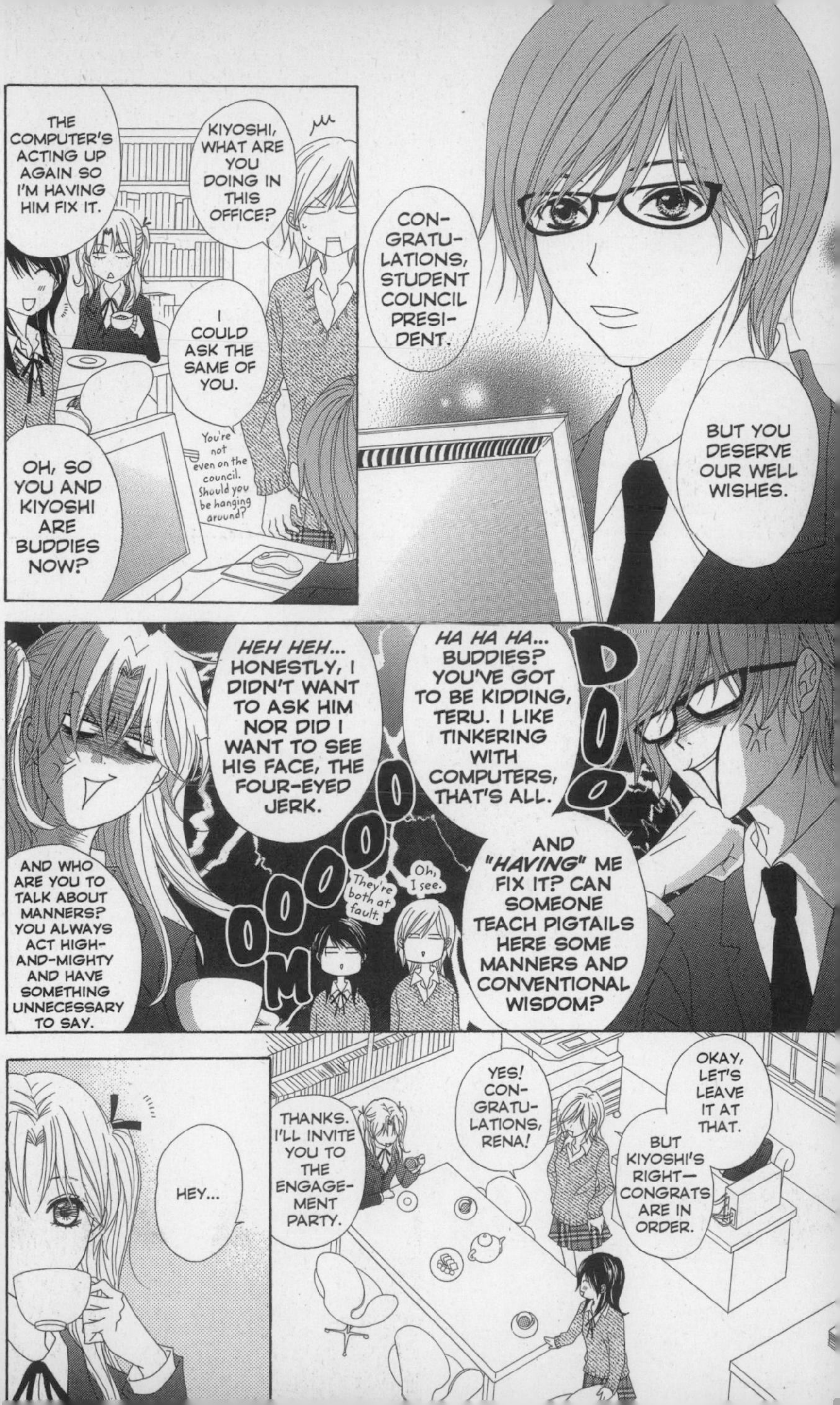
CON-GRATU-LATIONS, STUDENT COUNCIL PRESI-DENT.
BUT YOU DESERVE OUR WELL WISHES.
KIYOSHI, WHAT ARE YOU DOING IN THIS OFFICE?
THE COMPUTER'S ACTING UP AGAIN SO I'M HAVING HIM FIX IT.
I COULD ASK THE SAME OF YOU.
You're not even on the council. Should you be hanging around?
OH, SO YOU AND KIYOSHI ARE BUDDIES NOW?
DOOOOOOOOM
HA HA HA... BUDDIES? YOU'VE GOT TO BE KIDDING, TERU. I LIKE TINKERING WITH COMPUTERS, THAT'S ALL.
HEH HEH... HONESTLY, I DIDN'T WANT TO ASK HIM NOR DID I WANT TO SEE HIS FACE, THE FOUR-EYED JERK.
AND "HAVING" ME FIX IT? CAN SOMEONE TEACH PIGTAILS HERE SOME MANNERS AND CONVENTIONAL WISDOM?
Oh, I see.
They're both at fault.
AND WHO ARE YOU TO TALK ABOUT MANNERS? YOU ALWAYS ACT HIGH-AND-MIGHTY AND HAVE SOMETHING UNNECESSARY TO SAY.
OKAY, LET'S LEAVE IT AT THAT.
BUT KIYOSHI'S RIGHT—CONGRATS ARE IN ORDER.
YES! CON-GRATU-LATIONS, RENA!
THANKS. I'LL INVITE YOU TO THE ENGAGE-MENT PARTY.
HEY...

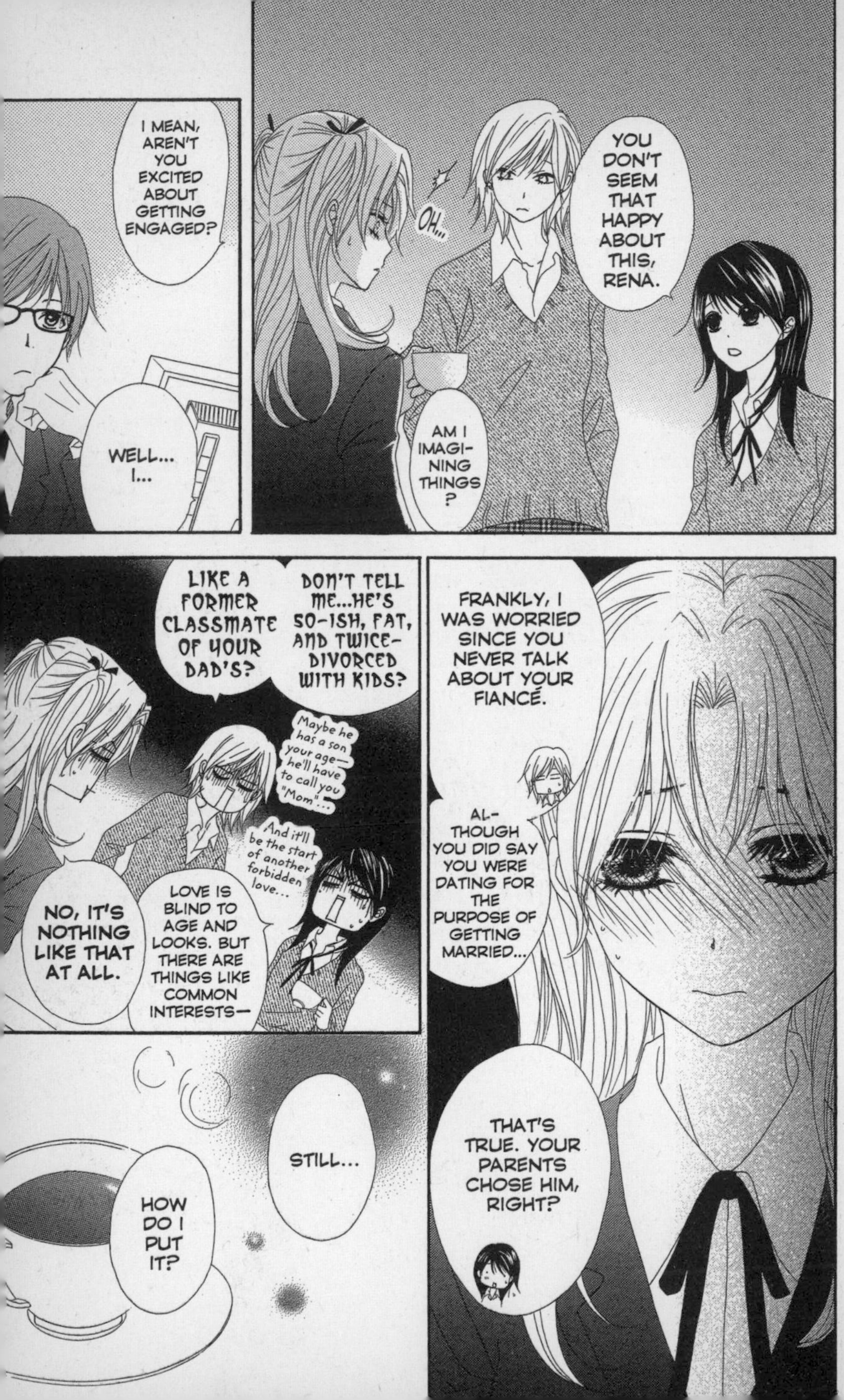
YOU DON'T SEEM THAT HAPPY ABOUT THIS, RENA.
OH...
AM I IMAGINING THINGS?
I MEAN, AREN'T YOU EXCITED ABOUT GETTING ENGAGED?
WELL... I...
FRANKLY, I WAS WORRIED SINCE YOU NEVER TALK ABOUT YOUR FIANCÉ.
ALTHOUGH YOU DID SAY YOU WERE DATING FOR THE PURPOSE OF GETTING MARRIED...
THAT'S TRUE. YOUR PARENTS CHOSE HIM, RIGHT?
DON'T TELL ME...HE'S 50-ISH, FAT, AND TWICE-DIVORCED WITH KIDS?
LIKE A FORMER CLASSMATE OF YOUR DAD'S?
Maybe he has a son your age—he'll have to call you "Mom"...
And it'll be the start of another forbidden love...
LOVE IS BLIND TO AGE AND LOOKS. BUT THERE ARE THINGS LIKE COMMON INTERESTS—
NO, IT'S NOTHING LIKE THAT AT ALL.
STILL...
HOW DO I PUT IT?

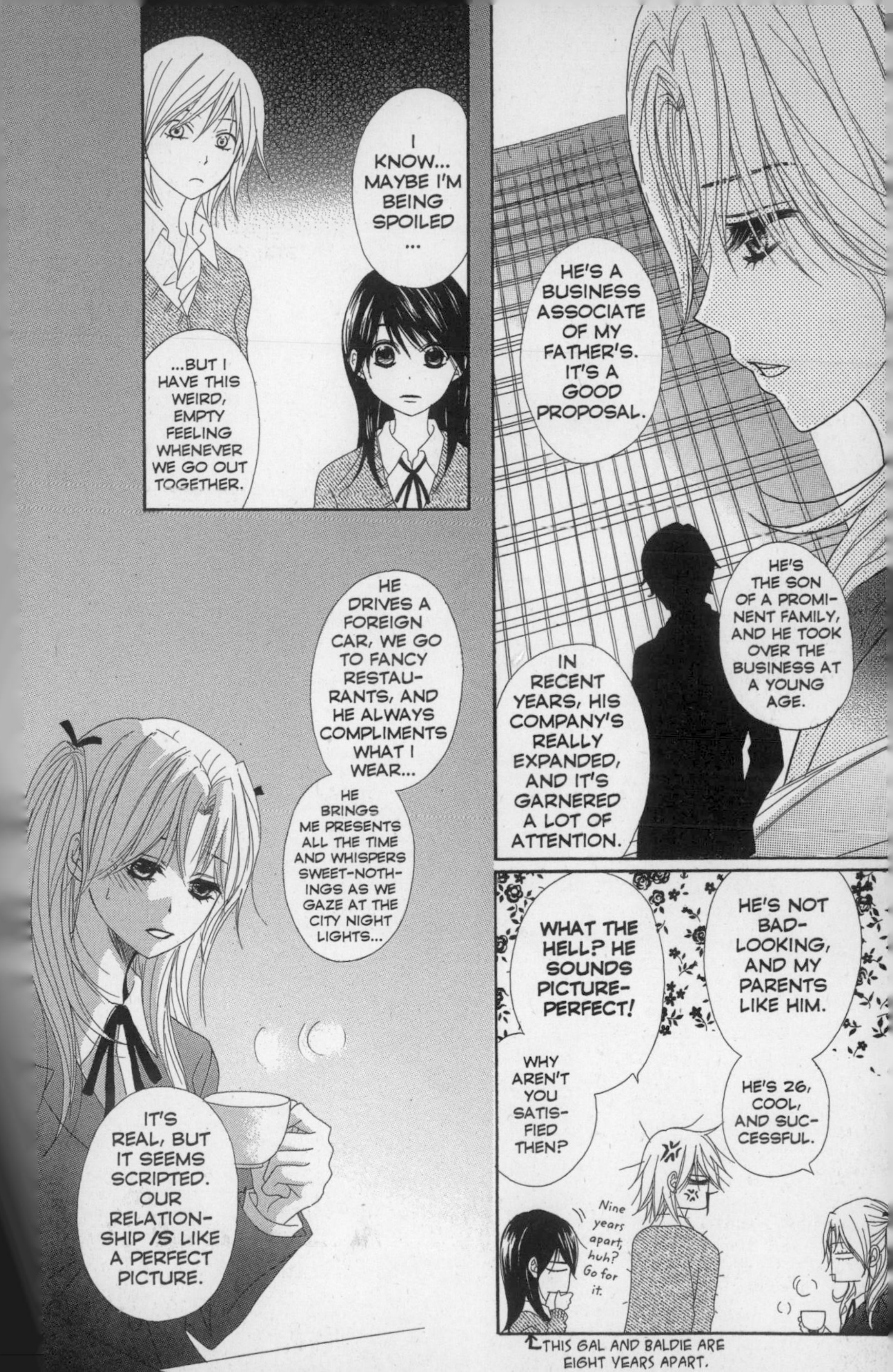
HE'S A BUSINESS ASSOCIATE OF MY FATHER'S. IT'S A GOOD PROPOSAL.
HE'S THE SON OF A PROMI-NENT FAMILY, AND HE TOOK OVER THE BUSINESS AT A YOUNG AGE.
IN RECENT YEARS, HIS COMPANY'S REALLY EXPANDED, AND IT'S GARNERED A LOT OF ATTENTION.
HE'S NOT BAD-LOOKING, AND MY PARENTS LIKE HIM.
HE'S 26, COOL, AND SUC-CESSFUL.
WHAT THE HELL? HE SOUNDS PICTURE-PERFECT!
WHY AREN'T YOU SATIS-FIED THEN?
Nine years apart, huh? Go for it.
THIS GAL AND BALDIE ARE EIGHT YEARS APART.
I KNOW... MAYBE I'M BEING SPOILED ...
...BUT I HAVE THIS WEIRD, EMPTY FEELING WHENEVER WE GO OUT TOGETHER.
HE DRIVES A FOREIGN CAR, WE GO TO FANCY RESTAU-RANTS, AND HE ALWAYS COMPLIMENTS WHAT I WEAR...
HE BRINGS ME PRESENTS ALL THE TIME AND WHISPERS SWEET-NOTH-INGS AS WE GAZE AT THE CITY NIGHT LIGHTS...
IT'S REAL, BUT IT SEEMS SCRIPTED. OUR RELATION-SHIP IS LIKE A PERFECT PICTURE.

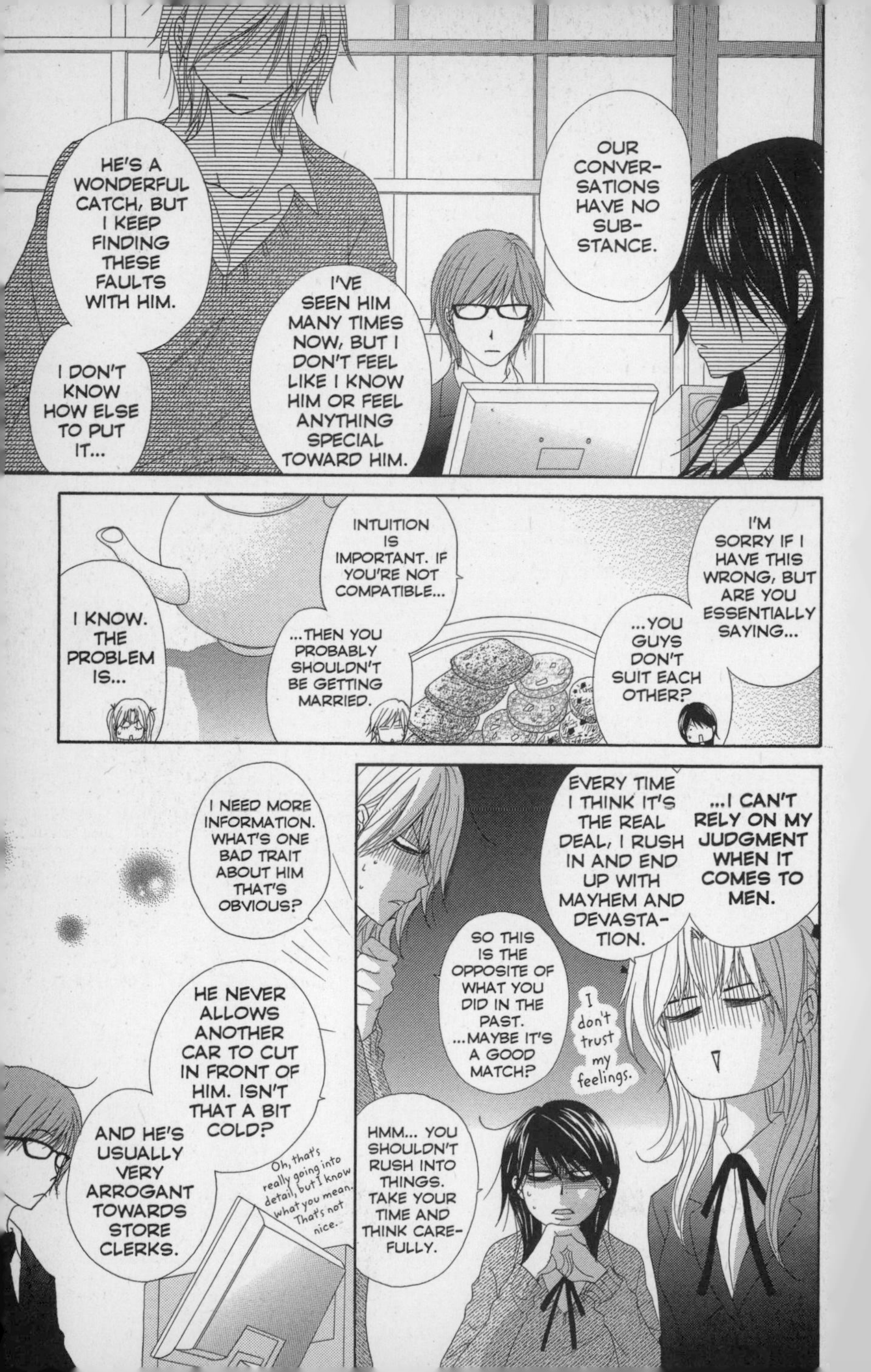
OUR CONVERSATIONS HAVE NO SUBSTANCE.
I'VE SEEN HIM MANY TIMES NOW, BUT I DON'T FEEL LIKE I KNOW HIM OR FEEL ANYTHING SPECIAL TOWARD HIM.
HE'S A WONDERFUL CATCH, BUT I KEEP FINDING THESE FAULTS WITH HIM.
I DON'T KNOW HOW ELSE TO PUT IT...
I'M SORRY IF I HAVE THIS WRONG, BUT ARE YOU ESSENTIALLY SAYING...
...YOU GUYS DON'T SUIT EACH OTHER?
INTUITION IS IMPORTANT. IF YOU'RE NOT COMPATIBLE...
...THEN YOU PROBABLY SHOULDN'T BE GETTING MARRIED.
I KNOW. THE PROBLEM IS...
...I CAN'T RELY ON MY JUDGMENT WHEN IT COMES TO MEN.
EVERY TIME I THINK IT'S THE REAL DEAL, I RUSH IN AND END UP WITH MAYHEM AND DEVASTATION.
I don't trust my feelings.
SO THIS IS THE OPPOSITE OF WHAT YOU DID IN THE PAST. ...MAYBE IT'S A GOOD MATCH?
HMM... YOU SHOULDN'T RUSH INTO THINGS. TAKE YOUR TIME AND THINK CAREFULLY.
I NEED MORE INFORMATION. WHAT'S ONE BAD TRAIT ABOUT HIM THAT'S OBVIOUS?
HE NEVER ALLOWS ANOTHER CAR TO CUT IN FRONT OF HIM. ISN'T THAT A BIT COLD?
AND HE'S USUALLY VERY ARROGANT TOWARDS STORE CLERKS.
Oh, that's really going into detail, but I know what you mean. That's not nice.

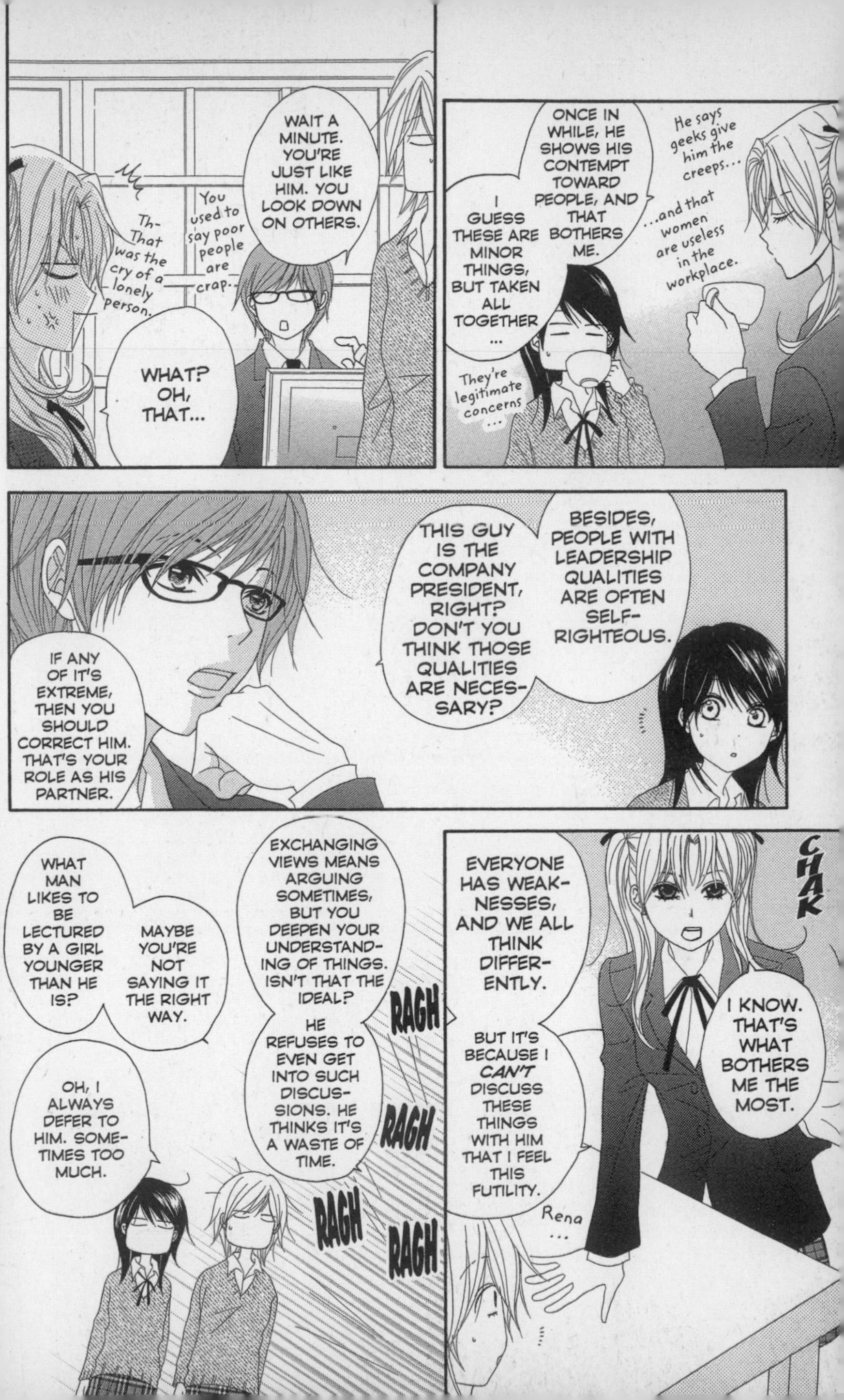
He says geeks give him the creeps...
...and that women are useless in the workplace.
ONCE IN WHILE, HE SHOWS HIS CONTEMPT TOWARD PEOPLE, AND THAT BOTHERS ME.
I GUESS THESE ARE MINOR THINGS, BUT TAKEN ALL TOGETHER ...
They're legitimate concerns ...
WAIT A MINUTE. YOU'RE JUST LIKE HIM. YOU LOOK DOWN ON OTHERS.
You used to say poor people are crap...
Th- That was the cry of a lonely person.
WHAT? OH, THAT...
BESIDES, PEOPLE WITH LEADERSHIP QUALITIES ARE OFTEN SELF-RIGHTEOUS.
THIS GUY IS THE COMPANY PRESIDENT, RIGHT? DON'T YOU THINK THOSE QUALITIES ARE NECES-SARY?
IF ANY OF IT'S EXTREME, THEN YOU SHOULD CORRECT HIM. THAT'S YOUR ROLE AS HIS PARTNER.
CHAK
EVERYONE HAS WEAK-NESSES, AND WE ALL THINK DIFFER-ENTLY.
I KNOW. THAT'S WHAT BOTHERS ME THE MOST.
BUT IT'S BECAUSE I *CAN'T* DISCUSS THESE THINGS WITH HIM THAT I FEEL THIS FUTILITY.
Rena ...
EXCHANGING VIEWS MEANS ARGUING SOMETIMES, BUT YOU DEEPEN YOUR UNDERSTAND-ING OF THINGS. ISN'T THAT THE IDEAL?
WHAT MAN LIKES TO BE LECTURED BY A GIRL YOUNGER THAN HE IS?
MAYBE YOU'RE NOT SAYING IT THE RIGHT WAY.
HE REFUSES TO EVEN GET INTO SUCH DISCUS-SIONS. HE THINKS IT'S A WASTE OF TIME.
RAGH
RAGH
RAGH
RAGH
OH, I ALWAYS DEFER TO HIM. SOME-TIMES TOO MUCH.

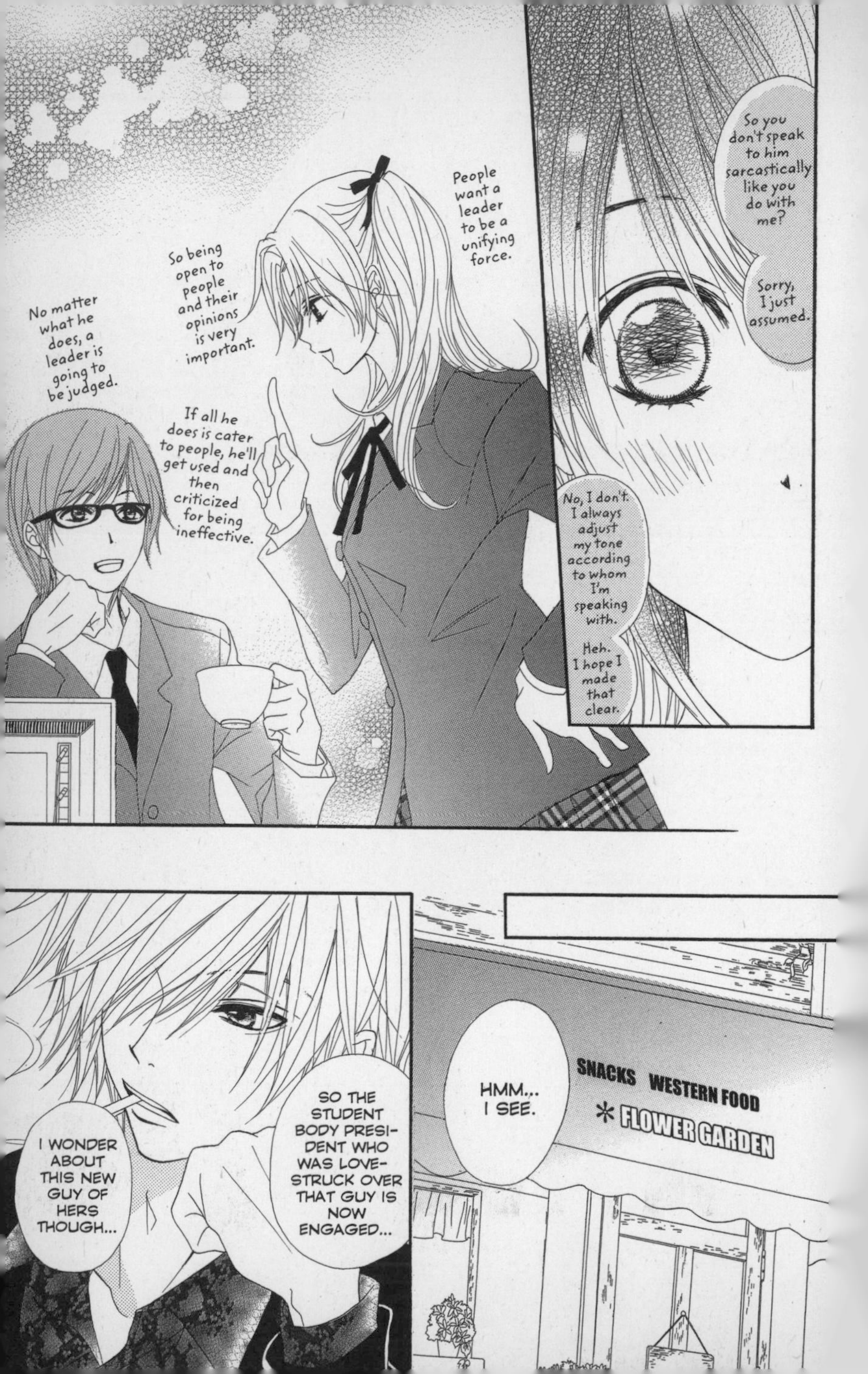
So you don't speak to him sarcastically like you do with me?
Sorry, I just assumed.
No, I don't. I always adjust my tone according to whom I'm speaking with.
Heh. I hope I made that clear.
People want a leader to be a unifying force.
So being open to people and their opinions is very important.
No matter what he does, a leader is going to be judged.
If all he does is cater to people, he'll get used and then criticized for being ineffective.
SNACKS WESTERN FOOD
* FLOWER GARDEN
HMM... I SEE.
SO THE STUDENT BODY PRESI-DENT WHO WAS LOVE-STRUCK OVER THAT GUY IS NOW ENGAGED...
I WONDER ABOUT THIS NEW GUY OF HERS THOUGH...

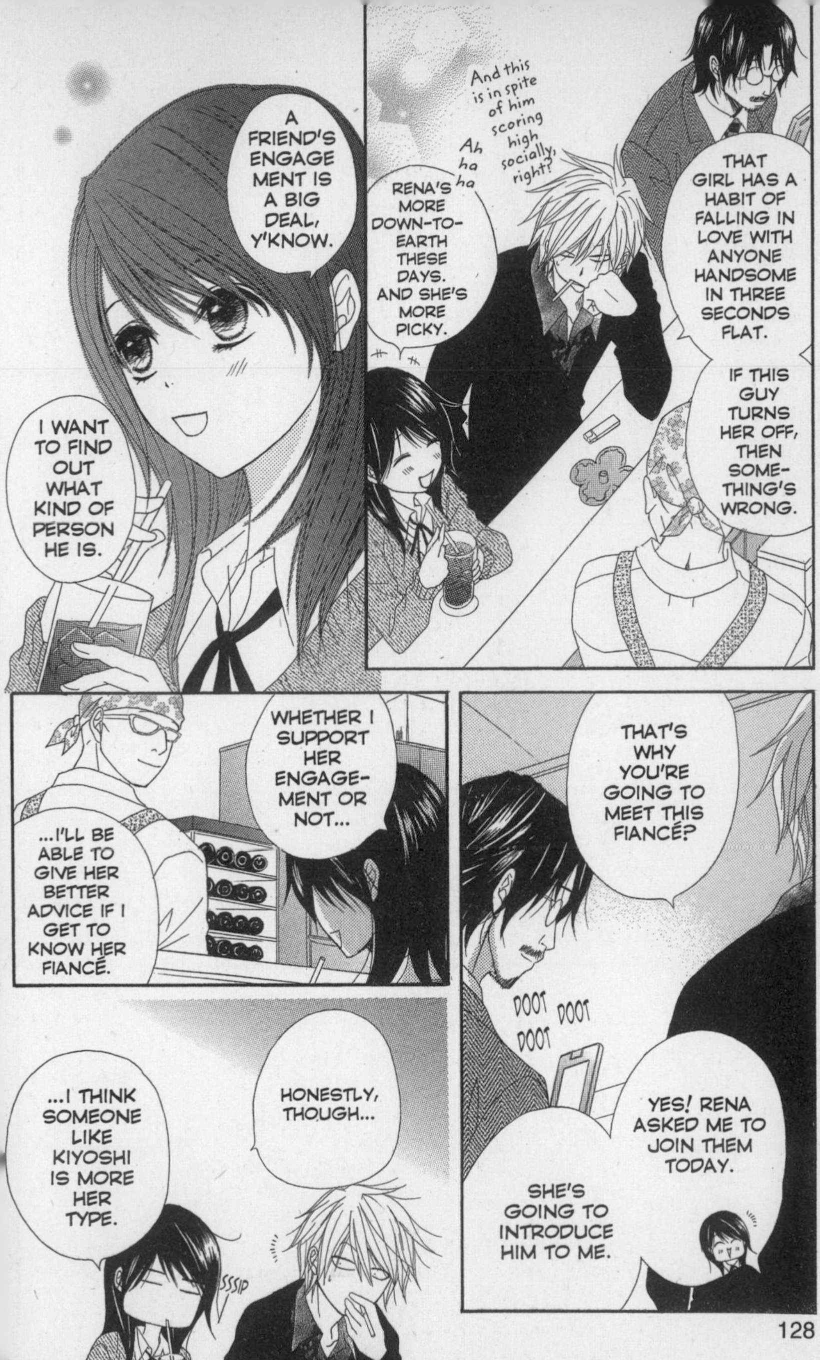
THAT GIRL HAS A HABIT OF FALLING IN LOVE WITH ANYONE HANDSOME IN THREE SECONDS FLAT.
And this is in spite of him scoring high socially, right?
Ah ha ha
RENA'S MORE DOWN-TO-EARTH THESE DAYS. AND SHE'S MORE PICKY.
IF THIS GUY TURNS HER OFF, THEN SOMETHING'S WRONG.
A FRIEND'S ENGAGEMENT IS A BIG DEAL, Y'KNOW.
I WANT TO FIND OUT WHAT KIND OF PERSON HE IS.
THAT'S WHY YOU'RE GOING TO MEET THIS FIANCÉ?
DOOT DOOT DOOT
YES! RENA ASKED ME TO JOIN THEM TODAY.
SHE'S GOING TO INTRODUCE HIM TO ME.
WHETHER I SUPPORT HER ENGAGEMENT OR NOT...
...I'LL BE ABLE TO GIVE HER BETTER ADVICE IF I GET TO KNOW HER FIANCÉ.
HONESTLY, THOUGH...
...I THINK SOMEONE LIKE KIYOSHI IS MORE HER TYPE.
SSSIP

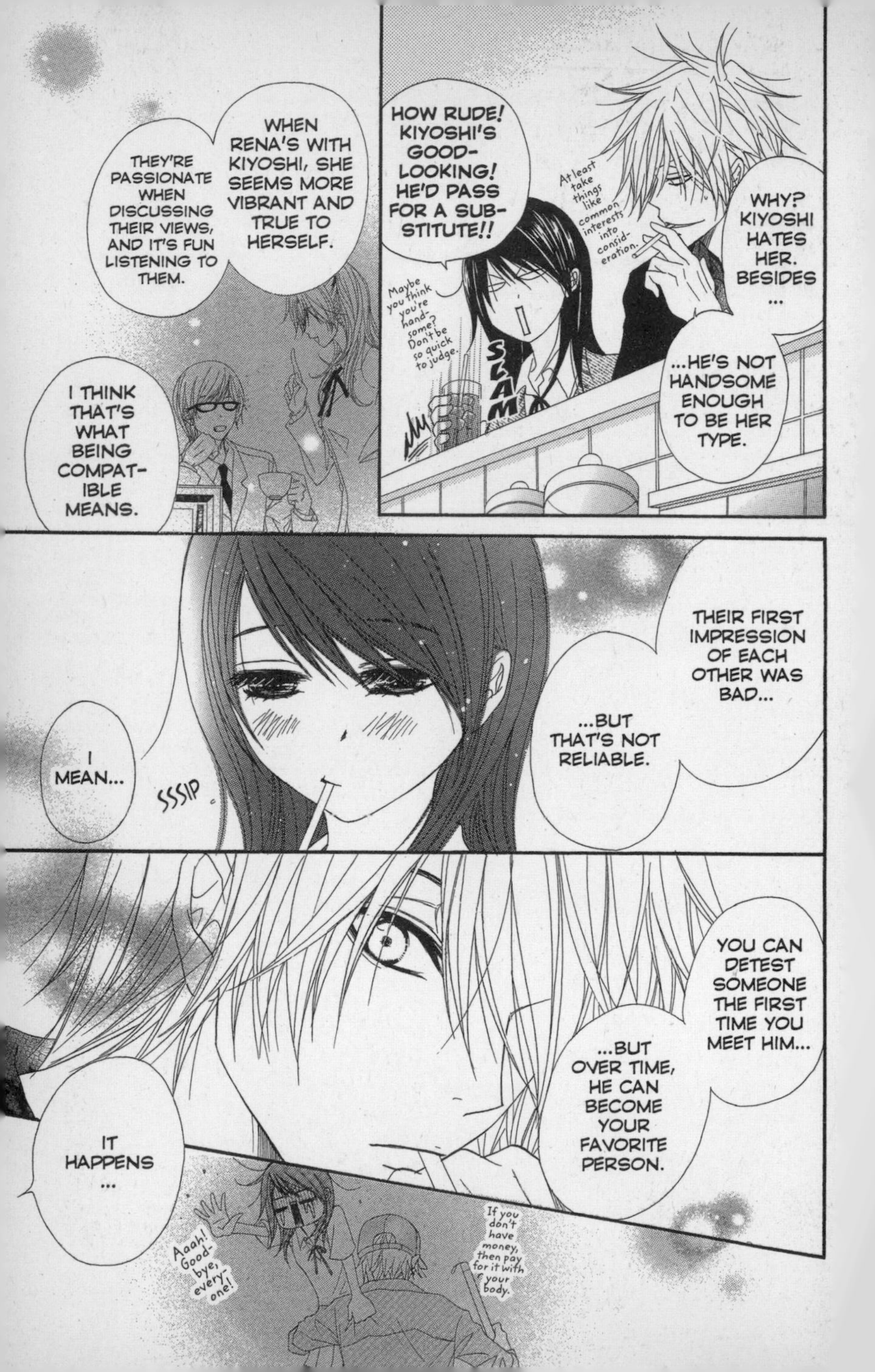
WHY? KIYOSHI HATES HER. BESIDES...
...HE'S NOT HANDSOME ENOUGH TO BE HER TYPE.
At least take things like common interests into consideration.
HOW RUDE! KIYOSHI'S GOOD-LOOKING! HE'D PASS FOR A SUB-STITUTE!!
Maybe you think you're hand-some? Don't be so quick to judge.
SLAM
WHEN RENA'S WITH KIYOSHI, SHE SEEMS MORE VIBRANT AND TRUE TO HERSELF.
THEY'RE PASSIONATE WHEN DISCUSSING THEIR VIEWS, AND IT'S FUN LISTENING TO THEM.
I THINK THAT'S WHAT BEING COMPAT-IBLE MEANS.
THEIR FIRST IMPRESSION OF EACH OTHER WAS BAD...
...BUT THAT'S NOT RELIABLE.
SSSIP
I MEAN...
YOU CAN DETEST SOMEONE THE FIRST TIME YOU MEET HIM...
...BUT OVER TIME, HE CAN BECOME YOUR FAVORITE PERSON.
IT HAPPENS...
If you don't have money, then pay for it with your body.
Aaah! Good-bye, every-one!

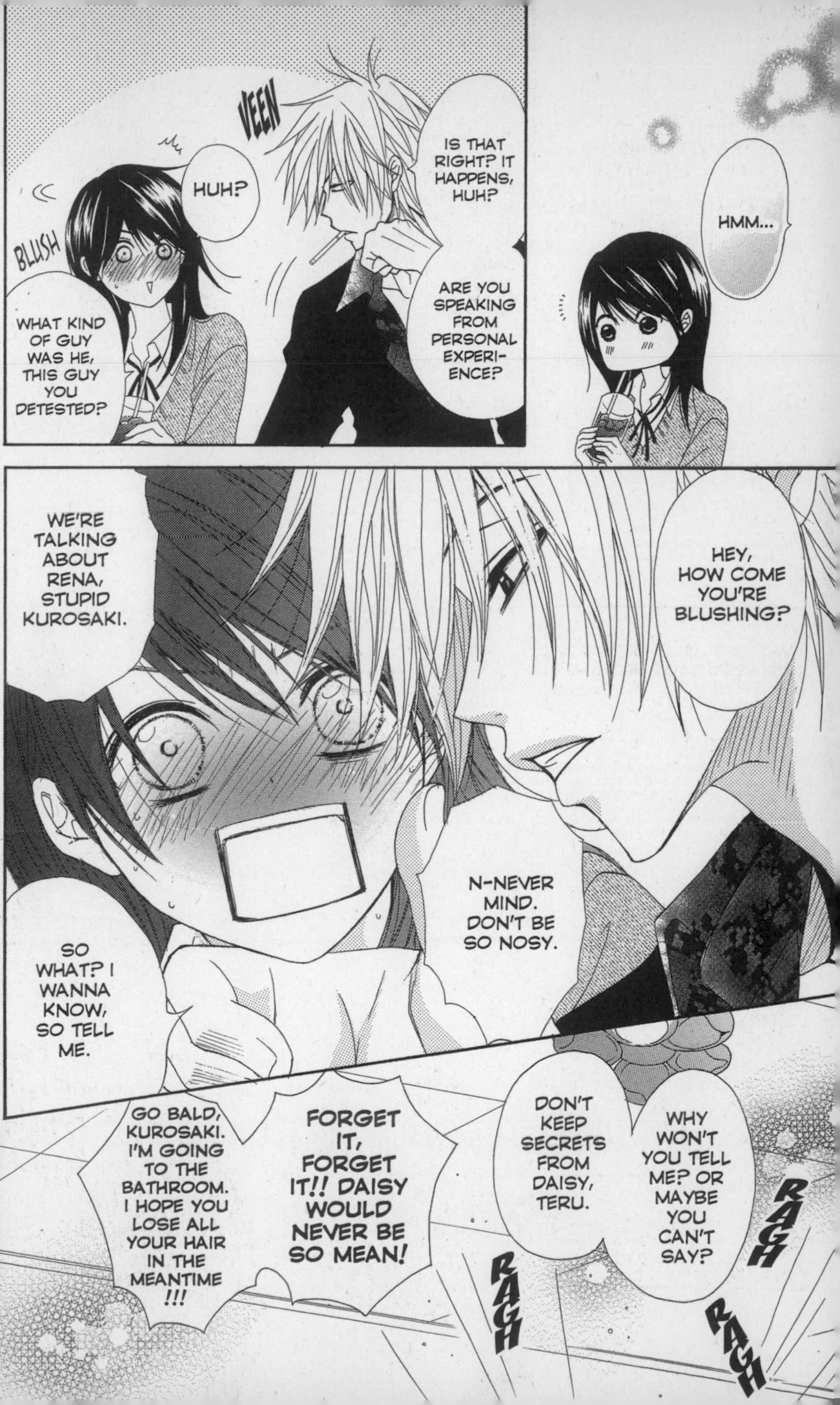
HMM...
IS THAT RIGHT? IT HAPPENS, HUH?
VEEN
HUH?
ARE YOU SPEAKING FROM PERSONAL EXPERIENCE?
BLUSH
WHAT KIND OF GUY WAS HE, THIS GUY YOU DETESTED?
HEY, HOW COME YOU'RE BLUSHING?
WE'RE TALKING ABOUT RENA, STUPID KUROSAKI.
N-NEVER MIND. DON'T BE SO NOSY.
SO WHAT? I WANNA KNOW, SO TELL ME.
WHY WON'T YOU TELL ME? OR MAYBE YOU CAN'T SAY?
RAGH
RAGH
DON'T KEEP SECRETS FROM DAISY, TERU.
RAGH
FORGET IT, FORGET IT!! DAISY WOULD NEVER BE SO MEAN!
GO BALD, KUROSAKI. I'M GOING TO THE BATHROOM. I HOPE YOU LOSE ALL YOUR HAIR IN THE MEANTIME!!!

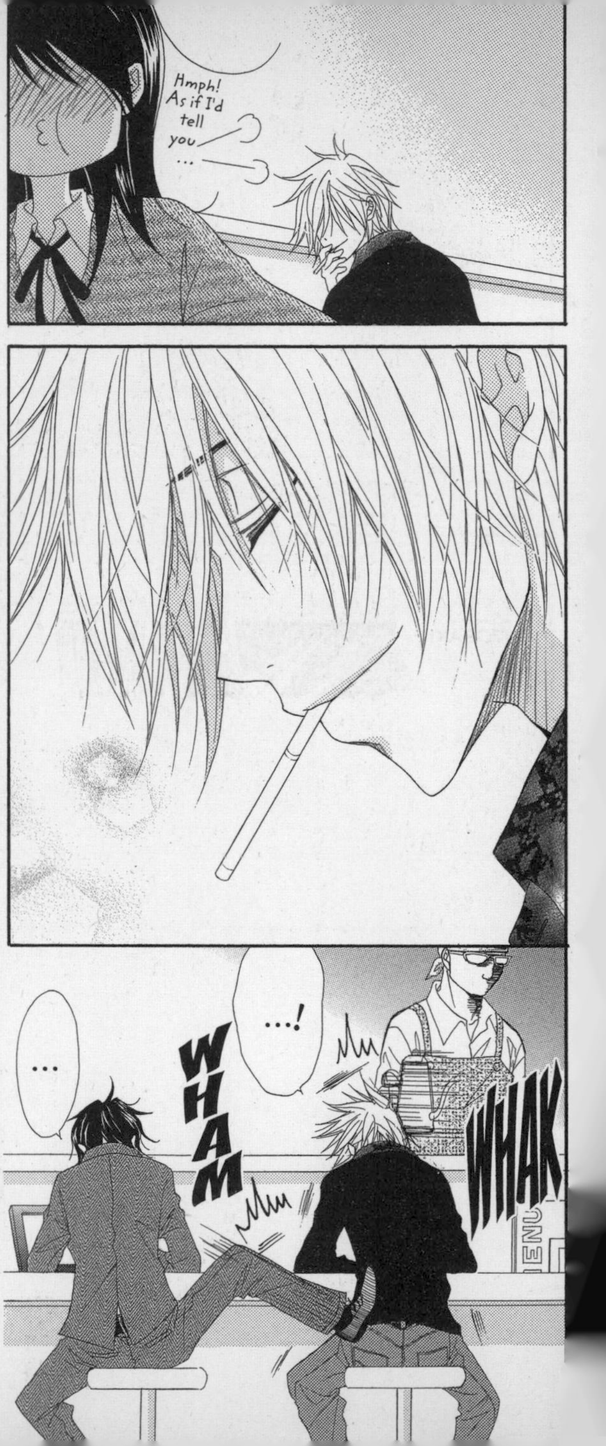
Hmph! As if I'd tell you...
WHAK
Mu
...!
WHAM
Mu
...

DENGEKI DAISY
QUESTION CORNER

BALDLY ASK!!

④

Q.
I THOUGHT ABOUT THIS AFTER SEEING KUROSAKI CLEAN THE ROOFTOP IN THE RAIN IN VOLUME 4. DOES THE PERVERT HAVE A THING WITH NECKS IN ADDITION TO LIKING TINY BREASTS? AND WHAT IS TERU'S FETISH?

(A.F., OSAKA PREFECTURE)

A.
WELL, LET'S SEE. A FETISH FOR TINY BREASTS AND NECKS. HE LIKES EARS, TOO. AND HE LIKES PANTIES AND SCHOOL SWIMSUITS A LOT. AS FOR TERU, IT'S NOT QUITE A FETISH, BUT IT SEEMS SHE HAS A TENDENCY TO STARE AT KUROSAKI'S ADAM'S APPLE. WHILE NO ONE HAS ASKED, THIS AUTHOR LIKES "THE ARM JOINT OF A SLENDER MAN WHERE IT BULGES AND FEELS SOLID," BUT PEOPLE TELL ME THEY DON'T UNDERSTAND WHAT KIND OF INTEREST THAT IS. A LOT OF PEOPLE AROUND ME LIKE MEN'S BUTTOCKS. I GUESS THERE ARE MANY KINDS OF FETISHES.

Q.
IN VOLUME 2, PAGE 40, KUROSAKI'S HAND IS DEFINITELY TOUCHING TERU'S CHEST. (HIS THUMB IS ESPECIALLY SUSPECT.) AT THAT TIME, WAS KUROSAKI THINKNG, "OOPS, I DID IT"?

(MISAKI@, MIYAGI PREFECTURE)

A.
WELL...IT'S PRETTY OBVIOUS FROM THE SMIRK ON HIS FACE THAT THIS WAS PREMEDITATED. TO BE HONEST, THE AUTHOR REGRETS THIS.

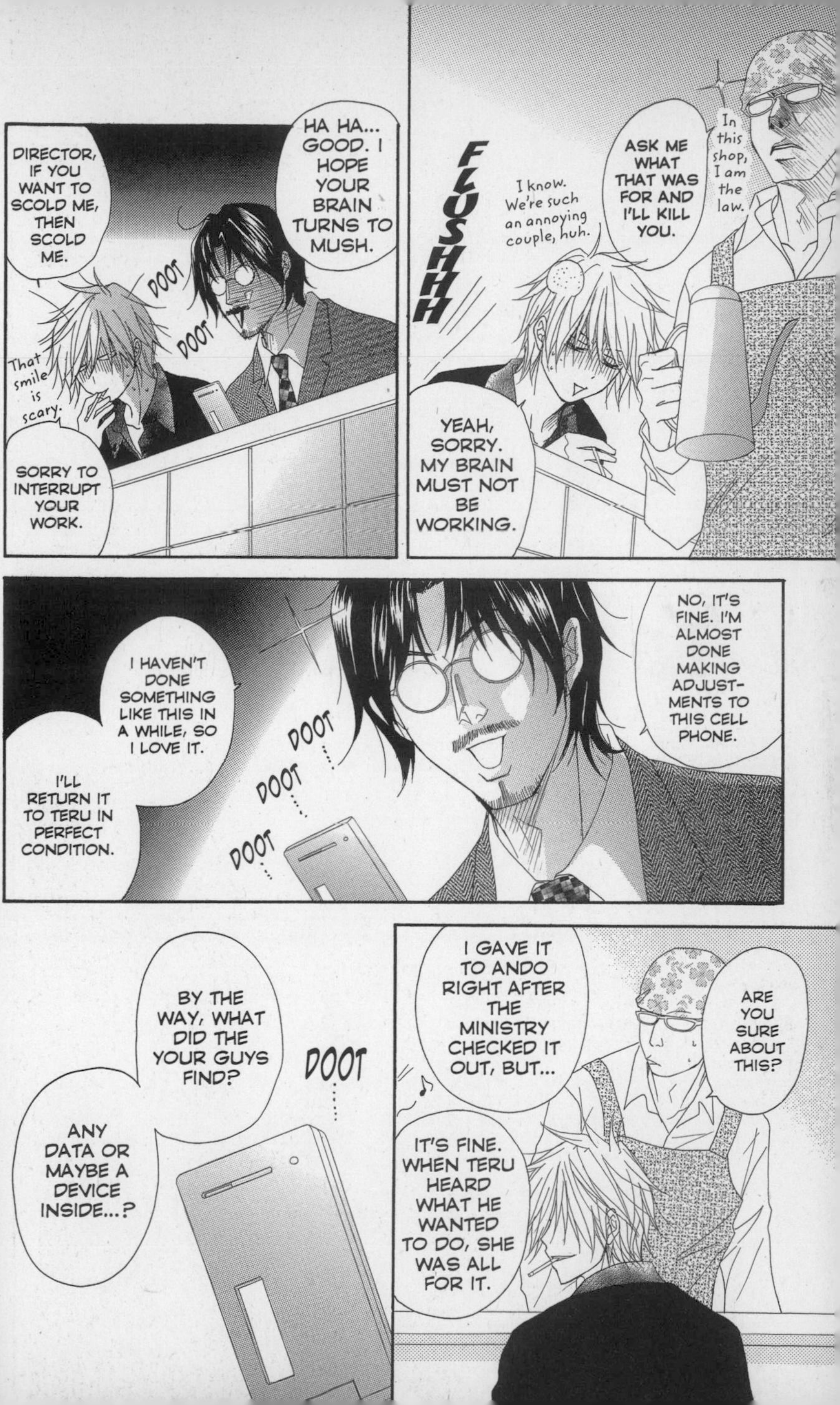
In this shop, I am the law.
ASK ME WHAT THAT WAS FOR AND I'LL KILL YOU.
FLUSHHH
I know. We're such an annoying couple, huh.
YEAH, SORRY. MY BRAIN MUST NOT BE WORKING.
HA HA... GOOD. I HOPE YOUR BRAIN TURNS TO MUSH.
DIRECTOR, IF YOU WANT TO SCOLD ME, THEN SCOLD ME.
DOOT
DOOT
That smile is scary.
SORRY TO INTERRUPT YOUR WORK.
NO, IT'S FINE. I'M ALMOST DONE MAKING ADJUST-MENTS TO THIS CELL PHONE.
DOOT...
DOOT...
DOOT...
I HAVEN'T DONE SOMETHING LIKE THIS IN A WHILE, SO I LOVE IT.
I'LL RETURN IT TO TERU IN PERFECT CONDITION.
ARE YOU SURE ABOUT THIS?
I GAVE IT TO ANDO RIGHT AFTER THE MINISTRY CHECKED IT OUT, BUT...
IT'S FINE. WHEN TERU HEARD WHAT HE WANTED TO DO, SHE WAS ALL FOR IT.
BY THE WAY, WHAT DID THE YOUR GUYS FIND?
DOOT...
ANY DATA OR MAYBE A DEVICE INSIDE...?

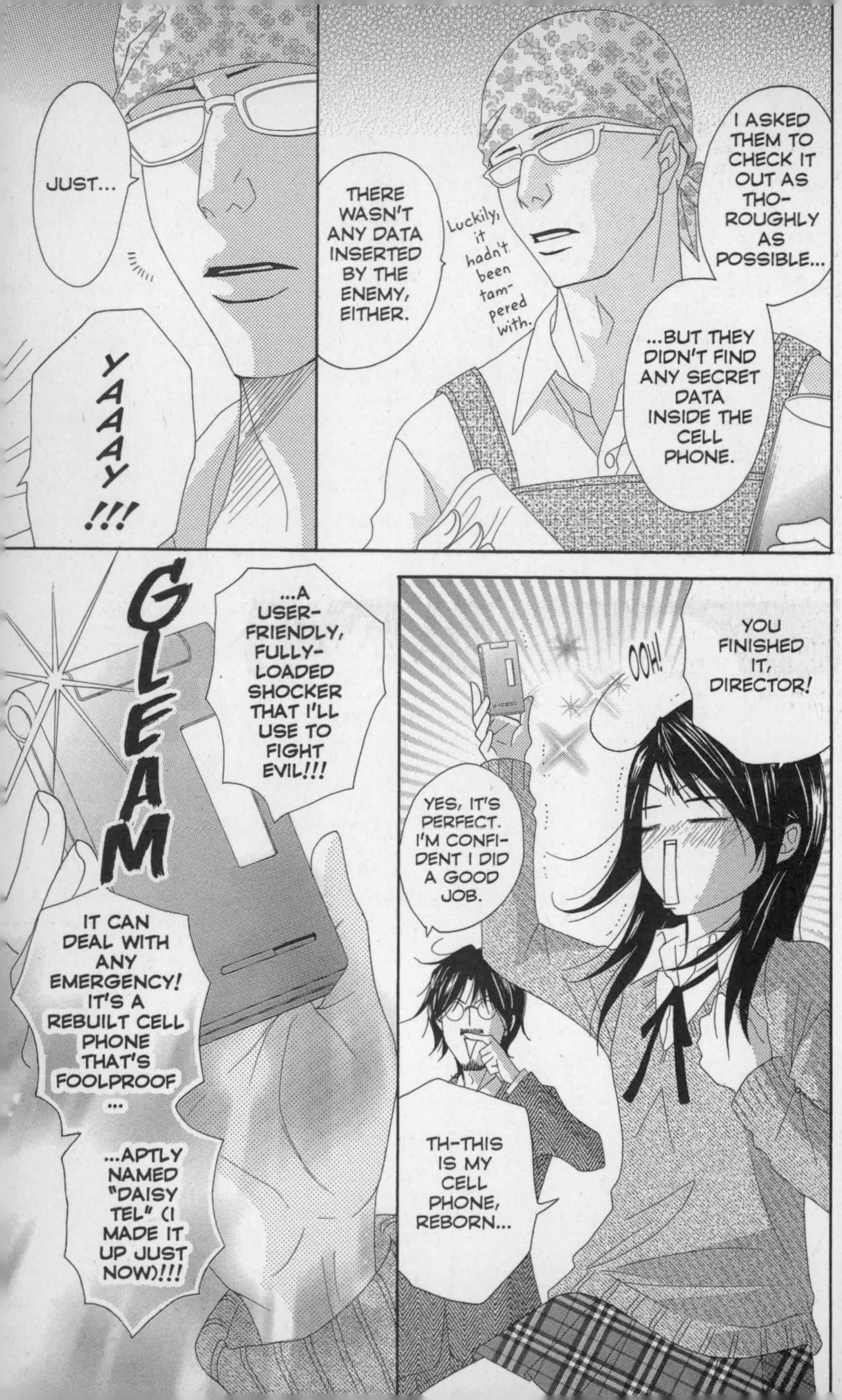
I ASKED THEM TO CHECK IT OUT AS THO-ROUGHLY AS POSSIBLE...
...BUT THEY DIDN'T FIND ANY SECRET DATA INSIDE THE CELL PHONE.
THERE WASN'T ANY DATA INSERTED BY THE ENEMY, EITHER.
Luckily, it hadn't been tam-pered with.
JUST...
YAAAAY!!!
YOU FINISHED IT, DIRECTOR!
OOH!
YES, IT'S PERFECT. I'M CONFI-DENT I DID A GOOD JOB.
TH-THIS IS MY CELL PHONE, REBORN...
...A USER-FRIENDLY, FULLY-LOADED SHOCKER THAT I'LL USE TO FIGHT EVIL!!!
GLEAM
IT CAN DEAL WITH ANY EMERGENCY! IT'S A REBUILT CELL PHONE THAT'S FOOLPROOF ...
...APTLY NAMED "DAISY TEL" (I MADE IT UP JUST NOW)!!!

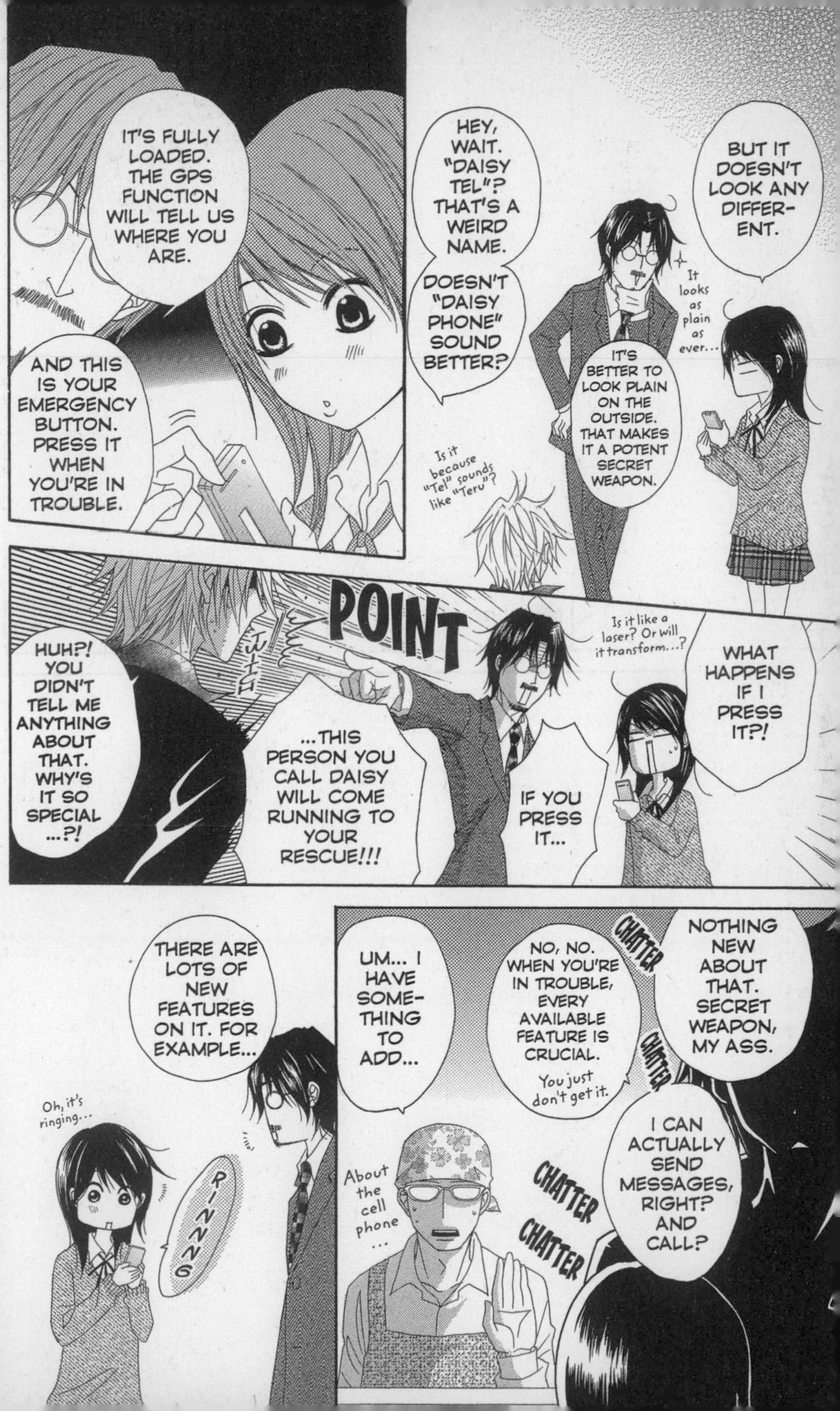

BUT IT DOESN'T LOOK ANY DIFFER-ENT.
It looks as plain as ever...
HEY, WAIT. "DAISY TEL"? THAT'S A WEIRD NAME.
DOESN'T "DAISY PHONE" SOUND BETTER?
IT'S BETTER TO LOOK PLAIN ON THE OUTSIDE. THAT MAKES IT A POTENT SECRET WEAPON.
Is it because "Tel" sounds like "Teru"?
IT'S FULLY LOADED. THE GPS FUNCTION WILL TELL US WHERE YOU ARE.
AND THIS IS YOUR EMERGENCY BUTTON. PRESS IT WHEN YOU'RE IN TROUBLE.
WHAT HAPPENS IF I PRESS IT?!
Is it like a laser? Or will it transform...?
IF YOU PRESS IT...
POINT
...THIS PERSON YOU CALL DAISY WILL COME RUNNING TO YOUR RESCUE!!!
HUH?! YOU DIDN'T TELL ME ANYTHING ABOUT THAT. WHY'S IT SO SPECIAL ...?!
NOTHING NEW ABOUT THAT. SECRET WEAPON, MY ASS.
CHATTER
CHATTER
I CAN ACTUALLY SEND MESSAGES, RIGHT? AND CALL?
NO, NO. WHEN YOU'RE IN TROUBLE, EVERY AVAILABLE FEATURE IS CRUCIAL.
You just don't get it.
UM... I HAVE SOME-THING TO ADD...
About the cell phone ...
CHATTER
CHATTER
THERE ARE LOTS OF NEW FEATURES ON IT. FOR EXAMPLE...
Oh, it's ringing...
RINNNG

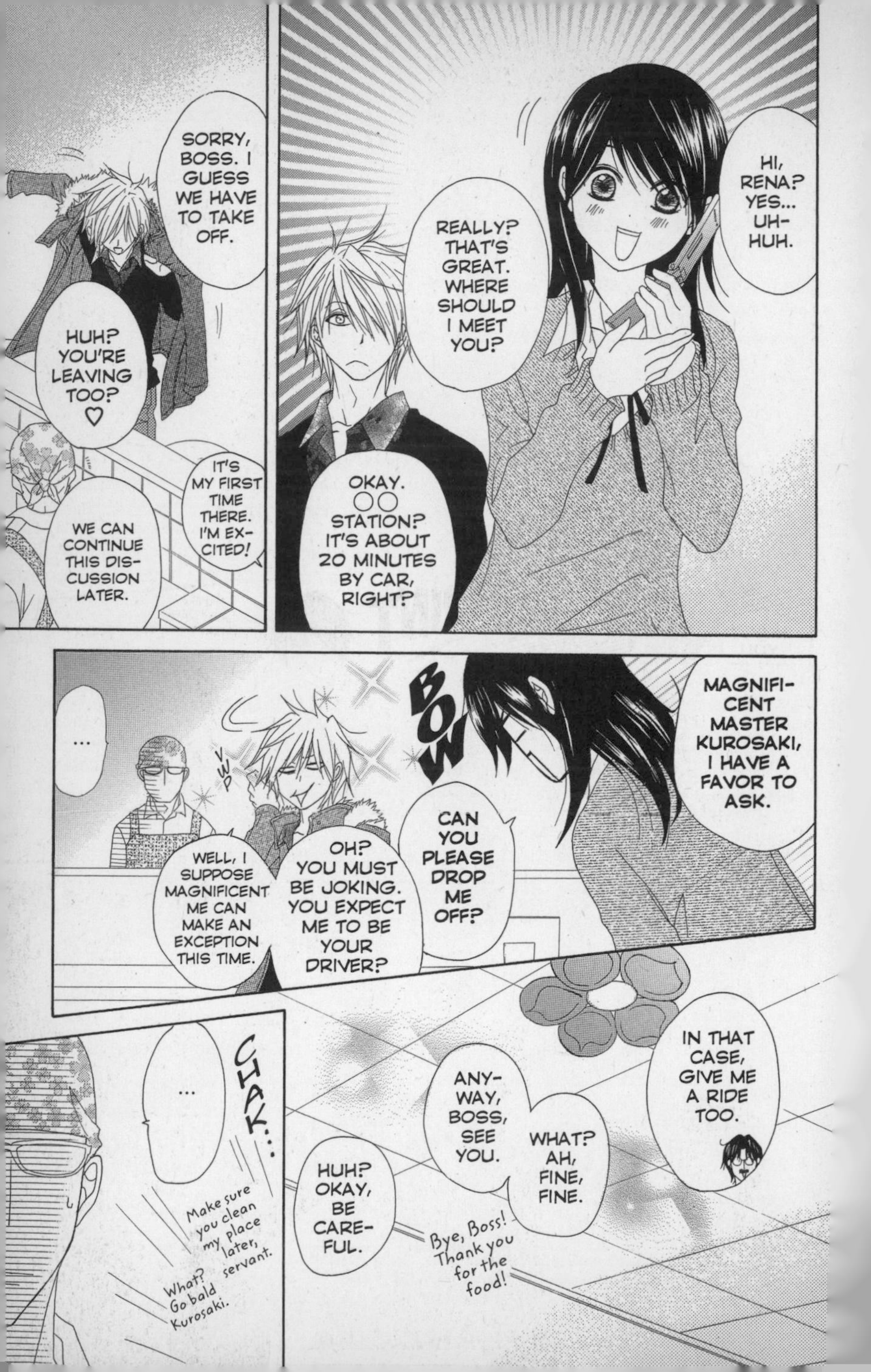
HI, RENA? YES... UH-HUH.
REALLY? THAT'S GREAT. WHERE SHOULD I MEET YOU?
OKAY. ○○ STATION? IT'S ABOUT 20 MINUTES BY CAR, RIGHT?
SORRY, BOSS. I GUESS WE HAVE TO TAKE OFF.
HUH? YOU'RE LEAVING TOO? ♡
IT'S MY FIRST TIME THERE. I'M EXCITED!
WE CAN CONTINUE THIS DISCUSSION LATER.
MAGNIFICENT MASTER KUROSAKI, I HAVE A FAVOR TO ASK.
BOW
CAN YOU PLEASE DROP ME OFF?
OH? YOU MUST BE JOKING. YOU EXPECT ME TO BE YOUR DRIVER?
VWP
WELL, I SUPPOSE MAGNIFICENT ME CAN MAKE AN EXCEPTION THIS TIME.
...
IN THAT CASE, GIVE ME A RIDE TOO.
WHAT? AH, FINE, FINE.
ANYWAY, BOSS, SEE YOU.
Bye, Boss! Thank you for the food!
HUH? OKAY, BE CAREFUL.
Make sure you clean my place later, servant.
What? Go bald Kurosaki.
CHAK...
...

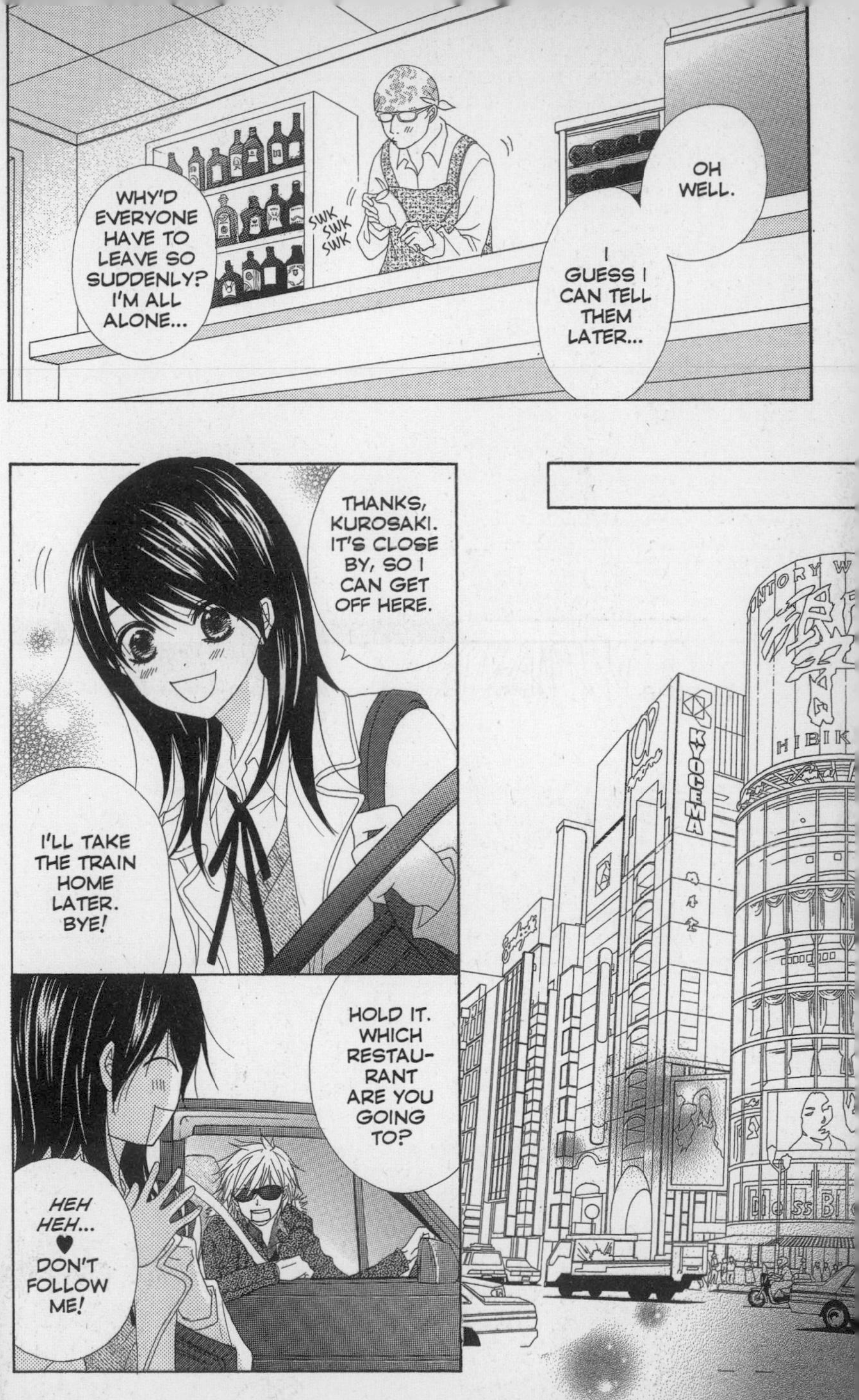
OH WELL.
I GUESS I CAN TELL THEM LATER...
SWK SWK SWK
WHY'D EVERYONE HAVE TO LEAVE SO SUDDENLY? I'M ALL ALONE...
THANKS, KUROSAKI. IT'S CLOSE BY, SO I CAN GET OFF HERE.
I'LL TAKE THE TRAIN HOME LATER. BYE!
HOLD IT. WHICH RESTAU-RANT ARE YOU GOING TO?
HEH HEH... ♥ DON'T FOLLOW ME!

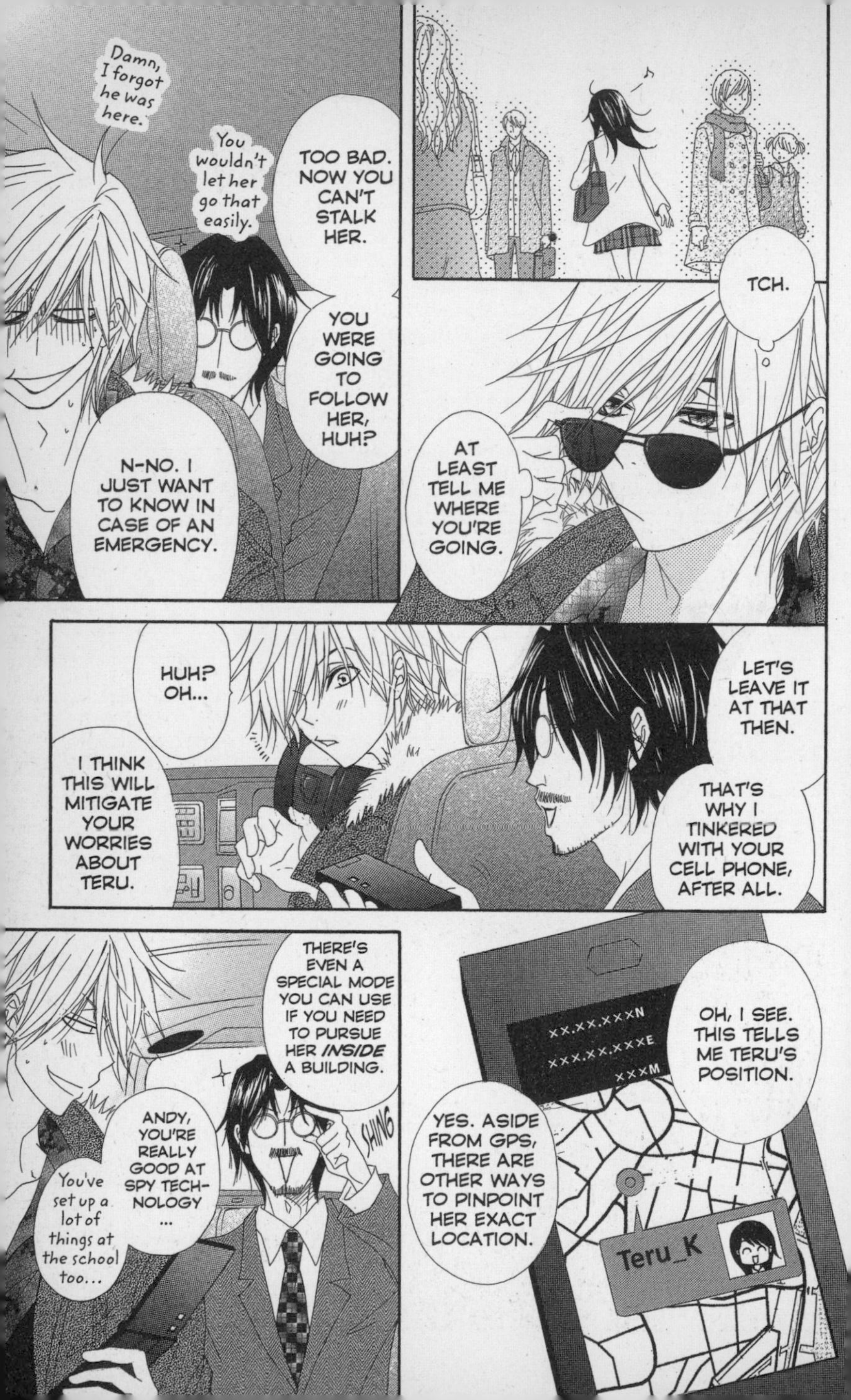
♪
TCH.
AT LEAST TELL ME WHERE YOU'RE GOING.
TOO BAD. NOW YOU CAN'T STALK HER.
YOU WERE GOING TO FOLLOW HER, HUH?
N-NO. I JUST WANT TO KNOW IN CASE OF AN EMERGENCY.
You wouldn't let her go that easily.
Damn, I forgot he was here.
LET'S LEAVE IT AT THAT THEN.
HUH? OH...
I THINK THIS WILL MITIGATE YOUR WORRIES ABOUT TERU.
THAT'S WHY I TINKERED WITH YOUR CELL PHONE, AFTER ALL.
xx.xx.xxxN
xxx.xx.xxxE
xxxM
Teru_K
OH, I SEE. THIS TELLS ME TERU'S POSITION.
YES. ASIDE FROM GPS, THERE ARE OTHER WAYS TO PINPOINT HER EXACT LOCATION.
THERE'S EVEN A SPECIAL MODE YOU CAN USE IF YOU NEED TO PURSUE HER *INSIDE* A BUILDING.
SHING
ANDY, YOU'RE REALLY GOOD AT SPY TECH-NOLOGY ...
You've set up a lot of things at the school too...

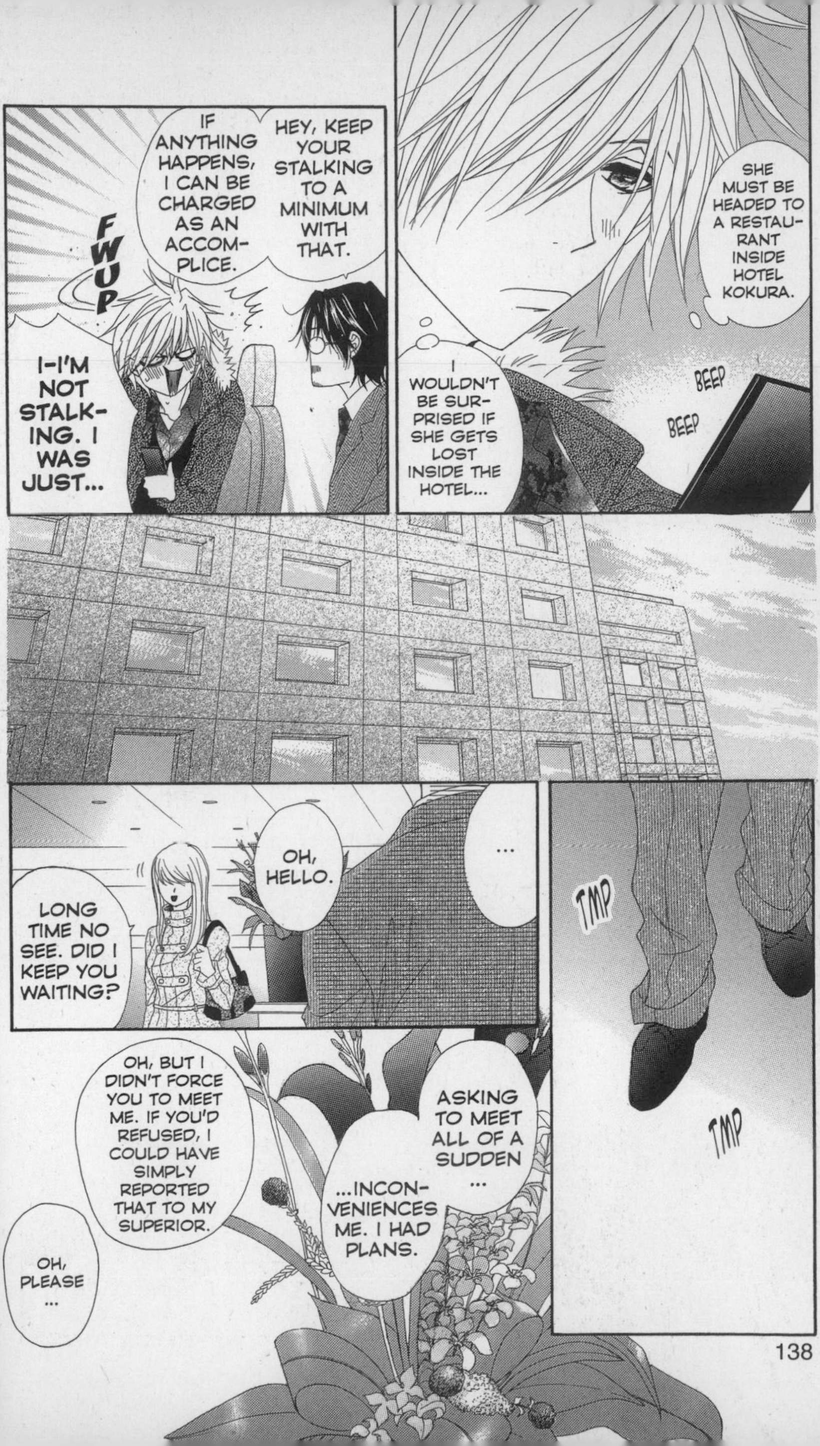
SHE MUST BE HEADED TO A RESTAURANT INSIDE HOTEL KOKURA.
BEEP
BEEP
I WOULDN'T BE SURPRISED IF SHE GETS LOST INSIDE THE HOTEL...
HEY, KEEP YOUR STALKING TO A MINIMUM WITH THAT.
IF ANYTHING HAPPENS, I CAN BE CHARGED AS AN ACCOMPLICE.
FWUP
I-I'M NOT STALKING. I WAS JUST...
TMP
TMP
...
OH, HELLO.
LONG TIME NO SEE. DID I KEEP YOU WAITING?
ASKING TO MEET ALL OF A SUDDEN ...
...INCONVENIENCES ME. I HAD PLANS.
OH, BUT I DIDN'T FORCE YOU TO MEET ME. IF YOU'D REFUSED, I COULD HAVE SIMPLY REPORTED THAT TO MY SUPERIOR.
OH, PLEASE ...

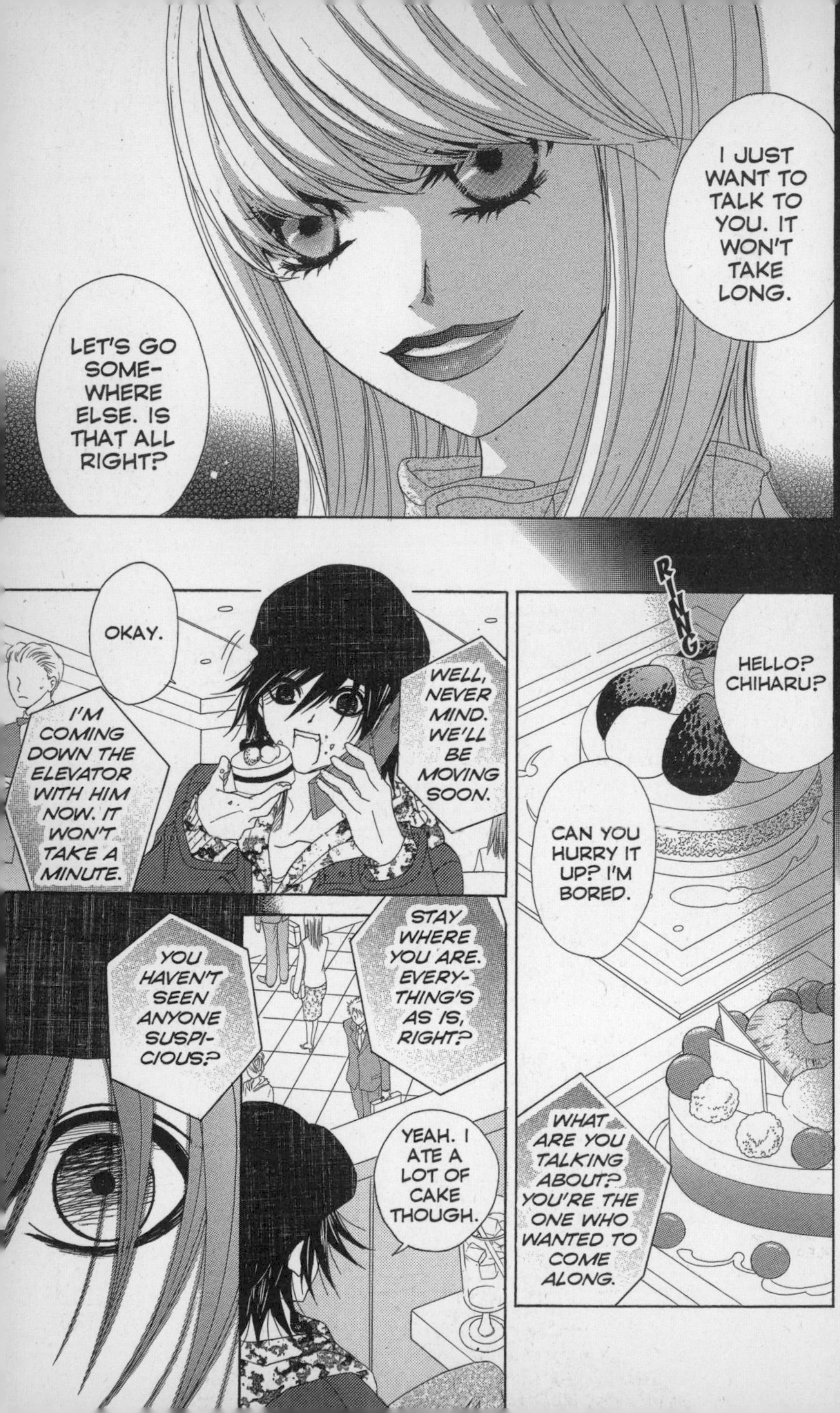
I JUST WANT TO TALK TO YOU. IT WON'T TAKE LONG.
LET'S GO SOME-WHERE ELSE. IS THAT ALL RIGHT?
RING
HELLO? CHIHARU?
CAN YOU HURRY IT UP? I'M BORED.
WHAT ARE YOU TALKING ABOUT? YOU'RE THE ONE WHO WANTED TO COME ALONG.
OKAY.
WELL, NEVER MIND. WE'LL BE MOVING SOON.
I'M COMING DOWN THE ELEVATOR WITH HIM NOW. IT WON'T TAKE A MINUTE.
STAY WHERE YOU ARE. EVERY-THING'S AS IS, RIGHT?
YOU HAVEN'T SEEN ANYONE SUSPI-CIOUS?
YEAH. I ATE A LOT OF CAKE THOUGH.

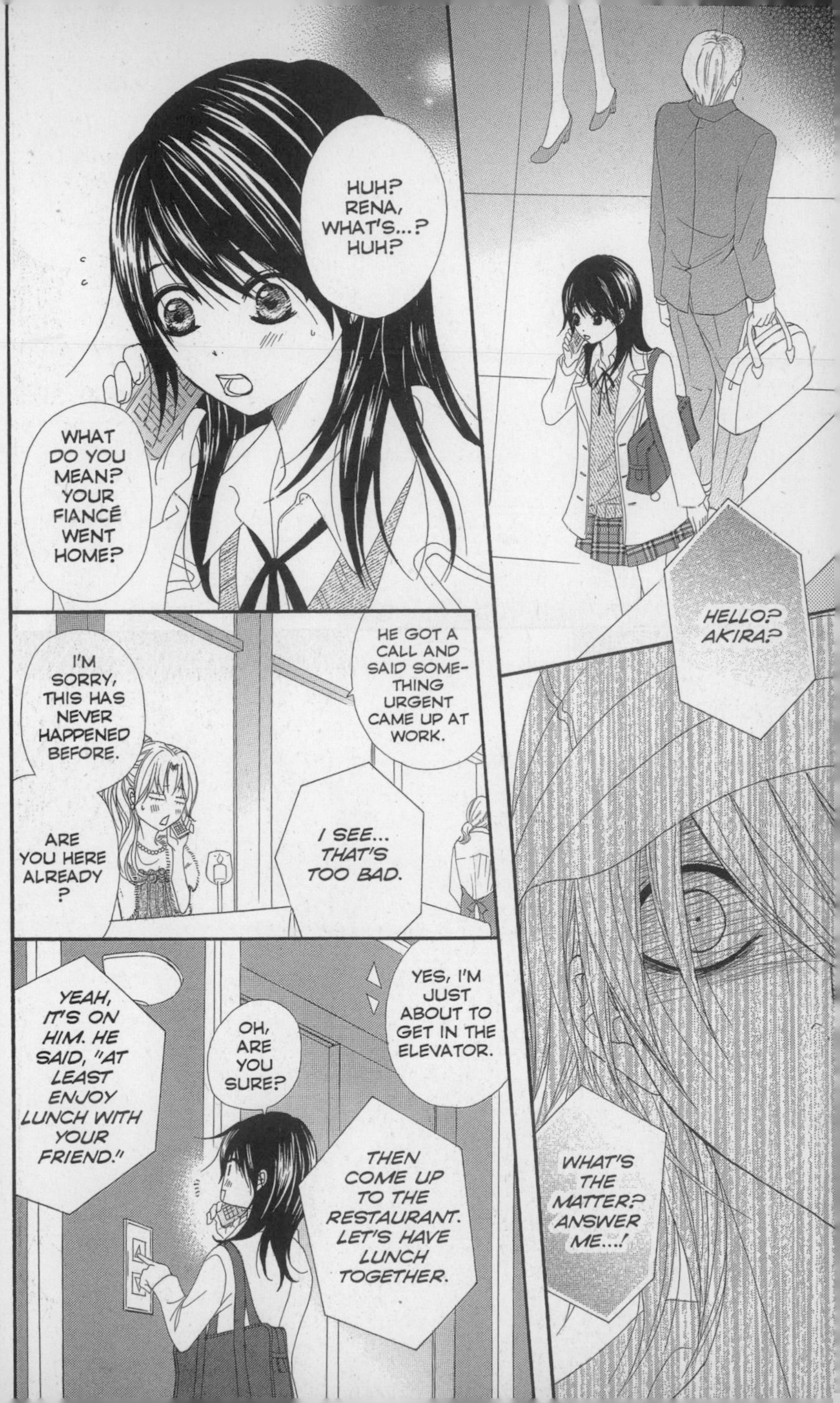
HELLO? AKIRA?
HUH? RENA, WHAT'S...? HUH?
WHAT DO YOU MEAN? YOUR FIANCÉ WENT HOME?
WHAT'S THE MATTER? ANSWER ME...!
HE GOT A CALL AND SAID SOME-THING URGENT CAME UP AT WORK.
I'M SORRY, THIS HAS NEVER HAPPENED BEFORE.
I SEE... THAT'S TOO BAD.
ARE YOU HERE ALREADY?
YES, I'M JUST ABOUT TO GET IN THE ELEVATOR.
OH, ARE YOU SURE?
YEAH, IT'S ON HIM. HE SAID, "AT LEAST ENJOY LUNCH WITH YOUR FRIEND."
THEN COME UP TO THE RESTAURANT. LET'S HAVE LUNCH TOGETHER.

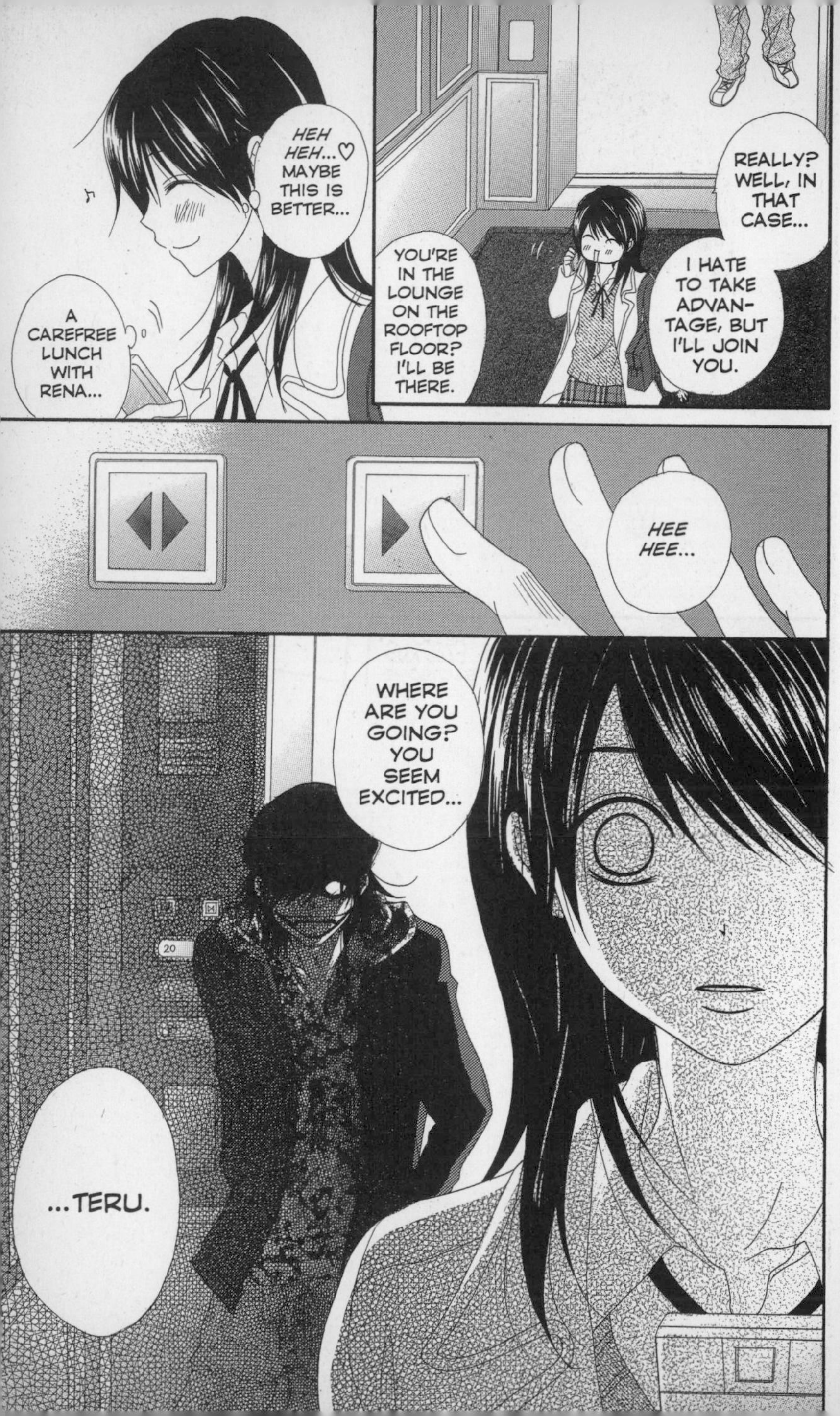
REALLY? WELL, IN THAT CASE...
I HATE TO TAKE ADVANTAGE, BUT I'LL JOIN YOU.
YOU'RE IN THE LOUNGE ON THE ROOFTOP FLOOR? I'LL BE THERE.
HEH HEH...♡ MAYBE THIS IS BETTER...
A CAREFREE LUNCH WITH RENA...
HEE HEE...
WHERE ARE YOU GOING? YOU SEEM EXCITED...
...TERU.

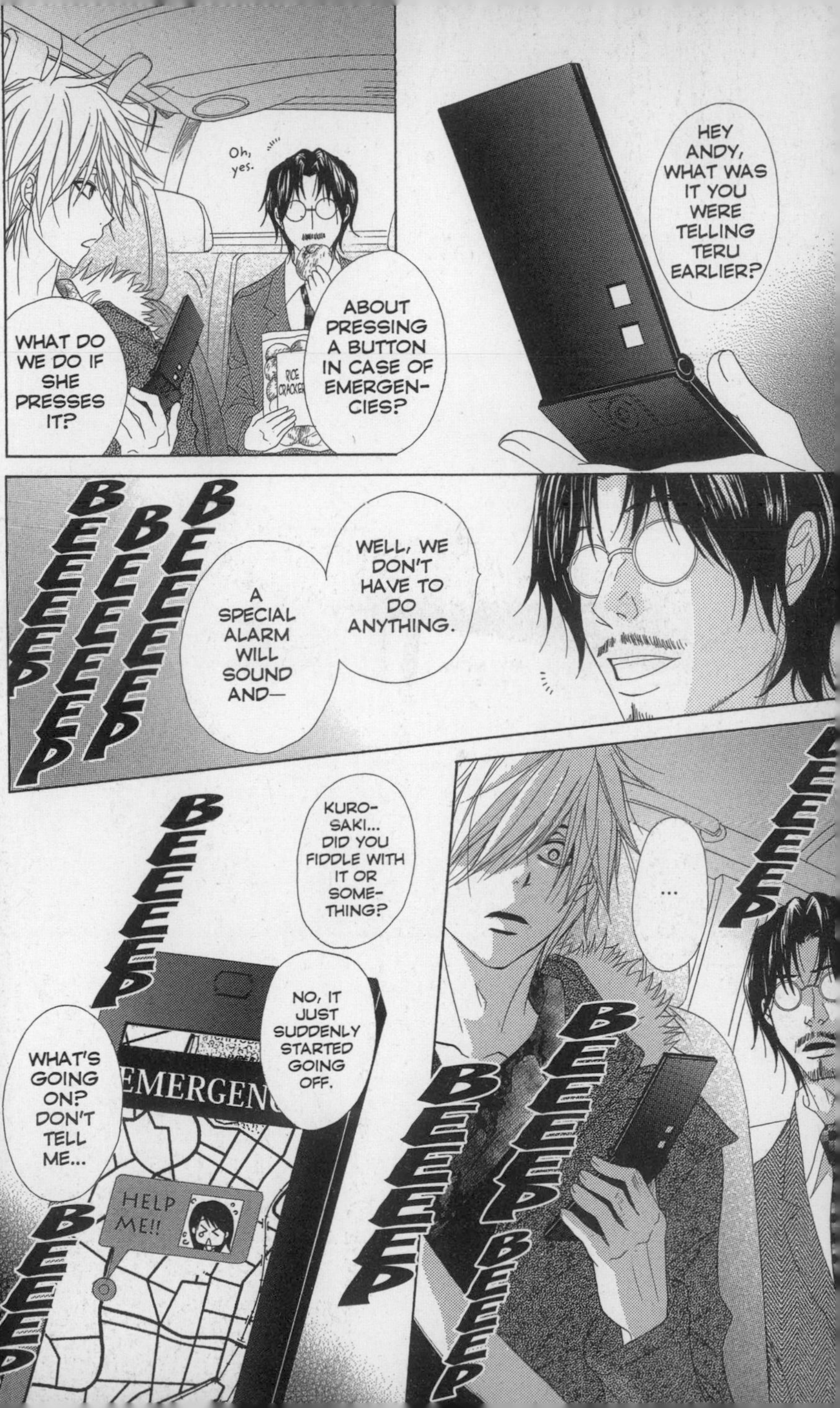
HEY ANDY, WHAT WAS IT YOU WERE TELLING TERU EARLIER?
Oh, yes.
ABOUT PRESSING A BUTTON IN CASE OF EMERGEN-CIES?
RICE CRACKERS
WHAT DO WE DO IF SHE PRESSES IT?
WELL, WE DON'T HAVE TO DO ANYTHING.
A SPECIAL ALARM WILL SOUND AND—
BEEEEEP
BEEEEEP
BEEEEEP
BEEEEEP
...
KURO-SAKI... DID YOU FIDDLE WITH IT OR SOME-THING?
BEEEEEP
BEEEEEP
BEEEEEP
NO, IT JUST SUDDENLY STARTED GOING OFF.
WHAT'S GOING ON? DON'T TELL ME...
EMERGENC
HELP ME!!
BEEEEP

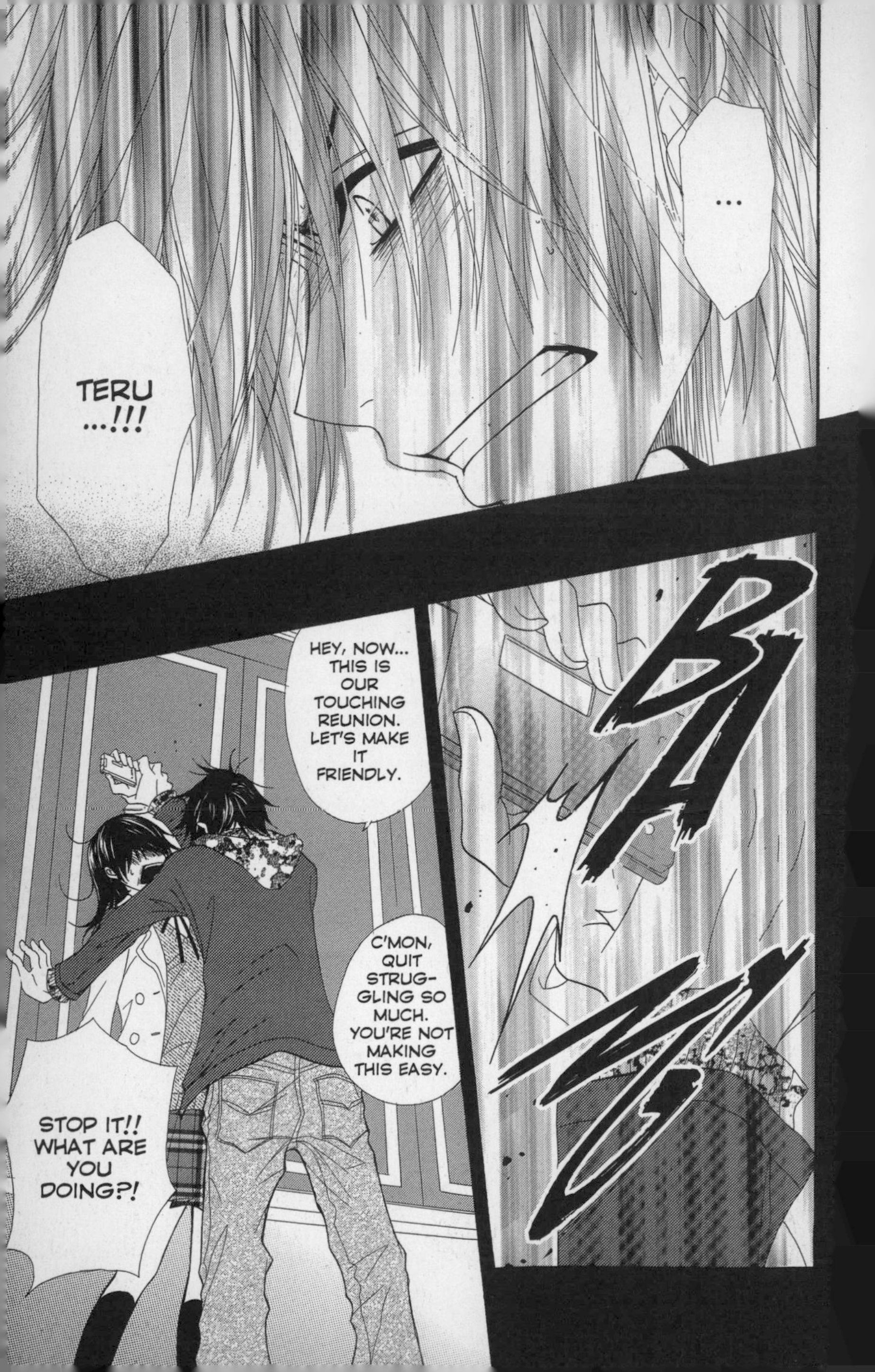
...
TERU ...!!!
BAM
HEY, NOW... THIS IS OUR TOUCHING REUNION. LET'S MAKE IT FRIENDLY.
C'MON, QUIT STRUG-GLING SO MUCH. YOU'RE NOT MAKING THIS EASY.
STOP IT!! WHAT ARE YOU DOING?!

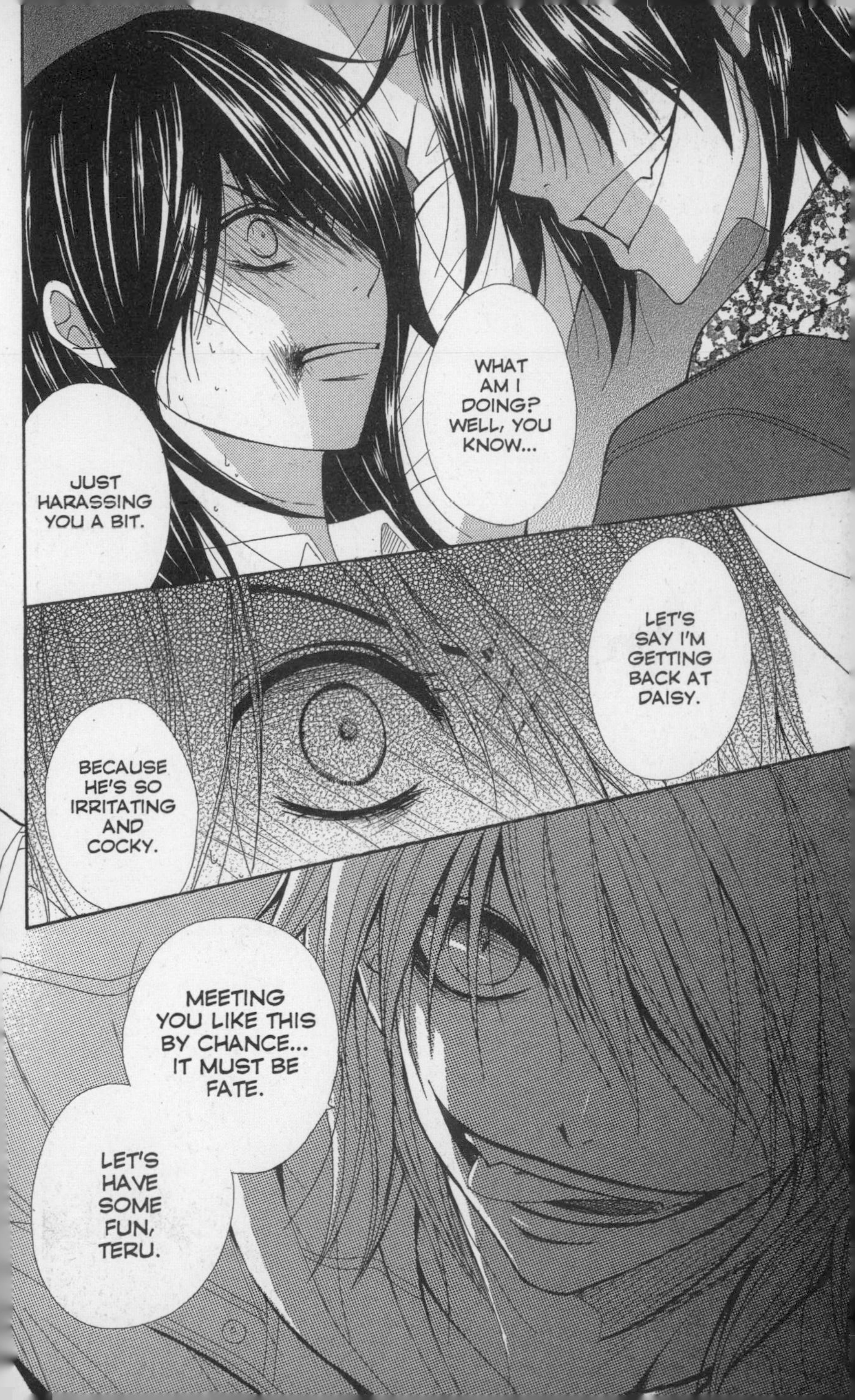
WHAT AM I DOING? WELL, YOU KNOW...
JUST HARASSING YOU A BIT.
LET'S SAY I'M GETTING BACK AT DAISY.
BECAUSE HE'S SO IRRITATING AND COCKY.
MEETING YOU LIKE THIS BY CHANCE... IT MUST BE FATE.
LET'S HAVE SOME FUN, TERU.

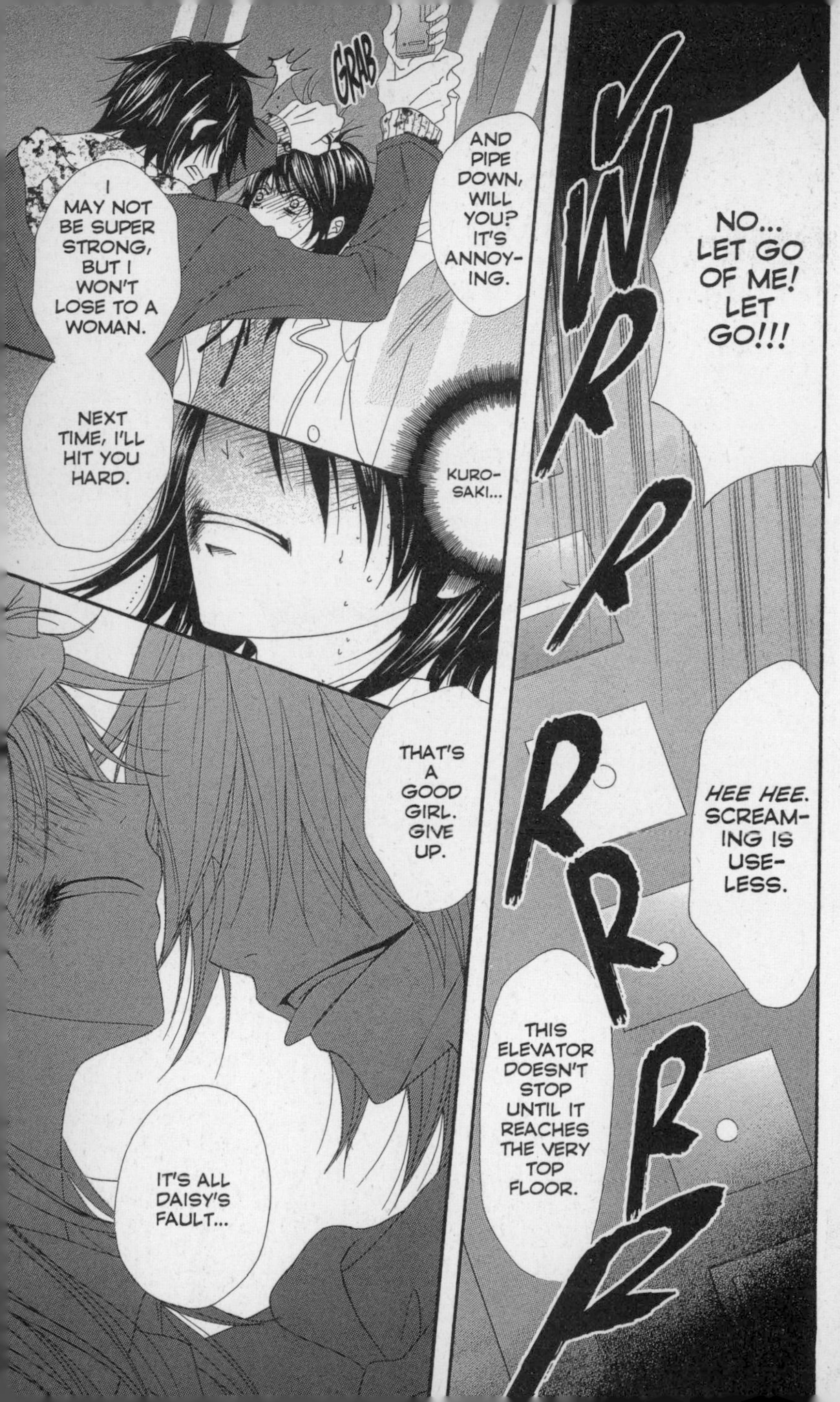
NO... LET GO OF ME! LET GO!!!
HEE HEE. SCREAMING IS USELESS.
THIS ELEVATOR DOESN'T STOP UNTIL IT REACHES THE VERY TOP FLOOR.
GRAB
AND PIPE DOWN, WILL YOU? IT'S ANNOYING.
I MAY NOT BE SUPER STRONG, BUT I WON'T LOSE TO A WOMAN.
NEXT TIME, I'LL HIT YOU HARD.
KUROSAKI...
THAT'S A GOOD GIRL. GIVE UP.
IT'S ALL DAISY'S FAULT...

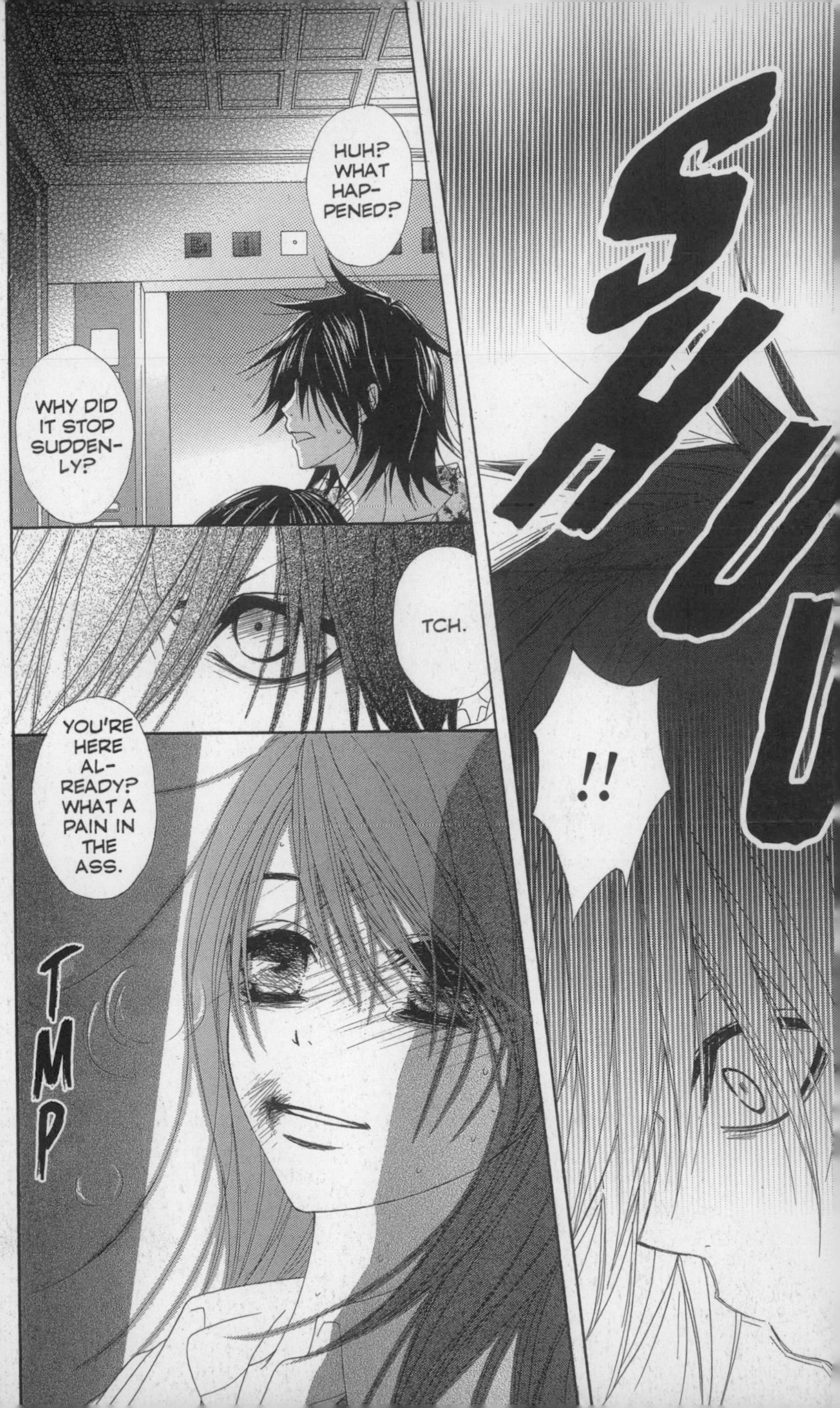
SHUUU
!!
HUH? WHAT HAP-PENED?
WHY DID IT STOP SUDDEN-LY?
TCH.
YOU'RE HERE AL-READY? WHAT A PAIN IN THE ASS.
TMP

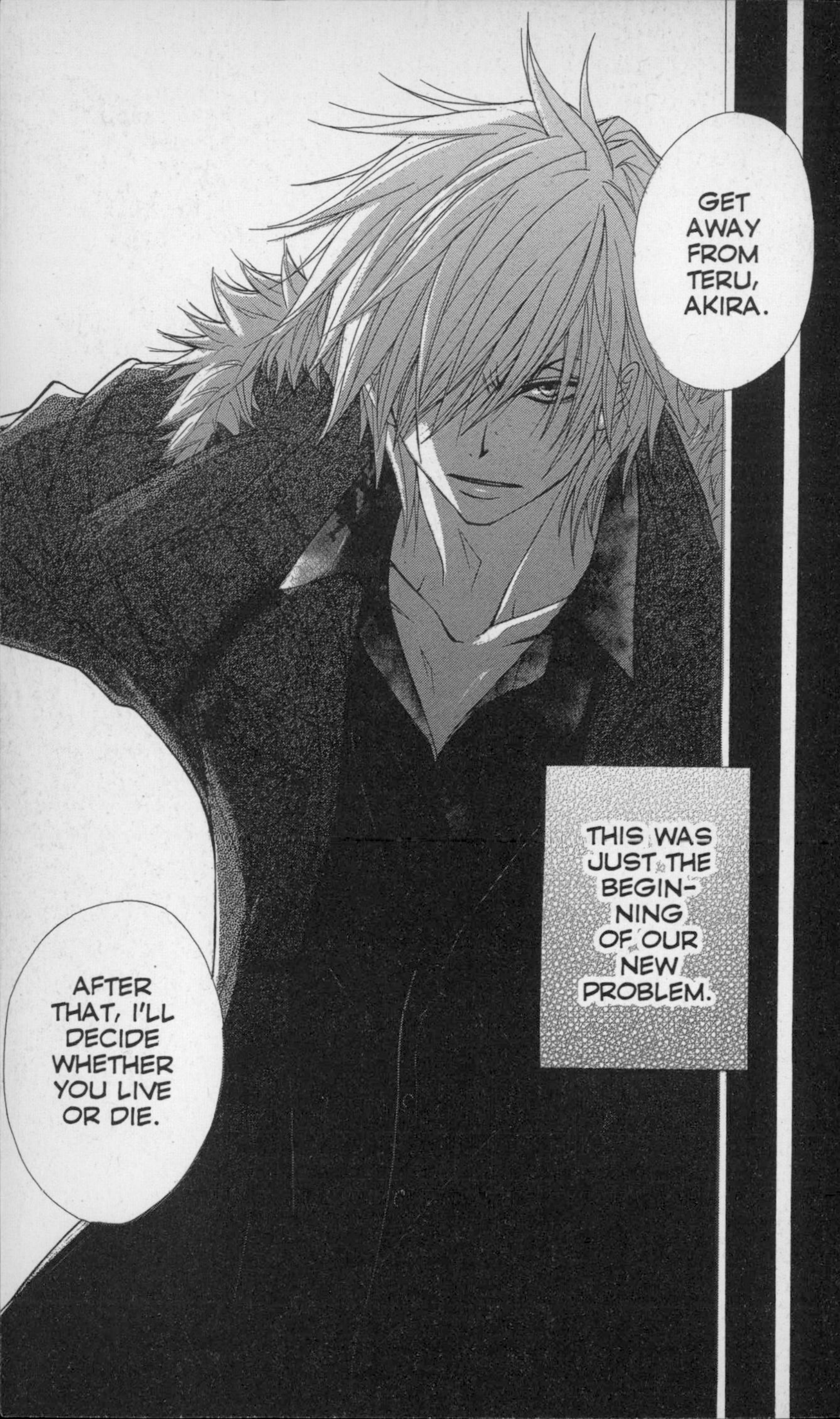
GET AWAY FROM TERU, AKIRA.
THIS WAS JUST THE BEGIN-NING OF OUR NEW PROBLEM.
AFTER THAT, I'LL DECIDE WHETHER YOU LIVE OR DIE.

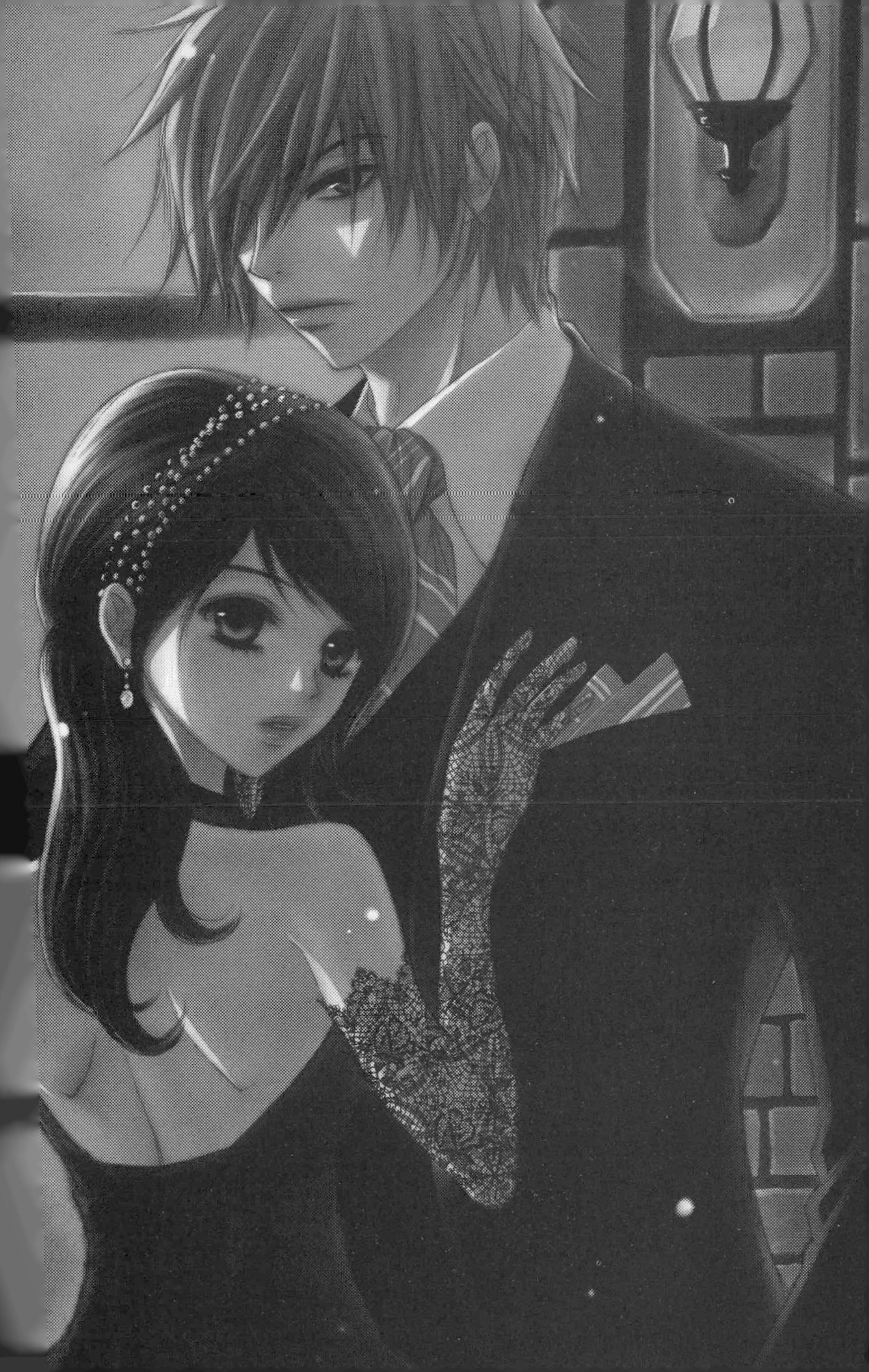

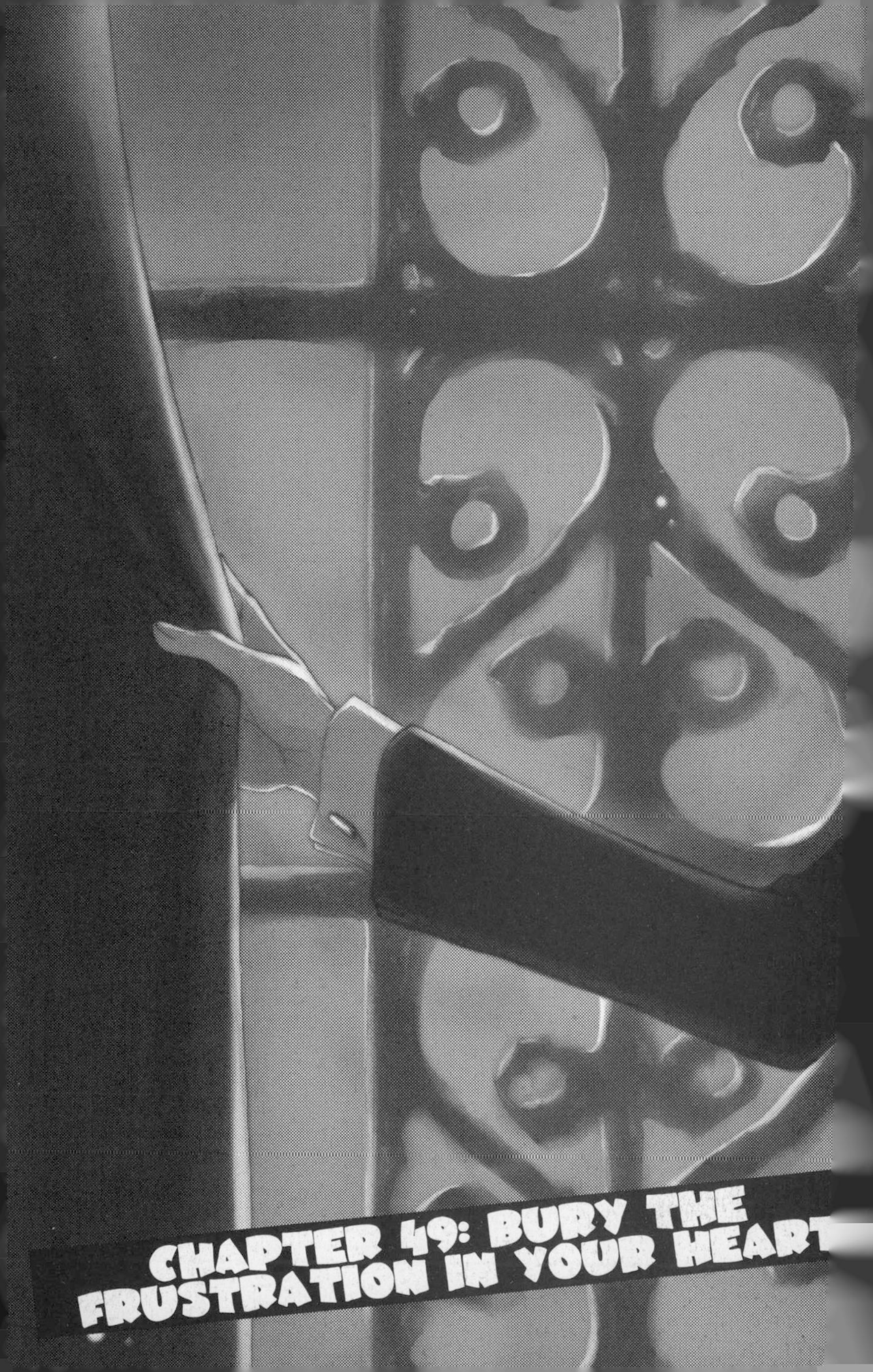
CHAPTER 49: BURY THE
FRUSTRATION IN YOUR HEART

THE BEST ☆ OF ☆ THE SECRET SCHOOL CUSTODIAN OFFICE ♥

THE 5TH OF THIS SUPER POPULAR SECTION ♥

THERE IS A *DENGEKI DAISY* FAN SEGMENT BOLDLY FEATURED IN *BETSUCOMI* THAT IS APTLY TITLED "THE SECRET SCHOOL CUSTODIAN OFFICE ♥"!
WITH ARBITRARY EYES, WE EXAMINED ALL THE GREAT WORK FEATURED THERE AND PICKED THE "BEST" AMONG THEM THAT WE WANTED TO LEAVE FOR POSTERITY!

THE "BEST OF" FOR VOLUME 10... "USE THEM WISELY! YOUR SWITCHABLE DUST COVER AND BOOKMARK SET!"

THIS IS A LECTURE ON HOW TO USE THE "SWITCHABLE DUST COVER AND BOOKMARK SET" SUPPLEMENT FROM THE JULY 2011 ISSUE OF *BETSUCOMI*. GOOD CHILDREN SHOULD NOT COPY EXAMPLE NUMBER THREE.

USE THEM WISELY! YOUR SWITCHABLE DUST COVER AND BOOKMARK SET!!

FOR READERS UNSURE OF HOW TO USE THE SUPPLEMENT, WE ASKED FOR THE BEST METHODS!

METHOD 1

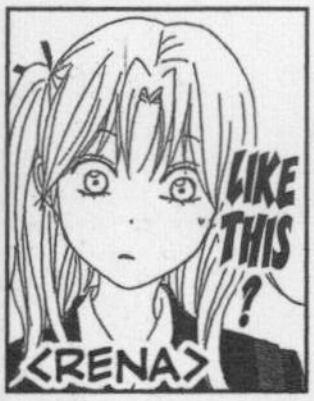
LIKE THIS?
<RENA>

RATING
★★★★★
USE IT TO COVER YOUR FAVORITE VOLUME! MARK YOUR FAVORITE SCENE WITH THE BOOKMARK, AND READ THE VOLUME.

METHOD 2

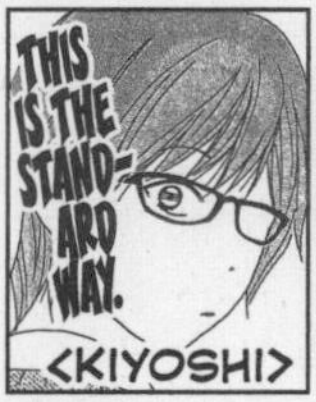
THIS IS THE STANDARD WAY.
<KIYOSHI>

RATING
★★★★★
USE IT TO COVER THE LATEST VOLUME. USE THE BOOKMARK TO MARK THE PLACE WHERE YOU ARE READING. A STRAIGHTFORWARD METHOD, SO TYPICAL OF KIYOSHI.

METHOD 3

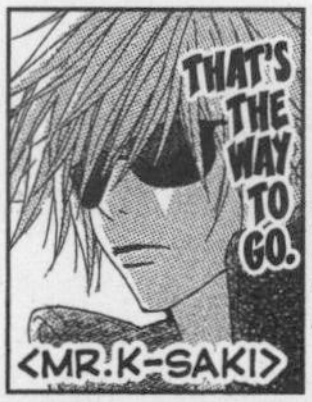
THAT'S THE WAY TO GO.
<MR. K-SAKI>

RATING
★☆☆☆☆
GET ENOUGH SETS FOR EVERY VOLUME AND MARK THE PAGES WHERE TERU'S PANTIES ARE SHOWING.

...NO COMMENT.

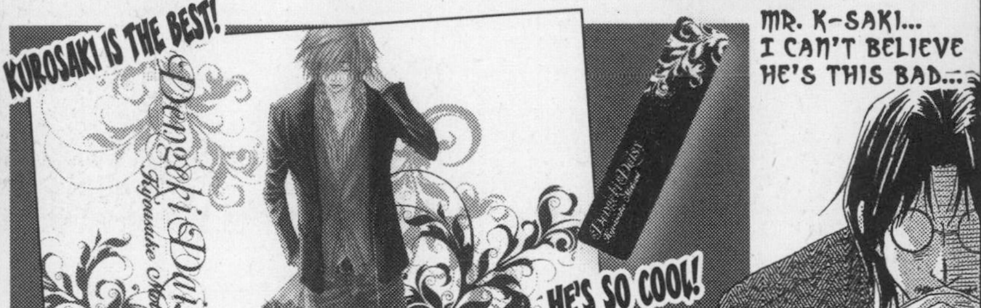
MR. K-SAKI... I CAN'T BELIEVE HE'S THIS BAD...
KUROSAKI IS THE BEST!
HE'S SO COOL!

JUDGES' COMMENTS

- I UNDERSTAND HOW MR. K-SAKI FEELS, BUT THERE HAVE ONLY BEEN TWO SCENES WHERE TERU'S PANTIES WERE VISIBLE. (WITHOUT EXCEPTION.) (HEAD JUDGE: KYOUSUKE MOTOMI)
- OUT OF 49 CHAPTERS ACROSS 10 VOLUMES, TERU'S PANTIES WERE VISIBLE IN ONLY TWO SCENES! TALK ABOUT AN IMMEDIATE REPLY. LEAVE IT TO THE AUTHOR. I VOTE FOR THE STRAIGHTFORWARD KIYOSHI. (JUDGE: *DAISY* EDITOR)

BETSUCOMI, THE MAGAZINE THAT SERIALIZES *DAISY*, GOES ON SALE EVERY MONTH AROUND THE 13TH!
PLEASE LOOK FOR IT IF YOU WANT TO READ "THE SECRET SCHOOL CUSTODIAN OFFICE"! ♥

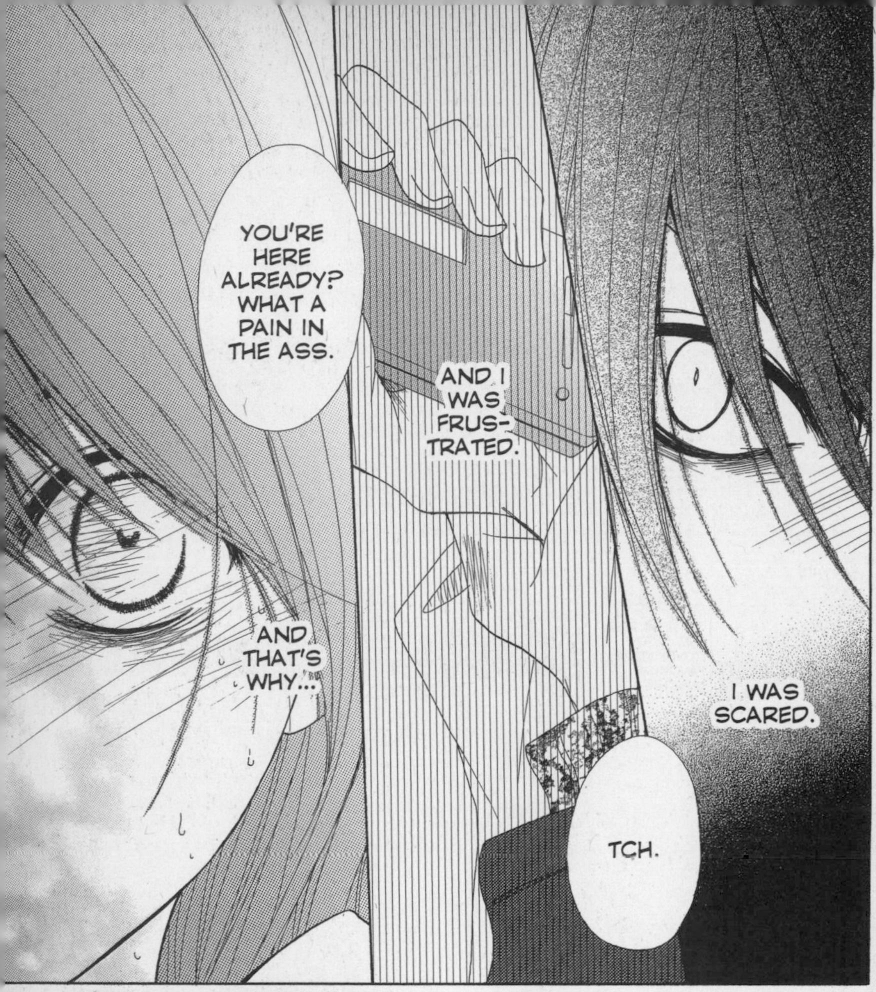
I WAS SCARED.
TCH.
AND I WAS FRUS-TRATED.
YOU'RE HERE ALREADY? WHAT A PAIN IN THE ASS.
AND THAT'S WHY...

TOWARDS THE END OF CHAPTER 48...

THE CAR THAT KUROSAKI AND THE OTHERS ARE RIDING IN IS RIGHT IN FRONT OF TERU'S HOTEL, AND ANDY IS SUPPOSED TO HACK INTO THE ELEVATOR CONTROLS TO MAKE IT STOP. DURING THAT TIME, KUROSAKI MAKES AN ULTRA-ROCKET-SPEED DASH TO TERU...

...BUT C'MON, KUROSAKI GOT THERE WAY TOO FAST... I MENTIONED IT TO THE EDITOR AND WAS TOLD, "IT'S ALL RIGHT!! IT'S THE POWER OF LOVE!!!" AND THAT MADE ME FEEL BOLDER. SO, I'M GOING TO BE BRAVE AND PRETEND I DIDN'T NOTICE ANYTHING. THE POWER OF LOVE MAKES THE IMPOSSIBLE POSSIBLE. IT'S REALLY AMAZING.

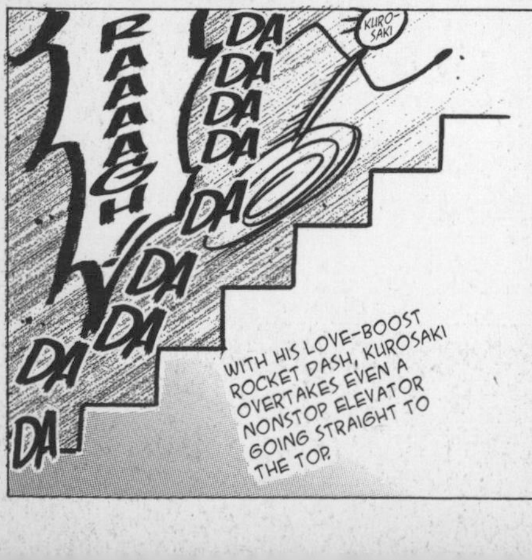
KURO-SAKI
DA DA DA DA DA DA DA
DA DA
DA DA
RAAAAAGH!!
WITH HIS LOVE-BOOST ROCKET DASH, KUROSAKI OVERTAKES EVEN A NONSTOP ELEVATOR GOING STRAIGHT TO THE TOP.

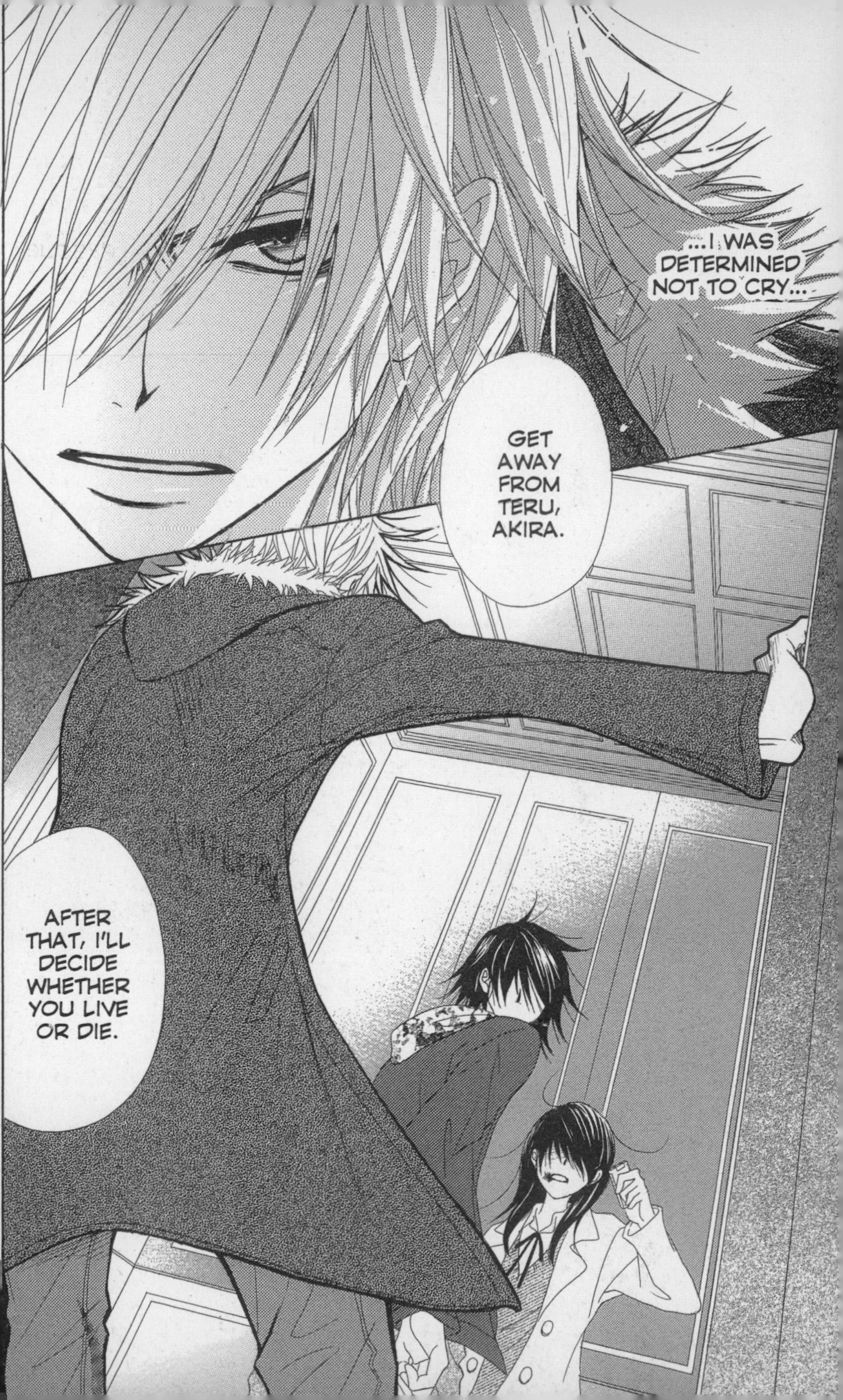
...I WAS DETERMINED NOT TO CRY...
GET AWAY FROM TERU, AKIRA.
AFTER THAT, I'LL DECIDE WHETHER YOU LIVE OR DIE.

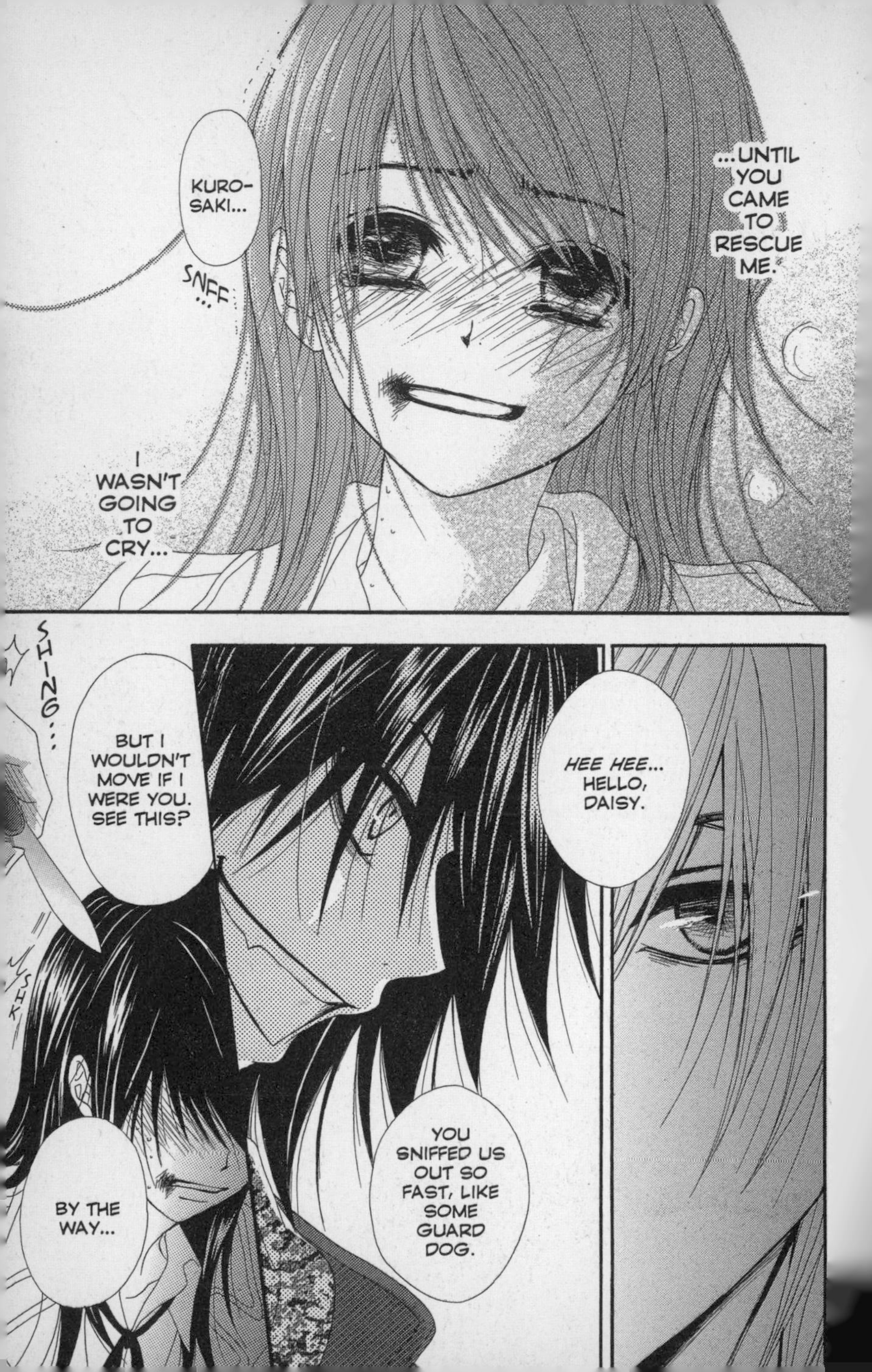
KURO-SAKI...
SNFF...
I WASN'T GOING TO CRY...
...UNTIL YOU CAME TO RESCUE ME.
HEE HEE... HELLO, DAISY.
YOU SNIFFED US OUT SO FAST, LIKE SOME GUARD DOG.
BY THE WAY...
SHING...
SHK
BUT I WOULDN'T MOVE IF I WERE YOU. SEE THIS?

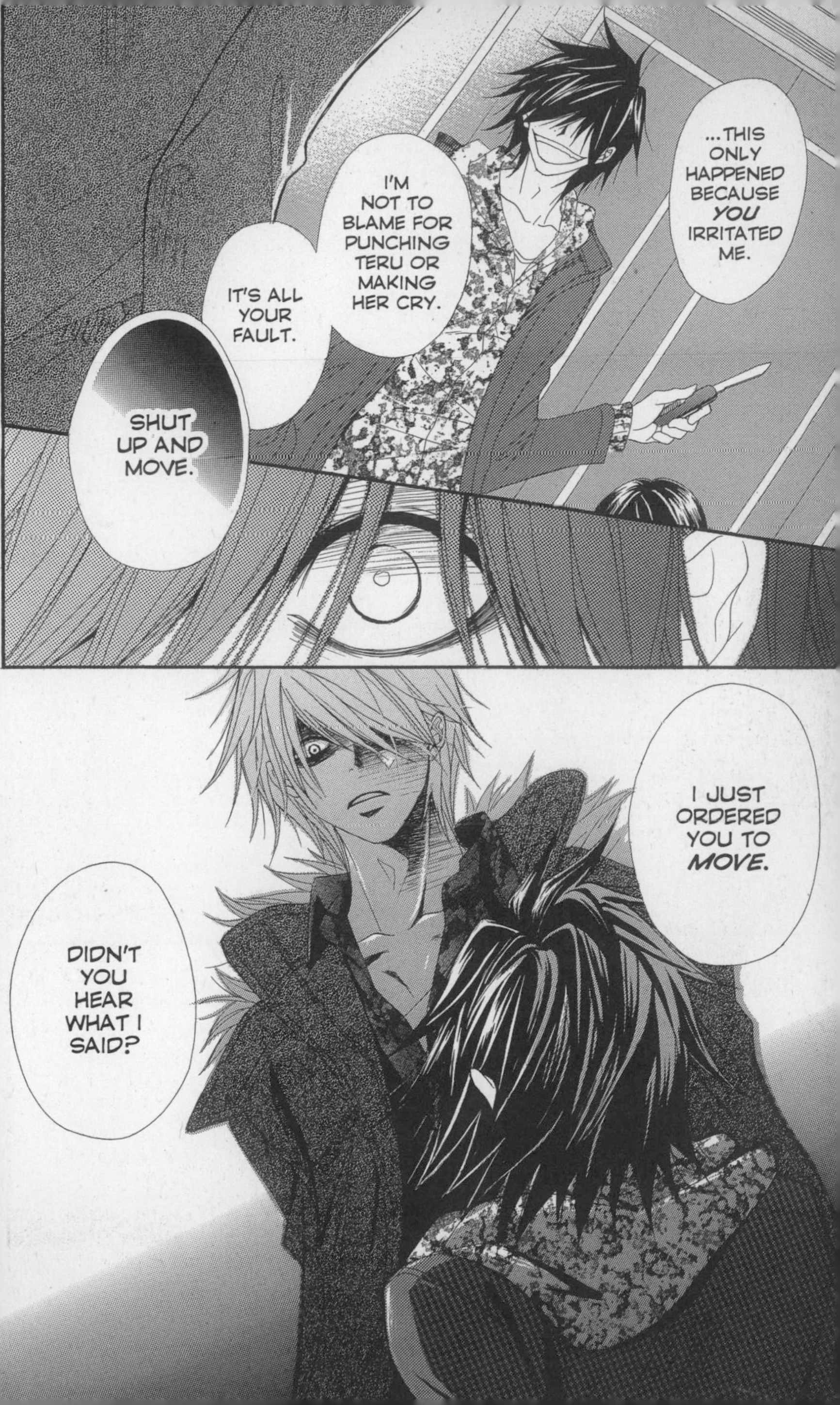
...THIS ONLY HAPPENED BECAUSE *YOU* IRRITATED ME.
I'M NOT TO BLAME FOR PUNCHING TERU OR MAKING HER CRY.
IT'S ALL YOUR FAULT.
SHUT UP AND MOVE.
I JUST ORDERED YOU TO *MOVE*.
DIDN'T YOU HEAR WHAT I SAID?

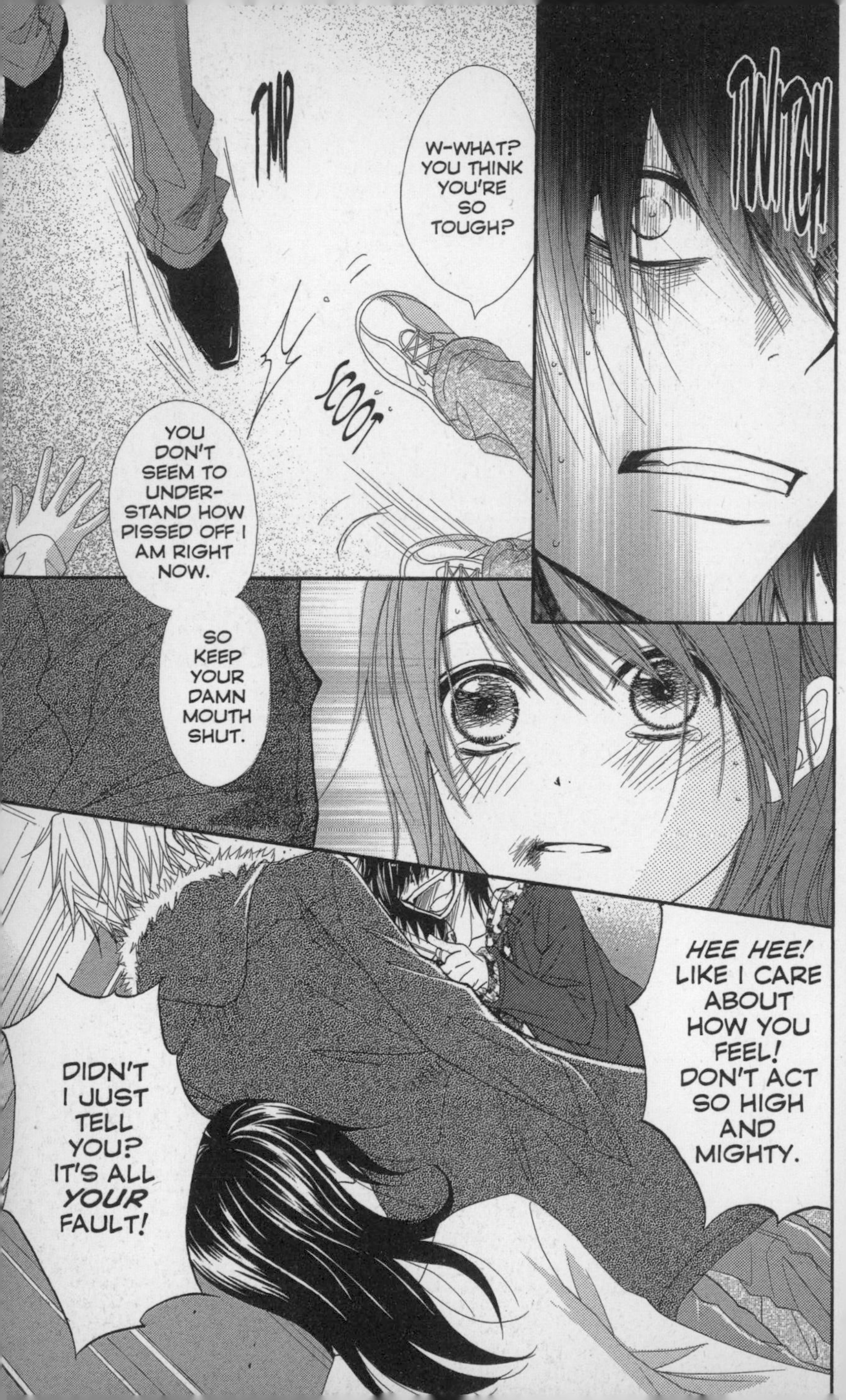
TWITCH
W-WHAT? YOU THINK YOU'RE SO TOUGH?
TMP
SCOOT
YOU DON'T SEEM TO UNDER-STAND HOW PISSED OFF I AM RIGHT NOW.
SO KEEP YOUR DAMN MOUTH SHUT.
HEE HEE! LIKE I CARE ABOUT HOW YOU FEEL! DON'T ACT SO HIGH AND MIGHTY.
DIDN'T I JUST TELL YOU? IT'S ALL ***YOUR*** FAULT!

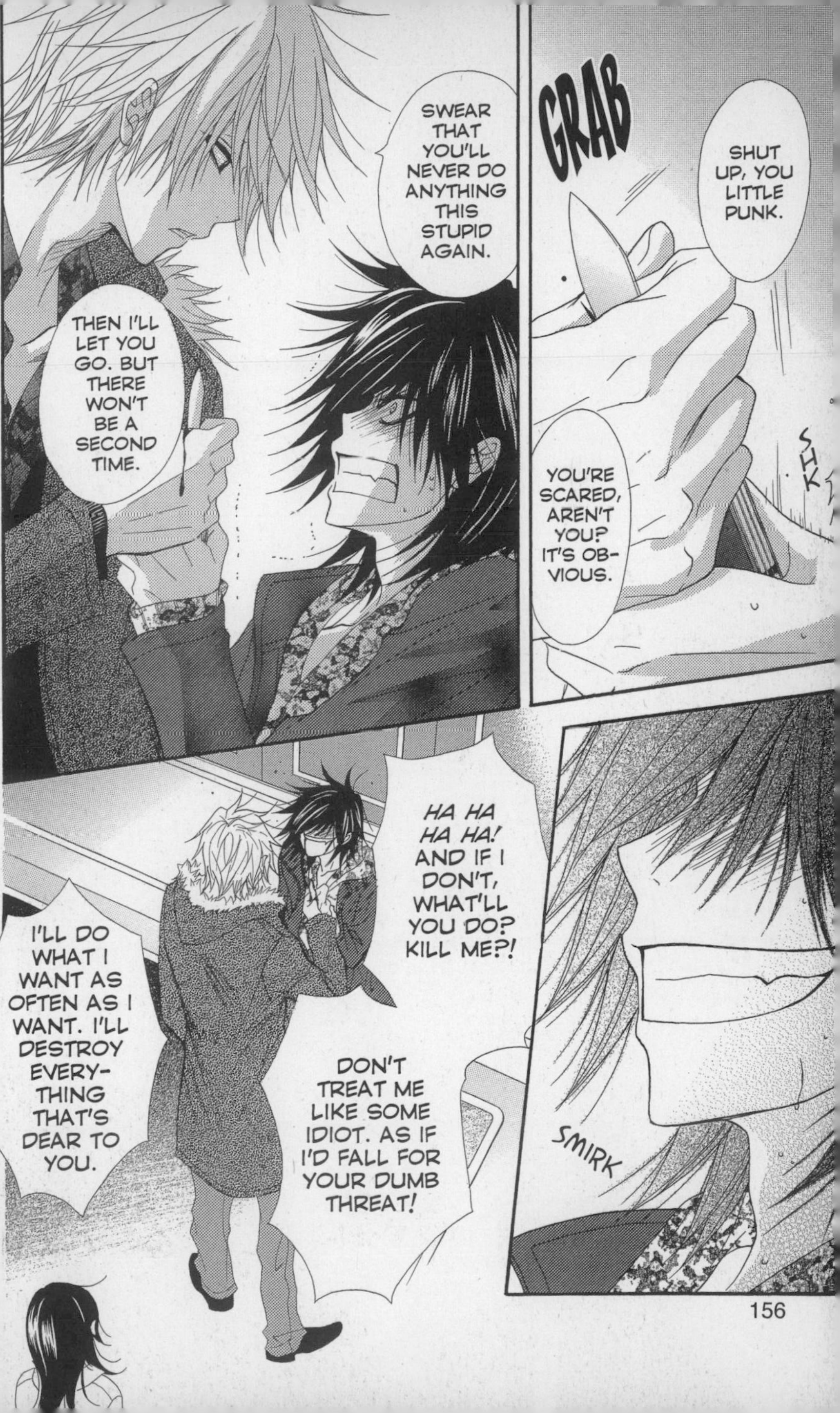
GRAB
SHUT UP, YOU LITTLE PUNK.
SHK
YOU'RE SCARED, AREN'T YOU? IT'S OB-VIOUS.
SWEAR THAT YOU'LL NEVER DO ANYTHING THIS STUPID AGAIN.
THEN I'LL LET YOU GO. BUT THERE WON'T BE A SECOND TIME.
SMIRK
HA HA HA HA! AND IF I DON'T, WHAT'LL YOU DO? KILL ME?!
I'LL DO WHAT I WANT AS OFTEN AS I WANT. I'LL DESTROY EVERY-THING THAT'S DEAR TO YOU.
DON'T TREAT ME LIKE SOME IDIOT. AS IF I'D FALL FOR YOUR DUMB THREAT!

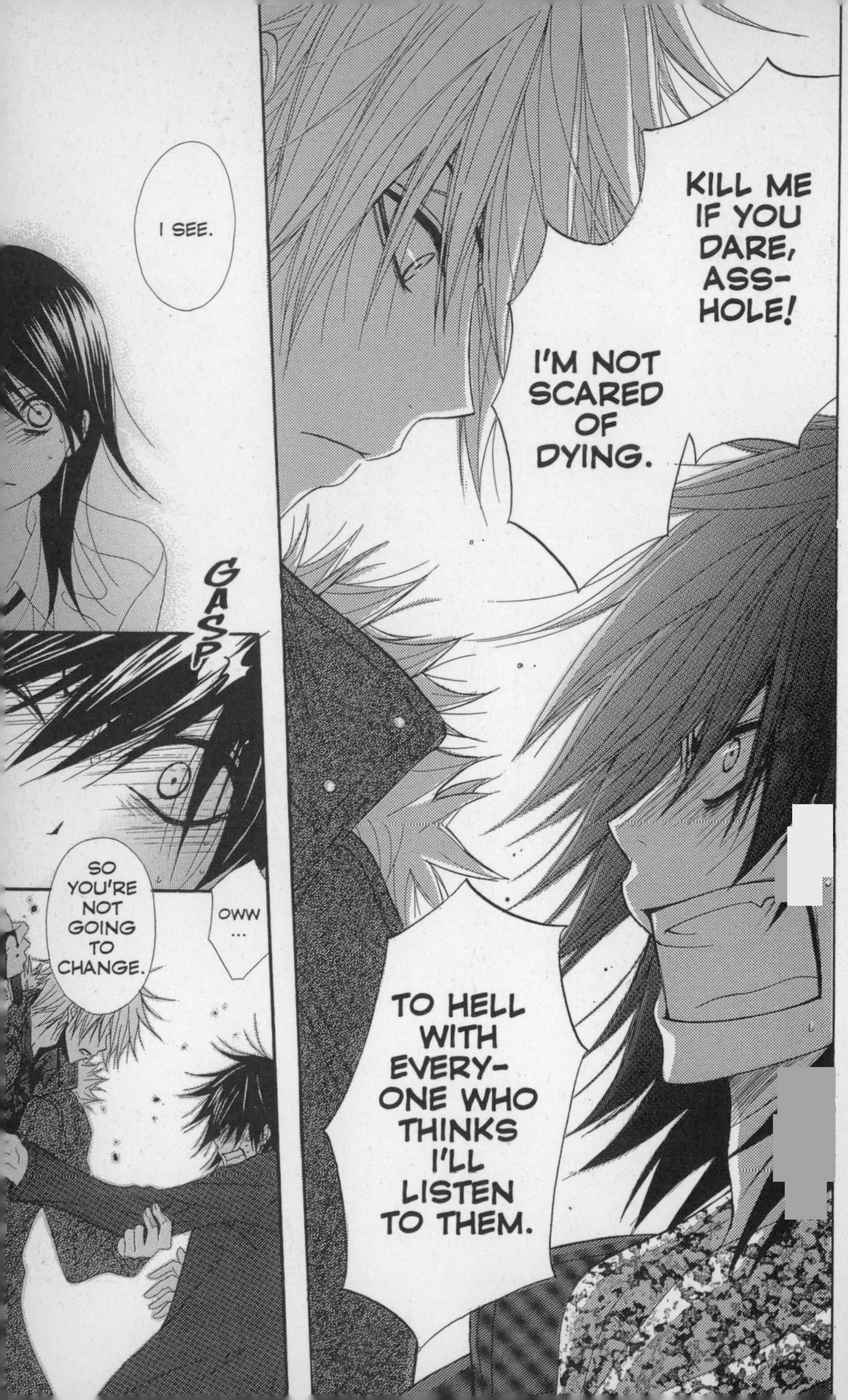
KILL ME IF YOU DARE, ASS-HOLE!
I'M NOT SCARED OF DYING.
TO HELL WITH EVERY-ONE WHO THINKS I'LL LISTEN TO THEM.
I SEE.
GASP
OWW ...
SO YOU'RE NOT GOING TO CHANGE.

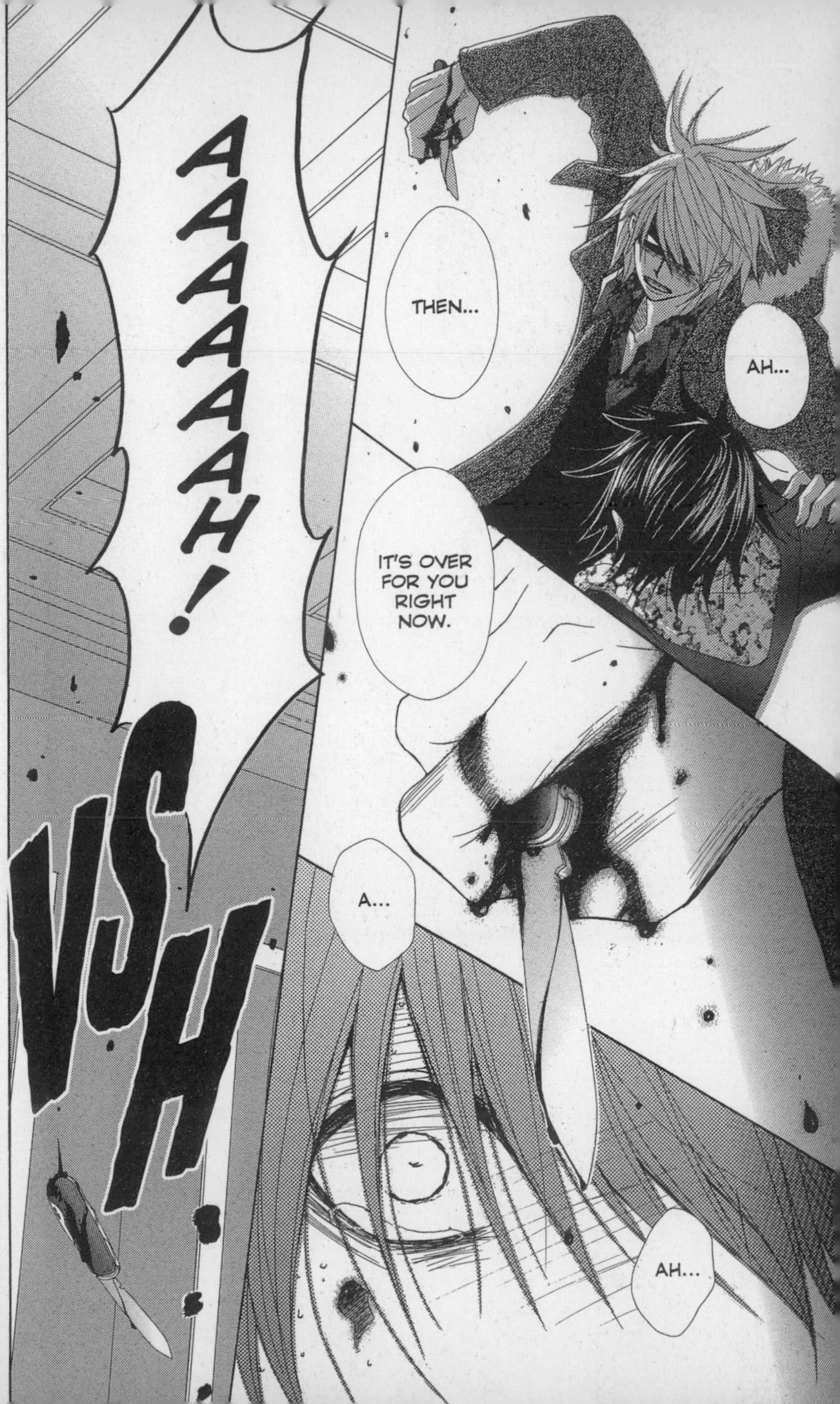
AH...
THEN...
IT'S OVER FOR YOU RIGHT NOW.
A...
AH...
AAAAAAH!
VSH

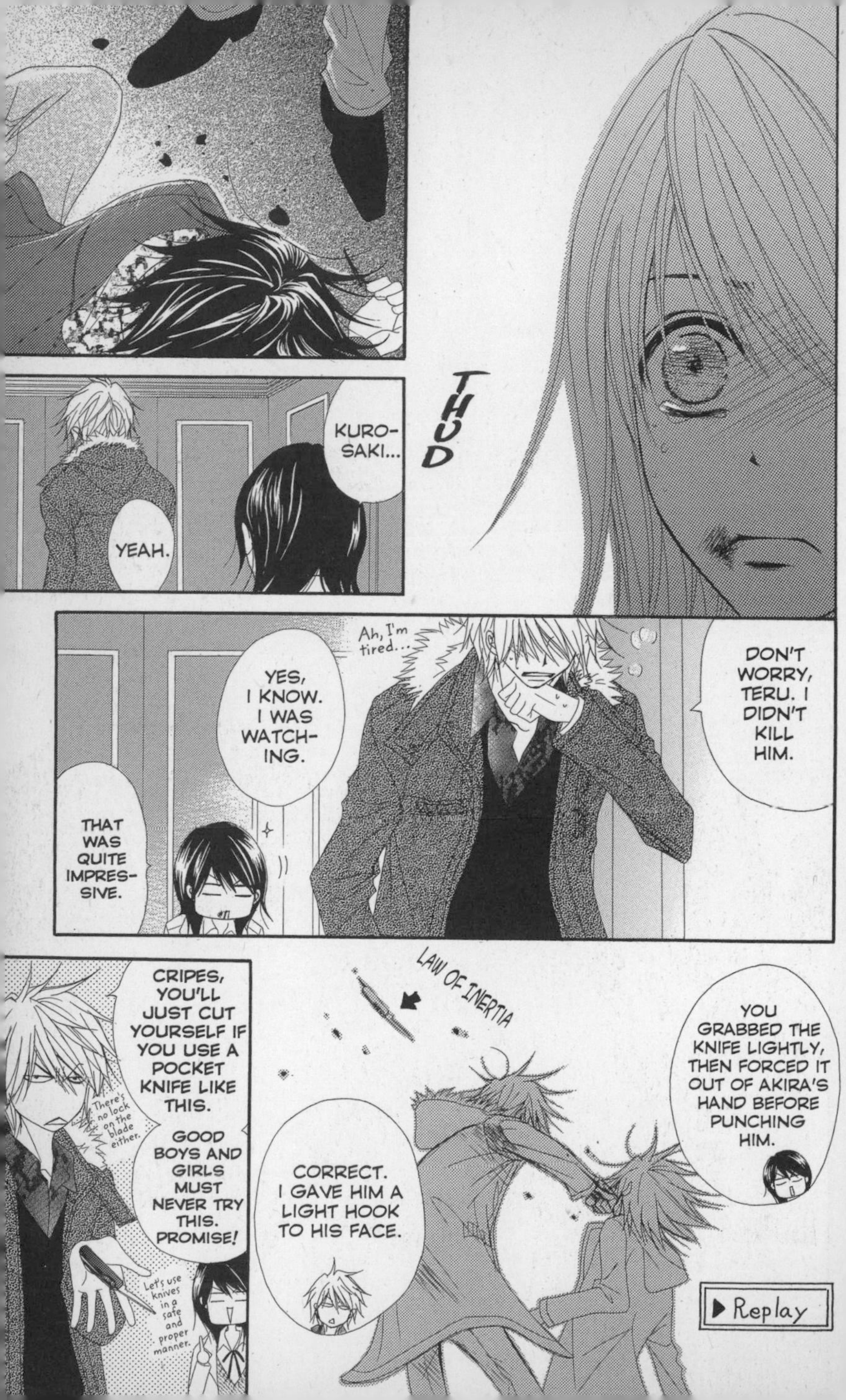
THUD
KURO-SAKI...
YEAH.
DON'T WORRY, TERU. I DIDN'T KILL HIM.
Ah, I'm tired...
YES, I KNOW. I WAS WATCHING.
THAT WAS QUITE IMPRESSIVE.
Replay
YOU GRABBED THE KNIFE LIGHTLY, THEN FORCED IT OUT OF AKIRA'S HAND BEFORE PUNCHING HIM.
LAW OF INERTIA
CORRECT. I GAVE HIM A LIGHT HOOK TO HIS FACE.
CRIPES, YOU'LL JUST CUT YOURSELF IF YOU USE A POCKET KNIFE LIKE THIS.
There's no lock on the blade either.
GOOD BOYS AND GIRLS MUST NEVER TRY THIS. PROMISE!
Let's use knives in a safe and proper manner.

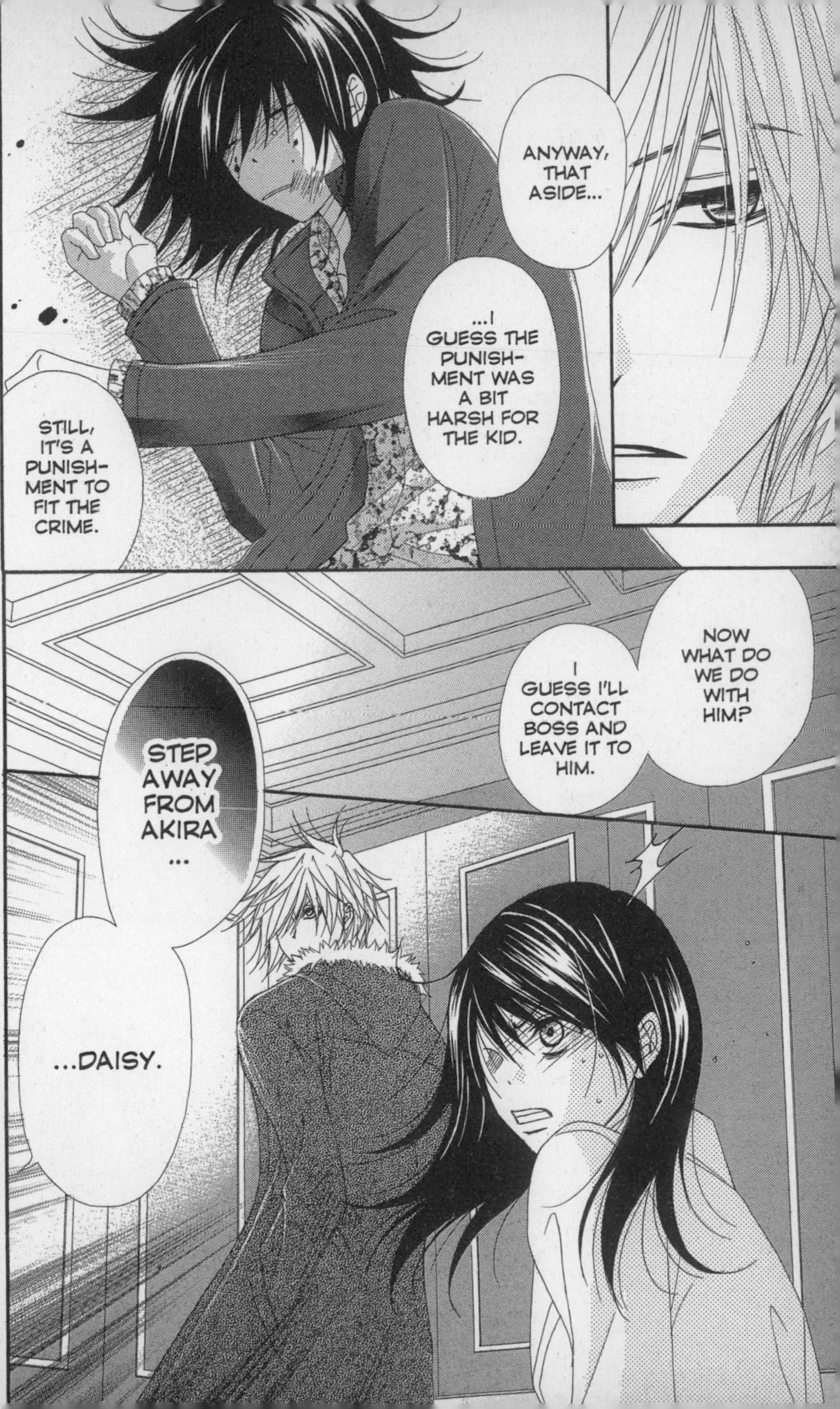
ANYWAY, THAT ASIDE...
...I GUESS THE PUNISHMENT WAS A BIT HARSH FOR THE KID.
STILL, IT'S A PUNISHMENT TO FIT THE CRIME.
NOW WHAT DO WE DO WITH HIM?
I GUESS I'LL CONTACT BOSS AND LEAVE IT TO HIM.
STEP AWAY FROM AKIRA ...
...DAISY.

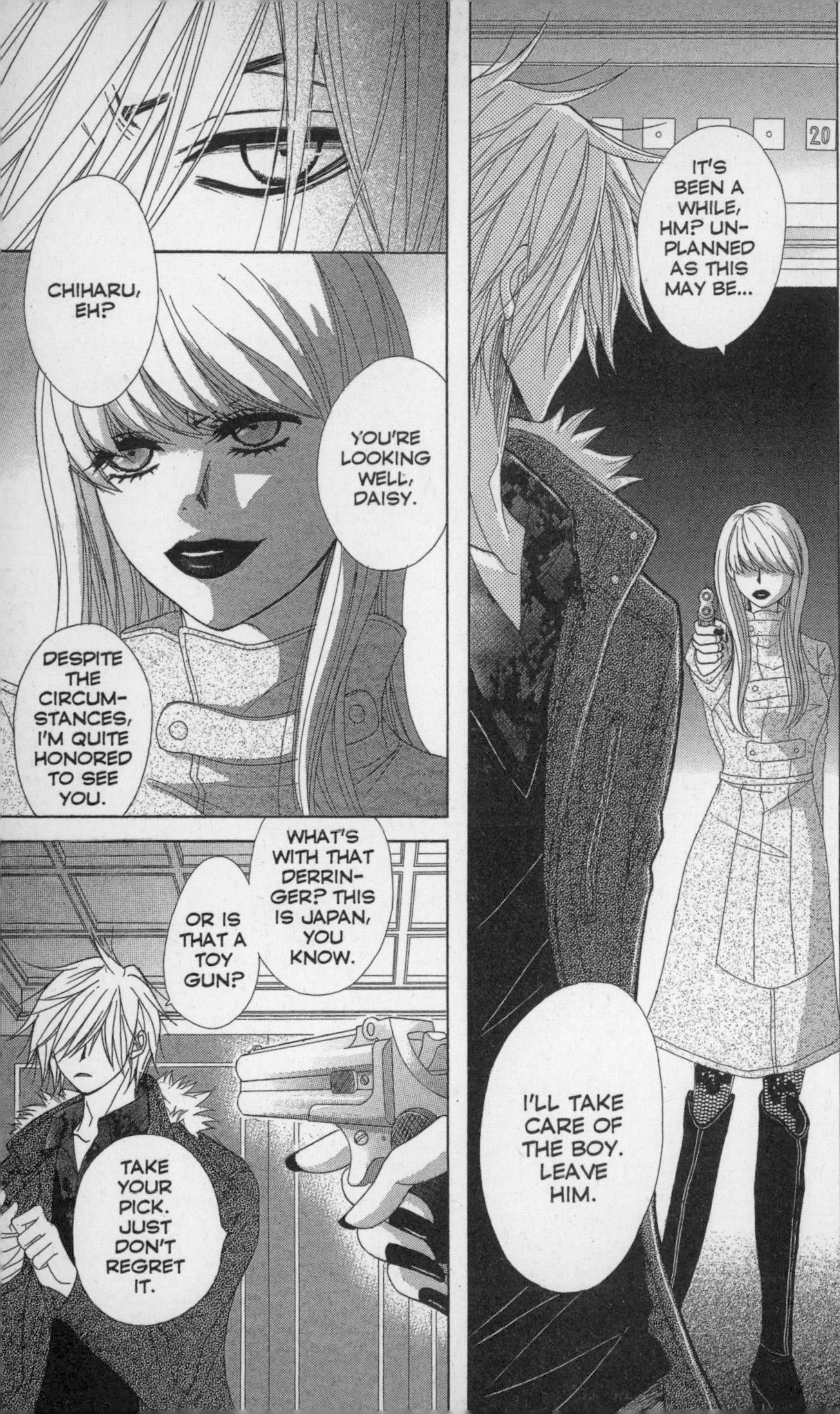
IT'S BEEN A WHILE, HM? UN-PLANNED AS THIS MAY BE...
I'LL TAKE CARE OF THE BOY. LEAVE HIM.
CHIHARU, EH?
YOU'RE LOOKING WELL, DAISY.
DESPITE THE CIRCUM-STANCES, I'M QUITE HONORED TO SEE YOU.
WHAT'S WITH THAT DERRIN-GER? THIS IS JAPAN, YOU KNOW.
OR IS THAT A TOY GUN?
TAKE YOUR PICK. JUST DON'T REGRET IT.

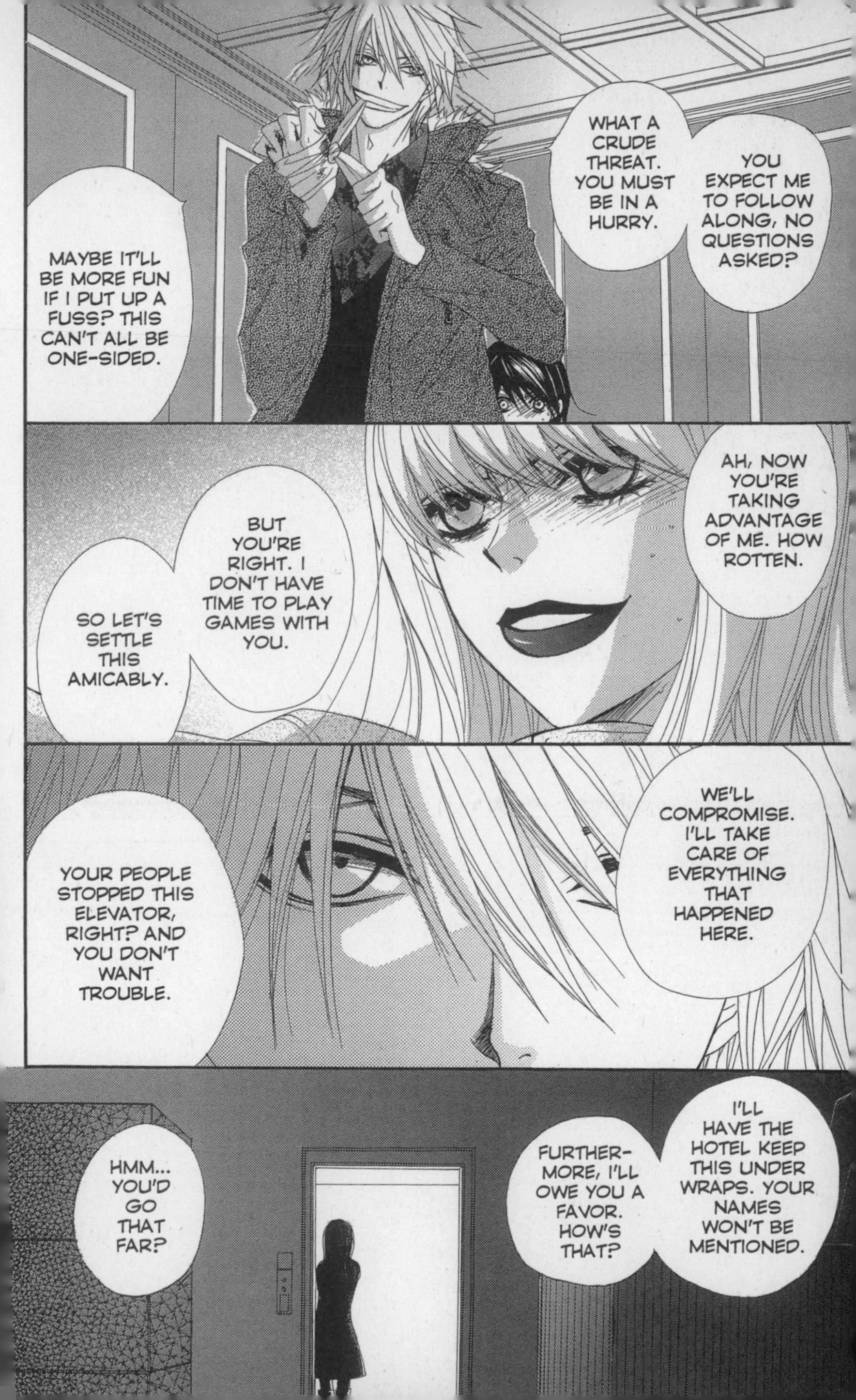
YOU EXPECT ME TO FOLLOW ALONG, NO QUESTIONS ASKED?
WHAT A CRUDE THREAT. YOU MUST BE IN A HURRY.
MAYBE IT'LL BE MORE FUN IF I PUT UP A FUSS? THIS CAN'T ALL BE ONE-SIDED.
AH, NOW YOU'RE TAKING ADVANTAGE OF ME. HOW ROTTEN.
BUT YOU'RE RIGHT. I DON'T HAVE TIME TO PLAY GAMES WITH YOU.
SO LET'S SETTLE THIS AMICABLY.
WE'LL COMPROMISE. I'LL TAKE CARE OF EVERYTHING THAT HAPPENED HERE.
YOUR PEOPLE STOPPED THIS ELEVATOR, RIGHT? AND YOU DON'T WANT TROUBLE.
I'LL HAVE THE HOTEL KEEP THIS UNDER WRAPS. YOUR NAMES WON'T BE MENTIONED.
FURTHER-MORE, I'LL OWE YOU A FAVOR. HOW'S THAT?
HMM... YOU'D GO THAT FAR?

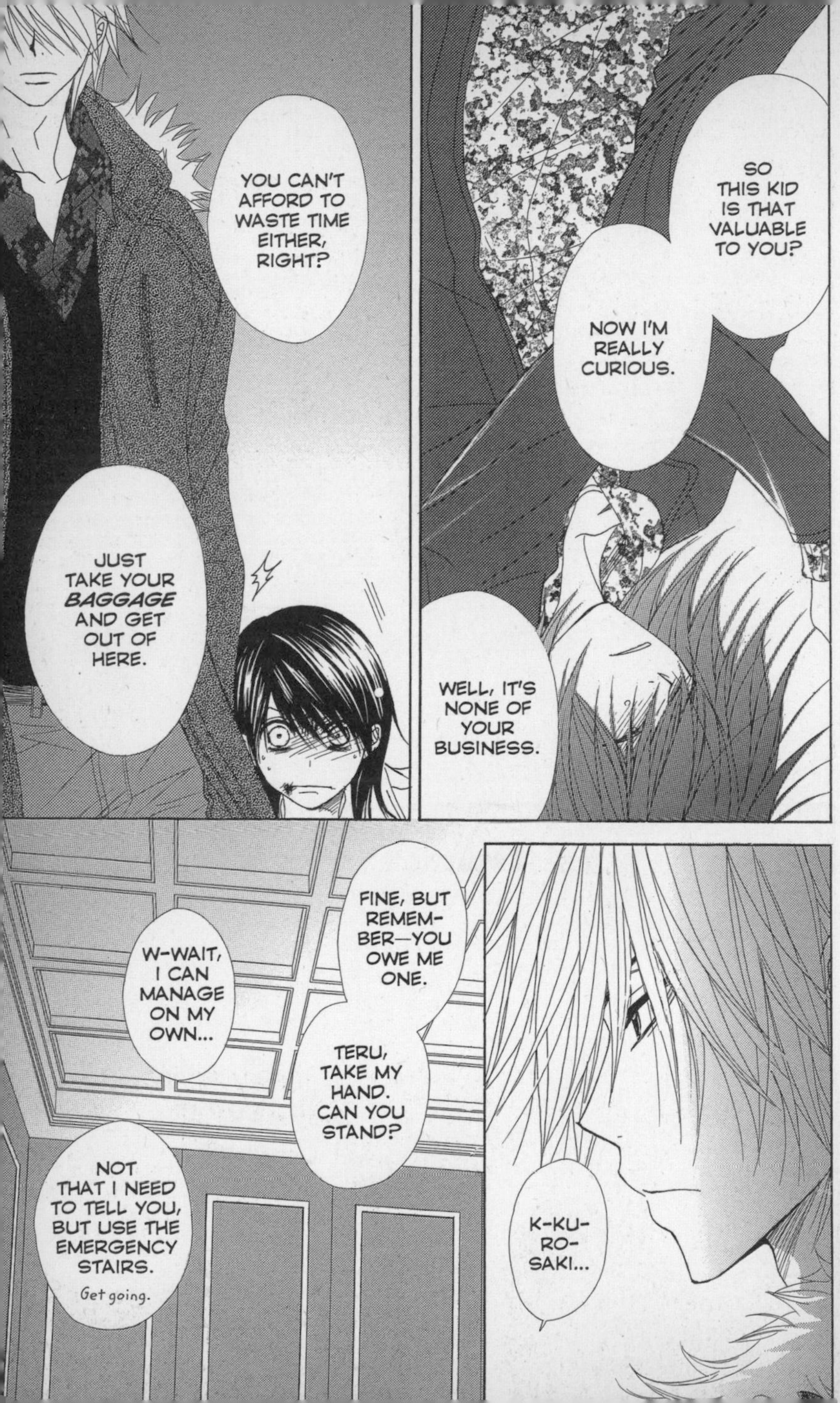
SO THIS KID IS THAT VALUABLE TO YOU?
NOW I'M REALLY CURIOUS.
WELL, IT'S NONE OF YOUR BUSINESS.
YOU CAN'T AFFORD TO WASTE TIME EITHER, RIGHT?
JUST TAKE YOUR *BAGGAGE* AND GET OUT OF HERE.
K-KU-RO-SAKI...
FINE, BUT REMEMBER—YOU OWE ME ONE.
W-WAIT, I CAN MANAGE ON MY OWN...
TERU, TAKE MY HAND. CAN YOU STAND?
NOT THAT I NEED TO TELL YOU, BUT USE THE EMERGENCY STAIRS.
Get going.

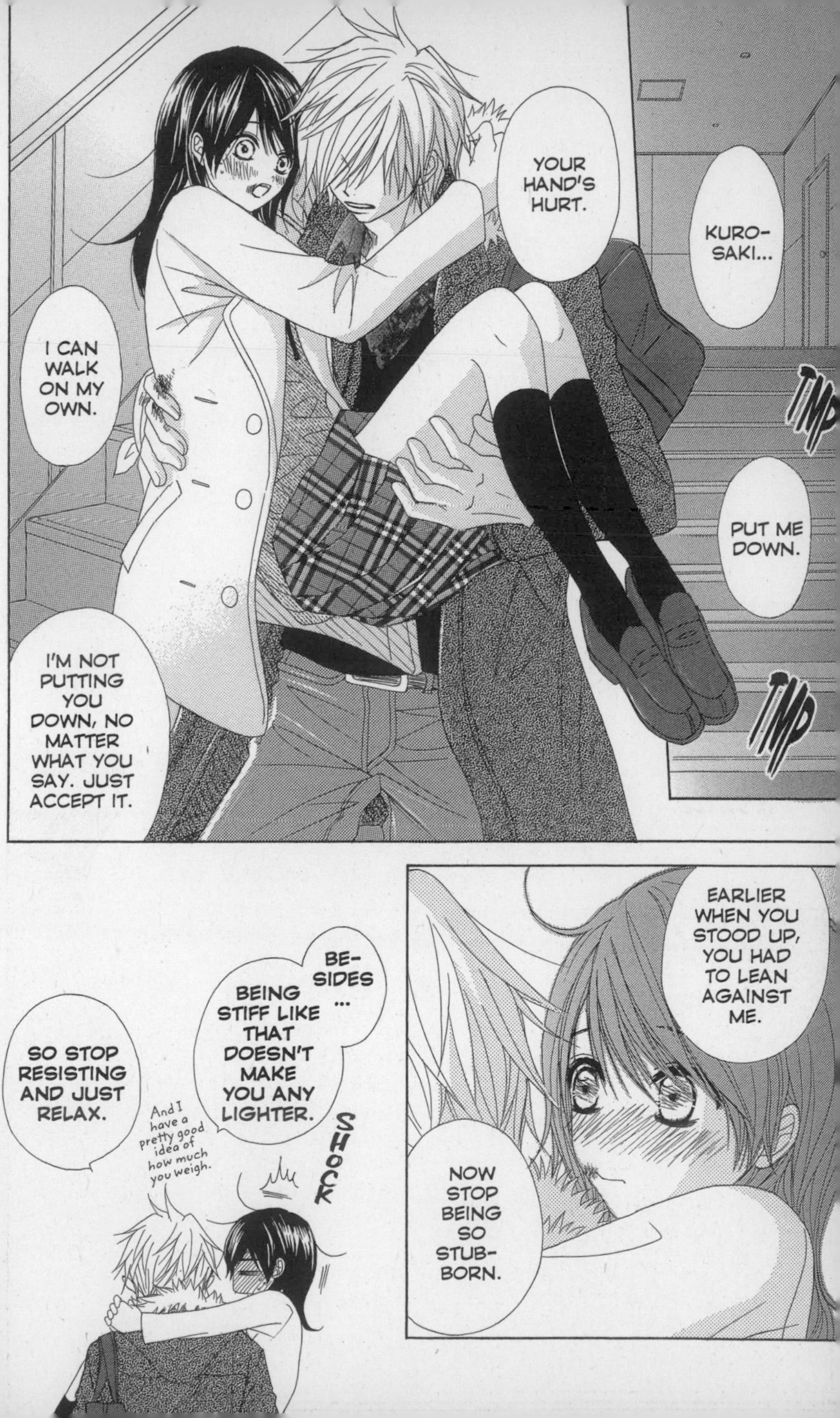
KURO-SAKI...
YOUR HAND'S HURT.
TMP
PUT ME DOWN.
TMP
I CAN WALK ON MY OWN.
I'M NOT PUTTING YOU DOWN, NO MATTER WHAT YOU SAY. JUST ACCEPT IT.
EARLIER WHEN YOU STOOD UP, YOU HAD TO LEAN AGAINST ME.
NOW STOP BEING SO STUB-BORN.
BE-SIDES...
BEING STIFF LIKE THAT DOESN'T MAKE YOU ANY LIGHTER.
SHOCK
SO STOP RESISTING AND JUST RELAX.
And I have a pretty good idea of how much you weigh.

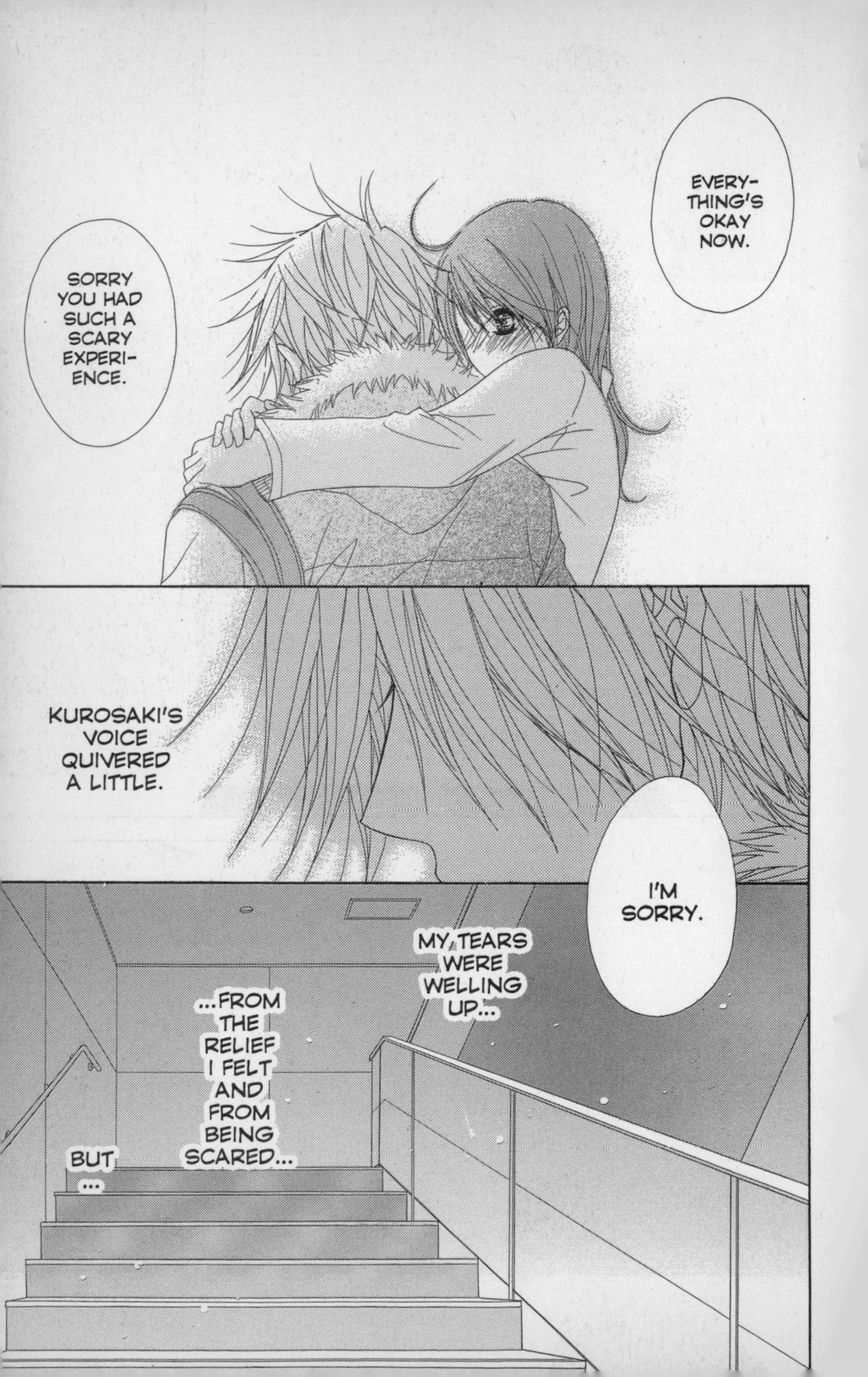
EVERYTHING'S OKAY NOW.
SORRY YOU HAD SUCH A SCARY EXPERIENCE.
KUROSAKI'S VOICE QUIVERED A LITTLE.
I'M SORRY.
MY TEARS WERE WELLING UP...
...FROM THE RELIEF I FELT AND FROM BEING SCARED...
BUT ...

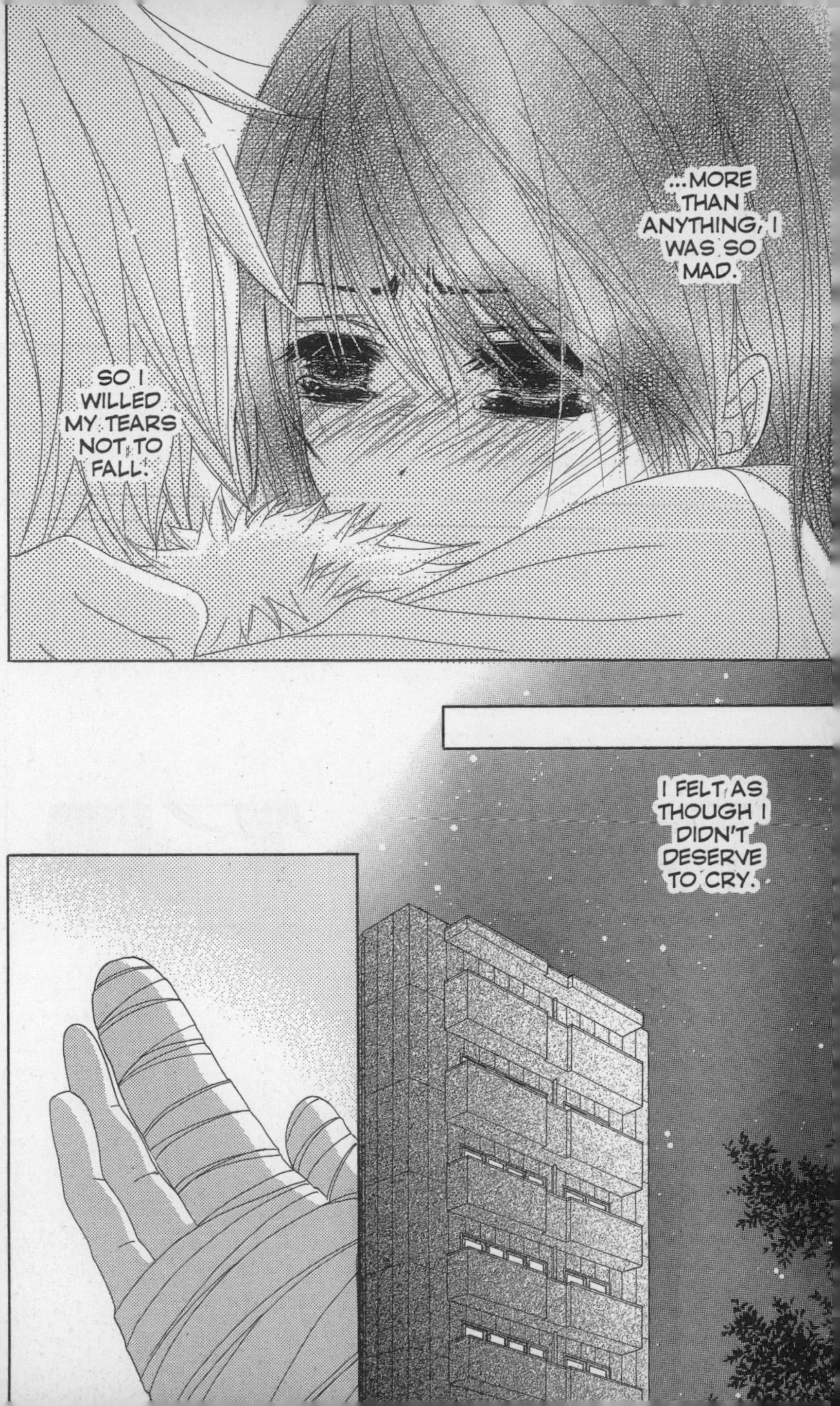
...MORE THAN ANYTHING, I WAS SO MAD.
SO I WILLED MY TEARS NOT TO FALL.
I FELT AS THOUGH I DIDN'T DESERVE TO CRY.

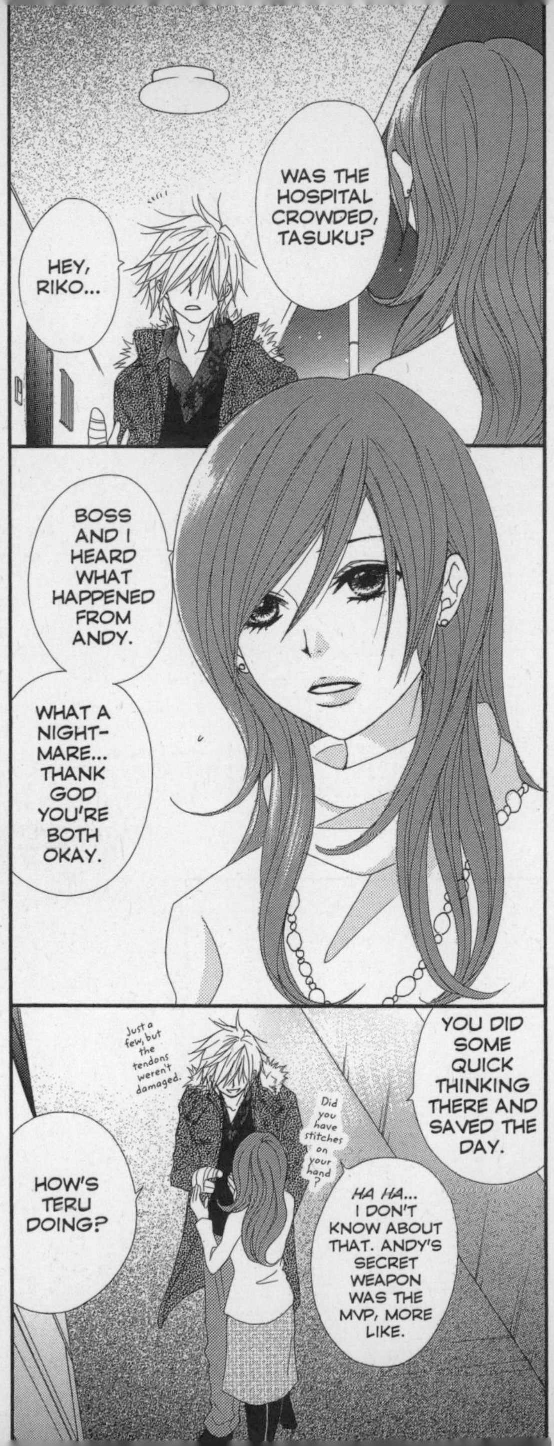
WAS THE HOSPITAL CROWDED, TASUKU?
HEY, RIKO...
BOSS AND I HEARD WHAT HAPPENED FROM ANDY.
WHAT A NIGHT-MARE... THANK GOD YOU'RE BOTH OKAY.
YOU DID SOME QUICK THINKING THERE AND SAVED THE DAY.
Did you have stitches on your hand?
HA HA... I DON'T KNOW ABOUT THAT. ANDY'S SECRET WEAPON WAS THE MVP, MORE LIKE.
Just a few, but the tendons weren't damaged.
HOW'S TERU DOING?

DENGEKI DAISY QUESTION CORNER

BALDLY ASK!! ⑤

Q. WHEN KUROSAKI CAUGHT TERU WHILE SHE WAS RUNNING AWAY AND READING HIS TEXT MESSAGES OUT LOUD, WHAT KIND OF PUNISHMENT WAS HE THINKING OF?

(KAMAKIRI, HOKKAIDO)

A. *DENGEKI DAISY* IS A SHOJO MANGA, SO I CAN'T GIVE OUT DETAILS. IT WOULD BE AWFUL IF I UPSET THE PERVERT.

Q. IF A BAND WERE TO BE FORMED, WHAT ROLE WOULD EACH CHARACTER PLAY?

(COSMO HOSHIMARU, AICHI PREFECTURE)

A. THIS WAS AN INTERESTING QUESTION, AND YOU HAD ME THINKING.

- VOCALS...KIYOSHI (HE'S PROBABLY THE BEST SINGER AMONG THE GROUP.)
- GUITAR...YOSHI AND KEN (THEY ARE IN A LIGHT MUSIC BAND.)
- BASS...BOSS (HE'S STABLE.)
- DRUMS...RIKO (SHE'S DYNAMIC.)
- KEYBOARD...ANDY (HE SEEMS TO LIKE YMO.)
- CASTANETS...TERU
- TAMBOURINE...SOICHIRO (THEY WOULD KEEP THE BEAT WITH EVERYTHING THEY'VE GOT.)
- SOMEONE WHO CAN MAKE QUICK REPLACEMENTS WHEN THE GUITAR STRING BREAKS AND WHATNOT... KUROSAKI

THAT'S IT FOR THIS VOLUME!! WE'LL CONTINUE IN THE NEXT ONE!!

IF I DIDN'T USE YOUR QUESTION, MY APOLOGIES! THANK YOU VERY MUCH.♥

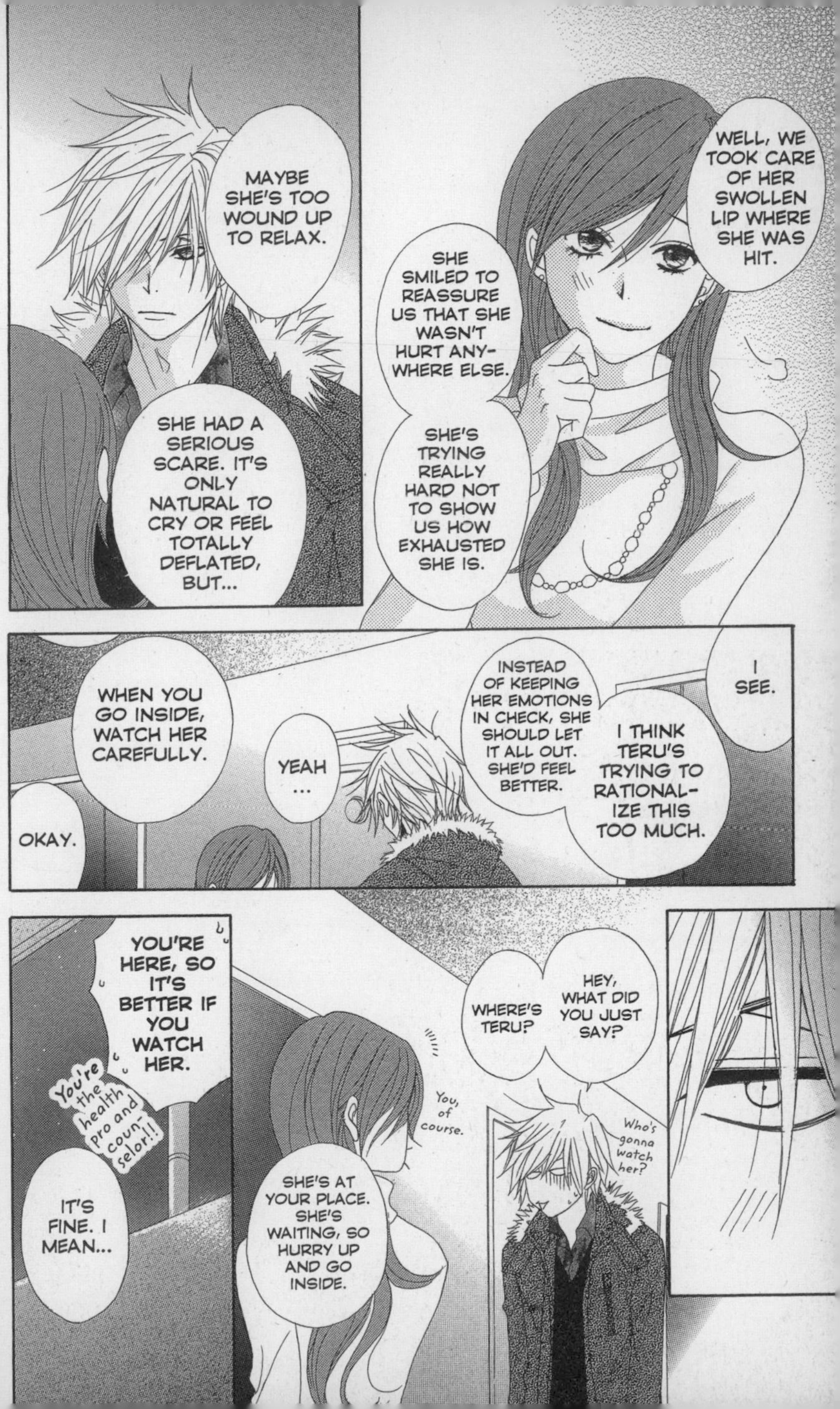
WELL, WE TOOK CARE OF HER SWOLLEN LIP WHERE SHE WAS HIT.
SHE SMILED TO REASSURE US THAT SHE WASN'T HURT ANY-WHERE ELSE.
SHE'S TRYING REALLY HARD NOT TO SHOW US HOW EXHAUSTED SHE IS.
MAYBE SHE'S TOO WOUND UP TO RELAX.
SHE HAD A SERIOUS SCARE. IT'S ONLY NATURAL TO CRY OR FEEL TOTALLY DEFLATED, BUT...
I SEE.
INSTEAD OF KEEPING HER EMOTIONS IN CHECK, SHE SHOULD LET IT ALL OUT. SHE'D FEEL BETTER.
I THINK TERU'S TRYING TO RATIONAL-IZE THIS TOO MUCH.
WHEN YOU GO INSIDE, WATCH HER CAREFULLY.
YEAH ...
OKAY.
HEY, WHAT DID YOU JUST SAY?
WHERE'S TERU?
Who's gonna watch her?
You, of course.
YOU'RE HERE, SO IT'S BETTER IF YOU WATCH HER.
You're the health pro and coun-selor!!
SHE'S AT YOUR PLACE. SHE'S WAITING, SO HURRY UP AND GO INSIDE.
IT'S FINE. I MEAN...

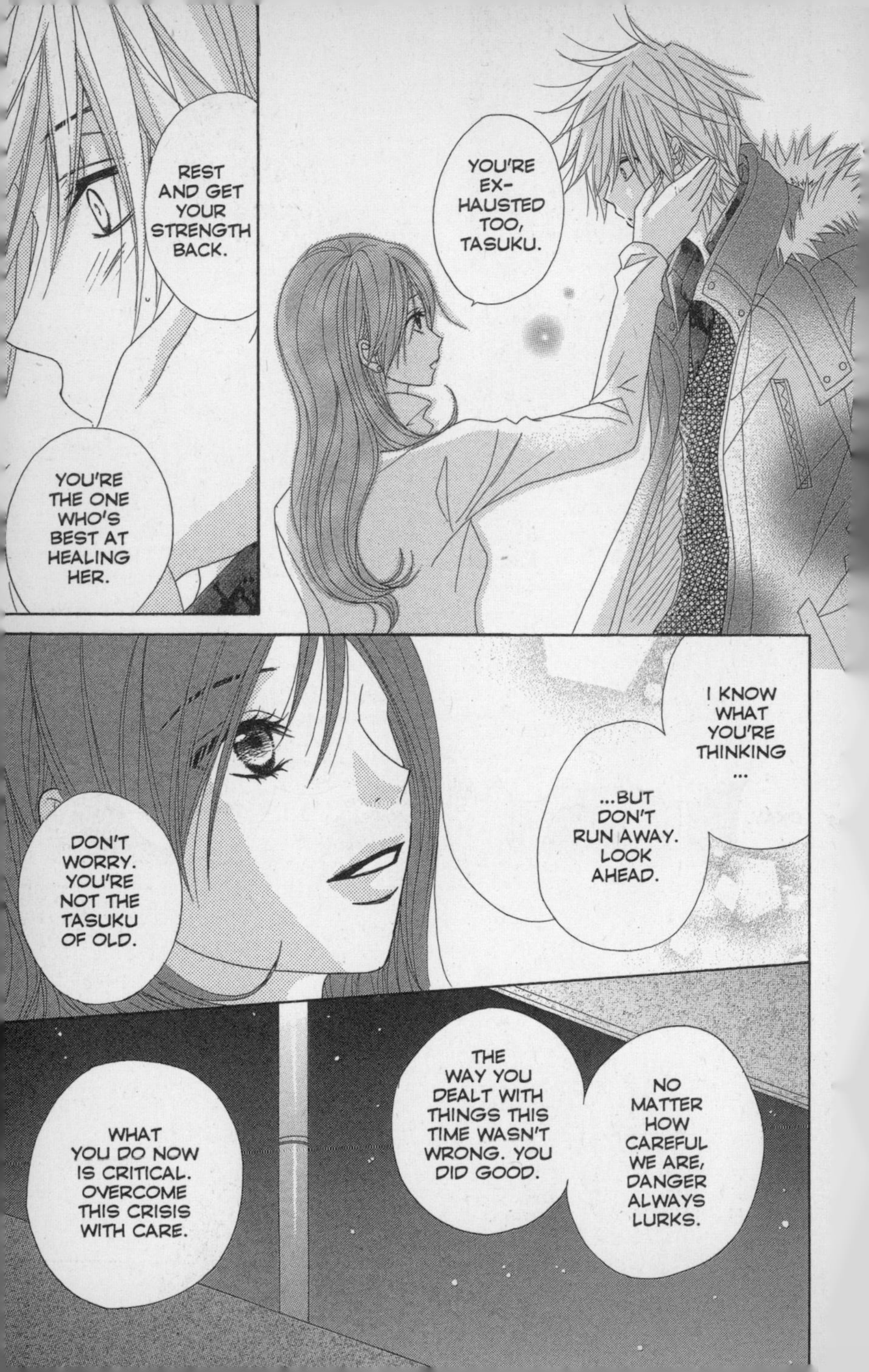
YOU'RE EX-HAUSTED TOO, TASUKU.
REST AND GET YOUR STRENGTH BACK.
YOU'RE THE ONE WHO'S BEST AT HEALING HER.
I KNOW WHAT YOU'RE THINKING ...
...BUT DON'T RUN AWAY. LOOK AHEAD.
DON'T WORRY. YOU'RE NOT THE TASUKU OF OLD.
NO MATTER HOW CAREFUL WE ARE, DANGER ALWAYS LURKS.
THE WAY YOU DEALT WITH THINGS THIS TIME WASN'T WRONG. YOU DID GOOD.
WHAT YOU DO NOW IS CRITICAL. OVERCOME THIS CRISIS WITH CARE.

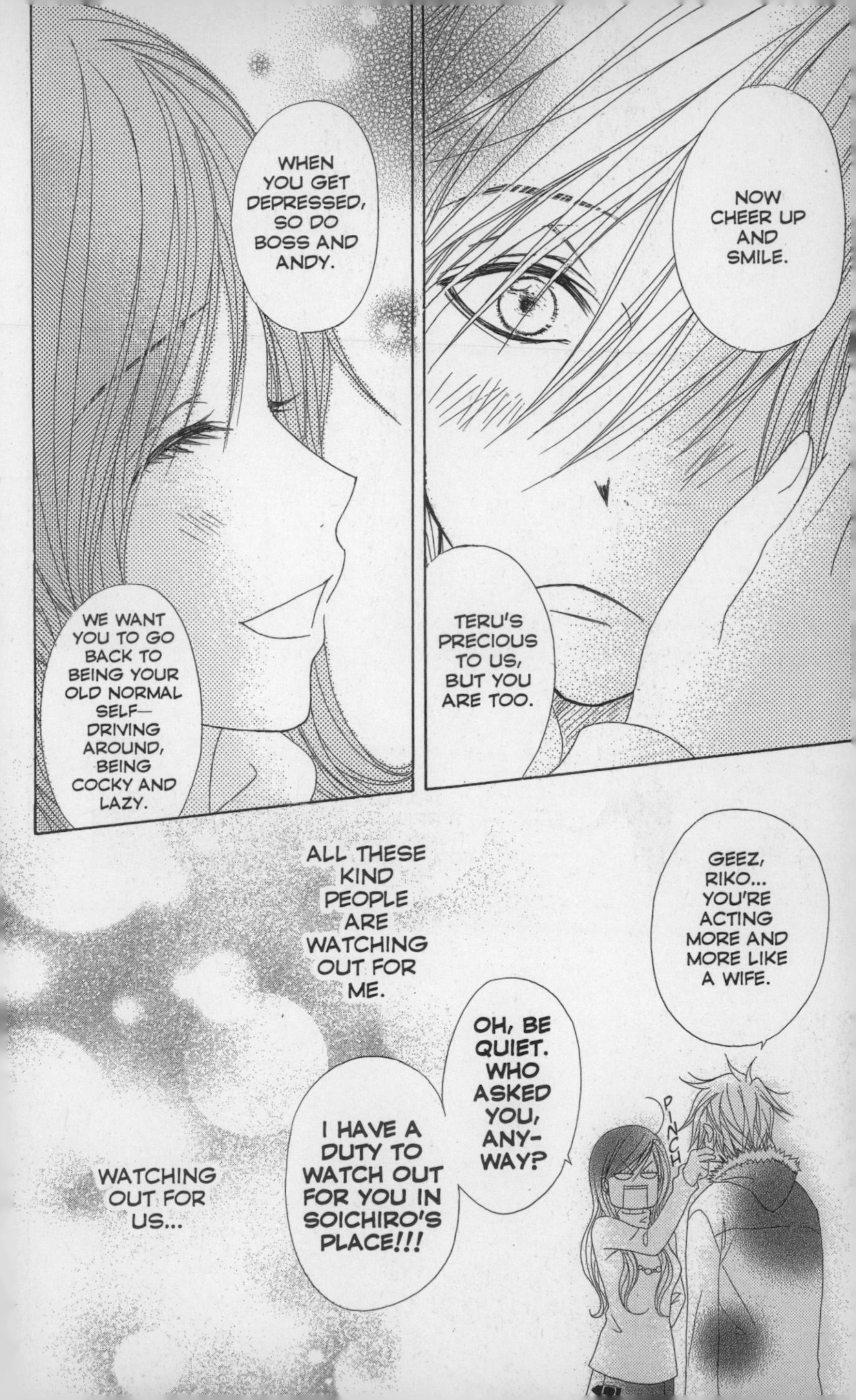
NOW CHEER UP AND SMILE.
TERU'S PRECIOUS TO US, BUT YOU ARE TOO.
WHEN YOU GET DEPRESSED, SO DO BOSS AND ANDY.
WE WANT YOU TO GO BACK TO BEING YOUR OLD NORMAL SELF— DRIVING AROUND, BEING COCKY AND LAZY.
GEEZ, RIKO... YOU'RE ACTING MORE AND MORE LIKE A WIFE.
ALL THESE KIND PEOPLE ARE WATCHING OUT FOR ME.
PINCH
OH, BE QUIET. WHO ASKED YOU, ANY- WAY?
I HAVE A DUTY TO WATCH OUT FOR YOU IN SOICHIRO'S PLACE!!!
WATCHING OUT FOR US...

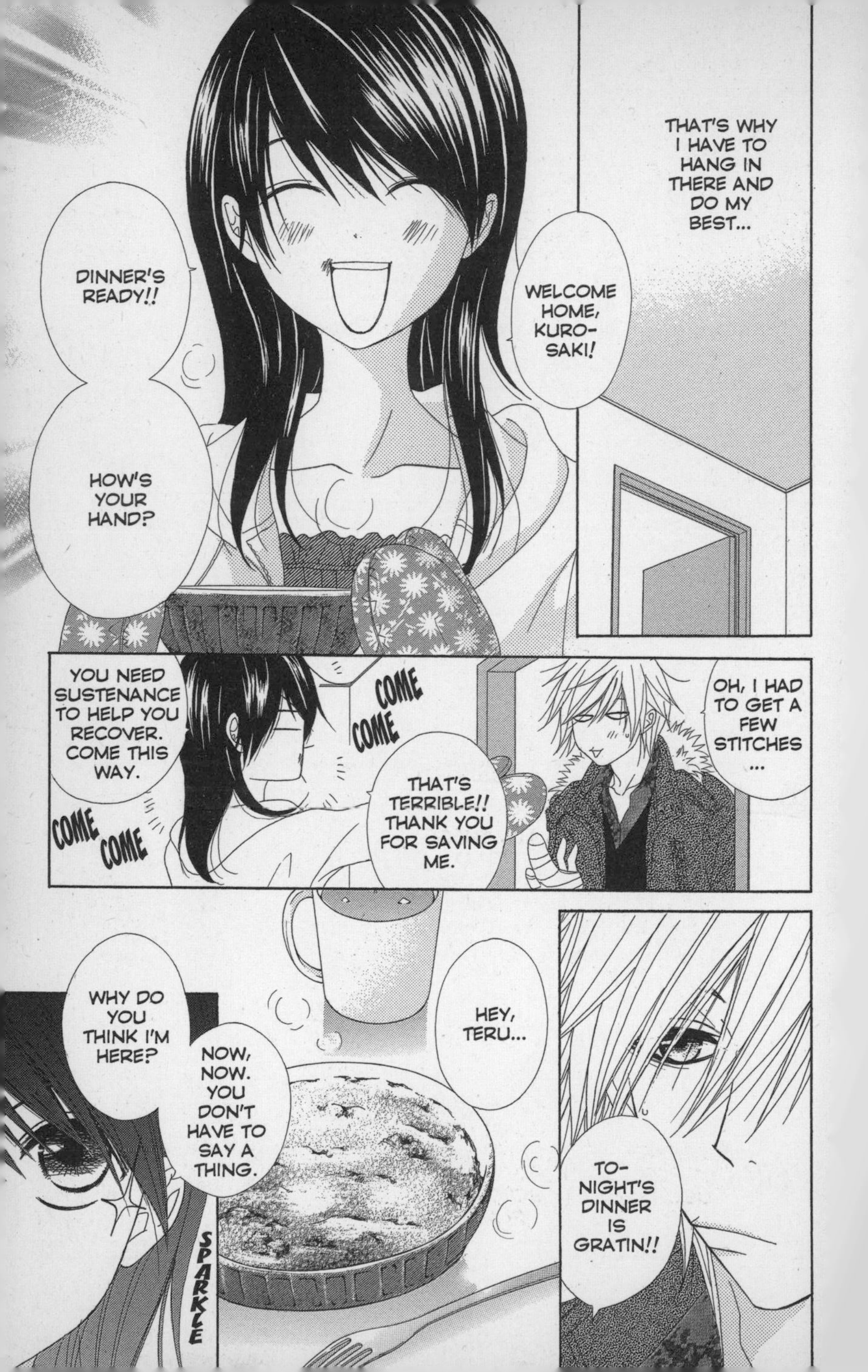

THAT'S WHY I HAVE TO HANG IN THERE AND DO MY BEST...
WELCOME HOME, KURO-SAKI!
DINNER'S READY!!
HOW'S YOUR HAND?
OH, I HAD TO GET A FEW STITCHES...
THAT'S TERRIBLE!! THANK YOU FOR SAVING ME.
COME COME
YOU NEED SUSTENANCE TO HELP YOU RECOVER. COME THIS WAY.
COME COME
HEY, TERU...
WHY DO YOU THINK I'M HERE?
NOW, NOW. YOU DON'T HAVE TO SAY A THING.
TO-NIGHT'S DINNER IS GRATIN!!
SPARKLE

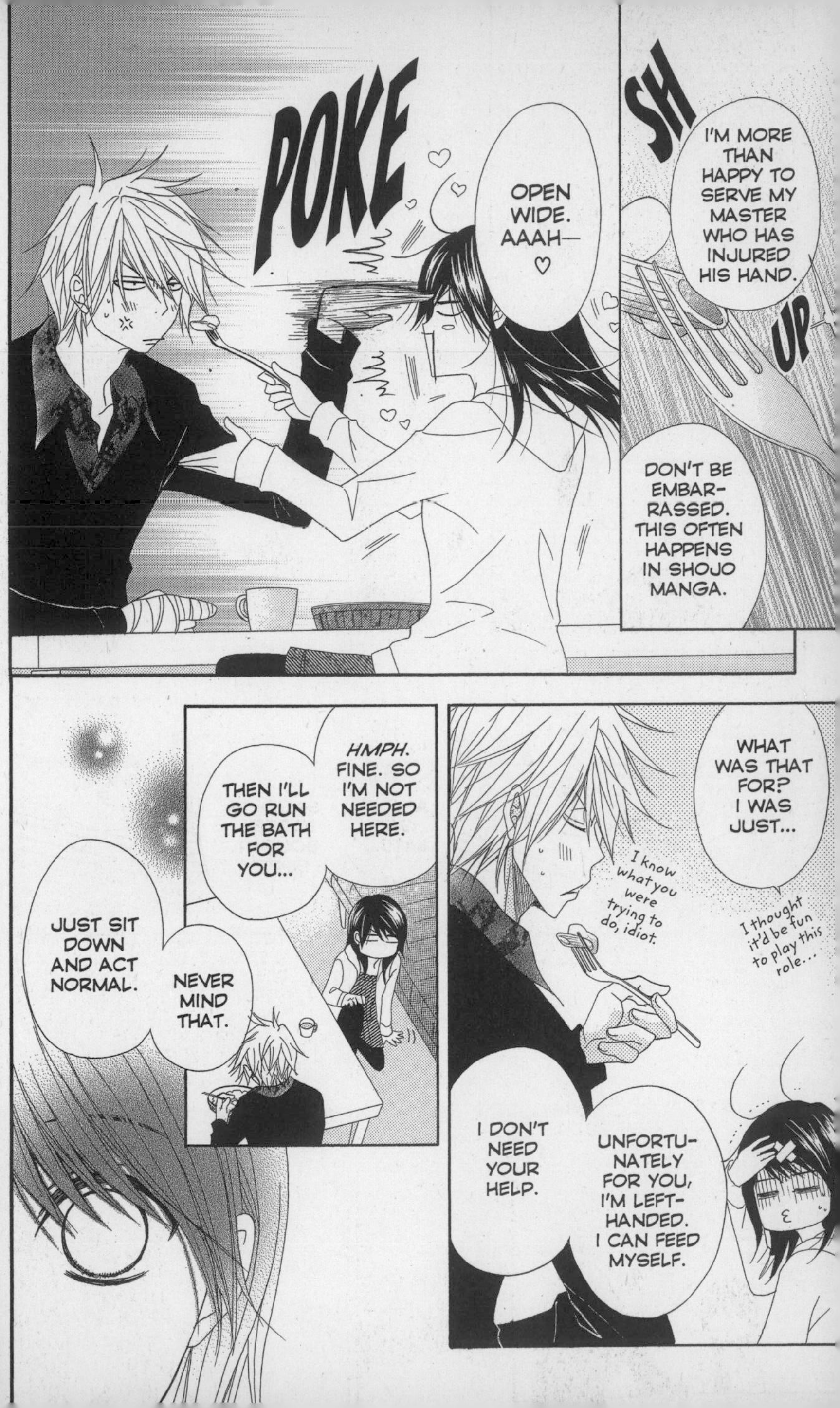
SH
I'M MORE THAN HAPPY TO SERVE MY MASTER WHO HAS INJURED HIS HAND.
UP
DON'T BE EMBARRASSED. THIS OFTEN HAPPENS IN SHOJO MANGA.
POKE
OPEN WIDE. AAAH— ♡
WHAT WAS THAT FOR? I WAS JUST...
I know what you were trying to do, idiot.
I thought it'd be fun to play this role...
UNFORTUNATELY FOR YOU, I'M LEFT-HANDED. I CAN FEED MYSELF.
I DON'T NEED YOUR HELP.
HMPH. FINE. SO I'M NOT NEEDED HERE.
THEN I'LL GO RUN THE BATH FOR YOU...
NEVER MIND THAT.
JUST SIT DOWN AND ACT NORMAL.

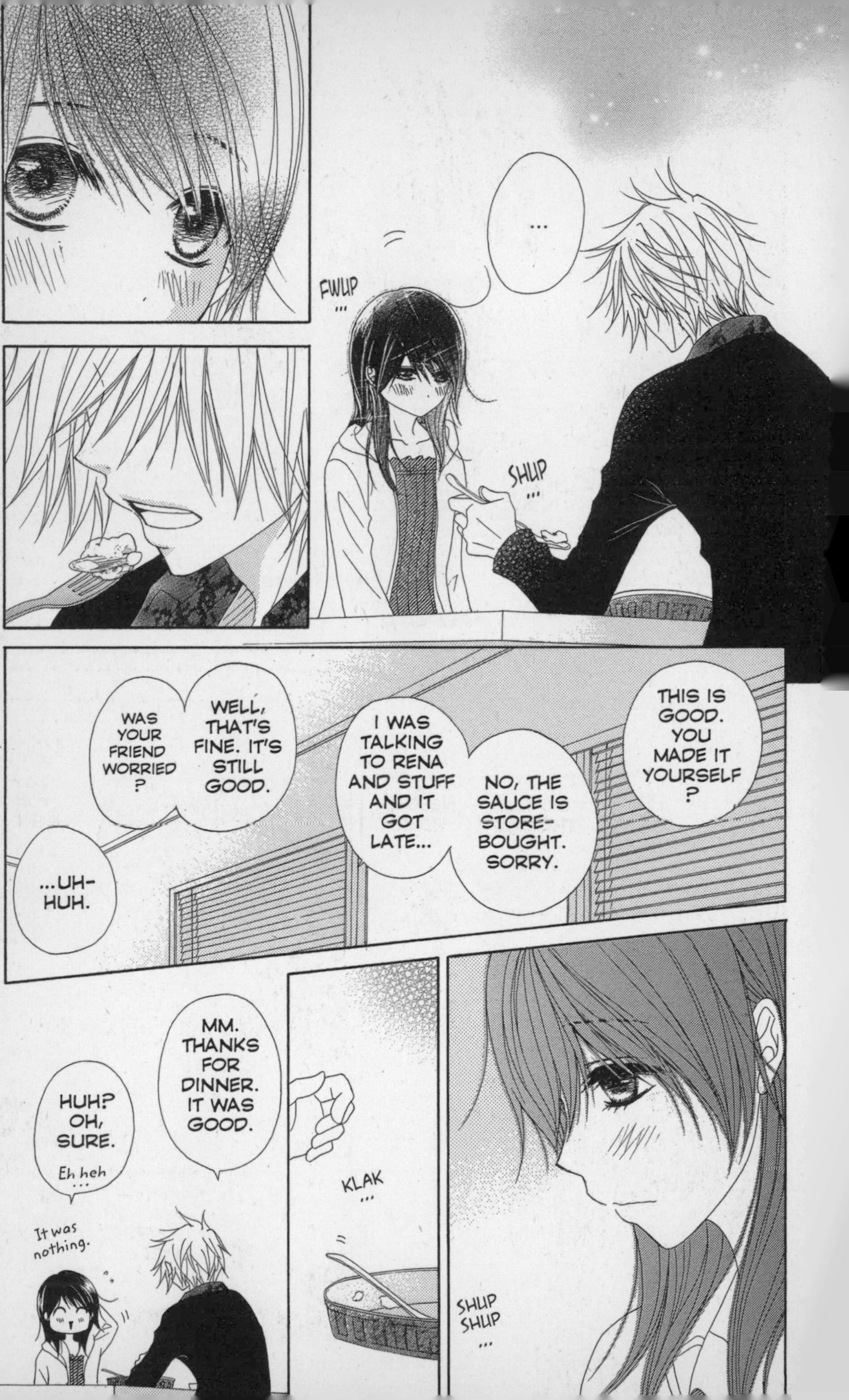
...
FWUP...
SHUP...
THIS IS GOOD. YOU MADE IT YOURSELF?
NO, THE SAUCE IS STORE-BOUGHT. SORRY.
I WAS TALKING TO RENA AND STUFF AND IT GOT LATE...
WELL, THAT'S FINE. IT'S STILL GOOD.
WAS YOUR FRIEND WORRIED?
...UH-HUH.
SHUP SHUP...
KLAK...
MM. THANKS FOR DINNER. IT WAS GOOD.
HUH? OH, SURE.
Eh heh...
It was nothing.

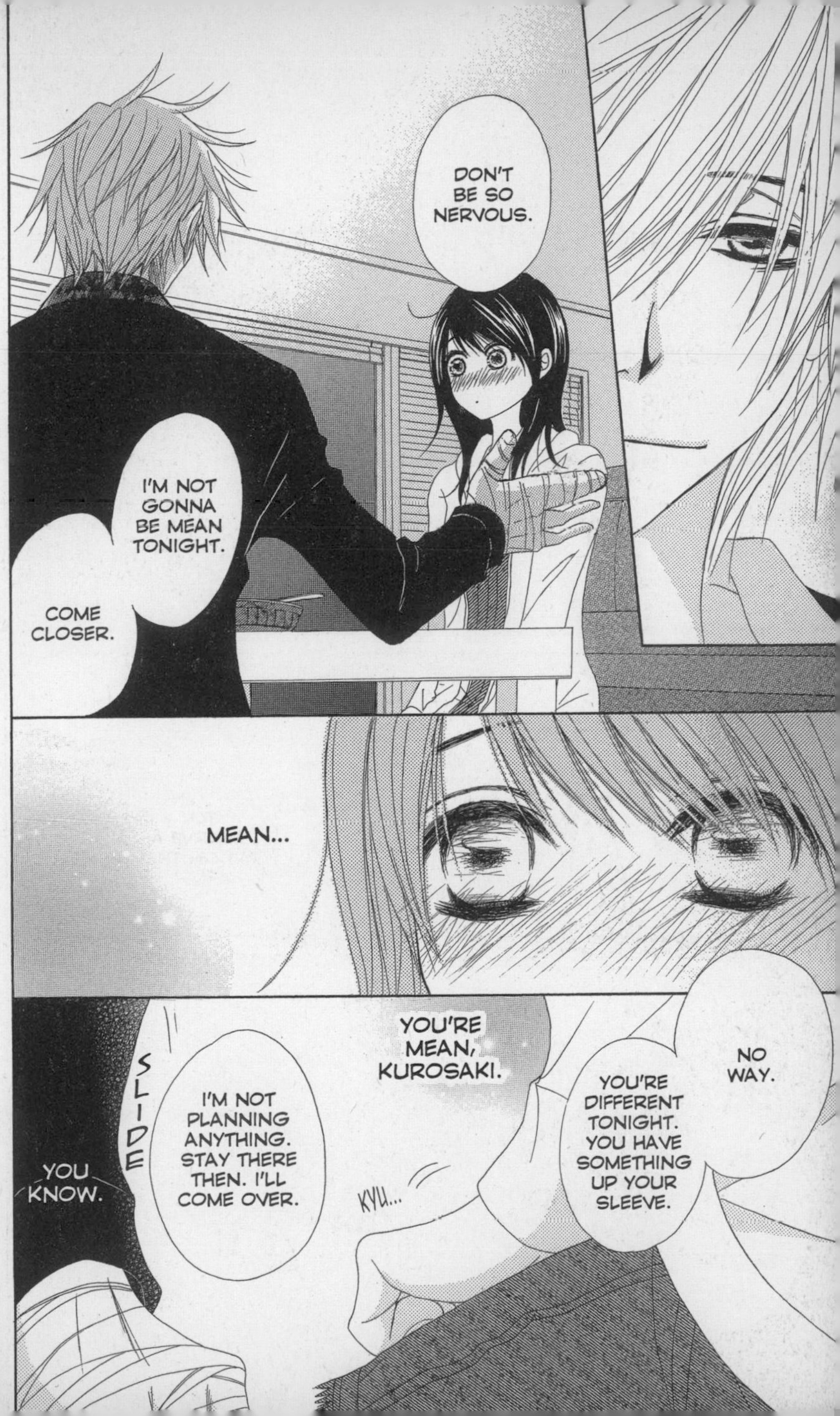
DON'T BE SO NERVOUS.
I'M NOT GONNA BE MEAN TONIGHT.
COME CLOSER.
MEAN...
NO WAY.
YOU'RE DIFFERENT TONIGHT. YOU HAVE SOMETHING UP YOUR SLEEVE.
YOU'RE MEAN, KUROSAKI.
KYU...
I'M NOT PLANNING ANYTHING. STAY THERE THEN. I'LL COME OVER.
SLIDE
YOU KNOW.

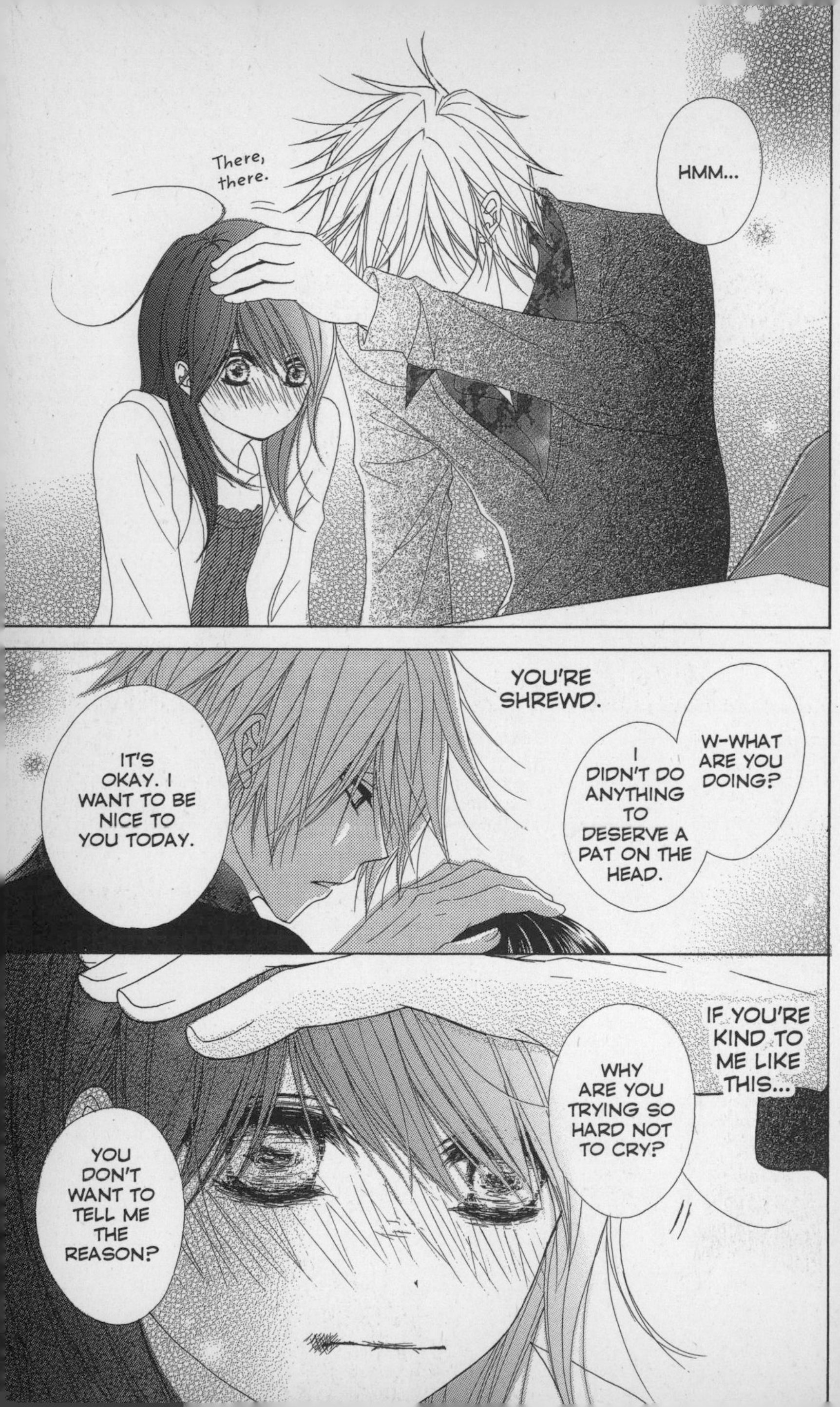
HMM...
There, there.
W-WHAT ARE YOU DOING?
I DIDN'T DO ANYTHING TO DESERVE A PAT ON THE HEAD.
YOU'RE SHREWD.
IT'S OKAY. I WANT TO BE NICE TO YOU TODAY.
IF YOU'RE KIND TO ME LIKE THIS...
WHY ARE YOU TRYING SO HARD NOT TO CRY?
YOU DON'T WANT TO TELL ME THE REASON?

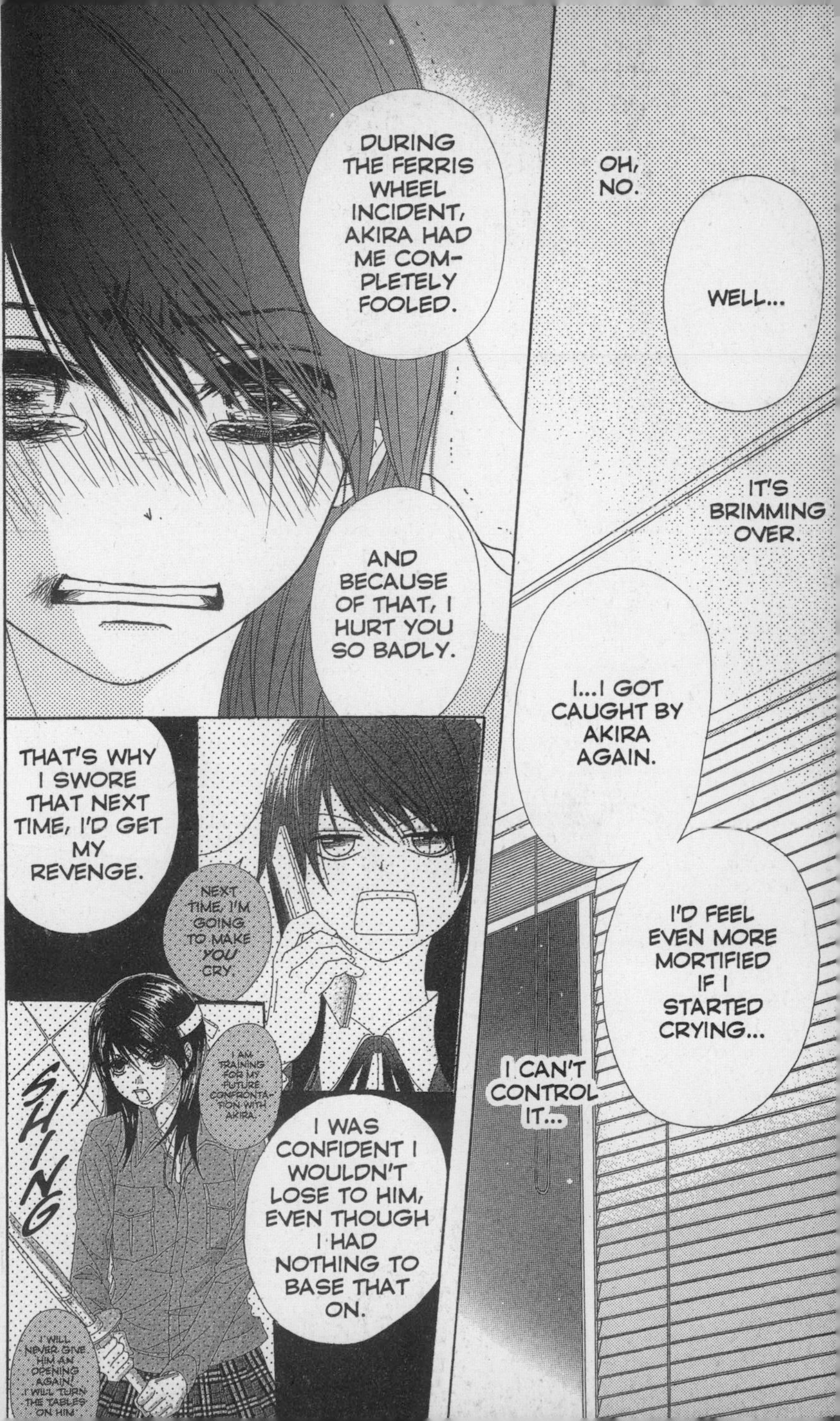
OH, NO.
WELL...
IT'S BRIMMING OVER.
I...I GOT CAUGHT BY AKIRA AGAIN.
I'D FEEL EVEN MORE MORTIFIED IF I STARTED CRYING...
I CAN'T CONTROL IT...
DURING THE FERRIS WHEEL INCIDENT, AKIRA HAD ME COM-PLETELY FOOLED.
AND BECAUSE OF THAT, I HURT YOU SO BADLY.
THAT'S WHY I SWORE THAT NEXT TIME, I'D GET MY REVENGE.
NEXT TIME, I'M GOING TO MAKE *YOU* CRY.
I AM TRAINING FOR MY FUTURE CONFRONTA-TION WITH AKIRA.
I WAS CONFIDENT I WOULDN'T LOSE TO HIM, EVEN THOUGH I HAD NOTHING TO BASE THAT ON.
SHING
I WILL NEVER GIVE HIM AN OPENING AGAIN! I WILL TURN THE TABLES ON HIM

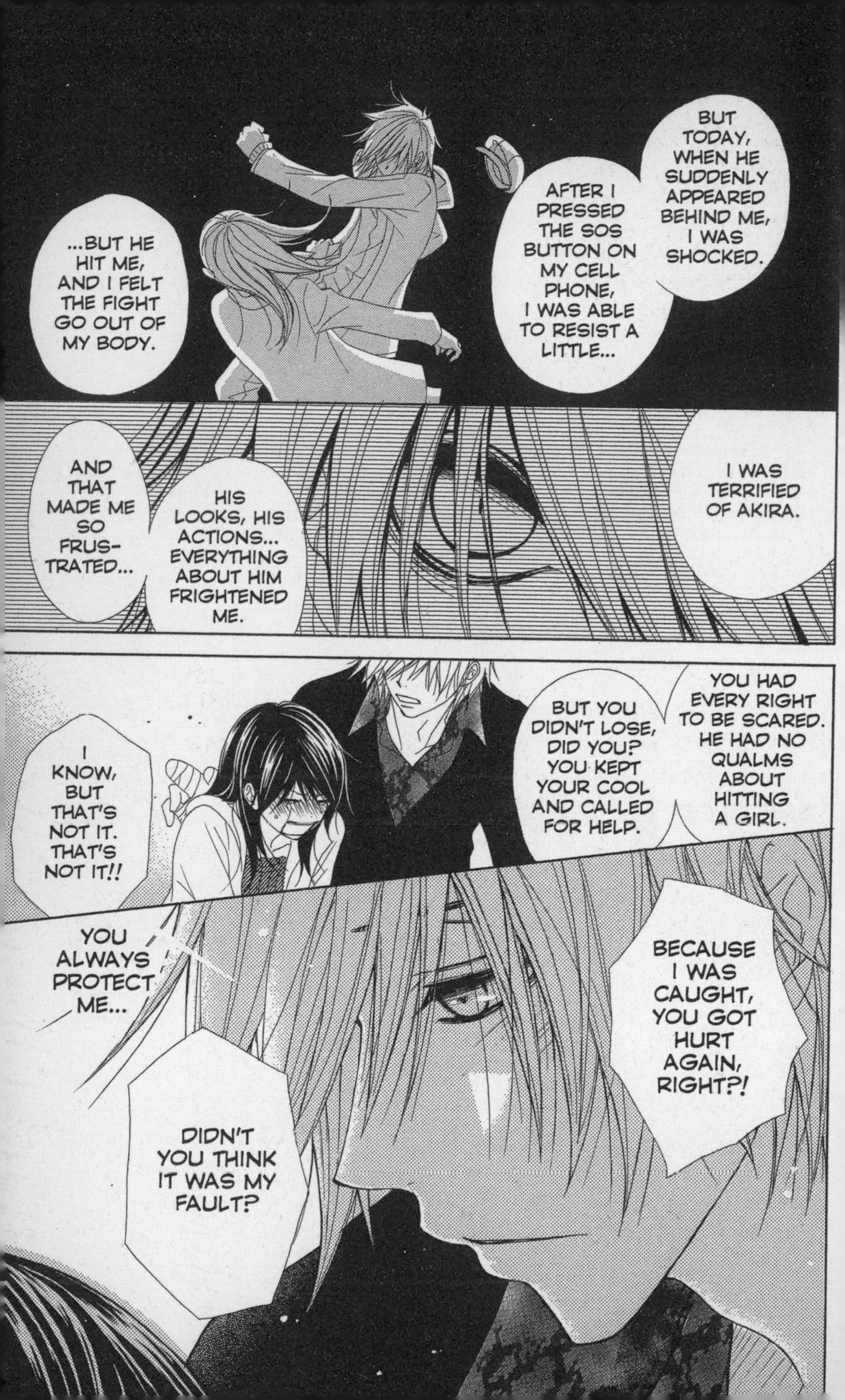
BUT TODAY, WHEN HE SUDDENLY APPEARED BEHIND ME, I WAS SHOCKED.
AFTER I PRESSED THE SOS BUTTON ON MY CELL PHONE, I WAS ABLE TO RESIST A LITTLE...
...BUT HE HIT ME, AND I FELT THE FIGHT GO OUT OF MY BODY.
I WAS TERRIFIED OF AKIRA.
HIS LOOKS, HIS ACTIONS... EVERYTHING ABOUT HIM FRIGHTENED ME.
AND THAT MADE ME SO FRUS-TRATED...
YOU HAD EVERY RIGHT TO BE SCARED. HE HAD NO QUALMS ABOUT HITTING A GIRL.
BUT YOU DIDN'T LOSE, DID YOU? YOU KEPT YOUR COOL AND CALLED FOR HELP.
I KNOW, BUT THAT'S NOT IT. THAT'S NOT IT!!
BECAUSE I WAS CAUGHT, YOU GOT HURT AGAIN, RIGHT?!
YOU ALWAYS PROTECT ME...
DIDN'T YOU THINK IT WAS MY FAULT?

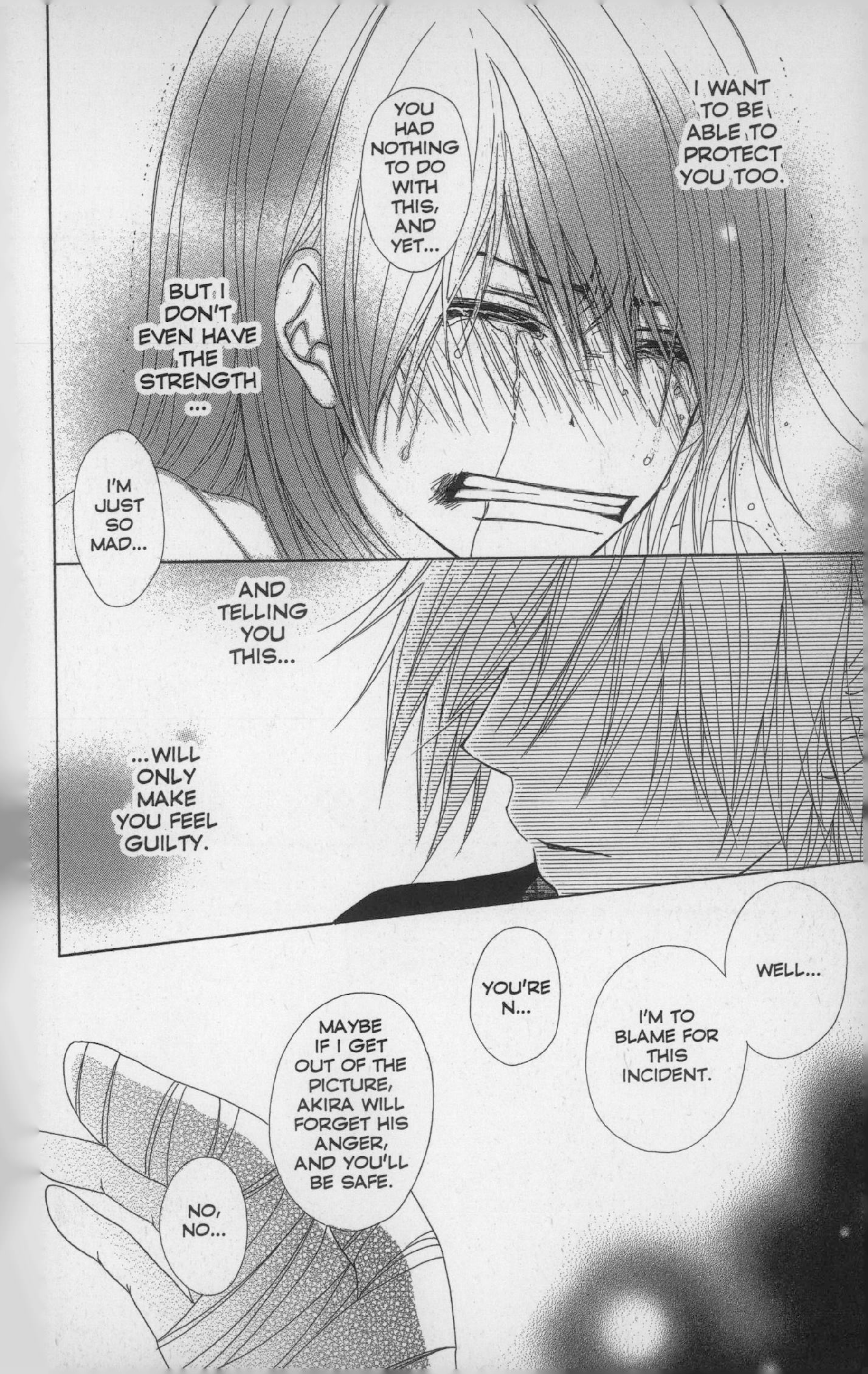
I WANT TO BE ABLE TO PROTECT YOU TOO.
YOU HAD NOTHING TO DO WITH THIS, AND YET...
BUT I DON'T EVEN HAVE THE STRENGTH...
I'M JUST SO MAD...
AND TELLING YOU THIS...
...WILL ONLY MAKE YOU FEEL GUILTY.
WELL...
I'M TO BLAME FOR THIS INCIDENT.
YOU'RE N...
MAYBE IF I GET OUT OF THE PICTURE, AKIRA WILL FORGET HIS ANGER, AND YOU'LL BE SAFE.
NO, NO...

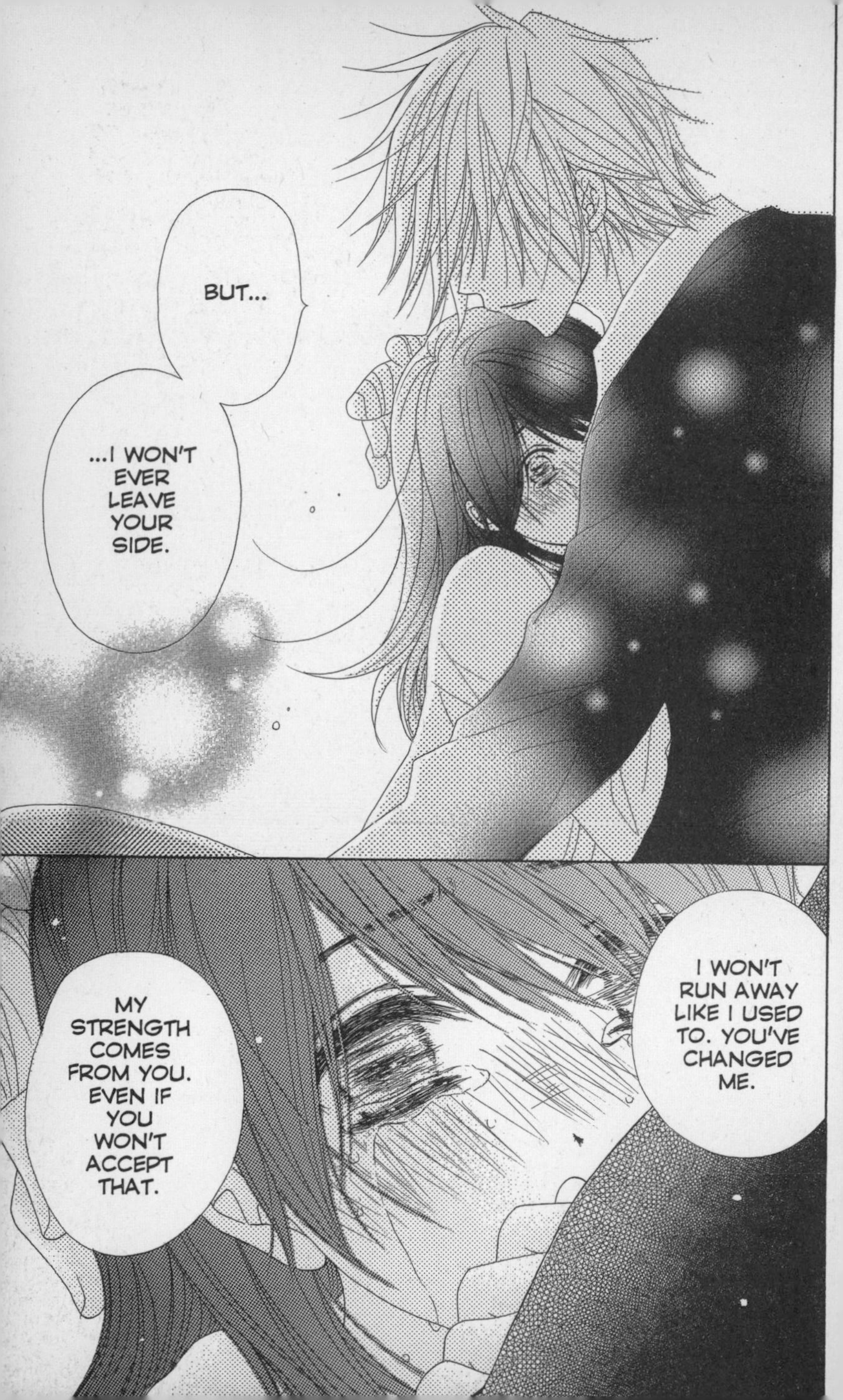
BUT...
...I WON'T EVER LEAVE YOUR SIDE.
I WON'T RUN AWAY LIKE I USED TO. YOU'VE CHANGED ME.
MY STRENGTH COMES FROM YOU. EVEN IF YOU WON'T ACCEPT THAT.

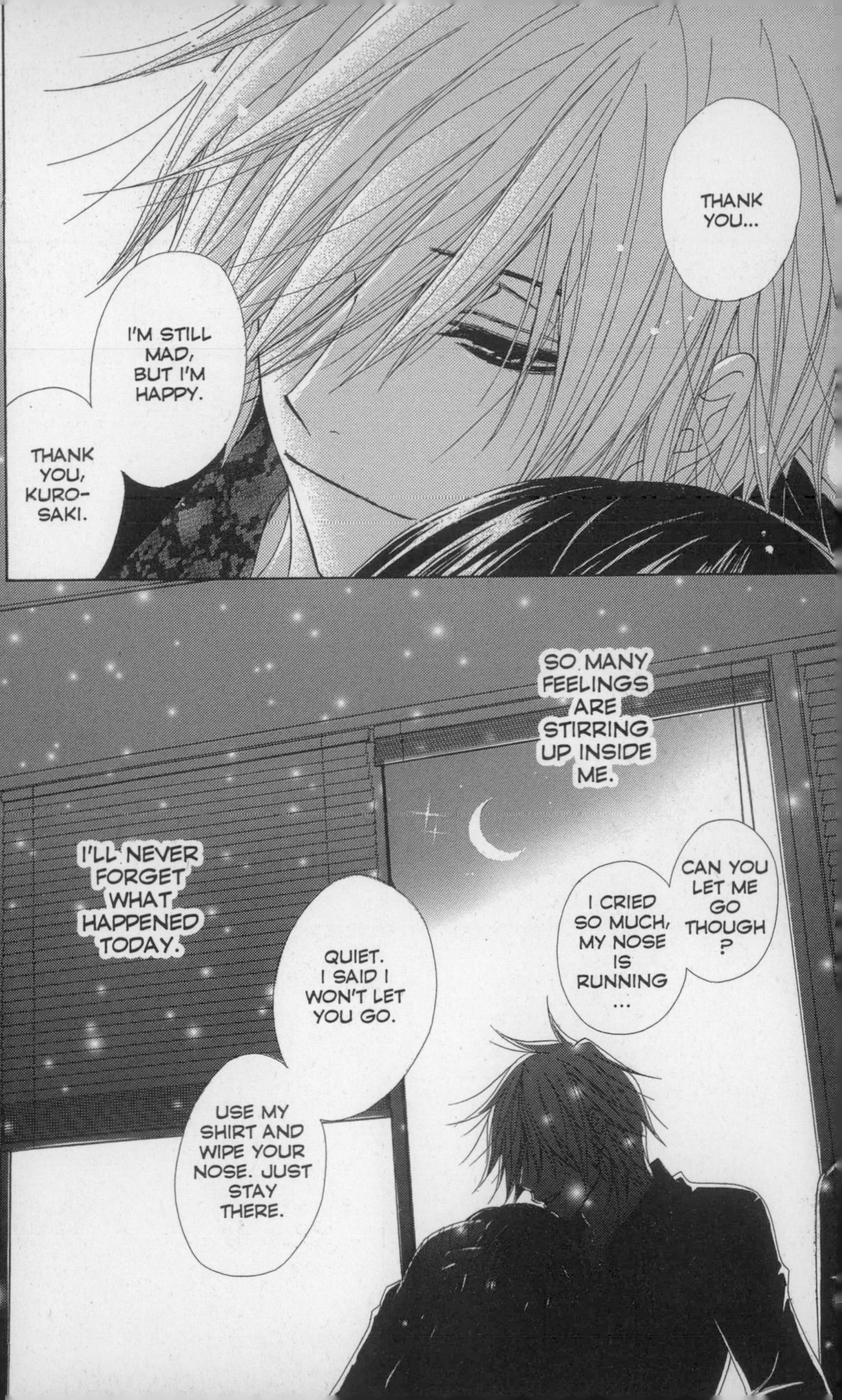
THANK YOU...
I'M STILL MAD, BUT I'M HAPPY.
THANK YOU, KURO-SAKI.
SO MANY FEELINGS ARE STIRRING UP INSIDE ME.
I CRIED SO MUCH, MY NOSE IS RUNNING...
CAN YOU LET ME GO THOUGH?
QUIET. I SAID I WON'T LET YOU GO.
USE MY SHIRT AND WIPE YOUR NOSE. JUST STAY THERE.
I'LL NEVER FORGET WHAT HAPPENED TODAY.

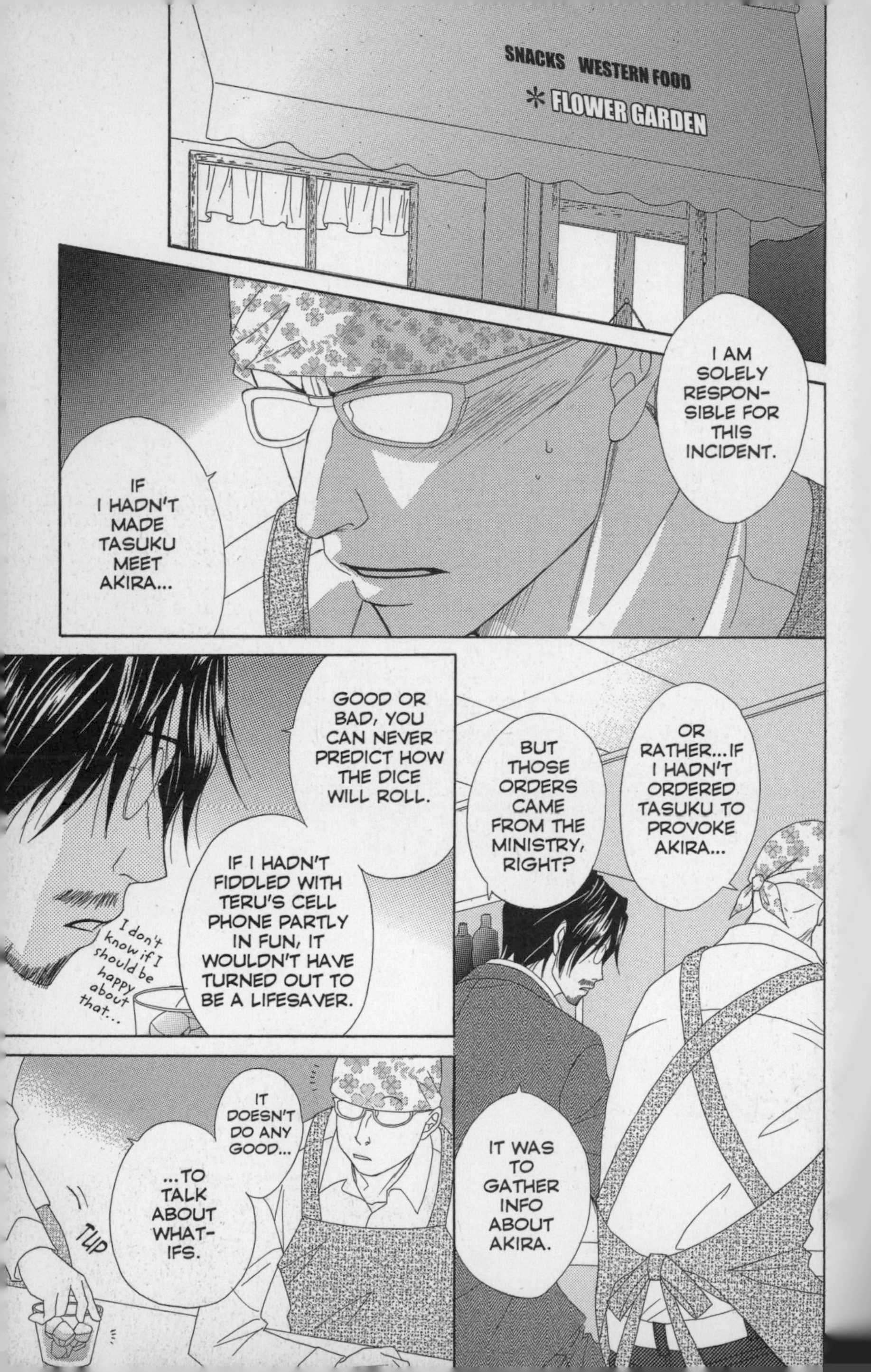
SNACKS WESTERN FOOD
FLOWER GARDEN
I AM SOLELY RESPONSIBLE FOR THIS INCIDENT.
IF I HADN'T MADE TASUKU MEET AKIRA...
OR RATHER...IF I HADN'T ORDERED TASUKU TO PROVOKE AKIRA...
BUT THOSE ORDERS CAME FROM THE MINISTRY, RIGHT?
IT WAS TO GATHER INFO ABOUT AKIRA.
GOOD OR BAD, YOU CAN NEVER PREDICT HOW THE DICE WILL ROLL.
IF I HADN'T FIDDLED WITH TERU'S CELL PHONE PARTLY IN FUN, IT WOULDN'T HAVE TURNED OUT TO BE A LIFESAVER.
I don't know if I should be happy about that...
IT DOESN'T DO ANY GOOD...
...TO TALK ABOUT WHAT-IFS.
TUP

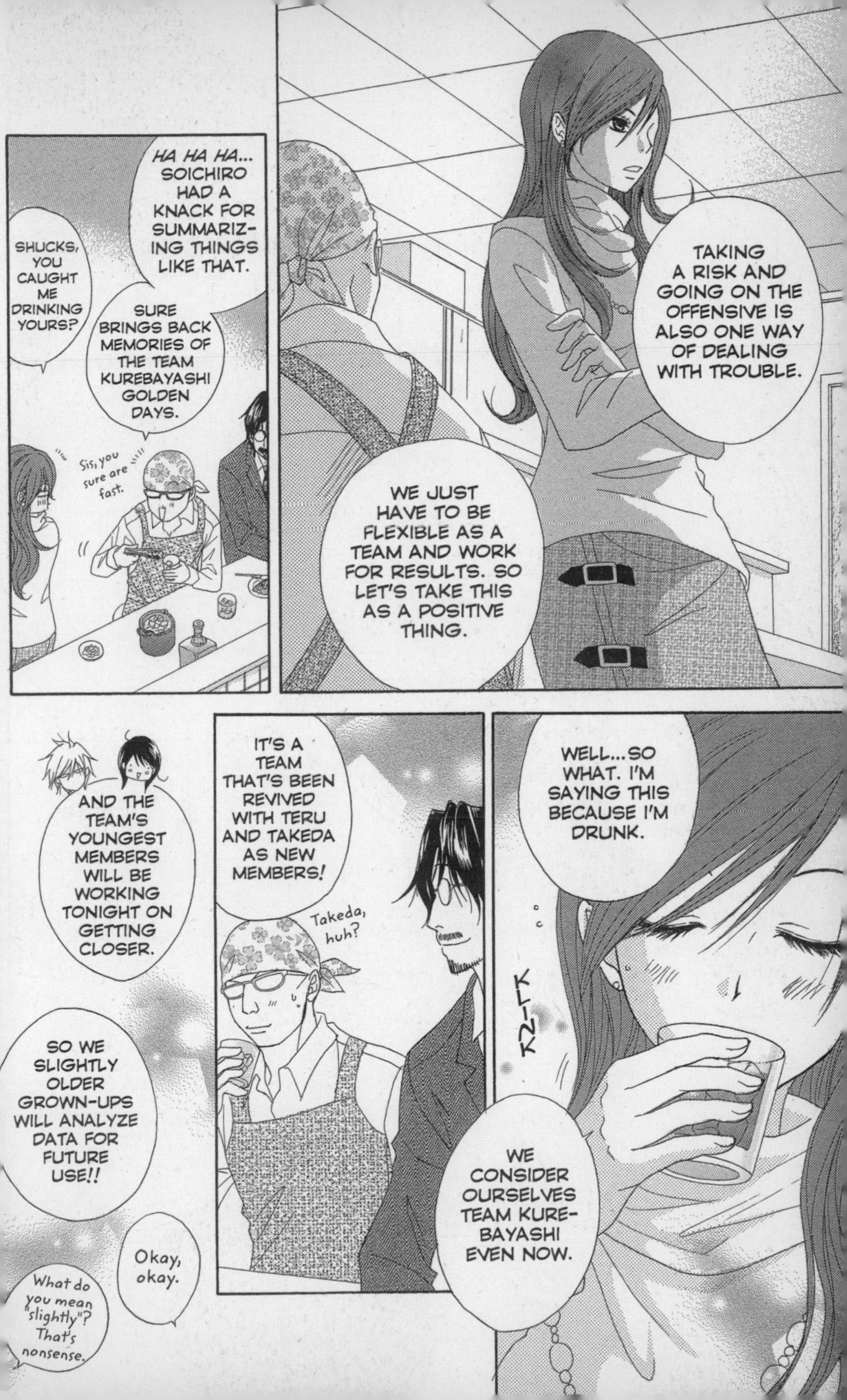
TAKING A RISK AND GOING ON THE OFFENSIVE IS ALSO ONE WAY OF DEALING WITH TROUBLE.
WE JUST HAVE TO BE FLEXIBLE AS A TEAM AND WORK FOR RESULTS. SO LET'S TAKE THIS AS A POSITIVE THING.
HA HA HA... SOICHIRO HAD A KNACK FOR SUMMARIZING THINGS LIKE THAT.
SURE BRINGS BACK MEMORIES OF THE TEAM KUREBAYASHI GOLDEN DAYS.
SHUCKS, YOU CAUGHT ME DRINKING YOURS?
Sis, you sure are fast.
WELL...SO WHAT. I'M SAYING THIS BECAUSE I'M DRUNK.
KLINK
WE CONSIDER OURSELVES TEAM KURE-BAYASHI EVEN NOW.
IT'S A TEAM THAT'S BEEN REVIVED WITH TERU AND TAKEDA AS NEW MEMBERS!
Takeda, huh?
AND THE TEAM'S YOUNGEST MEMBERS WILL BE WORKING TONIGHT ON GETTING CLOSER.
SO WE SLIGHTLY OLDER GROWN-UPS WILL ANALYZE DATA FOR FUTURE USE!!
Okay, okay.
What do you mean "slightly"? That's nonsense.

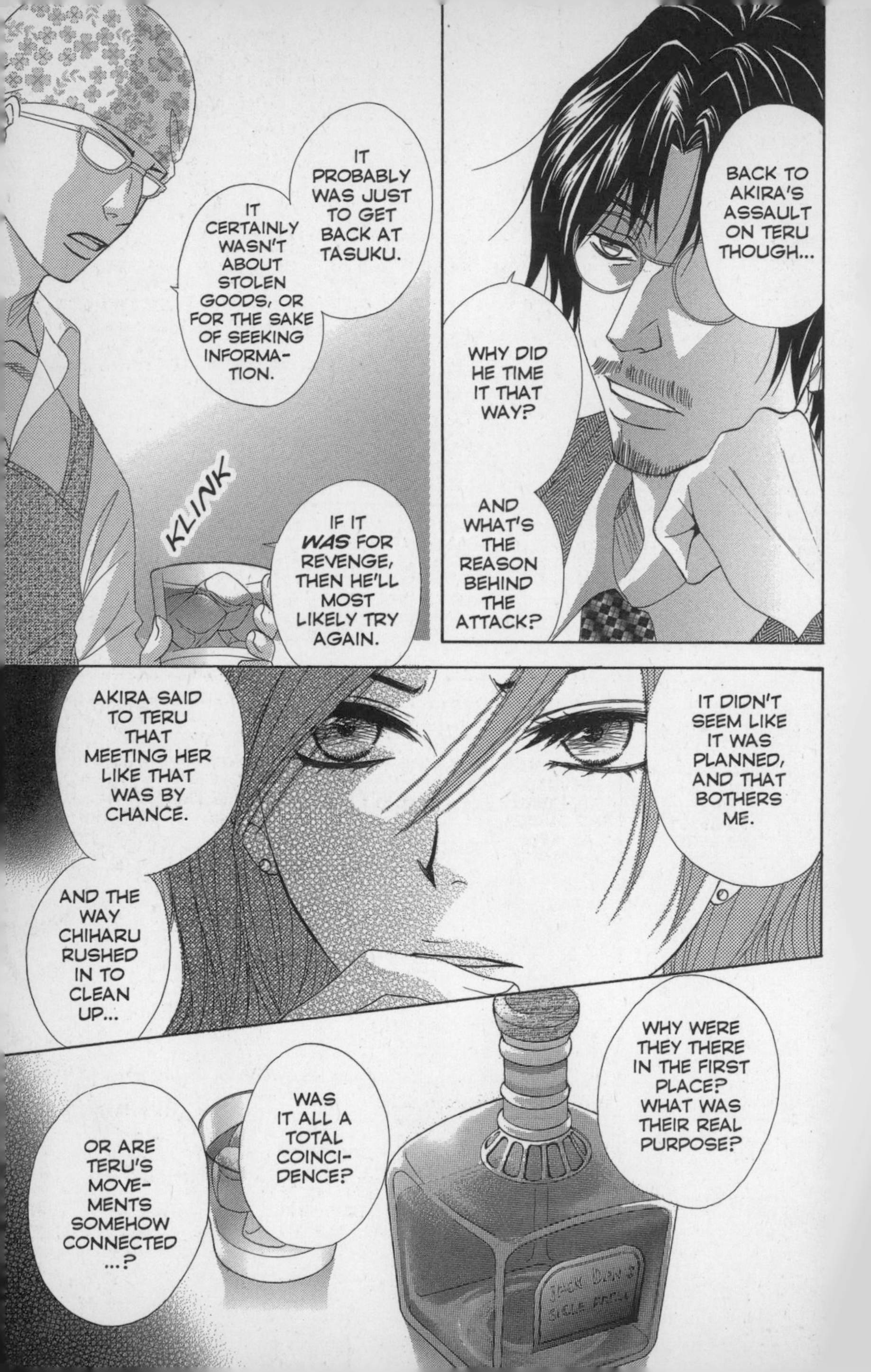
BACK TO AKIRA'S ASSAULT ON TERU THOUGH...
WHY DID HE TIME IT THAT WAY?
AND WHAT'S THE REASON BEHIND THE ATTACK?
IT PROBABLY WAS JUST TO GET BACK AT TASUKU.
IT CERTAINLY WASN'T ABOUT STOLEN GOODS, OR FOR THE SAKE OF SEEKING INFORMATION.
KLINK
IF IT *WAS* FOR REVENGE, THEN HE'LL MOST LIKELY TRY AGAIN.
IT DIDN'T SEEM LIKE IT WAS PLANNED, AND THAT BOTHERS ME.
AKIRA SAID TO TERU THAT MEETING HER LIKE THAT WAS BY CHANCE.
AND THE WAY CHIHARU RUSHED IN TO CLEAN UP...
WHY WERE THEY THERE IN THE FIRST PLACE? WHAT WAS THEIR REAL PURPOSE?
WAS IT ALL A TOTAL COINCIDENCE?
OR ARE TERU'S MOVEMENTS SOMEHOW CONNECTED...?

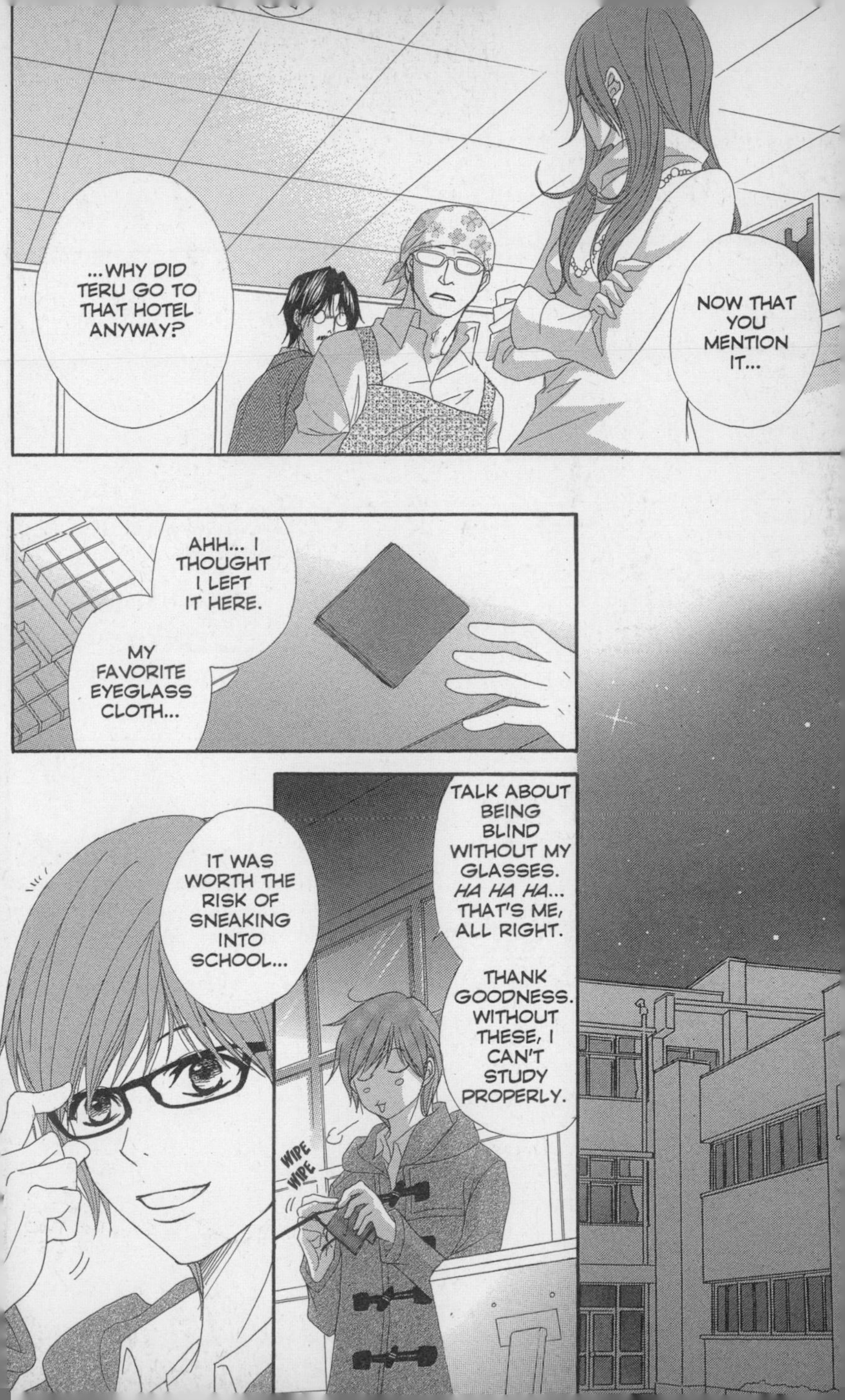
NOW THAT YOU MENTION IT...
...WHY DID TERU GO TO THAT HOTEL ANYWAY?
AHH... I THOUGHT I LEFT IT HERE.
MY FAVORITE EYEGLASS CLOTH...
TALK ABOUT BEING BLIND WITHOUT MY GLASSES. *HA HA HA*... THAT'S ME, ALL RIGHT.
THANK GOODNESS. WITHOUT THESE, I CAN'T STUDY PROPERLY.
WIPE WIPE
IT WAS WORTH THE RISK OF SNEAKING INTO SCHOOL...

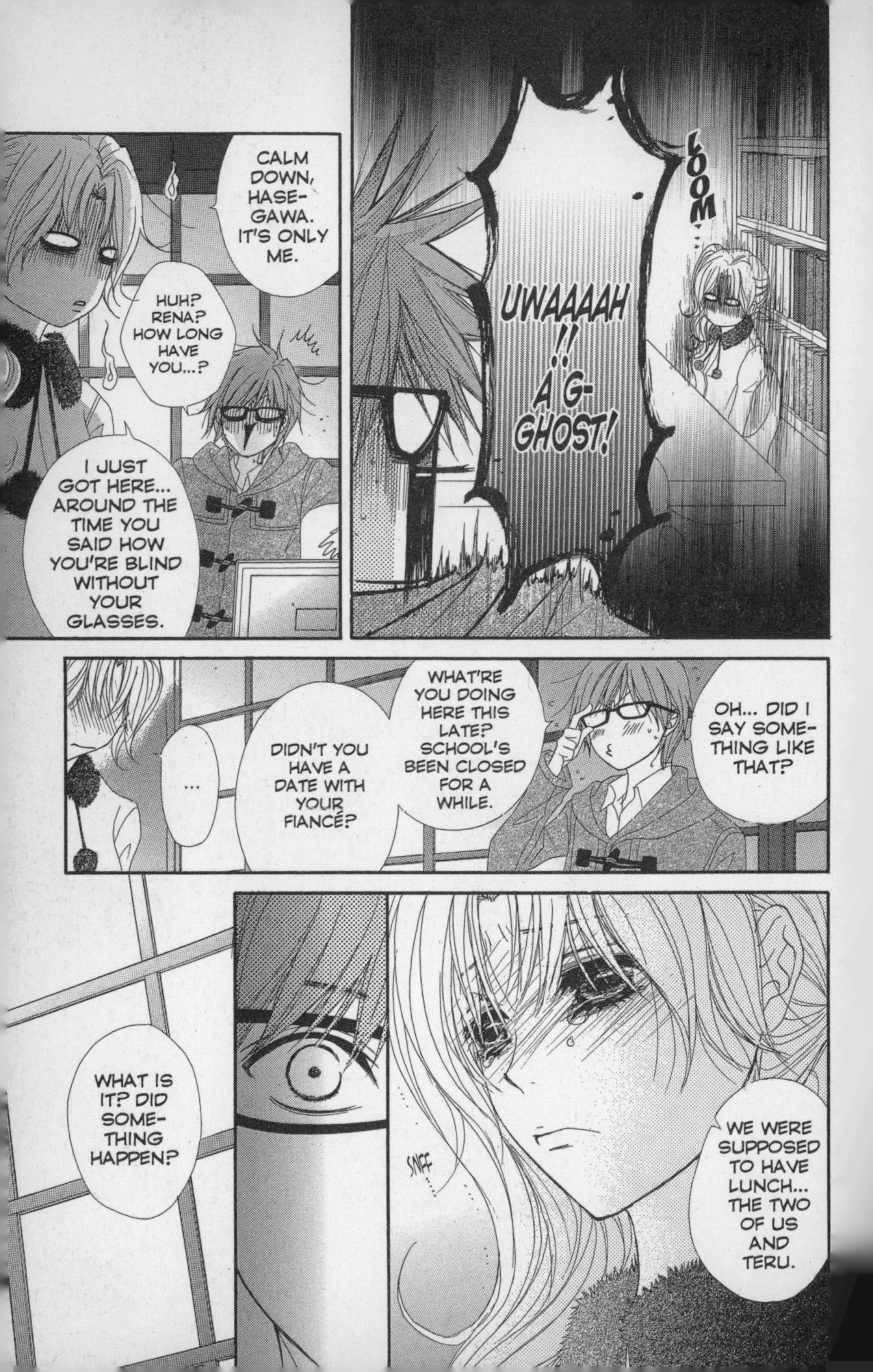
LOOM...
UWAAAAH!! A G-GHOST!
CALM DOWN, HASEGAWA. IT'S ONLY ME.
HUH? RENA? HOW LONG HAVE YOU...?
I JUST GOT HERE... AROUND THE TIME YOU SAID HOW YOU'RE BLIND WITHOUT YOUR GLASSES.
OH... DID I SAY SOMETHING LIKE THAT?
WHAT'RE YOU DOING HERE THIS LATE? SCHOOL'S BEEN CLOSED FOR A WHILE.
DIDN'T YOU HAVE A DATE WITH YOUR FIANCÉ?
...
WE WERE SUPPOSED TO HAVE LUNCH... THE TWO OF US AND TERU.
SNIFF...
WHAT IS IT? DID SOMETHING HAPPEN?

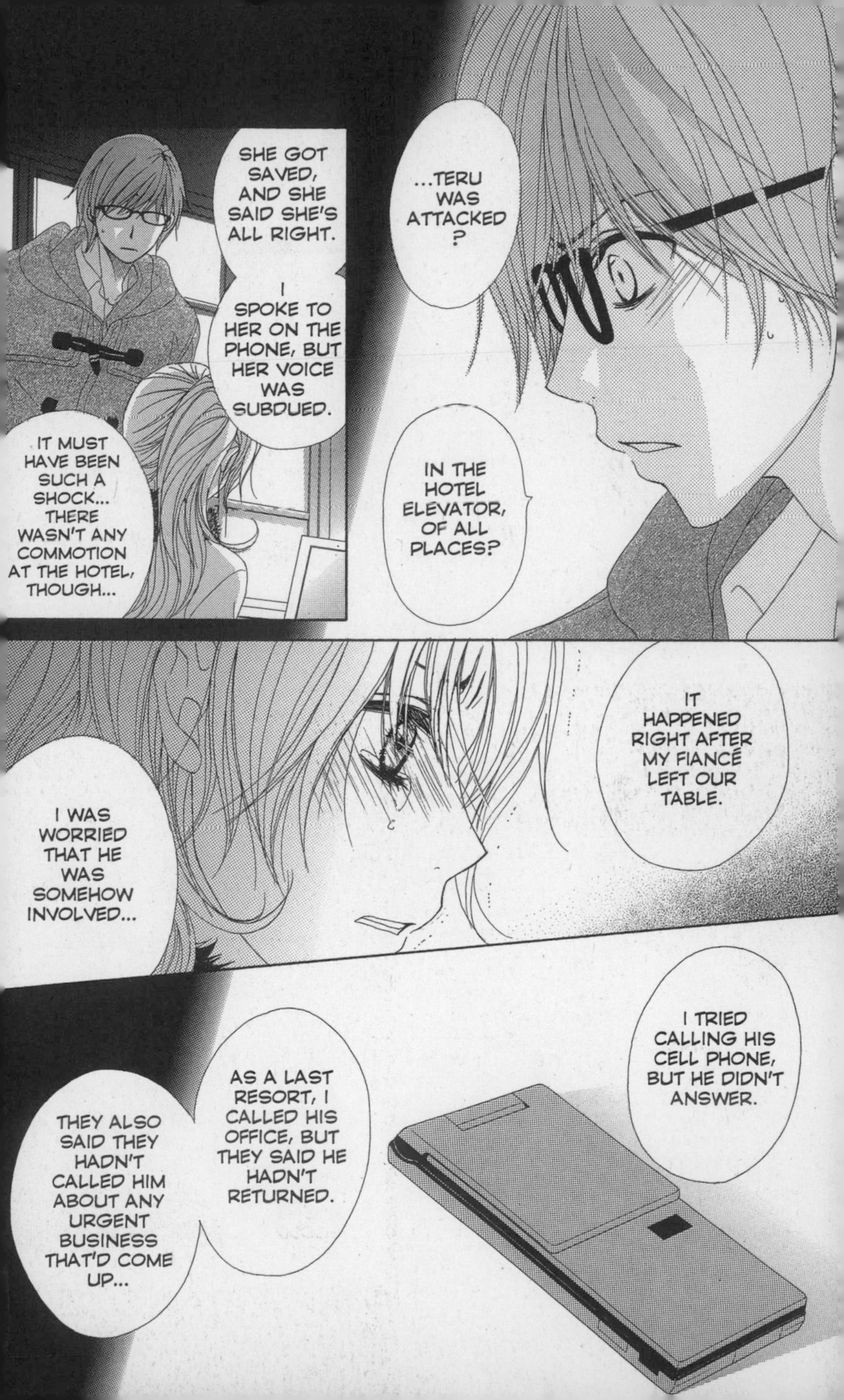
...TERU WAS ATTACKED?
IN THE HOTEL ELEVATOR, OF ALL PLACES?
SHE GOT SAVED, AND SHE SAID SHE'S ALL RIGHT.
I SPOKE TO HER ON THE PHONE, BUT HER VOICE WAS SUBDUED.
IT MUST HAVE BEEN SUCH A SHOCK... THERE WASN'T ANY COMMOTION AT THE HOTEL, THOUGH...
IT HAPPENED RIGHT AFTER MY FIANCÉ LEFT OUR TABLE.
I WAS WORRIED THAT HE WAS SOMEHOW INVOLVED...
I TRIED CALLING HIS CELL PHONE, BUT HE DIDN'T ANSWER.
AS A LAST RESORT, I CALLED HIS OFFICE, BUT THEY SAID HE HADN'T RETURNED.
THEY ALSO SAID THEY HADN'T CALLED HIM ABOUT ANY URGENT BUSINESS THAT'D COME UP...

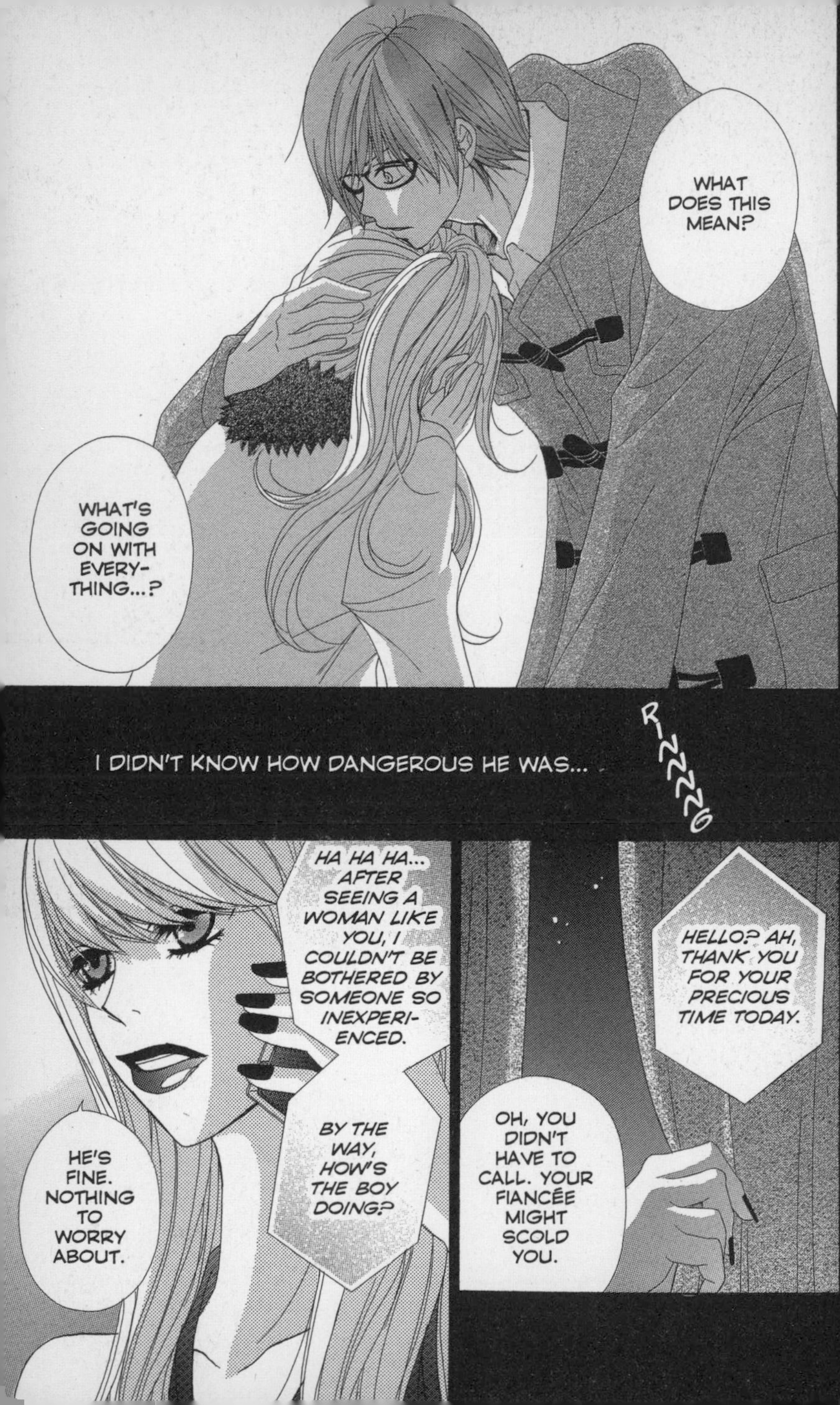
WHAT DOES THIS MEAN?
WHAT'S GOING ON WITH EVERY-THING...?
RINNNNG
I DIDN'T KNOW HOW DANGEROUS HE WAS...
HELLO? AH, THANK YOU FOR YOUR PRECIOUS TIME TODAY.
OH, YOU DIDN'T HAVE TO CALL. YOUR FIANCÉE MIGHT SCOLD YOU.
HA HA HA... AFTER SEEING A WOMAN LIKE YOU, I COULDN'T BE BOTHERED BY SOMEONE SO INEXPERI-ENCED.
BY THE WAY, HOW'S THE BOY DOING?
HE'S FINE. NOTHING TO WORRY ABOUT.

OH, DON'T BE SO DISTANT NOW.
THAT BOY IS THE... NO, I'LL KEEP THAT A SECRET.
I THINK WE'LL HAVE A NICE PART-NERSHIP, YOU AND I.
THIS PERSON I'M TRYING TO STAND UP TO...
I'M COUNTING ON YOU FROM NOW ON.
BEEP
BEEP
BEEP
I WONDER WHO HE IS...
DENGEKI DAISY 10 *THE END*

AFTERWORD

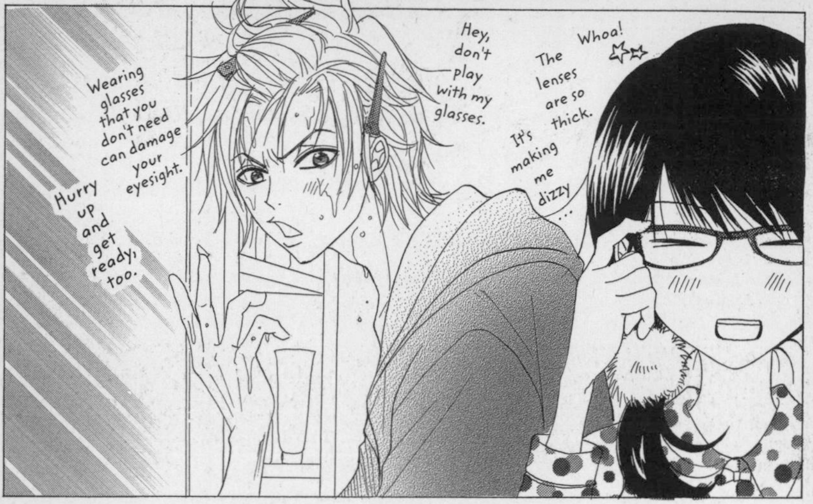

Whoa!
The lenses are so thick.
It's making me dizzy...
Hey, don't play with my glasses.
Wearing glasses that you don't need can damage your eyesight.
Hurry up and get ready, too.

ERR...YES! THIS IS THE END OF *DENGEKI DAISY* VOLUME 10.

THANK YOU FOR STAYING WITH IT UNTIL THE END!!
THIS MANGA, WHICH I THOUGHT WOULD ALREADY BE IN THE DEAD FILE, IS MIRACULOUSLY IN ITS TENTH VOLUME. IT HAS DASHED THE PREDICTIONS OF MANY AND CONTINUES TO BE SERIALIZED!!!!!

ONCE AGAIN, THERE SEEMS TO BE A ~~SNAG~~ HINT OF ANOTHER HEART-STOPPING INCIDENT. I'LL CONTINUE TO DO MY BEST, TAKING THINGS STEP-BY-STEP, AND REINING IN THAT RECKLESS SEXUAL ATTRACTION DURING CRITICAL TIMES. I HOPE WE CAN MEET AGAIN IN THE NEXT VOLUME. SEE YOU THEN!!

最富キョウスケ
KYOUSUKE MOTOMI

DENGEKI DAISY
C/O VIZ MEDIA
P.O. BOX 77010
SAN FRANCISCO, CA 94107

← IF YOU HAVE ANY QUESTIONS, PLEASE SEND THEM HERE. FOR REGULAR FAN MAIL, PLEASE SEND THEM TO THE SAME ADDRESS BUT CHANGE THE ADDRESSEE TO:

KYOUSUKE MOTOMI
C/O DENGEKI DAISY EDITOR

...AND THAT'S IT. THANK YOU VERY MUCH!!

MY MOTHER GAVE ME AN EDO KIRIKO GLASS.

WATER SEEMS TO TASTE BETTER FROM IT.

I keep bragging about being unhealthy, so this time, let me tell you about an important health regimen that I've continued for a little while: Drink ice water to wash away morning grogginess. It's an easy but pretty effective pick-me-up. I recommend it.

-Kyousuke Motomi

Born on August 1, Kyousuke Motomi debuted in *Deluxe Betsucomi* with *Hetakuso Kyupiddo* (No-Good Cupid) in 2002. She is the creator of *Otokomae! Biizu Kurabu* (Handsome! Beads Club), and her latest work, *Dengeki Daisy*, is currently being serialized in *Betsucomi*. Motomi enjoys sleeping, tea ceremonies and reading Haruki Murakami.